BRIDGING THE DISTANCE

BRIDGING THE DISTANCE

COMMON ISSUES OF THE RURAL WEST

Edited by David B. Danbom

Foreword by David M. Kennedy

A Project of the
Bill Lane Center for the American West

The University of Utah Press
Salt Lake City

2/17
$30-

The Defiance House Man colophon is a registered trademark of the University of Utah Press. It is based on a four-foot-tall Ancient Puebloan pictograph (late PIII) near Glen Canyon, Utah.

19 18 17 16 15 1 2 3 4 5

LIBRARY OF CONGRESS CATALOGING-IN-PUBLICATION DATA
Bridging the distance : common issues of the rural West / edited by David B. Danbom ; foreword by David M. Kennedy.
pages cm
A project of the Bill Lane Center for the American West.
Includes bibliographical references and index.
ISBN 978-1-60781-455-9 (paperback : alkaline paper)
ISBN 978-1-60781-456-6 (ebook)
1. West (U.S.)—Rural conditions. 2. Social problems—West (U.S.) 3. Community life—West (U.S.) 4. West (U.S.)—Economic conditions. 5. Land use—West (U.S.) 6. West (U.S.)—Environmental conditions. I. Danbom, David B., 1947- II. Bill Lane Center for the American West.
HN79.A17B75 2015
306.0978—dc23

2015022954

Parts of chapter 15, "Skull Valley Goshutes and the Politics of Place, Identity, and Sovereignty in Rural Utah," were published in "Skull Valley Goshutes and the Politics of Nuclear Waste: Environment, Economic Development, and Tribal Sovereignty," in *Native Americans and the Environment: Perspectives on the Ecological Indian*, edited by Michael E. Harkin and David Rich Lewis. Reprinted with permission of the University of Nebraska Press and the board of regents of the University of Nebraska.

Printed and bound by Sheridan Books, Inc., Ann Arbor, Michigan

Contents

Illustrations and Tables

Illustrations

Tables

Foreword

This volume is composed of papers presented at a conference on the rural West sponsored by Stanford University's Bill Lane Center for the American West in October 2012 in Ogden, Utah. It represents a major milestone for the Rural West Initiative, a long-term research project sponsored by the Lane Center. The center launched the initiative in 2009, one hundred years after the scholars assembled by President Theodore Roosevelt issued their landmark *Report of the Country Life Commission.*[1]

Prompted largely by the agrarian upheavals that had convulsed the American countryside during the preceding decade, the 1909 *Report* confirmed Populists' complaints about the alarmingly diverging ways of life that were rapidly separating rural Americans from their urban counterparts. It highlighted several "deficiencies" that afflicted rural communities, including population drain to the cities, underemployment, economic insecurity, inadequate health care, poor schools, shaky banks, rutted roads, cultural torpor, and the near-total absence of increasingly common urban amenities like electricity, indoor plumbing, and telephones.

Many of those deficiencies (or their modern-day equivalents) have stubbornly persisted in rural America. As the essays that follow make clear, nowhere are they more problematic than in the sprawling, isolated western hinterlands that stretch from the Pacific coastal mountain ranges to the midcontinental prairies. There the inexorable logic of what the Australian historian Geoffrey Blainey has aptly called "the tyranny of distance" is an often-punishing fact of everyday life.

The American West was once a mythical beacon of hope for sodbusters, cowboys, prospectors, and lumberjacks. It is still a place where their ways of life flourish and hope continues to track the setting sun. Yet great swaths of the rural West remain remote, both physically and culturally, from the region's—and the nation's—metropolitan centers. Much of today's western interior is the landscape of loneliness and isolation, of anemic public services, weak Internet connectivity, scarce financial institutions, poor medical facilities, shrinking opportunity, and environmental degradation—not to mention some of that old-fashioned Populist disenchantment.

The Bill Lane Center's Rural West Initiative seeks to document and understand western rural life in the twenty-first century and to help improve it. It highlights those issues that have for too long gone understudied by scholars, underreported in the mainstream media, and underappreciated by urban and suburban dwellers. It focuses especially on the kinds of deficiencies that the *Report of the Country Life Commission* identified more than a century ago. Through careful reporting and scholarly analysis, we hope to begin conversations that will generate salutary results.

Let's begin with population, and a paradox. In 1893, little more than a decade before the publication of the *Report of the Country Life Commission*, the young historian Frederick Jackson Turner stepped up to a podium at the Chicago World's Fair to deliver what is arguably the single-most-influential paper in the annals of American historical scholarship and one that has long dominated thinking about the West: "The Significance of the Frontier in American History."

"In a recent bulletin of the Superintendent of the Census for 1890," Turner began, "appear these significant words: 'Up to and including 1880 the country had a frontier of settlement, but at present the unsettled area has been so broken into by isolated bodies of settlement that there can hardly be said to be a frontier line. In the discussion of its extent, its westward movement, etc., it cannot, therefore, any longer have a place in the census reports.' This brief official statement," Turner declared, "marks the closing of a great historic movement."[2] Or did it?

Turner believed that the three-century-long process of pushing the frontier westward had constituted an epic march through time that had peopled the continent while deeply molding the nation's values, institutions, and its very character. Now that the frontier was officially closed, he famously wondered what forces might shape the next chapters in the nation's history.

Turner conceived of the frontier not simply as a boundary that demarcated physical space on the map. For him it was above all a place of renewal, where the confrontation with untamed and largely unpeopled nature repeatedly catalyzed the unfolding of American democracy and nurtured America's singular genius.[3] Populating the transfrontier region represented the triumph of the future, understood as "civilization," over the past, understood as empty or "free" land that awaited the quickening touch of Europeans before it could enter the stream of history.[4]

But when he spoke in Chicago, Turner could not have imagined that the next century would see both a robustly rejuvenated westward movement and the stalling—or even the reversal—of time's vector on America's last frontier, leaving vast tracts of the rural West on the outermost margins of the civilizing process that he assumed was irresistible.

Westward movement did in fact come to a near halt in Turner's time as the line of settlement approached the fabled hundredth meridian, beyond which lay the arid lands of the West. There the arrival of large populations awaited the federal government's enormous investments in dams and interstate highways in the twentieth century. In a development that Turner could not have foreseen, World War II triggered a stupendous resurgence of the westward movement—a massive human migration that made westerners out of one-third of Americans by the dawn of the twenty-first century.

Turner might have been even more perplexed that most of those modern westerners lived in cities; indeed, the West has been the most urbanized of America's four major regions since the 1880s. So here is a great paradox: the West is now both the most urban region (measured by where people live) as well as the most rural region (measured by how much territory is classified as rural).

But the most stunning demonstration of how vulnerable Turner's basic assumptions were lies in the most recent census data on population distribution in the American West. It shows something that Turner would have had great difficulty imagining in 1893: history—or at least demographic history—has reversed itself throughout much of the rural West. According to the nineteenth-century definition of "unsettled area" that the superintendent of the census and Turner relied on (fewer than two inhabitants per square mile), the transfrontier pattern of settlement has never fully disappeared from the West, especially in the intermountain Great Basin. And in a broad, wedge-shaped zone stretching from central Montana and the western Dakotas through much of Wyoming, Nebraska, Kansas, Colorado, and down to the Texas and Oklahoma panhandles, the population of many rural counties has reverted to prefrontier, nineteenth-century densities.

The depopulation of the American heartland has perplexed and concerned many contemporary observers. It would have astonished the young Turner. Its causes and consequences remain to be fully understood—an important part of our agenda at the Rural West Initiative.

The persistence of a transfrontier unsettled area and the steady depopulation of many rural counties have already prompted some unorthodox proposals, including a plan to hasten the work of human removal and reconstitute the north-central plains as a "buffalo commons," where million-head bison herds will once again rumble across the grasslands. It seems unlikely that this vision will be fully realized. But the existence of an extensive, empty rural West a century after Turner and the superintendent of the census declared it to be—well—history is a powerful reminder that history can still deliver some surprises. The essays in this volume contain many of these surprises, and we hope to deliver still more in future reports from the Bill Lane Center's Rural West Initiative.

— David M. Kennedy

Notes

1. Liberty Hyde Bailey, *Report of the Country Life Commission* (Washington, DC: Government Printing Office, 1909)
2. Frederick Jackson Turner, "The Significance of the American Frontier in American History," in *Annual Report of the American Historical Association for the Year 1893* (Washington, DC: Government Printing Office and American Historical Association, 1894), 199–227.
3. As Turner should have known (indeed, he did know it but chose not to acknowledge it as relevant), but as historians over the last few decades have emphatically insisted, there *were* inhabitants in all those blank spaces on the map—Indians. As Patricia Limerick in particular has eloquently argued, Turner's uncritical reliance on the superintendent of the census's categories of measurement facilitated a narrative of expansion and development and the spread of civilization, rather than a narrative of encounters, displacement, and conquest. Patricia Nelson Limerick, *The Legacy of Conquest: The Unbroken Past of the American West* (New York: W. W. Norton, 1987).
4. Westerners themselves, on the other hand, have been known to suggest that the frontier did not mark the place where the West began but the place where the East petered out.

Acknowledgments

This volume owes its existence to the efforts of a number of people and institutions. The conference that gave birth to the essays in this collection was held at the David Eccles Conference Center in Ogden, Utah, where the conferees enjoyed the hospitality and support of the Spence and Cleone Eccles family. The conference was organized by the Bill Lane Center for the American West at Stanford University. David M. Kennedy, then faculty director of the Bill Lane Center, conceived the conference and the book that resulted from it. The staff of the center, especially John McChesney and Kathy Zonana, contributed mightily to the success of the conference. John Alley of the University of Utah Press was an advocate for this project from the beginning. The readers he secured—William Rowley and Brian Cannon—suggested changes and revisions that improved the essays significantly, and the staff at the press moved it efficiently toward completion. Of special note was the work of copyeditor Barbara Bannon, who, along with Kathy Zonana, stepped into the breach at a crucial time when I was hiding in Europe. Most of all I would like to thank the authors, who suffered the process in general and my requests and deadlines in particular with grace, good humor, and efficiency. Not all editors are so lucky.

Introduction

DAVID B. DANBOM

The essays in *Bridging the Distance* are based on papers presented at an October 2012 conference in Logan, Utah, sponsored by the Bill Lane Center for the American West at Stanford University. This conference was part of the Bill Lane Center's Rural West Initiative, which aims to identify challenges confronting the rural West and suggest ways to resolve them.

The authors of these essays do not address all of the challenges facing the rural West, nor do they all suggest solutions. But they do highlight some of the critical problems in the region and initiate what we hope will be fruitful conversations about our future.

The first section of this volume deals with defining the rural West. While each of us may have a mental picture of the rural West—often involving a rider on horseback and wide-open spaces—no single image captures the geographical and demographic diversity of the region. To some degree, the rural West may be defined by a common culture, history, environment, set of problems, and means of addressing those problems. Or it may be defined by what it lacks in the way of social services, modern conveniences, communications and transportation infrastructure, and amenities. Or perhaps a combination of characteristics—positive and negative—creates a meaningful definition of the region. Rural westerners themselves define the region by what it gives them as individuals and families—a sense of place, a familiar landscape, close and sustaining human communities, and, most of all, an identity. Many rural westerners are willing to make material sacrifices to enjoy these nonmaterial benefits, but they must still cope with the challenges presented by modern social, economic, political, and environmental developments.

The old saying that all politics is local also applies to the critical challenges facing the rural West. Problems may be regional, national, or international, but they all have local manifestations, and they are frequently dealt with locally. This is the theme of the second section of this volume, which focuses on community.

Anyone who has much acquaintance with small communities will agree that the ones that effectively address problems and take advantage of opportunities have strong local leadership. But the ability to recognize a problem or an opportunity, to define it, and to marshal citizens behind a plan of action is too often absent in the rural West and elsewhere. Sometimes citizens are reluctant to challenge the thinking of most of their peers or step out from the group to take a leadership role. Communities are often divided along lines of class, race, ethnicity, religion, and economic interests. Sometimes very small communities split along the fault lines of ideology or even ancient feuds and grudges.

In addition to these realities endemic to so many communities are the stresses that result from rapid economic change, shrinking resource bases, and altered demographic composition. Rural communities in the West may appear to be static and unchanging to the outside observer, but nothing is further from the truth. And, while change presents opportunities as well as challenges, dealing with both requires effective leadership.

Every discussion of the challenges facing the rural West must include the issue of economic development. While improved economic performance will not solve all of the region's problems, addressing them effectively depends on having access to the resources a healthy economy provides.

Nature is at the heart of the rural western economy. Gold and silver under the ground, land for grazing animals and growing crops, and timber-covered mountains drew the early settlers into the region. The relative decline of the natural-resources economy and its negative effects—a boom-and-bust economic cycle and environmental degradation—are the major factors leading westerners to search for alternative ways to profit from nature. Today the West beckons tourists for brief visits and lures permanent residents who appreciate the amenities and experiences provided by rural living.

The present emphasis on attracting tourists and amenity-seeking residents, with its concomitant environmental benefits, must not blind us to the fact that the exploitation of natural resources remains significant in the western economy. Much of the nation's timber remains in the West, where it helps sustain local economies. Mining continues to be important, and the significance of rare earth elements to modern high-tech industrial production suggests that it may become even more prominent. Fossil-fuel production is increasingly significant in much of the rural West, but especially in Colorado, Wyoming, Montana, and North Dakota. Renewable energy, which takes advantage of the abundance of wind and sun in the West, is also growing in importance. And the West remains a major producer of grazing animals and crops, especially in irrigated areas.

The centrality of nature in the western economy is at once a benefit and a detriment because that economy continues to be vulnerable to business cycles, environmental degradation, depletion of finite resources, and government regulation. And looming over everything is the growing scarcity of water and the unknowable, but ominous, effects of climate change.

One thing that the West has in abundance is land, and struggles over who will control it and what they will do with it are an old story in the region. Many conflicts arise from the reality that the federal government owns much of the land in the West—more than 80 percent in Nevada and 60 percent in Idaho and Utah, with substantial shares in other states as well. For many decades, the federal government was a relatively benevolent landlord, allowing grazing, mining, oil drilling, and timber cutting under generally permissive terms. But by the 1960s, pressure from environmentalists and the tourist trade forced the government to put curbs on economic exploitation and emphasize multiple use of public land. The multiple-use approach has not satisfied established interests in the rural West; perhaps it has pleased nobody at all.

Federal control of western lands has never been completely benign. After World War II, the government conducted atmospheric atomic testing in Nevada, threatening nearby residents with nuclear contamination. And for years the military has used the Dugway Proving Ground in Utah to test nerve gas, anthrax, and other chemical and biological agents. In 1968, more than six thousand grazing sheep died when nerve gas drifted beyond the confines of Dugway. Rural westerners have become increasingly concerned about using government lands for these purposes and have thwarted the federal government's efforts to establish storage of spent nuclear material at Yucca Mountain, Nevada. Still, western communities with limited economic-development options continue to consider hosting storage of hazardous wastes.

We do not claim that the issues on which these essays focus are the only ones deserving attention. We don't believe we have asked all the relevant questions, and we certainly haven't come up with all of the answers. What we hope we have done is stimulate conversation about the rural West and its future. This is a conversation that we must have, not only for the sake of the rural West but for all of us.

DEFINING THE RURAL WEST

Plenty of people have a mental picture of the rural West, but a definition that fits most of the region is not easy to come by. Is the rural West central Nevada or eastern Wyoming, where one can drive for miles without seeing an occupied dwelling or even another car? Is it western North Dakota and eastern Montana, where oil-company vehicles dominate the roads and workers crowd the towns? Is it Grand Canyon, Zion, Death Valley, Yellowstone, and the other natural attractions for which the region is known? Is it the Napa Valley of California with its wineries, or the Arkansas Valley of Colorado with its rich, irrigated farms? Is it the world-class ski resorts like Sun Valley, Park City, and Aspen? Is it some of these, all of these, or something else altogether? Defining the rural West is no easy task, and the more one knows about the region, the harder it gets.

In this section, Jon Lauck explores some of the historical factors that helped set the West apart as a distinct region with a unique identity, and he makes an eloquent plea for preserving the characteristics that make the West what it is.

Geoff McGhee takes a different approach. He defines the rural West not by what it has, but by what it lacks—retail centers, post offices, libraries, and especially broadband service. It is these absences that define the rural West in McGhee's mind, and gaining access to them is essential if the rural West is to keep pace with a country and a world increasingly dependent on rapid communication.

Finding the Rural West

JON K. LAUCK

Finding the particular rhythms of the rural West first requires determining the dimensions of the West as a whole, or at least roughly approximating its boundaries and discussing their validity. While a definitive answer remains elusive, the process of determining some working parameters for the rural West bears other fruit. To discuss the dimensions of the West is to engage in a form of regional thinking and makes one more fully aware of a regional sensibility. Despite the recurring belief that regional attachments have largely vanished in the United States, a second look reveals that impulses toward regionalism still exist and that they correspond to regional realities, but they are not always easy to recognize. This essay seeks to evoke some older voices of regionalism to advance this worthy search and elevate regional consciousness.

The West and Its Regional Characteristics

When attempting to define the rural West, it is important to underscore how difficult that is and how contested the conclusion can be. Albert Hurtado notes that the West is "a place on the map with political boundaries as arbitrary as Africa's" and wonders if it is "too riven with historical, cultural, and environmental differences to allow for boundaries that are equally satisfying to all surveyors in the field."[1] Hurtado raises an important question, and it is necessary to approach any definition with caution and humility and not with the idea of arriving at one incontrovertible answer.

The longtime University of Montana historian Dave Emmons echoes this cautionary note and explains that there is no consensus about the parameters of the West, but he does make a valiant effort to derive some reasonable ones and distinguish the West from other regions.[2] Emmons's inclusion of much of the Midwest in his definition—in particular the "corn-belt West" of Minnesota, Iowa, Missouri, Nebraska, and Kansas—is also particularly helpful.[3] The Midwest has suffered in recent decades by being excluded from studies of the trans-Appalachian United States despite its history as the "original West" and its crucial role in first developing a western body of historical research and, more generally, a regional identity.[4]

An expansive view of the region is in keeping with the older concept of a "Great West" embraced by Frederick Jackson Turner, a designation he used in his famous essay on the frontier. If our definition is to be comprehensive, we need to recognize that the original West was the colonial backcountry: the immediate region beyond the Alleghenies and across the Ohio River. As Clarence Carter once noted, one of the earliest acts of Congress, the Northwest Ordinance, was "devised in the first instance to fit the immediate situation in the 'Western' Territory, as it was originally known, where settlements were few, weak, and widely dispersed."[5]

Understanding these early experiences in what is now the Midwest will also illuminate the farther West since much of what happened in the Midwest was repeated there in later decades and was in fact shaped by these earlier experiences. As some western historians have explained, "Just so did the Northwest become old Northwest, and that in turn become Middle West and even—for some—East. Much of western history has always been about ceasing to be west—that is to say, making the long transition from frontier *to region* [italics added]."[6] While we embrace the concept of the Great West, it is no great sin to give "special attention to the 'last' West in the vast and arid trans-Mississippi region" because of its even stronger regional characteristics, but the early West should not be forgotten.[7]

When embracing a broader definition of the American West, in other words, it is helpful to divide it into regions and subregions. The regions include the Old Northwest, the prairie Midwest, the prairie plains or the "short-grass country," the various mountain ranges, the Great Basin, and the more arid regions and deserts. The subregions encompass the Sandhills of Nebraska, the Willamette Valley of Oregon, the West River country of South Dakota, the Grand Prairie of Illinois, the canyonlands of Utah, and so the list goes on.[8] This division satisfies the concept of the West as a Great West or "many Wests," as recent scholars have called it, but it preserves a broader regional vision and recognizes the general qualities that unite the area.[9] In his conversations with Wallace Stegner, Richard Etulain called this a "fragmented unity."[10]

One caveat that may be added to this description involves California, which is arguably difficult to include in the West because of its singular characteristics. The longtime University of Colorado historian Robert Athearn once quipped that he "wouldn't let California into the West with a search warrant."[11] Despite certain reservations about fitting California into the region, it probably has to be included because of its agriculture, mountains, deserts, and other identifiably western landscapes, but it should be recognized as perhaps a highly unique half brother. Gene Gressley once said that "California is to the West what Jackson Hole is to Wyoming."[12] This description clarifies some intraregional tensions about California's influence over—or, some would say, incursions into—parts of the rural West that are explored in this volume.

So what are the unifying characteristics of this region, what Michael Malone once called the "regional bonding forces" that make the parts of the West fit together?[13] First, the region has a highly natural resource–focused economy that includes farming, mining, timber harvesting, and energy production. Second, given this focus on natural resources, the West is, as Bill Cronon has noted, the nation's "most 'land centered' region."[14] Third, since the region becomes increasingly arid as one moves west, access to water becomes increasingly important. Fourth, the region is highly diverse ethnically and includes the largest number of the nation's Indian reservations and many Hispanic and Asian immigrants, which makes issues relating to federal reservations and immigration policies more important. Fifth, because its American history largely postdates the American Revolution, the region shares a heritage with American territorial and frontier settlement.

Finally, it is important to point out the region's space and sparsity. The West is big, and in some places there are not many people, a fact that creates a number of logistical complications for life and of course constitutes one of the reasons many people prefer living there. Western space can be vast, which, as William Least Heat Moon notes, makes things "more noticeable. *Things show up out here* [italics in original]."[15] As Wallace Stegner once said, "people have the dignity of rareness" in the rural West that makes it distinct from urban cores and suburbs.[16]

These characteristics color life in the rural West in ways that they do not in other parts of the country. That these characteristics and attendant social and economic issues are more prominent in the rural West affirms that regionalism still matters. Paying greater attention to regional trends can help us contextualize concerns that may appear localized or isolated, such as the growing pressure on water resources, which is reflected in the varying political attitudes underlying surface-water and groundwater irrigation efforts in Kansas and Nebraska; the way the news is reported and disseminated in small towns such as Norwood, Colorado; state taxation issues stemming from new development in the energy-rich West; the efforts of rural communities in Oregon and the rest of the West to promote economic development of their resources; the experience of one band of Goshute Indians with economic development, nuclear waste, and local and regional reaction to their plans; the pressures of in-migration and "rural gentrification" in the Yellowstone area evidenced by cultural friction over water use and wolf reintroduction; the complexities of health-care delivery generally in the West and, more specifically, the challenges of reaching Latino immigrants; local opposition to rules promulgated by federal authorities and the government's control of land in the West; and ways a ranch family in Nevada may cope with the shifting fortunes of Great Basin topography, changing federal land policies, and even the nuclear age.

Recognizing Regionalism and the Problem of Homogenization

Recognition of regional characteristics and the formation of regional identity are not new. Perhaps most famously, Frederick Jackson Turner recognized the importance of regional identity and affiliation.[17] He focused, in particular, on how certain geographic places and the people who settled them shaped regions and forged regional identities. Turner also went beyond just examining the formation of regional identity; he focused on "state resistance to the nationalizing process" and regional "resistance to national homogeneity."[18] When he retired from Harvard, Turner gave a speech to the Wisconsin Historical Society in which he emphasized various forms of regional heritage. When the nation's leaders made decisions on a national level, Turner said, they could not overlook "the fact of a vast and varied Union of unlike sections."[19]

In Turner's Midwest, the first West, his regional vision led to the creation of a school of historians who advanced his work and research interests for several decades.[20] Since he led the effort to get American historians focused on the West beyond the Ohio River, Turner is, as Martin Ridge notes, "justly named the father of western history."[21] Other prominent regionalists followed Turner, including Walter Prescott Webb, Bernard DeVoto, James Malin, and Wallace Stegner, and these voices collectively gave the West greater definition and a sense of regional identity.[22]

According to the now-old prairie folk singer, "You don't know what you've got 'til it's gone," and, indeed, the concentration of writers and historians on regionalism has been driven in part by concerns over diminishing regional attachments.[23] As early as the 1890s, Turner's graduate-school friend, Woodrow Wilson, was discussing the "homogenization" that would change the Great West and make it less distinct.[24] Lord Bryce, who famously visited the United States in 1887 and saw the West as "the most American part of America"—or the least linked to the mother countries of Europe—returned in 1910 and noted "a phase of life which is now swiftly disappearing and may never be again seen anywhere." He described the way the western "regions are now becoming more like the older parts of the Republic."[25]

Between Bryce's visits, the pioneer Californian and later Harvard philosopher Josiah Royce also expressed his fear that the coming flood of mass culture would homogenize American life.[26] Royce called for preserving the "independence" and "organic life" of the "provinces."[27] He promoted the work of the interior's intellectuals, rejected the "West's subservience to the East," and generally celebrated decentralization and the "diversity and cultural pluralism" that the provinces preserved.[28] Midwesterners such as Hamlin Garland similarly sought to "combat literary centralization," especially in New York, and "to build up local centres" by recognizing the literature from the "great interior spaces."[29]

The effort to maintain local traditions in the face of "suffocating sameness" bolstered regionalism.[30] Turner, for example, believed that regions were "restraints upon a deadly uniformity" that he saw growing in the country.[31] While Turner saw regions forming in the West, others were skeptical. Some worried that the West was so new and its institutions and culture so derivative that there would not be enough time for regional roots to sprout. They were concerned that before regional sentiments could take hold in the West, the region would be overwhelmed by national culture: radio (and later television), syndicated newspaper stories, chain stores, and styles springing from New York and Hollywood.[32]

As these concerns indicate, identifying and promoting regional traditions are difficult tasks. Writing in the 1930s for the University of Nebraska's literary journal *Prairie Schooner*, English professor Lowry Charles Wimberly warned readers about the difficulties of preserving regionalism in a homogenizing world. He was not against regional characteristics; indeed he seemed to appreciate them and noted that they represented a "Western movement," but he thought they were fading fast.[33] "There was a day," Wimberly said, "when a mountainous region or a prairie country played an important part in determining man's point of view or philosophy of life. But as a force in molding American mind and character, physical environment counts for little nowadays and will count for less and less as time goes on."[34] The "forces" and "materials" of regionalism, he thought, had "virtually spent themselves."[35] Wimberly was identifying valid concerns, but his eulogy was premature.

Eastern Hostility

In addition to attempts to hold onto a fading past, regionalism was also encouraged by the neglect and at times abuse of other regions by the concentrated cultural and economic power of the American Northeast. These feelings quickly emerged in the first American West just beyond the Ohio River.[36] The Iowan Herbert Quick felt stifled because "the great editors" in the East failed to be moved, for example, by the idea of an Iowa literature.[37] The Idaho writer Vardis Fisher, for another example, urged westerners to resist the power of the northeastern "literary establishment," which dominated book publishing, reviewing, and awarding prizes and was too cozy, urban, and alienated from the West to understand the area.[38] Fisher noted the comment of one *Harper's* magazine editor, who said, "Vardis Fisher doesn't seem to be speaking to me."[39] Fisher and the editor's outlooks did not align. Fisher said of this editor, "His mind and interests are so urban and traditional, mine so rural and non-conformist that we really have little in common."[40] Fisher thought people should recognize the "difference between country and city minds" and, based on his time in Manhattan, concluded that "it would be unreasonable of me to expect New Yorkers to like the kind of books I wanted to write."[41] There was too much separation of space, culture, and economic focus; in other words, there were critical regional differences. Stegner once noted all the acquaintances and connections he had made in the East but commented that when he moved to the West, "that was cut off as if by guillotine."[42]

Fisher's criticisms of the literary establishment, the dominance of the East, and the sneering directed at the rural West by some commentators and writers are good to remember. They underscore the distinctions between regions. Fisher is right—many people in Manhattan really do not understand the rural West, nor do they care to. That is certainly their choice, but it is important to acknowledge that, as the *Harper's* magazine editor said, writers grounded in the rural West do not speak to him, and therefore his attention to western matters is necessarily cursory, dismissive, or even hostile. Fisher's Populist regionalism, in other words, reminds us of the value of our own unapologetic regional attachments, which can be embraced without fear of censure from a distant set of cultural critics who do not really understand the region.

The western writer Mary Austin noted of New York that the "people I met were seldom interested in the things that interested me."[43] She protested the "centralization of publishing trades in and around Manhattan" and the fact that most cultural criticism was nothing more than what "a small New York group thinks ought to be written and thought."[44] A half century later, the cultural critic Christopher Lasch, who was born in Omaha but embraced a more cosmopolitan outlook that dismissed regional attachments early in his career, rebelled against the constrictions of eastern intellectual life and began a serious tabulation of the costs of hostility to regionalism and a search for regional rootedness that provided a deeper meaning to an atomized age.[45]

In short, Turner, Fisher, Lasch and many others can help us see the rural West. They can help us find its rhythms and texture. They can help defend the culture of the rural West against either abuse or neglect by the nation's metropolitan centers and the homogenizing effects of mass culture. If we want to understand the rural West and preserve its regional distinctiveness and independence, identifying and promoting the region's voices—such as Turner, Fisher, and Lasch—and recalling the older organs of regionalism—such as the journals *Frontier*, *The Midland*, and *Southwest Review*—are a first step.

The Persistence of Regionalism

The overt warnings and inherent skepticism in Lowry Charles Wimberly's commentary about the disappearance of regionalism cannot be forgotten, but this attitude has become too prominent. Regional impulses are still detectable, and we should become better at finding them. Scholars should take off their academic mortarboards for a moment and just absorb what they see. Despite the monotonous generica we encounter in our travels, it is still obvious that Laredo, Texas, is not Boston and Seattle is not Charleston, South Carolina.[46] Geography and history and place still matter.[47] To think more broadly, there are reasons why we see constant headlines about the impending implosion of the euro, secession in Catalonia and Quebec, and the decision to subsidize Belgian draft horses in Flanders to "preserve regional identity."[48]

Wallace Stegner once noted that rootedness is more difficult in the West with its tradition of migration and mobility. But he also recognized that roots could grow and be valuable. He recognized the "physical and spiritual bonds that develop within a place and a society" and promote "communities and traditions" and the "gods that make places holy."[49] Stegner urged us to look past the cities of the West—which are similar in many ways to other cities[50]—and see the *rural West*, "out in the boondocks where the interstates do not reach, mainline planes do not fly, and branch plants do not locate."[51] He called our attention to the "winter wheat towns on the subhumid edge, whose elevators and bulbous silver water towers announce them miles away, or county towns in ranch country," which are "bounded by weedy prairie" and are "scruffy and indispensable."[52] "I know how precious is the safety of a few known streets and vacant lots and familiar houses," Stegner recalled.[53]

While Stegner worried that there was too much instability and movement and dislocation in the West—more than he wished there would be, anyway—he also noted the more settled places, where regional attachments were stronger. In contrast to the more atomized parts of the West, Stegner recognized, for example, the "unity" of the "corn Midwest."[54] This is a testament to Stegner's ability to search out dynamics that others cannot see but also to his Iowa roots. He was born in Lake Mills, Iowa, after all, next to the Minnesota border, and his grandfather was a classic Norwegian Lutheran immigrant who settled in the Midwest and sought "to build a little piece of Norway in Iowa."[55] As a young man, Stegner took his "grandfather's Old Country name and signed it in all my schoolbooks."[56]

He was attracted to ranching in the West because it was more stable and closer to farming and the midwestern small-town tradition, but he understood that the latter will always be underappreciated because the "horseman is always more romantic than the plowman or the townsman."[57] But the latter had the ingredients of a "continuous, forming life" and "a local character, a local literature" that could create a "regional culture."[58] In contrast to the amorphous churning of parts of western culture, in other words, Stegner recognized the "healthy provincialism of Iowa."[59] He saw that, in addition to the individualism and mobility often associated with the West, there also existed, as Michael Steiner and David Wrobel have noted, a "counterdesire for stability and more intimate places of identity."[60]

In short, Stegner helps us see that places are different. They have their own tempo and cultural dynamics and institutions and their own sense of place and regionalism or lack of rootedness. In Utah, as Stegner explained, the Mormon culture of the Great Basin was remarkably settled after a long period of dislocation, whereas Californians are much less rooted.[61] A psychiatrist once came to a book talk I gave in Fargo, North Dakota, and commented that he had moved his practice from the L.A. suburbs because his wife had started a new job. He said the first thing that struck him was that people in North Dakota knew exactly where they were from—which fjord in Norway their grandparents had migrated from, where they had settled on the plains, which 160 acres had been the family's patch of earth, and which little towns they had organized their lives around. He said people in California simply did not talk or think that way. He saw them as completely without roots and wider connections.[62]

He said this had caused him to think differently about the psychological maladies that afflicted people. Specifically, he began to think about the psychological consequences of rootlessness and appreciate the concerns of those who worried about the erosion of rural folkways and the once-strong agrarian tradition.[63] He was discovering what Lucy Lippard calls the "lure of the local," or the "geographical component of the need to belong somewhere, one anti-dote to a prevailing alienation," or what Cleanth Brooks describes as the "strength to be gained" from a "sense of belonging to a living community and the special focus upon the world bestowed by one's having a precise location in time and history."[64]

Los Angeles is an exception to the rest of the West, but it makes the point about the persistence of regionalism in other parts of the country, especially, I would highlight, in the rural West.[65] It helps us to see regional attachments that are right in front of us but we are not recognizing because we are not used to seeing them.[66] The raft of books about red versus blue states are often perceived in partisan terms as in-the-moment blips to feed the cable-news commentary–industrial complex and not as evidence of something deeper about historical development and regional orientation. But the varied political attitudes of the states are unique and can tell us much about the way they are shaped by historical forces and regionalism.[67]

More specifically, regional dynamics are at work in the western caucus in the United States Senate and legislative battles such as the farm bill, which is largely fought regionally.[68] They are apparent in the 2012 Montana Senate race, for example, where the candidates argued about who was the real farmer or rancher.[69] They are obvious in the controversy over the California game commissioner who hunted mountain lions in Idaho, where the sport is uncontroversial, but which caused a firestorm in California (and gives meaning to Idaho bumper stickers such as "Don't Californicate Idaho" and "Keep Idaho beautiful; go back to California").[70] In short, attention needs to be paid to recent scholars who have emphasized that the "regionalist impulse is still very much alive."[71]

It should also be noted that regionalism is not limited to those with deep personal and historical connections to a place, although those connections can certainly deepen regional sentiments. Yi-Fu Tuan distinguishes between "rootedness," which is historic, traditional, and deep and may not even be recognized consciously because it is so embedded, and a "sense of place," which is more self-conscious and the product of learning, research, and a purposeful absorption in one's surroundings.[72] A sense of place, Tuan explains, "implies a certain distance between self and place that allows the self to appreciate a place."[73] Therefore, regionalism is not as exclusionary as some critics fear—people can learn to love a place, even though they were initially foreign to it. More importantly, all people can find a place, both those who are new and those who are old timers but not aware of it.

Even natives may need help finding their home. They should look around and pay attention to their surroundings and the culture that still breathes and affects them in ways they do not recognize. Michael Steiner and David Wrobel, two brilliant scholars who have noted the persistence of regionalism in American culture—albeit a waxing and waning one—state that regionalism is often a "largely unconscious source of identity."[74] "Unreflective immersion in landscape or movement through space are more common than deliberate sense of place," they explain, "and a degree of environmental blindness is inevitable and even necessary to function smoothly in the world."[75]

People are busy and distracted, in other words. But with a nudge, they can begin to see what is all around them and has been part of their entire lives, and they can become more active ingredients in a regional ferment. All people can find a place, in short, both those who are new to it and those who are products of it but not aware of their roots. To find a place, however, one must first see it, as John Brinkerhoff Jackson has demonstrated through his attention to the small towns and rural spaces of the American interior.[76] The problem of "placelessness," Lucy Lippard argues, "may simply be place ignored, unseen, or unknown."[77]

So while regionalism may not be as strong as it once was, it does live on—and it can emerge in new ways. That's a good thing and leads me to offer five pieces of advice designed to foster regional consciousness.

Don't Fear the Local

First, people should control their fear of the local, which can be especially strong for academics and other elite information analysts. For a long time, a part of being modern, according to Daniel Bell, was a "detachment from place and time" and an embrace of "social and geographical mobility."[78] To be cosmopolitan was to be antiprovincial and against local-yokel small-town boosters. It's important not to fall into this trap—to be smart and educated and liberal and liberated and therefore against the local.

Minnesota historian Theodore Blegen once rightly noted the provincialism of the supposed cosmopolitans and saw regionalism as its reverse because it sought to "view the region in relation to the nation and the world."[79] Regionalism, in other words, helps us to see other places better.[80] Regionalism places people in a broader perspective. Also some people—those in the rural West, for example—can be lost or excluded from a common form of cosmopolitanism. This form obstructs "a complete picture of the American scene" and, as one analyst noted, obscures "our buried cultures and our submerged classes."[81]

Grant Wood, a well-known spokesman for regionalism, rightly dismissed the charges of boosterism used to undermine regional ethos: "This is no mere chauvinism. If it is patriotic, it is so because a feeling for one's own milieu and for the validity of one's own life and its surrounding is patriotic."[82] Wood's use of the term *patriotism* is telling because of the age of nationalism and state-organized political terror that he was living through. He did not mean patriotism in that sense. He meant it as George Orwell did—as in opposition to blind nationalism and its thirst for power and control over others. Orwell thought patriotism "mean[t] devotion to a particular place and a particular way of life, which one believes to be the best in the world but has no wish to force on other people. Patriotism is of its nature defensive, both militarily and culturally."[83]

Wood and Orwell were making the point that an attachment to a region, as Robert Dorman has explained, is primarily a "soft" form of cultural identity, which often consists of magazines, journals, art, works of history, museums, public forums, and civic inclinations, not a politically rebellious, separatist, secessionist, or racial movement. It respects American federalism and genuine intellectual pluralism and seeks a place for all the nation's subcultures.[84]

A Capacity for Resistance

Second, based in part on a life with young children, I feel we need better cultural defenses. I feel as if I am in constant combat mode against the invasion of Dora the Explorer, Elmo, Thomas the Train, and the Wiggles. And I know that they are just the advance scouts of a much larger and more menacing blitzkrieg of mass culture featuring desperate and real housewives, sex in various cities, and the bewildering world of absurdity and self-absorption that defines boardwalks in New Jersey. In a few years, the forms of this invasion will change because—by their nature—the elements of this culture are created by those who, as one regionalist put it, are "attracted by any cheap and 'smarty' fashion that can be made to sound shocking" at the moment.[85]

The historian Joe Amato and his son, Anthony, describe this sense of invasion and the inability to protect and save what we think is important when they write about rural Minnesota:

> Nothing restrains the forces of the outside world. Unresisted and undeflected, they intrude on the countryside in unprecedented ways. Opinions, images, sensibilities, and even strangers themselves enter the rural mind as if they were without barrier.... The agents of change enter the rural community without knocking and, trafficking in the contraband of wishes and daydreams, they steal minds and hearts.[86]

"Various forms of media homogenize ideas, feelings, and language," they explain, "and place no longer defines mind or morals."[87] Limiting electronic media (see Iowa's fight against MTV or the V-chip debate as examples) is a big part of the solution, of course, but Twitter and Facebook and iPhones are so ubiquitous now that the situation borders on the uncontrollable. Lord Bryce would be stunned.

While I understand the challenges of this invasion, I think steps can be taken to develop resistance. Building personal levies against the electronic flood is important, and, as noted, recognizing regional intellectual and scholarly voices is helpful. It is also essential to focus on the popular sphere, which includes such basic components of community life as a strong, locally oriented newspaper. Unfortunately, local reporting has suffered lately. Local newspapers are cutting staff and space, and more generic and national stories are filling the paper.[88] Local Associated Press bureaus are also being cut. National reporting isn't going to be much help, either. An editor at the *New York Times* recently told me that the newspaper is basically using one reporter to cover eight midwestern/Great Plains states.

So it is important to support locally oriented news—both traditional newspapers and their newer websites and blogs—and maintain healthy skepticism about what passes for news in the national media. The writer Frederick Manfred perhaps put it best when discussing eastern attitudes toward regional writing, offering the reminder that "most of the nation's communication media are in the hands of aliens."[89] In other words, national news is disconnected from local life. Engaging with local and regional news and events, on the other hand, signals a sense of being home and centered and placed and rooted. "Home is where you know what's going on," says the Iowa folksinger Greg Brown.[90]

Another way to stave off the outside flood is, I think, recognizing and resisting snubs. The jabs and slams and jokes from Hollywood in movies such as *Napoleon Dynamite, Fargo,* and *About Schmidt* get stale and deserve pushback.[91] E.J. Dionne's new book, *Our Divided Political Heart,* makes the point that the smug dismissals of the rural West as "fly-over country" and "Jesusland" need to be abandoned by the intelligentsia.[92] One aspect of this resistance is the recent country-music song, "Fly over States," by Jason Aldean.[93] Similarly Thomas Frank's book attacking Kansas was countered by Nebraska-grown writer Denis Boyles's gracefully argued book about his father's hometown of Superior, Nebraska.[94] Another American interior author, in a witty act of mockery and dissent against the coastal domination of culture, donned a T-shirt reading, "MINOR REGIONAL NOVELIST."[95]

The Western History Problem and Regionalism

A third dimension of a revived attention to regionalism is a balanced approach to western history, which was once the norm. Because they often felt neglected by easterners in the profession, historians in the Midwest, under the leadership of Frederick Jackson Turner, organized a western history association that focused on the history of the Mississippi Valley.[96] Once this western-oriented history began to grow, some historians farther west sought a greater focus on their region and ultimately formed the Western History Association in 1961.[97] This successful venture brought academics and popular western writers and regionalists together and focused attention on the story of the western United States.

But in the 1980s, the New Western Historians began to emphasize a different side of the West: failure, oppression, and racism. As Eric Foner and Jon Weiner gleefully reported in *The Nation,* these historians "hammered the final nail into the coffin of Frederick Jackson Turner's 'frontier thesis.'"[98] This overemphasis on the negative naturally causes regional attachments to suffer, and the objections of those who criticized this approach deserve to be heard.

This new wave of history was too bound up in the political causes of the 1960s and not focused enough on the unique features of the American West. It was too "ideologically driven" and wedded to promoting social reforms.[99] It wanted to create a "new past" or a "usable past" to advance a particular set of causes.[100] In short, it was too much of a myth-busting exercise and not enough of a good-faith attempt to understand the American West as a region and map its subregions. The leading proponent of this New Western History, Patricia Nelson Limerick, said her goal was to make western history as grim as the history of the American South.[101] It should be perfectly clear, however, that the West is not the South; it does not have the South's historical burdens, so we should not be trying to invent them.

There are costs associated with the overeager age of debunking the alleged myths of the American West. If untrue myths persist, they should be corrected. But there has been a tendency to dismiss the positives in the West too quickly and emphasize the negatives. Recent research on Dakota Territory, for example, indicates that there is much to recommend in the more traditional views of western settlement and Turner's writing.[102]

The emphasis on the negative is also harmful to regionalism. When debunking supposed myths goes too far, "it strips people of social memory, of loyalty to their own remembered past," as Edward Ayers has noted.[103] It causes people to disconnect from their region. The University of Utah historian Robert Goldberg once chided scholars who "play it safe and pay homage to the New Western Canon that disparages any sense of the positive to balance negatives."[104] He was affirming that it was acceptable to acknowledge accomplishments in the West and not be swept away by the trendy tide of critical western scholarship.

There has been, of late, a more careful consideration of the costs of this overzealous myth busting. William Deverell, for example, has been sympathetic to the work of historians—the New Western Historians in particular—who "seek to defamiliarize the field and its icons" and "to disassemble that which was once solid."[105] Still, Deverell does reluctantly acknowledge that "there may be some truth behind that caricature of the decent western lawman out to do good, some reality shadowing the memories we have of the independent farmer, the rugged cowboy, the schoolteacher."[106]

This is an important concession, and it echoes comments made at a panel discussion of New Western Historians in Oakland in 2011. Richard White wondered about the costs of all this debunking and regretted the "collateral damage" that he and others might have caused.[107] Patricia Nelson Limerick has also lessened the intensity of her criticism in recent years. Stegner once said that "repudiation and parody" had gone "too far" and that the critics had "cut out something that was valuable; they throw out the baby with the bath water."[108] Stegner's warning may be getting more of a hearing.[109] The more recent emphasis on balance is a good sign for western regionalism.

If the bias against studying the frontier process and older historians such as Turner can be overcome, then we will be able to understand western regionalism better. David Wrobel emphasizes that the frontier process was essential to the later sense of place that emerged and that the two are tightly intertwined.[110] Focusing on pioneer societies that formed later, Wrobel explains how pioneers "were connected by their shared experience, remained connected through shared memory of that experience, developed a shared sense of westernness in relation to that experience and an emotional connection to a particular place."[111] Western history done well, historians sympathetic to Turner have noted, can explain how a frontier becomes a region, how the frontier process has produced "locales and regions as different as the fishing villages of Nova Scotia, the hill country of Appalachia, the Corn Belt of the Midwest, the cattle lands of the High Plains, the Navajo sheep pastures of the desert Southwest, and the irrigated agroindustrial empire of Southern California."[112] Regionalism is grounded in the frontier process that Turner explained, in other words, and when the frontier and Turner are denigrated, it naturally follows that regionalism suffers. Bashing Turner, then, needs to end. He can teach us much about regionalism, and he deserves to be heard, not propped up as a rhetorical foil.

Understanding Antistatism

One of the central leaders in western history and a dissenter from the New Western History group leads us to a fourth piece of advice. Gene Gressley, who served the University of Wyoming for many years, was not enthused about the New Western History and the way it distorted the view of the West held by nonwesterners. More importantly, Gressley grasped the importance of understanding western regionalism and that westerners were concerned about what the federal state had done to it. The westerner, Gressley once reminded us, was "far more Brandeisian in his emphasis on limiting and managing the federal government than he was intrigued by the New Nationalism of the enormously popular Theodore Roosevelt."[113] Gressley noted westerners' concern about the "decentralized transfer of localism into the maws of a central bureaucratic state."[114] This concern was based on the "westerner's romance with localism" and "fear of bureaucracy and government planning."[115] Gressley remarked that in 1900, the federal government consumed 2 percent of the gross domestic product

(GDP), but by 1980, it was using 30 percent (and it is now headed for 40 percent).[116] Gressley observed that the various acts of resistance to federal power in recent decades were "expressions of anguish" from people "desperately trying to avoid the vortex of the whirlpool of federal centralization."[117] Most importantly, regions—those unique and often rural places around our nation—were "more than dust swirling around the gravitational pull of the Washingtonian cosmic black hole."[118] They were specific places with local cultures and identities and always at risk of losing their heritage because of expanding outside control.

This control relates to governmental power. Since the beginning of the Great West, the territories and later states of the West have resisted federal encroachments on local decision making. While this is true of states generally, this resistance assumes greater significance in the West because the national government controls substantial resources in the region. Turner is again instructive on this preference for decentralization in the West. While noting the problem of potential fragmentation, Turner thought American regionalism was preferable, as Michael Steiner explains, to "inflexible nationalism and the consolidation of life into an ever-widening, undifferentiated mass" and an "unvarying urban-industrial order."[119] Turner, Steiner says, was suspicious of the "leviathan nation-state" because he wanted to preserve regional diversity.[120] In his recent book about Turner and the midwestern historical tradition, David Brown notes that what united the first group of historians in the West—now the Midwest—was, in essence, their "concerns about the centrality of power and politics in eastern hands."[121]

The midwestern historians were also acutely aware that local people had formed new democratic governments in their new states that could help revive the democratic spirit in the East. In the agrarian territories and states of the West, Thomas Jefferson believed, the republican principles and practices of the American Revolution would be renewed: "By enlarging the empire of liberty, we multiply its auxiliaries, and provide new sources of renovation, should its principles at any time degenerate in those portions of our country which gave them birth."[122]

Not only would these western states and territories be a source of democratic renewal and innovation, but they would advance the decentralization that the founders of the country had promoted. Peter Onuf explains that regionalism is rooted in the beginnings of the republic and the founders' emphasis on empowering the "expanding periphery" as a counterweight to "metropolitan authority" and an "imperial center."[123]

We need to understand the dynamics of federal power and resistance to it on the local level better than we do. Perhaps our lack of understanding is due to recent shortcomings in western history.[124] Whatever the cause, a greater focus on these dynamics may help us understand national politics better.

Regionalism, Community, and Politics

Politics leads us to a final point—regionalism promotes community and civic life. Community involvement and communal interaction and participation in civic affairs stem in part from confidence in and loyalty to regions and their cultures.[125] If you are attached to a place, you care more about how it is governed and its future. Turner, Lasch, Gressley, and others have noted the importance of local community and the costs of statism. The Californian Robert Nisbet also famously defended the importance of local and "intermediary institutions."[126] It seems significant that Nisbet was a westerner, the son of a lumberyard worker, and grew up in a small town where local community institutions were important (his dad embraced the local poker game and his mom, the local church). Nisbet's philosophy of community was "premised on protection of the social order—'family, neighborhood, local community, and *region foremost* [italics added].'"[127]

Regionalism, in short, can promote community by preserving local and traditional life and self-governance, what Josiah Royce saw as a healthy provincialism conducive to local civic energies and democratic action.[128] Lewis Mumford, whose work intrigued Lasch and inspired other regionalists, similarly saw regionalism as a means of fostering local control and as a break against monopoly and colonialism. As John Thomas explained, it offered a healthy "counter-doctrine to modern bureaucracy, economic consolidation, and political centralism."[129]

Surrender to outside forces, on the other hand, weakens democracy. Elite condescension toward the provinces and local obeisance to coastal intellectuals, the Iowan Ruth Suckow worried, sapped smaller-scale democratic energies and the capacity for regional resistance. Their persistence, she thought, too often gave "despair to our intelligentsia" and dampened the "spirit of participation" in the institutions of the common, local life.[130] Without strong local culture, as E. Bradford Burns explained in his treatment of Iowa regionalism, regions are open "to every sort of external exploitation."[131] With it democracy is vigorous and more durable.

Conclusion—against Subordination

I offer one final word of caution. We don't want to take regionalism too far. Turner has been fairly criticized for finding too much uniqueness in the West and not paying enough attention to what westerners borrowed from the East. Using the West as a category of analysis can also be tricky when so much of what happens unfolds in similar ways in other regions. The historian Robert Johnston has recently argued that scholars should "radically subordinate" regionalism because it causes them to lose sight of other more important transregional factors in American life and causes otherwise important research to be treated less seriously because of its designation as western history.[132]

While Johnston usefully cautions against the dangers of overdoing regionalism, there are significant regional dimensions to our lives, and we should recognize and encourage them. To radically suppress these regional sentiments is at best unwise and snobbish and at worst mildly totalitarian. Recognizing regionalism, finding regional voices, preserving some capacity for the maintenance of regional cultures, protecting regionalism against the flood of outside generica and coercion, and recognizing its stimulating effects on local community and political participation are all worthy goals for those engaged in life and civic affairs in the rural West. They deserve emphasis and focus, not suppression and subordination.

Notes

1. Albert L. Hurtado, "The Proffered Paradigm: Finding the West in Time and Space," *Western Historical Quarterly* 25, no. 4 (Winter 1994): 469.
2. David M. Emmons, "Constructed Province: History and the Making of the Last American West," *Western Historical Quarterly* 25, no. 4 (Winter 1994), 436–59.
3. Ibid., 447.
4. Jon K. Lauck, *The Lost Region: Toward a Revival of Midwestern History* (Iowa City: University of Iowa Press, 2013).
5. Clarence E. Carter, "Colonialism in Continental United States," *South Atlantic Quarterly* 47 (January 1948): 19.
6. William Cronon, George Miles, and Jay Gitlin, "Becoming West: Toward a New Meaning for Western History," in *Under an Open Sky: Rethinking*

America's Western Past, ed. William Cronon, George Miles, and Jay Gitlin (New York: W. W. Norton, 1992), 26.

7. When discussing the views of the authors of *Under an Open Sky* (26, 6), John Mack Faragher notes that "western history is the study of 'the Great West,' with special attention to the 'last' West in the vast and arid trans-Mississippi region, an approach that obviously owes a great deal to Turner." Faragher, "The Frontier Trail: Rethinking Turner and Reimagining the American West," *American Historical Review* 98, no. 1 (February 1993): 117. See also Frederic Logan Paxson, *When the West Is Gone* (New York: Henry Holt and Company, 1930), 78.
8. Frederick C. Luebke, "Regionalism and the Great Plains: Problems of Concept and Method," *Western Historical Quarterly* 15, no. 1 (January 1984): 28–29.
9. "More than such compact and geographically distinct regions as New England, the Deep South, or the Upper Midwest, the West is a sprawling amalgamation of diverse subregions." Michael P. Malone, introduction to *Historians and the American West*, ed. Michael P. Malone (Lincoln: University of Nebraska Press, 1983), 1. See also Wallace Stegner and Richard Etulain, *Stegner: Conversations on History and Literature*, rev. ed. (Reno: University of Nevada Press, 1996), 156; and Robert L. Dorman, *Hell of a Vision: Regionalism and the Modern American West* (Tucson: University of Arizona Press, 2012), 4. The idea of many Wests, however, is not new. See Paxson, *When the West Is Gone*, 15.
10. Stegner and Etulain, *Stegner*, xv. On the difficulties of defining the West, see Walter Nugent, "Where Is the American West? Report on a Survey," *Montana: The Magazine of Western History* 42 (Summer 1992): 2–23.
11. Robert Athearn, quoted in Emmons, "Constructed Province," 436. "One thing Athearn was also clear about: California was not true West." Howard R. Lamar, "Commentary," in *Writing the History of the American West*, ed. Martin Ridge (Worcester: American Antiquarian Society, 1991), 114.
12. Gene Gressley, "The American West, the World, and the Twenty-First Century," in *The American West in 2000: Essays in Honor of Gerald D. Nash*, ed. Richard W. Etulain and Ferenc Morton Szasz (Albuquerque: University of New Mexico Press, 2003), 175. See also Stegner and Etulain, *Stegner*, x.
13. Michael P. Malone, "Beyond the Last Frontier: Toward a New Approach to Western History," *Western Historical Quarterly* 20, no. 4 (November 1989): 426.
14. William G. Robbins, "Western History: A Dialectic on the Modern Condition," *Western Historical Quarterly* 20, no. 4 (November 1989): 433.
15. William Least Heat Moon, *Blue Highways: A Journey into America* (New York: Fawcett Crest, 1982), 136.
16. Stegner and Etulain, *Stegner*, xviii.
17. See Donald G. Holtgrieve, "Frederick Jackson Turner as a Regionalist," *Professional Geographer* 17 (May 1974), 159–65.
18. Frederick Jackson Turner, "Is Sectionalism in America Dying Away," *American*

Journal of Sociology 13, no. 5 (March 1908): 661–62; Dorman, *Hell of a Vision*, 13–14.

19. Turner, quoted in Richard W. Etulain, *Re-Imagining the Modern West: A Century of Fiction, History, and Art* (Tucson: University of Arizona Press, 1996), 107.
20. Jon K. Lauck, "The Prairie Historians and the Foundations of Midwestern History," *Annals of Iowa: A Quarterly Journal of History* 71, no. 2 (Spring 2012), 137–173; Lauck, *The Lost Region*.
21. Martin Ridge, "Frederick Jackson Turner and His Ghost: The Writing of Western History," in *Writing the History of the American West*, 67.
22. Etulain, *Re-Imagining the Modern West*, 104–18; see also Dorman, *Hell of a Vision*.
23. Joni Mitchell, "Big Yellow Taxi," from the album *Ladies of the Canyon* (1970). Mitchell is of Norwegian ancestry (Anderson) and grew up on the prairies of Alberta and Saskatchewan and in western Canada generally. "My years there were glorious, really. I loved growing up in Saskatchewan. We always lived on the edge of small towns, so I had the luxury of riding my bicycle into the country, looking for beautiful places, which usually constituted a grove of trees." See Mary Aikins, "Heart of a Prairie Girl," *Reader's Digest*, July 2005.
24. David M. Wrobel, "Beyond the Frontier-Region Dichotomy," *Pacific Historical Review* 65, no. 3 (August 1996): 417–18.
25. Bryce, quoted in Richard W. Etulain, "Shifting Interpretations of Western American Cultural History," in *Historians and the American West*, 415.
26. Josiah Royce, "Provincialism," in Royce, *Race Questions, Provincialism, and Other American Problems* (1908; repr. Freeport, New York: Books for Libraries Press, Inc., 1967), 57–108; Dorman, *Hell of a Vision*, 9, 64. On the "long series of death knells for the West and other American regions," (1), see Michael C. Steiner and David M. Wrobel, "Many Wests: Discovering a Dynamic Western Regionalism," in *Many Wests: Place, Culture, and Identity*, ed. Michael C. Steiner and David M. Wrobel (Lawrence: University Press of Kansas, 1997), 1–30.
27. "Phi Beta Kappa Address; Provincialism the Cure for Mob Spirit; Professor Royce of Harvard Discusses Interesting Problems in Scholarly Manner," *Daily Iowan*, June 12, 1902; E. Bradford Burns, *Kinship with the Land: Regionalist Thought in Iowa, 1894–1942* (Iowa City: University of Iowa Press, 1996), 25; Robert V. Hine, "A Centennial for Josiah Royce," *California History* 66, no. 2 (June 1987): 90, 93.
28. Robert V. Hine, "The Western Intellectual Josiah Royce," *Montana: The Magazine of Western History* 41, no. 3 (Summer 1991): 71; Stow Persons, *The Decline of American Gentility* (New York: Columbia University Press, 1973), 250–52.
29. Robert L. Dorman, *Revolt of the Provinces: The Regionalist Movement in America, 1920–1945* (Chapel Hill: University of North Carolina Press, 1993), 17.
30. Wrobel, "Beyond the Frontier-Region Dichotomy," 426.
31. Ibid., 420.

32. John W. Caughey, *The American West: Frontier & Region* (Los Angeles: Ward Ritchie Press, 1969), 4.
33. Lowry Charles Wimberly, "The New Regionalism," *Prairie Schooner* 6, no. 3 (Summer 1932), 214. On Wimberly's leadership of *Prairie Schooner* and his critique of regionalism, see Kathleen A. Boardman, "Lowry Charles Wimberly and the Retreat of Regionalism," *Great Plains Quarterly* 11 (Summer 1991): 143–56.
34. Wimberly, "The New Regionalism," 220.
35. Ibid., 221. See also Wallace Stegner, *The American West as Living Space* (Ann Arbor: University of Michigan Press, 1987), 71. On the decline of regional thinking, see Terry G. Jordan, "The Concept and Method," in *Regional Studies: The Interplay of Land and People*, ed. Glen E. Lich (College Station: Texas A&M University Press, 1992), 9–10, 18.
36. Jon K. Lauck, "Why the Midwest Matters," *Midwest Quarterly* 54, no. 2 (Winter 2013), 175–77.
37. Ruth Suckow, "Middle Western Literature," *English Journal* 21, no. 3 (March 1932): 175. On the dismissal and false categorization of regional literature, see Jon K. Lauck, "The Myth of the Midwestern 'Revolt from the Village,'" *Mid-America* 40 (2013): 39–85.
38. Vardis Fisher, "The Western Writer and the Eastern Establishment," *Western American Literature* 1 (Winter 1967): 244, 254–56. The journal *Western American Literature* was founded in 1965 to advance regional writing. Etulain, "Shifting Interpretations of Western American Cultural History," 422. Fisher's English class inspired Stegner to write. Stegner and Etulain, *Stegner*, 24.
39. Fisher, "The Western Writer and the Eastern Establishment," 246.
40. Ibid.
41. Ibid., 252. See John R. Milton on the difficulty of "getting the professors and critics (and often they are the same persons) to put aside the long-established misconceptions" of western writing. Milton, "The Western Novel—A Symposium," *South Dakota Review* 2, no. 1 (Autumn 1964), 4. Milton was a Minnesotan who founded *South Dakota Review*. See Milton, "The West and Beyond: *South Dakota Review*," *South Dakota History* 13, no. 4 (Winter 1983): 334.
42. Stegner and Etulain, *Stegner*, xxi.
43. Mary Austin, quoted in Dorman, *Revolt of the Provinces*, 39.
44. Austin, "New York: Dictator of American Criticism," *The Nation*, July 31, 1920. After settling in New Mexico, Austin promoted a "number of prominent regionalists scattered across the awakening West." Dorman, *Revolt of the Provinces*, 39.
45. Jon K. Lauck, "The Prairie Populism of Christopher Lasch," *Great Plains Quarterly* 32, no. 3 (Summer 2012): 183–205.
46. Chuck Thompson, *Better Off without 'Em: A Northern Case for Southern Secession* (New York: Simon and Schuster, 2012). Note also the strong critique offered by Barton Swaim, "A New Turn in the South," *Wall Street Journal*, August 10, 2012.
47. Robert Kaplan argues that "we all need to recover a sensibility about time

and space that has been lost in the jet and information ages" or face greater foreign-policy challenges from the "revenge of geography." Robert D. Kaplan, *The Revenge of Geography: What the Map Tells Us about Coming Conflicts and the Battle against Fate* (New York, Random House, 2012), xix, 28.

48. James Kanter, "To Preserve Regional Tradition, Flanders Subsidizes Horse Breeding," *New York Times*, August 27, 2012.
49. Stegner, *The American West as Living Space*, 22.
50. Ibid., 71; Stegner and Etulain, *Stegner*, xiv.
51. Stegner, *The American West as Living Space*, 25.
52. Ibid.
53. Ibid.
54. Stegner and Etulain, *Stegner*, xv.
55. Ibid., 146.
56. Ibid., 148.
57. Ibid.
58. Ibid.
59. Ibid., 190.
60. Steiner and Wrobel, "Many Wests," 7.
61. Wallace Stegner's first book was about Utah. Stegner, *Mormon Country* (New York: Duell, Sloan & Pearce, 1942).
62. Pico Iyer calls California "a society built on quicksand, where everyone is getting new lives every day." Pico Iyer, *The Global Soul: Jet Lag, Shopping Malls, and the Search for Home* (New York: Alfred A. Knopf, 2000), 5. For a brilliant recent description of feelings of homesickness—or the loss of roots—from a historical perspective, see Susan Matt, *Homesickness: An American History* (New York: Oxford University Press, 2011); and Matt, "Home, Sweet Home," *New York Times*, April 19, 2012.
63. See Jon K. Lauck, "'The Silent Artillery of Time': Understanding Social Change in the Rural Midwest," *Great Plains Quarterly* 19, no. 4 (Fall 1999): 245–55; and Lauck, *American Agriculture and the Problem of Monopoly: The Political Economy of Grain Belt Farming, 1953–1980* (Lincoln: University of Nebraska Press, 2000).
64. Lucy R. Lippard, *The Lure of the Local: Senses of Place in a Multicentered Society* (New York: New Press, 1997), 7; Cleanth Brooks, "Regionalism in American Literature," *Journal of Southern History* 26, no. 1 (February 1960): 36.
65. For an overview of regional persistence, see Raymond D. Gastil, *Cultural Regions of the United States* (Seattle: University of Washington Press, 1975).
66. Nathan Glazer, foreword to *Cultural Regions of the United States*, viii; Steiner and Wrobel, "Many Wests," 6–7. Even geographers have difficulty seeing regional distinctions within the country, according to D. W. Meinig, "American Wests: Preface to a Geographical Interpretation," *Annals of the Association of American Geographers* 62, no. 2 (June 1972): 159.
67. See, for example, Jon K. Lauck, John E. Miller, and Don Simmons, eds., *The Plains Political Tradition: Essays on South Dakota Political Culture*, 2 vols. (Pierre: South Dakota State Historical Society Press, 2011–14); and Lauck,

Miller, and Edward Hogan, "The Contours of South Dakota Political Culture," *South Dakota History* 34, no. 2 (Summer 2004): 157–78.

68. On western caucuses, see F. Alan Coombs, "Twentieth-Century Western Politics," in *Historians and the American West*, 301. See also Ann R. Markusen, "The Economics of Regionalism," in *Regional Studies: The Interplay of Land and People*, 55–56. On persisting regionalism, see Cronon, Miles, and Gitlin, "Becoming West," 23; and Steiner and Wrobel, "Many Wests," 6.
69. Manu Raju, "Senate Battle Hits Big Sky Country," *Politico*, October 5, 2012.
70. Charles Mathesian, "California Values v. Idaho Values," *Politico*, August 8, 2012.
71. Wendy J. Katz and Timothy R. Mahoney, "Regionalism and the Humanities: Decline or Revival?" in *Regionalism and the Humanities*, ed. Wendy J. Katz and Timothy R. Mahoney (Lincoln: University of Nebraska Press, 2008), ix. See also Ira Sharkansky, *Regionalism in American Politics* (Indianapolis and New York: Bobbs-Merrill, 1970), 5.
72. Yi-Fu Tuan, "Rootedness versus Sense of Place," *Landscape* 24 (1980): 3–8.
73. Ibid., 4.
74. Steiner and Wrobel, "Many Wests," 6.
75. Ibid., 6–7.
76. Jackson first started to record regional differences after "seeing the American countryside with fresh eyes" after having battled his way across Europe with the American army during World War II, according to Helen Lefkowitz Horowitz, "J. B. Jackson and the Discovery of the American Landscape," in John Brinckerhoff Jackson, *Landscape in Sight: Looking at America*, ed. Helen Lefkowitz Horowitz (New Haven: Yale University Press, 1997), xix. Jackson said "I *see* [italics in original] things very clearly, and I rely on what I see... And I see things that other people don't see, and I call their attention to it." Horowitz, xxiv. Tuan's essay, cited in note 72, was published in *Landscape*, a journal Jackson founded in 1951. Horowitz, xx. On observing the small towns of the American interior, see Jackson's essay, "The Almost Perfect Town," in *Landscape in Sight*, 31–42.
77. Lippard, *The Lure of the Local*, 9; see also Jon. K. Lauck, "Born in a Small Town," special issue, *Claremont Review of Books* (Summer 2014): 1–3; and Lauck, "Finding Solace in the Midwest Where It Isn't Supposed to Be," *Flyover Country Review* 2, no. 2 (April 2015), http://www.flyovercountryreview.com/fiction/finding-solace-in-the-midwest-where-it-isnt-supposed-to-be/.
78. Daniel Bell, quoted by James M. Dennis, *Renegade Regionalists: The Modern Independence of Grant Wood, Thomas Hart Benton, and John Steuart Curry* (Madison: University of Wisconsin Press, 1998), 5.
79. Theodore C. Blegen, *Grassroots History* (Minneapolis: University of Minnesota Press, 1947), 12.
80. David C. Pierce and Richard C. Wiles, "A Place for Regionalism?" *Hudson Valley Regional Review* 11 (1994): 8.
81. B. A. Botkin, "Regionalism: Cult or Culture?" *English Journal* 25, no. 3 (March 1936): 185.

82. Dennis, *Renegade Regionalists,* 77.
83. George Orwell, "Notes on Nationalism" (1945) in Orwell, *Decline of the English Murder and Other Essays* (Harmondsworth, Middlesex, England: Penguin Books, 1970), 155–56. See also Pierce and Wiles, "A Place for Regionalism?," 9. On regionalism as a check on nationalism, see Robert Sayre, "Rethinking Midwestern Regionalism," *North Dakota Quarterly* 62, no. 2 (Spring 1994–95): 116.
84. Dorman, *Hell of a Vision,* 14; also see Jon. K. Lauck's review, *Western Historical Quarterly* (forthcoming); Royce, "Provincialism," 64; Michael C. Steiner, "Regionalism," in *The American Heritage Encyclopedia of American History,* ed. John Mack Faragher (New York: Henry Holt and Company, 1998), 775; Michael C. Steiner, "Region, Regionalism, and Place," in *Oxford Encyclopedia of Cultural and Intellectual History,* ed. Joan Shelley Rubin and Scott E. Casper (New York: Oxford University Press, 2013). The entry notes regionalism's "multiple loyalties" in comparison to "regionalism's evil twin, sectionalism".
85. Joseph E. Baker, "Regionalism in the Middle West," *American Review* 4 (March 1935), 606. Baker is discussing Ruth Suckow's novel, *The Folks.*
86. Joseph A. Amato and Anthony Amato, "Minnesota: A Different America?" *Daedalus* 129, no. 3 (Summer 2000): 71.
87. Ibid., 76; see also Jon. K. Lauck, "How Regionalism Dies: The Intellectual Journey of *The Minnesota Review,*" *Mid-America* 41 (2014): 80–87; Lauck, "The Death of the Midwest: Garrison Keillor's Impending Retirement as a Wake for Midwestern Regionalism," *Belt Magazine,* March 24, 2014, http://www.beltmag.com/death-midwest-garrison-keillors-impending-retirement-wake-midwestern-regionalism/; and Lauck, "An Interview with Garrison Keillor," *Salmagundi,* no. 184 (Fall 2014): 46–67.
88. See, for example, *Matching the Scenery: Journalism's Duty to the North American West,* Report of the Wallace Stegner Initiative of the Institute for Journalism & Natural Resources (Missoula: Institute for Journalism & Natural Resources, 2003), 25–31.
89. Frederick Manfred, "The Western Novel—A Symposium," *South Dakota Review* 2 no. 1 (Autumn 1964): 9; See also Arthur S. Brisbane, "Success and Risk as the *Times* Transforms," *New York Times,* August 25, 2012, where the paper's ombudsman criticizes its biases.
90. Greg Brown, quoted in Mary Swander, "The Roosting Tree," in *Imagining Home: Writing from the Midwest,* ed. Mark Vinz and Thom Tammaro (Minneapolis: University of Minnesota Press, 1995), 41.
91. Nicolaas Mink, "A (Napoleon) Dynamite Identity: Rural Idaho, the Politics of Place, and the Creation of a New Western Film," *Western Historical Quarterly* 39, no. 2 (Summer 2008): 154–75. Mink notes the tradition of depicting the rural West as "backward, hackneyed, and uncivilized" (159).
92. E. J. Dionne Jr., *Our Divided Political Heart: The Battle for the American Idea in an Age of Discontent* (New York, Bloomsbury, 2012), 261.
93. Jason Aldean, "Fly Over States," from the album *My Kinda Party* (2010).

94. Thomas Frank, *What's the Matter with Kansas? How Conservatives Won the Heart of America* (New York: Metropolitan Books, 2004). See also Jon K. Lauck's review of Frank's book in *Annals of Iowa: A Quarterly Journal of History* 64, no. 1 (Winter 2005): 93–94. Denis Boyles, *Superior, Nebraska: The Common Sense Values of America's Heartland* (New York: Doubleday, 2008). In response to Frank, see also Richard E. Wood, *Survival of Rural America: Small Victories and Bitter Harvests* (Lawrence: University Press of Kansas, 2008).
95. Edward Hoagland, "But Where Is Home?" *New York Times Book Review*, December 23, 1973. Hoagland thought the writer might have been Texan Larry McMurtry.
96. Lauck, "The Prairie Historians and the Foundations of Midwestern History," 137–73; Lauck, *The Lost Region.*
97. On the organization of the 1961 Santa Fe conference that launched the Western History Association, see FF 88, Box 34, James Olson Papers, Nebraska State Historical Society, Lincoln.
98. Eric Foner and Jon Wiener, "Fighting for the West," *The Nation*, July 29/August 5, 1991, 163–65.
99. Richard W. Etulain, "Western Stories for the Next Generation," *Western Historical Quarterly* 31, no. 1 (Spring 2000), 11; see also Ridge, "Frederick Jackson Turner and His Ghost," 76; Martin Ridge, "The New Western History and the National Myth," *Continuity: A Journal of History* no. 17 (Fall 1993): 4; Susan Rhoades Neel, "A Place of Extremes: Nature, History, and the American West," *Western Historical Quarterly* 25, no. 4 (Winter 1994): 488–505. Neel claims that "rejecting the idea of scholarship as neutral or objective, the new western historians have adopted the stance of social critics and reformers" (494).
100. Donald Worster pronounced that "we need a new past" in "A Country without Secrets," in *Under Western Skies: Nature and History in the American West* (New York: Oxford University Press, 1992), 253. Donald Pisani concluded that the "New Western Historians—like the New Left historians of the 1960s and 1970s—are far more concerned with ideology and the search for a 'usable past' than were earlier western historians." Donald J. Pisani, "Is There Life after Turner? The Continuing Search for the Grand Synthesis and an Autonomous West," *New Mexico Historical Review* 67 (1992): 294. Gerald Thompson saw the New Western Historians as seeking a "usable past for understanding and dealing with present-day problems in the West." Gerald Thompson, "The New Western History: A Critical Analysis," *Continuity: A Journal of History*, no. 17 (Fall 1993): 6. Limerick calls for a usable past in *Trails: Toward a New Western History*, ed. Patricia Nelson Limerick, Clyde A. Milner II, and Charles E. Rankin (Lawrence: University Press of Kansas, 1991), xii.
101. Jon K. Lauck, "How South Dakota Sparked the New Western History Wars: A Commentary on Patricia Nelson Limerick," *South Dakota History* 41, no. 3 (Fall 2011): 353–81.

102. Lauck, *Prairie Republic: The Political Culture of Dakota Territory, 1879–1889* (Norman: University of Oklahoma Press, 2010).
103. Edward L. Ayers, "The South, the West, and the Rest," *Western Historical Quarterly* 25, no. 4 (Winter 1994): 475.
104. Robert A. Goldberg, review of *The Cold War American West, 1945–1989*, ed. Kevin J. Fernlund, *Western Historical Quarterly* 30, no. 3 (Autumn 1999): 375.
105. William Deverell, "Fighting Words: The Significance of the American West in the History of the United States," *Western Historical Quarterly* 25, no. 2 (Summer 1994): 186.
106. Ibid., 195.
107. Richard White's remarks, panel discussion on the New Western History, Western History Association annual meeting, October 13–16, 2011, Oakland, California.
108. Stegner and Etulain, *Stegner*, 192.
109. Jon K. Lauck, "The Old Roots of the New History: The Intellectual Origins of Howard Lamar's *Dakota Territory*," *Western Historical Quarterly* 39, no. 3 (Autumn 2008): 261–81.
110. Wrobel, "Beyond the Frontier-Region Dichotomy," 401–29. See also Luebke, "Regionalism and the Great Plains," 31–33. For an early discussion of the "frontier" stage and the later "region" stage, see Paxson, *When the West Is Gone*, 28.
111. Wrobel, "Beyond the Frontier-Region Dichotomy," 413.
112. Cronon, Miles, and Gitlin, "Becoming West," 7. On the failure of New Western History to focus on regional diversity within the West, see Steiner and Wrobel, "Many Wests," 10.
113. Gene Gressley, "The West: Past, Present, and Future," *Western Historical Quarterly* 17, no. 1 (January 1986): 15. FDR, as a former state governor, also had more Brandeisian leanings than people remember. James T. Patterson, *The New Deal and the States: Federalism in Transition* (Princeton, NJ: Princeton University Press, 1969), 3. See also Steiner and Wrobel, "Many Wests," 6.
114. Gressley, "The West," 15. On regionalism and antistatism, see also John L. Thomas, "The Uses of Catastrophe: Lewis Mumford, Vernon L. Parrington, Van Wyck Brooks, and the End of American Regionalism," *American Quarterly* 42, no. 2 (June 1990): 225, 239; and Dorman, *Hell of a Vision*, 10.
115. Gressley, "The West," 16.
116. Ibid., 18.
117. Ibid., 19. Also see Dorman, *Hell of a Vision*, 154–58.
118. Gressley, "The West," 20.
119. Michael C. Steiner, "The Significance of Turner's Sectional Thesis," *Western Historical Quarterly* 10, no. 4 (October 1979): 460–61.
120. Michael C. Steiner, "Frontier to Region: Frederick Jackson Turner and the New Western History," *Pacific Historical Review* 64, no. 4 (November 1995): 492.
121. David S. Brown, *Beyond the Frontier: The Midwestern Voice in American Historical Writing* (Chicago: University of Chicago Press, 2009), 191; Jon K. Lauck,

"The 'Interior Tradition' in American Historical Writing," *Annals of Iowa: A Quarterly Journal of History* 69, no. 1 (Winter 2010): 82–93. On resistance to the federal government in North Dakota, see Howard R. Lamar, "Regionalism and the Broad Methodological Problem," in *Regional Studies: The Interplay of Land and People*, 31–32.

122. Gordon S. Wood, *Empire of Liberty: A History of the Early Republic, 1789–1815* (New York: Oxford University Press, 2011), 357; see also August C. Miller Jr., "Jefferson as an Agriculturalist," *Agricultural History* 16, no. 2 (April 1942): 65–78.

123. Edward L. Ayers, Patricia Nelson Limerick, Stephen Nissenbaum, and Peter S. Onuf, *All over the Map: Rethinking American Regions* (Baltimore: Johns Hopkins University Press, 1996), 13–19; Robert L. Dorman, "History's Divining Rod," *Reviews in American History* 25, no. 3 (September 1997): 369.

124. Karen Merrill notes the curious "absence of popular political protest in accounts of the rise of federal administrative power in the West." Karen R. Merrill, "In Search of the 'Federal Presence' in the American West," *Western Historical Quarterly* 30, no. 4 (Winter 1999): 455–23.

125. Glazer, foreword," *Cultural Regions of the United States*, viii–ix; Iyer, *The Global Soul*, 24.

126. Robert Nisbet, *The Quest for Community* (New York: Oxford University Press, 1953).

127. Robert Nisbet, *Prejudices: A Philosophical Dictionary* (Cambridge, MA: Harvard University Press, 1982), 55.

128. Hine, "The Western Intellectual Josiah Royce," 71.

129. John L. Thomas, "Lewis Mumford: Regionalist Historian," *Reviews in American History* 16, no. 1 (March 1988): 162. Thomas directed the dissertation of Robert Dorman, who became a leading historian of regionalism.

130. Ruth Suckow, "The Folk Idea in American Life," *Scribner's Magazine* 88 (September 1930): 246, 254.

131. Burns, *Kinship with the Land*, 16.

132. Robert D. Johnston, "'There's No "There" There': Reflections on Western Political Historiography," *Western Historical Quarterly* 42, no. 3 (Autumn 2011): 334.

Conquering Distance?

Broadband and the Rural West

GEOFF MCGHEE

One of the chief difficulties is the failure of country life, as it exists at present, to satisfy the higher social and intellectual aspirations of country people. Whether the constant draining away of so much of the best elements in the rural population into the towns is due chiefly to this cause or to the superior business opportunities of city life may be open to question. But no one familiar at all with farm life throughout the United States can fail to recognize the necessity for building up the life of the farm upon its social as well as upon its productive side.

—*Report of the Country Life Commission,* February 1909

In 1909, President Roosevelt's Country Life Commission warned of difficulties in rural America that were hastening migration to the nation's growing cities: problems with health care, schools, roads, and access to modern conveniences like indoor plumbing.[1] Due to grassroots efforts, federal government intervention, and improvements in technology, the decades to come brought a dramatic rise in living standards as roads, dams, telephones, and electricity reached deep into the American countryside—even into the rugged mountains, forests, and deserts of the rural West. The region is still remote, but airports, highways, television, radio, and telecommunications services have bound it more closely than ever to the rest of the nation.

However, in the early decades of the Internet age, a new technological divide may be returning economic and social isolation to rural communities across the western United States: the lagging expansion of high-speed online access into rural areas.

Broadband and the Rural West

For many Americans,
a world without broadband is unimaginable.

—Michael J. Copps

In two decades, the Internet and the World Wide Web have transformed American society. The web, which initially consisted of a text-focused information-retrieval and communication service, has since grown into an all-encompassing broadband entertainment, voice, and video-communication platform, commercial emporium, and social-service portal.

Already the web is supplanting traditional media. Newspapers as varied as the *Christian Science Monitor,*[2] the *Detroit News,* and the New Orleans *Times-Picayune* have eliminated or cut back print editions in favor of an expanded online presence. The online video-streaming service, Netflix, surpassed the pay-cable television channel HBO for the number of subscribers,[3] while educational institutions have seen the rise of the massive open online course (MOOC) and the "flipped classroom," where students do lab work at school and watch online video lectures at home. The social network, Facebook, has accumulated more than a billion users worldwide. And despite its troubled initial rollout, the Affordable Care Act's online insurance exchange is central to national health-care reform, along with less heralded forms of e-government that have quietly taken hold like electronic tax filing and access to online social services.

In short, both the American people and their government—to say nothing of the national-security apparatus—have seized the Internet and its possibilities with a zeal that previously characterized their embrace of the automobile, radio, television, and pro sports. We, as a nation, are all hooked and hooked up.

Falling Behind

As was true after the wide adoption of electrification, telephone service, and the interstate highway system—among other advances—the rural West faces challenges in keeping pace with the rest of the nation, ones that carry all of the economic, social, and cultural stakes of connectedness. As the geographer Edward J. Malecki wrote in 2003, "Telecommunications technologies and the Internet diminish, if they do not erase, the tyranny of space and distance."[4]

Rural America has been at this crossroads before: Congress's nineteenth-century mandate to the U.S. Post Office to offer rural free delivery and favorable postage rates to newspapers, especially local ones, helped connect rural residents to national and international news services and develop a thriving rural press that still counts several hundred rural western newspapers,[5] according to a 2011 study by the Rural West Initiative.[6] Parcel service, which the United States was the last industrialized nation to introduce in 1913, enabled rural residents to order consumer goods from all over the country.[7]

Accordingly, contemporary arguments for broadband Internet access draw parallels with the achievements of previous eras, often emphasizing the importance of government action to bring service to rural areas. "Such a transformation will rival the building of the roads, canals, and ports that made commerce possible in pre-Civil War America," the Federal Communication Commission's (FCC's) acting chairman, Michael J. Copps, wrote in a 2009 report on rural Internet service, "the transcontinental railroads that made us a continental power in the late nineteenth century; the national highway system that opened the way for rapid transportation and demographic migration in the last century; and the immense efforts to extend telephone and electrical service to the far corners of America."[8]

Grand Policy Precedents, Smaller Steps

If such language speaks of soaring ambitions associated with rural broadband access—and the very real national achievements of decades and centuries past—then the reality of government efforts has been more modest.

To begin with, the defining piece of legislation dealing with Internet access, the 1996 Telecommunications Act, was drafted prior to the explosive growth of the public Internet in a far different political and cultural climate from the New Deal that supported rural electrification or the Cold War that drove construction of the interstate highways. Drafted by a conservative Republican Congress and signed by President Clinton (who in his State of the Union address that January had famously declared that "the era of big government is over"[9]), the act was principally a deregulatory measure meant to unleash innovation and competition in highly regulated industries like telecommunications, broadcasting, and cable television.

But it also expanded the principle of universal telephone service—enshrined in the FCC's mission when it was created in 1934—to encompass "telecommunications and advanced services."[10] Though the principle fell well short of a guarantee of service, it introduced a direct surcharge to wired and cellular phone subscribers to support telecommunications grants via the so-called Universal Service Fund.

A guarantee of rural broadband service is just what some other countries have issued: in 2009, Australia began an eight-year program promising ultra-high-speed Internet access to 90 percent of homes and offices, and broadband access to sparsely populated areas;[11] France instituted a program designed to bring mobile broadband service to towns of 3,000 residents or fewer. Norway has set a target for every resident to have access to high-speed service by 2017.[12]

The 1996 act did facilitate Internet access for schools, libraries, and health-care providers through the universal schools and libraries program, also known as E-Rate, which offers support for discounted Internet access at a cost to the government of around $2.3 billion per year. In a 2006 study, the National Center for Education Statistics reported that nearly all U.S. public schools had Internet access, 97 percent of them with broadband; another study in 2006 found that 99 percent of public library branches were connected to the Internet, and 98 percent of them offered public access.[13]

The importance of public libraries as local computing centers is highlighted by an article by the Institute for Rural Journalism and Community Issues at the University of Kentucky,[14] which cited the steady increase in recorded visits to rural public libraries, which topped 167.6 million in 2011:

> With the Internet such an important part of every day life, and some rural residents still struggling to get connected, if all else fails, the one solution that keeps popping up in stories—applying for jobs, students preparing for standardized tests, enrolling in the Affordable Care Act—is to visit your local library for Internet access. That has led the Institute for Museum and Library Services to conduct what is believed to be the first of its kind report on computer use at rural libraries. This seems like a report that could be replicated in every community.[15]

The Telecommunications Act also instituted an aid program for hard-to-reach areas called the High Cost Program, designed to "ensure that communities in rural, insular and high cost areas have access to telecommunications services that are affordable and reasonably comparable to rates charged for similar service in urbanized areas."[16] The program, which does not specifically mention broadband, allocates more than $4 billion a year[17] in grants to improve telecom infrastructure and offset the higher costs of operating in less populated areas.[18]

But generally, government policy has been limited to creating incentives and lowering barriers for commercial operators. For example, the FCC has repeatedly called on local governments to reform policies on rights-of-way, tower siting, and utility-pole access that make it cumbersome to install broadband infrastructure.

Broadband Adoption Takes Off

Both owing to and in spite of U.S. telecommunications policy, broadband Internet access spread like wildfire beginning in the late 1990s, reaching more than eighty-three million households by 2013.[19] Also like a wildfire, it swept through some areas while leaving others completely untouched.

By 2008, it was becoming clear that many areas—especially rural ones—were underserved or completely unserved—but it was difficult to know how much. More information was needed on actual service figures, and these data were largely in the hands of private cable, telecom, satellite, and wireless providers. The 2008 Food, Conservation, and Energy Act, more popularly known as the Farm Bill, instructed the FCC to develop a comprehensive rural broadband strategy, and another law empowered the agency to collect data on broadband subscriptions across the country.

The report emerging a year later lamented,

> For years, large parts of rural America have languished on the sidelines of the digital revolution. Home to the homesteaders, pioneers, and the rich and diverse Native American cultures that contribute so much to our national identity, rural America has for most of our history been deemed too remote, too sparsely populated, or too inaccessible to be fully connected with our nation's infrastructures.[20]

Some help came in the form of the 2009 stimulus plan, the American Recovery and Reinvestment Act (ARRA), which brought new money.

"ARRA's attention to improving economic circumstances throughout the country," said the National Agricultural & Rural Development Policy Center report, "brought broadband services under its umbrella."[21]

In all, the ARRA allocated more than $7 billion in loans and loan guarantees for investment in broadband infrastructure, aimed at serving people in unserved and underserved areas and establishing public computing facilities or so-called third places for access. The lobbying group TechNet writes, "These funds have helped shore up many initiatives to encourage broadband adoption that have been around since the early 2000s, such as Computers for Youth (CFY), One Economy, One Community, Connected Nation, and others."[22]

Mapping Broadband's Reach

Through the National Broadband Map,[23] the United States got a better picture of Internet access. The map came online in 2011 to both praise and derision. A headline on the tech website *Engadget* snarked, "United States Gets National Broadband Map, Finds Much of Its Nation Doesn't Have Broadband."[24] But the map was the first result of regulations requiring Internet providers to disclose more detailed zip-code level (later census-tract level) information on the number of actual subscribers and technologies and speeds offered.[25]

The map also revealed for the first time the number of people with no broadband access at all, and rural populations figured largely. In 2010, broadband was unavailable to more than a quarter of noncore county populations (the Office of Management and Budget's definition of rural residents). As an October 2012 research report for the Hudson Institute and the Foundation for Rural Service wrote, "The single best predictor of 'have not' status is population density. Dividing America into urban and rural populations shows stark contrasts in broadband availability."[26]

The FCC duly reported to Congress in 2011 that "our data show that broadband deployment and adoption gaps in rural areas remain significant," citing statistics that revealed that three-quarters of the twenty-six million people without broadband lived in rural areas. "Moreover, other data indicate that rural consumers have fewer choices among broadband technologies and providers than other consumers have."[27]

This fact points to one of the weaknesses in telecommunications policy. Back in the late '90s, it was impossible to know which access technology would predominate, and regulators envisioned a future where phone,

U.S. Census Tracts with Broadband Internet Available

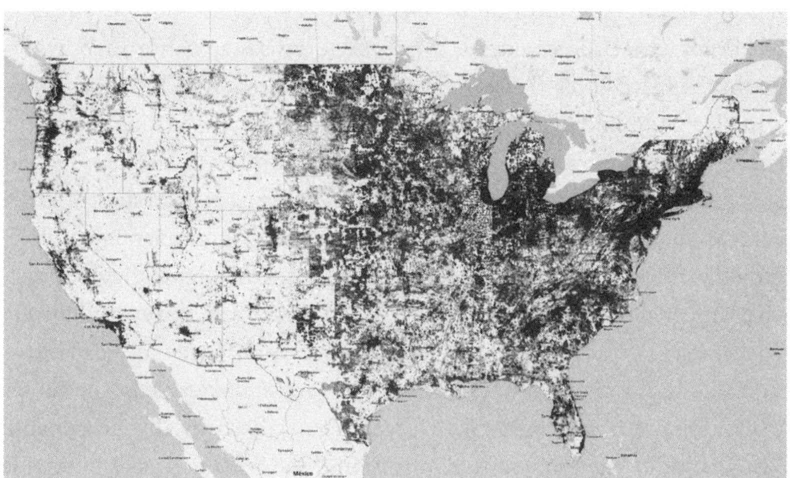

U.S. Census tracts with broadband Internet available on December 31, 2013. Source: BroadbandMap.gov.

cable, satellite, cellular, and even power companies would compete to bring Internet access to American households—forcing prices down and increasing service.[28] (This was one of several reasons that the Bush-era FCC decided to classify Internet access as a lightly regulated information service—like dialing in to CompuServe or a Bloomberg terminal—rather than a heavily regulated common carrier like voice telephone service. This decision set the stage for the current battle over "net neutrality," which debates whether Internet access should be a "dumb pipe" transmitting any data without bias to its content—like electricity—or whether its carriers should have the discretion to curate—in essence, to decide what content they make available to users and at what cost).

As it turned out, each technology that delivers Internet technology carries different costs and benefits, and those best positioned to offer service were the incumbent cable carriers, whose infrastructure required the least modification to reach the increasingly high speeds customers needed and expected. The telephone companies, on the other hand, enjoyed early success offering Internet via DSL that connected customers over their legacy copper wires, but they are finding that these cannot keep up with speed improvements available on cable or fiber-optic networks. Still, it is these DSL lines (whose performance degrades over distance from the central office) that are typically the best—or only—wired option for rural residents.

Shifting Definition of Broadband

In fact, the definition of *broadband* itself has been a moving target as technology has progressed and Internet use has become more bandwidth intensive. Until 2008, the FCC's minimum definition of broadband was a sluggish 200 kilobits per second (Kbps)—barely faster than dial-up. It raised the minimum rate several times, settling on 4 megabits per second (Mbps—4,000 Kbps) in 2010. Critics like the legal scholar and Internet analyst Susan Crawford think that this target is insufficient for future growth. In December 2012, she wrote, "It allows the digital divide to survive, and ensures that the U.S. will stagnate."[29] Instead, she argued for the widespread deployment of fiber-optic networks that are more expensive to install in the short term but infinitely more upgradeable in the future than common technologies like DSL and coaxial-based cable broadband. "This would mean 1,000 Mbps connections," she argues, "speeds hundreds of times faster than what most Americans have today."[30]

Many countries in the developed world have deployed broadband at speeds like those Crawford describes. In South Korea, for example, subscribers can get gigabit (1,000 Mbps) connections for just over thirty dollars a month, and 200 to 500 Mbps connections are common, if not standard, throughout Europe and Asia, at least for urban areas.[31]

What's at stake? The conventional vision of the future of broadband imagines the same things we do now—browse the web, watch video, play some games—just at higher speeds. But gigabit broadband offers something closer to true telepresence. According to Crawford, "One strand of fiber can convey not only 90,000 television channels but also potentially hundreds of thousands of lives being shared. Families, separated, having dinner together, screens bringing lives together. We don't yet know what this will be like."[32]

Private Investment in Broadband Already on the Wane

In the United States, however, broadband expansion has already begun to decline. In the second quarter of 2012, growth in the broadband user base was the lowest it had been in a decade. With the top seventeen cable and telecom providers controlling 93 percent of the broadband market, major players in the broadband build out were declaring, "Mission accomplished."[33]

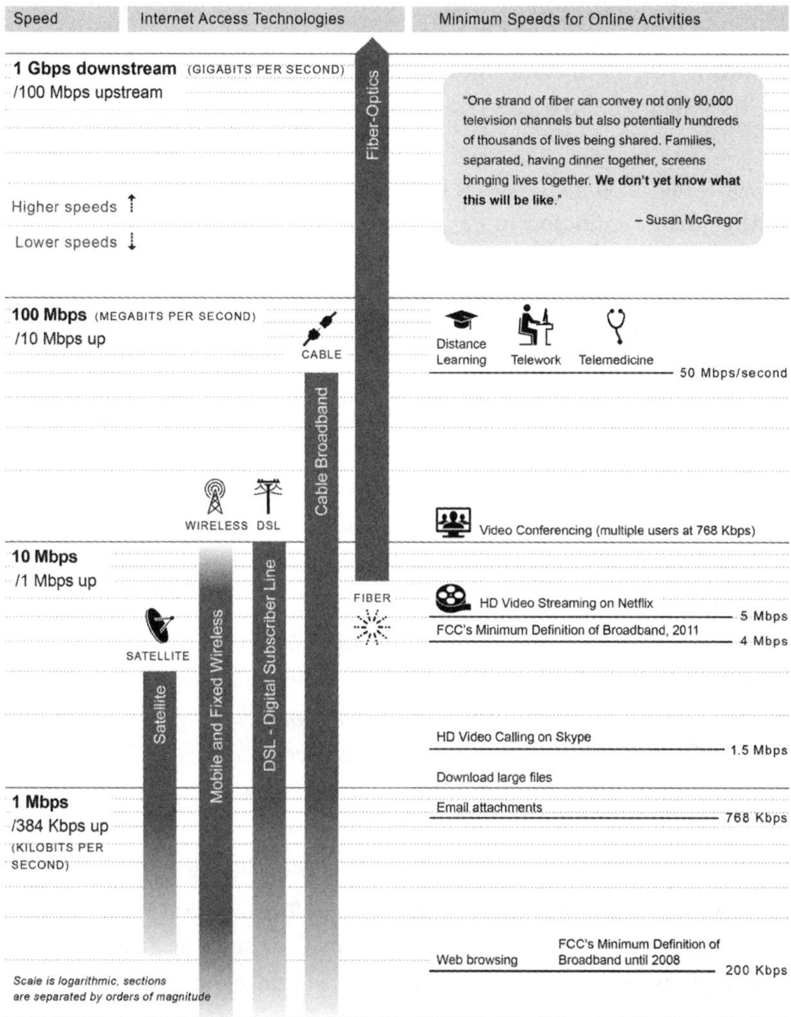

Broadband Internet available access speeds as of April 2014. Source: Government Accountability Office, Netflix, Federal Communications Commission, Speedtest.net, and Skype. Icons created by Irit Barzily, Benjamin Brandt, Joe Mortell, Diego Naive, Anton Noskov, Martha Ormiston, Stephen JB Thomas, Jakub Ukrop, Lance Weisser, and Gerald Wildmoser of thenounproject.com.

In late 2011, AT&T stated that it was finished building its ultra-high-speed fiber-optic service U-verse after putting it within reach of thirty million homes,[34] and Verizon followed with a similar announcement. The following year, both companies turned down government grants offering nearly $70 million to expand rural broadband.

Wireless Substitution for Rural Broadband

Rather than continuing to expand their landline broadband networks, both Verizon and AT&T have promoted wireless Internet access via cellular networks to rural households. These are relatively expensive compared to wired broadband and come with usage caps that make them impractical for household use. Maggie Reardon on the technology news site CNET writes, "They are likely inadequate for an entire household that expects to do more than check e-mail each day."[35] The New America Foundation, in its 2013 report *The Cost of Connectivity*, wrote, "The combination of high costs, slower and more unreliable speeds, and restrictive data caps mean that mobile broadband cannot be used as a substitute for home broadband in the U.S."[36]

But for rural residents too far from population centers, costly Internet service via cellular networks or satellite may be their only option. "Deregulation at the federal level," wrote Edward J. Malecki in 2003, "diminished the likelihood of 'universal service' for advanced services such as Internet access or broadband in favor of letting 'the market' determine what goes where."[37]

But rural Americans faced worse obstacles obtaining electrical service back in the twentieth century, only to overcome them through local initiatives and strenuous federal intervention. The Rural Electrification Administration (REA) helped form hundreds of rural electric cooperatives,[38] and by 1953, more than 90 percent of U.S. farms had electricity.[39] The REA went on to champion local telephone service through low-interest loans and technical assistance to local services starting in 1946.[40]

Community Broadband Efforts

Many of those services live on in the form of regional co-ops that have become central to developing local Internet services. One example is the Dakota Carrier Network (DCN), a consortium of rural telephone companies that was founded in 1996. The recipient of a $10.7 million grant from the National Telecommunications & Information Administration (NTIA),[41]

DCN says it and its member companies have committed $120 million a year toward building a fiber-optic network spanning North Dakota, enabling its members to offer gigabit-speed Internet service and television programming.[42]

By 2011, more than 130 cities were operating publicly built and owned broadband networks. Utilities offering fiber-optic broadband service include the Grant County Public Utility District in central Washington and California's smallest city, Vernon, population 114, which initiated service in November 2013.[43]

The telecom industry has lobbied hard against public networks, though, arguing that they are unfair competition. A 2011 report by the Institute for Local Self-Reliance, a community broadband-advocacy group, writes, "As municipal initiatives have succeeded, the telecommunications giants have used their political clout to persuade state legislatures to change the rules, barring or significantly inhibiting local efforts."[44] A 2014 article in the *New York Times* counted nineteen states that have enacted restrictions on municipal broadband services.[45] Nevada has banned cities larger than 25,000 from offering telecom services, while Utah, Colorado, and Washington have all erected obstacles to starting local broadband projects.[46]

Tom Wheeler, the chairman of the FCC, has spoken out in support of overturning state-level bans on community broadband, writing,

> If the people, acting through their elected local governments, want to pursue competitive community broadband, they shouldn't be stopped by state laws promoted by cable and telephone companies that don't want that competition.... Throughout the country where we have seen competitive broadband providers come in to a market, prices have gone down and broadband speeds have gone up. No wonder incumbent broadband providers want to legislate rather than innovate.[47]

Beyond Access: Other Barriers to Rural Internet Adoption

Whether delivered by commercial or public carriers, wired broadband service was within reach of 93 percent of the United States population in 2013, according to the NTIA.[48] However, only 62 percent of rural Americans had broadband at home, according to a survey by the Pew Internet &

American Life Project.[49] Evidence suggests that affordability may be an equally significant final hurdle; another Pew survey—of Americans without Internet at home—found that lack of availability was the least common reason cited, mentioned by only 7 percent of respondents. Instead, nearly one-fifth of those without Internet said the primary reason was cost.[50]

Data from the NTIA reveal that much rural use of broadband varies by income, education, and ethnicity. Of the 58 percent of rural households with broadband service in 2011, usage varied from a peak of around 80 percent among Asian Americans, households with more than fifty thousand dollars in income, and college graduates, down to the low 30 percent among African American and American Indian households, and to about a quarter of households where residents had less than a high-school education.[51]

Policy Options to Encourage Internet Access

"When is government intervention needed?" asked a 2013 report by the National Agricultural and Rural Development Policy Center (NARDeP). "How do we evaluate conditions of market failure as opposed to the 'normal' course of technological diffusion?"[52] The authors of the study suggested that training and outreach can be effective in bringing nonusers into the fold:

> Programs specifically focusing on the economic development potentials of broadband applications in highly public ways—through town meetings, public demonstrations, and through mobilizing local community change agents—may contribute to improved adoption levels. In particular, use of community anchor sites for broadband during these programs may help encourage Internet use among historically low adopters, which may in turn lead to future adoption at the household level.[53]

The federal government has also revisited existing policies to help promote rural broadband service. The FCC has begun to overhaul the E-Rate Program for schools and libraries, pointing out that funding requests have badly outstripped the program's budget and schools' broadband needs have increased drastically in recent years. In November 2014, Chairman Wheeler proposed raising the program's annual budget to $3.9 billion, partially by increasing the universal-service surcharge on consumers' phone bills. The Universal Service Fund, the *New York Times* says, has grown 20 percent since the Obama administration took office.[54]

As for the High-Cost Program, now called the Connect America Fund (CAF), the FCC in late 2014 solicited bids for its $100 million Rural Broadband Experiments program, where funds will be allocated to pilot projects demonstrating the feasibility of delivering very-high-speed (100 Mpbs) service to designated rural areas, and high-speed broadband (10 Mbps) to designated high-cost and extremely high-cost areas.[55] What remains to be seen is if the federal government will find money to support more investment if the pilot programs are successful. One estimate suggested that fully funding all of the 181 projects solicited by the program's request for proposals would cost in the neighborhood of $885 million.[56]

It is arguable that this sum is a mere drop in the bucket compared to the cost of wiring the whole country for fiber-optic service. "How much would it cost to bring fiber to the homes of all Americans?" asks Susan Crawford in the book *Captive Audience*, quoting an estimate of $50 to $90 billion in a study commissioned by the glass manufacturer, Corning, Inc.[57] "Think of what the $90 billion means in terms of the total US budget," she writes. "The Defense Department was given $80 billion in FY 2010 just for research, development, testing, and evaluation of new weapons systems. For the same amount that the country spends on defense research in one year, America could bring fiber networking to all Americans for generations."[58]

In fairness, a closer look at the Corning estimate shows that the budget only covers the densest 80 percent of the U.S. population; the authors say it is too hard to calculate the cost of reaching highly dispersed communities, which most likely represent a significant portion of the rural West's population.[59]

What Is at Stake for Rural Communities

To advocates of broadband adoption, the stakes are higher than merely the addition of a modern convenience to the home. As a 2010 article in the journal *Choices* argued,

> Why should communities across the nation care about this ongoing digital divide? Substantial research documents the positive economic and social benefits derived from access to high quality broadband service. [The authors of a 2009 report by the United

> States Department of Agriculture's Economic Research Service] provide examples for enhanced community interactions, telemedicine, distance education, and telework when discussing the relationship between rural area development and broadband. For rural businesses, broadband enables both cost savings and increased revenue potential.
>
> The corollary of this research implies there are potential negative consequences for communities lacking adequate access to broadband infrastructure.... Without access to high speed, high bandwidth Internet service, rural communities already suffering from the economic effects of industrial restructuring and the current economic crisis may continue to find their communities increasingly less competitive. This situation creates a vicious cycle that serves to widen the rural/urban digital divide.[60]

"Today the opportunity cost of not having broadband," wrote Hans Kuttner in a 2012 study for the Hudson Institute, "and not having access to robust broadband is disproportionately borne by those who live in rural America, and by the rural economy."[61]

In 2010, the Public Policy Institute of California (PPIC) estimated that employment growth was on average more than 6 percent higher in areas with broadband access—adding that the effect was particularly pronounced in rural areas:

> The relationship between broadband and employment growth is also stronger in some places than others. For example, the relationship is stronger for ZCTAs [zip codes] with lower population density (and, conversely, weaker for those with higher density)—consistent with the theory that smaller or more isolated areas may benefit more from high-speed connections, giving businesses in these areas access to larger markets.[62]

The research firm Headwaters Economics has also explored the relationship among population density, distance, and development. In a 2009 report, the authors described three categories of western counties: urban, "isolated," and "connected." The eighty rural western counties the authors defined as connected were characterized by being located within an hour of airports with regular commercial service. These connected areas, the authors hypothesized, were likely to attract "amenity migration" by entrepreneurs and professionals drawn by the quality of life, who needed to remain tethered to urban economic centers. The report was less optimistic for the 206 other nonmetropolitan counties, stating, "Others are truly remote and isolated (the 'isolated' counties) and therefore have limited opportunities, normally constrained to natural resources, such as farming, ranching and resource extraction."[63]

In the coming decades, however, may virtual connectivity play a bigger role relative to physical commuting? The PPIC report cites a California Public Utilities Commission estimate that "the [minimum] speed necessary for telecommuting...—3 mbps downstream—is fifteen times faster than what qualifies as broadband in the historical FCC definition."[64] The report refers to the FCC's original minimum threshold of 200 Kbps for broadband, but since 2010, that amount has risen to 4 Mbps, well above the necessary speed for telecommuting.

The rural scholar Don Albrecht is correspondingly bullish on electronic connectivity as a force for economic development:

> With computers, the Internet, and cell phones, it is now possible for individuals and firms to be connected to the global world while enjoying the benefits of rural living. Because of their amenity advantages, the rural West has an opportunity to reap great benefits from these societal changes. The disadvantages of the past have become the advantages of the present.[65]

The Choice

If it is the case that Internet connectedness will spur development in the rural West, policy makers still have work to do. According to a 2013 report by the USDA's Economic Research Service, population growth since 2010 in the Mountain West has slowed markedly for the first time in decades. The report suggests that "while metro proximity, attractive scenery, and recreation potential have historically contributed to population growth, the influence of those factors has weakened considerably." In general, 2012–13 saw no net employment growth in nonmetropolitan counties nationwide, compared to a steady recovery since 2009 in metropolitan areas.[66]

As the once-formidable Penn State football coach Joe Paterno said, "If you're not getting better, you're getting worse."[67] While debate continues over the future of rural broadband access in the United States, other bedrock institutions connecting the rural West to the rest of the country are falling on hard times. The twentieth-century vintage copper-wire telephone network is falling into disrepair as major carriers seek to divest from costly and heavily regulated wire-line infrastructure and move into profitable new areas like wireless voice and data services. "In rural Wisconsin and Minnesota, even 911 calls can get lost," says a report by the consumer advocacy group Stop the Cap![68] A local television station in Minneapolis described an FCC inquiry into dropped calls: "What shocked the FCC into calling this problem 'epic' earlier this year was the revelation that long distance calls between people as little as 15 miles away from each other often are routed through Siberia or other distant lands as long distance companies seek the cheapest possible way to route calls to boost profits."[69]

Postal distribution is also facing a cloudy future with rural newspapers facing the potential disruption of Saturday mail service. The United States Post Office (USPS) has proposed and withdrawn its discontinuance several times, most recently in the summer of 2013. Since the USPS lost $15.9 billion in 2012,[70] the future is hardly certain for mail service generally, for inexpensive service in particular, and for the future of locally delivered newspapers that bind communities together.

While it is not the main challenge facing Internet access in the rural West, the net neutrality debate is particularly significant for rural areas. By remaining classed as an information service, rather than an essential telecommunications utility, carriers can choose what content they offer and how much it costs users—tantamount to the way cable television bundles work. Such a scenario will accentuate the paucity of choices among carriers in rural areas. A separate, but related, issue is the bandwidth caps that Internet service providers are increasingly adopting: these will make telepresence, telemedicine, and telecommuting significantly more expensive and could limit starting new connectivity-driven businesses in rural areas.

Of course, the future of Internet access in the rural West is not yet written. As legacy networks like the copper-wire telephone and the postal system decline in usage and importance, the essential nature of broadband access may become more widely accepted. That scenario could awaken the power of the rural grassroots movement to effect change.

In 1873, for example, the USPS was also running significant deficits; in response, the postmaster general convinced Congress to eliminate all free mailing privileges. "When Congress reconvened, it was besieged with petitions, most representing rural interests, imploring it to reinstate the free mailing privilege for the press." Legislators relented early in the session, restoring and even expanding free in-county delivery.[71]

While small in number, rural Americans—and rural westerners—are not without political power. Rural states and congressional districts are regularly described as "punching above their weight," partially due to the allocation of two senators to every state, and partially due to what Stanford political scientist Jonathan Rodden calls "unintentional gerrymandering" by urban residents, who live in dense areas and thus form tightly packed congressional districts.[72]

Although the current Republican congressional leadership opposes increased regulation of Internet service providers,[73] shifting public opinion about broadband service in their heavily represented rural districts could affect their position. Some quintessentially rural groups are being impacted by halting broadband development. A *New York Times* story on municipal broadband quoted a North Carolina farmer who wanted to monitor growing conditions in his tobacco and sweet-potato crops but couldn't—because they were planted beyond the service boundary of his town's public network.[74] The increased use of information technology and remote sensing in agriculture, like that provided by unmanned aerial vehicles (drones), could bring farmers further into broadband advocacy.

Finally, explosive economic growth in regions like western North Dakota's Bakken oil and gas field has created new opportunities for rural areas to think big. In a recent speech, the Minneapolis Federal Reserve Bank chief remarked on the rapid growth of North Dakota's energy-fed permanent fund, which is expected to surpass $5 billion by 2015. He suggested the state could invest the windfall in science, technology, and engineering (STEM) education.[75]

This brings up another important constituency for broadband expansion: schools. The KQED public-media blog *MindShift* profiled Matt Akin, the superintendent of a rural school district in Alabama that purchased e-readers for students to use at home. "Late one night, when Akin was leaving the middle school, he saw students sitting on the steps of the school trying to use its Internet." It turned out that enough students lacked Internet access at home that the district arranged to spend ten thousand dollars a month to support mobile Internet hot spots. "'It was really not fair to say this homework requires Internet access, and if you don't have it, go to McDonald's,' Akin said. 'But it was the only option that we had.'" The article adds that the district used to offer only Spanish as a foreign language but now teaches five languages, including Chinese; it also expanded its advanced-placement offerings from two courses to eight.[76]

With the advent of broadband connectivity representing a more connected and diversified rural western economy, maybe communities in the rural West can find a way to achieve the goals of a Country Life Commission that sought to further not just economic but social and cultural growth in a beautiful and isolated region. In 2009, the FCC chairman, Michael J. Copps, closed his report on rural broadband with a vow, one that has yet to be entirely fulfilled either by the federal government or individual efforts and one that is a reminder of the importance of telecommunications to connecting the rural West with the rest of the nation.

> As long as a grade-school child living on a farm cannot research a science project, or a high school student living on a remote Indian reservation cannot submit a college application, or an entrepreneur in a rural hamlet cannot order spare parts, or a local law enforcement officer cannot download pictures of a missing child without traveling to a city or town that has broadband Internet access, we cannot turn back from these challenges.[77]

Notes

1. Liberty Hyde Bailey, *Report of the Country Life Commission* (Washington, DC: Government Printing Office, 1909), 5.
2. David Cook, "*Monitor* Shifts from Print to Web-based Strategy," *Christian Science Monitor*, October 29, 2008, http://www.csmonitor.com/USA/2008/1029/p25s01-usgn.html.
3. Justin Bachman, "Netflix Passes HBO in Subscribers! (If You Stop Counting at the Border)," *Bloomberg Business Week*, October 21, 2013, http://www.bloomberg.com/bw/articles/2013-10-21/netflix-passes-hbo-in-subscribers-as-long-as-you-stop-counting-at-the-border.
4. E.J. Malecki, "Digital Development in Rural Areas: Potentials and Pitfalls," *Journal of Rural Studies* 19, no. 2 (2003): 201–14, 201.
5. Richard B. Kielbowicz and Linda Lawson, "Protecting the Small-Town Press: Community, Social Policy and Postal Privileges, 1845–1977," *Canadian Review of American Studies* 19 (Spring 1988): 23–45.

6. Rural West Initiative, *Report: Community Journalism in the United States*, Rural West Initiative, Bill Lane Center for the American West, Stanford University, October 30, 2012, http://ruralwest.stanford.edu/newspapers/.
7. Kielbowicz and Lawson, "Protecting the Small-Town Press," 32.
8. Michael J. Copps, *Bringing Broadband to Rural America: Report on a Rural Broadband Strategy*, Federal Communications Commission, May 22, 2009, 4, http://apps.fcc.gov/edocs_public/attachmatch/DOC-291012A1.pdf.
9. Cable News Network, "CNN Transcript of President Clinton's Radio Address," January 27, 1996, http://www.cnn.com/US/9601/budget/01-27/clinton_radio/.
10. Federal Communications Commission, "Universal Service," Federal Communications Commission, December 5, 2014, http://www.fcc.gov/encyclopedia/universal-service.
11. Esme Vos, "Australia Plans 100 Mbps to 90 Percent of Homes and Offices," *MuniWireless*, April 7, 2009, http://www.muniwireless.com/2009/04/07/australia-plans-100mbps-national-network/.
12. Phillip Dampler, "Norway Bringing Gigabit Fiber Broadband to Rural Areas as Americans Struggle for Faster DSL," *Stop the Cap!*, December 11, 2013, http://www.stopthecap.com/2013/12/11/norway-bringing-gigabit-fiber-broadband-to-rural-areas-as-americans-struggle-for-faster-dsl/.
13. Bethany J. Lenz, ed., *Broadband and Rural America* (New York: Nova Science Publishers, 2010), 74.
14. Tim Mandell, "Computer Use at Libraries Is Rising in Rural Areas, Declining in Urban Areas," *The Rural Blog*, Institute for Rural Journalism and Community Issues, University of Kentucky, October 4, 2013, http://irjci.blogspot.com/2013/10/computer-use-at-libraries-is-rising-in.html.
15. Ibid.
16. Peter Stenberg, Mitch Morehart, Stephen Vogel, John Cromartie, Vince Breneman, and Dennis Brown, *Broadband Internet's Value for Rural America*, Economic Research Report No. 78, Economic Research Service, U.S. Department of Agriculture, August 2009, http://www.ers.usda.gov/publications/err-economic-research-report/err78.aspx.
17. Brian Whitacre, Roberto Gallardo, and Sharon Strover, *Rural Broadband Availability and Adoption: Evidence, Policy Challenges, and Options*, National Agricultural & Rural Development Policy Center, U.S. Department of Agriculture, March 18, 2013, 7, http://www.nardep.info/uploads/BroadbandWhitePaper.pdf.
18. Stenberg et al., *Broadband Internet's Value for Rural America*, 15.
19. Om Malik, "The U.S. Now Has over 83 Million Broadband Subscribers," *GigaOm*, November 29, 2013, https://gigaom.com/2013/11/29/u-s-now-has-over-83-million-broadband-subscribers/.
20. Lenz, *Broadband and Rural America*.
21. Whitacre, Gallardo, and Strover, *Rural Broadband Availability*, 8.

22. John B. Horrigan, "Broadband Adoption in 2012: Little Movement Since '09 & Stakeholders Can Do More to Spur Adoption," *TechNet*, March 20, 2012, http://www.technet.org/wp-content/uploads/2012/03/TechNet-NBP-Broad band-Report-3-20-2012-FINAL1.pdf.
23. Federal Communications Commission, "National Broadband Map," http://www.broadbandmap.gov/speed.
24. Vlad Savov, "United States Gets a National Broadband Map, Finds Much of Its Nation Doesn't Have Broadband," *Engadget*, February 18, 2011, http://www.engadget.com/2011/02/18/united-states-gets-a-national-broadband-map-finds-much-of-its-n/.
25. Martin H. Bosworth, "Congress Passes Broadband Data Improvement Act," *Consumer Affairs*, October 2, 2008, http://www.consumeraffairs.com/news04/2008/10/congress_broadband.html.
26. Hanns Kuttner, *Broadband for Rural America: Economic Impacts and Economic Opportunities*, Hudson Institute, October 15, 2012, 6, http://www.hudson.org/content/researchattachments/attachment/1072/ruraltelecom-kuttner-1012.pdf.
27. Julius Genachowski, *Bringing Broadband to Rural America: Update to Report on a Rural Broadband Strategy*, Federal Communications Commission, June 17, 2011, 7, http://www.fcc.gov/document/bringing-broadband-rural-america.
28. Susan P. Crawford, *Captive Audience: The Telecom Industry and Monopoly Power in the New Gilded Age* (New Haven, CT: Yale University Press, 2013).
29. Susan P. Crawford, "U.S. Internet Users Pay More for Slower Service," *Bloomberg Business Week*, December 27, 2012, http://www.bloomberg.com/news/2012-12-27/u-s-internet-users-pay-more-for-slower-service.html.
30. Ibid.
31. Hibah Hussain, Danielle Kehl, Patrick Lucey, and Nick Russo, *The Cost of Connectivity 2013*, New America Foundation, October 28, 2013, http://newamerica.net/publications/policy/the_cost_of_connectivity_2013.
32. Susan P. Crawford, "Remarks at US-Ignite's Next Generation Application Summit, Chicago Cultural Center, June 24, 2013," http://www.scrawford.net/remarks-at-us-ignites-next-generation-application-summit-chicago-cultural-center-june-24-2013/.
33. Om Malik, "US Broadband's New Reality: Slowing Growth," *Gigaom*, November 14, 2012, http://gigaom.com/2012/11/14/us-broadbands-new-reality-slowing-growth/.
34. Karl Bode, "AT&T: The U-Verse Build Is Over," *Broadband DSL Reports*, February 9, 2012, http://www.dslreports.com/shownews/ATT-The-UVerse-Build-is-Over-118297.
35. Marguerite Reardon, "Verizon Offers Rural Americans a Pricey 4G Broadband Alternative," *CNET News*, March 6, 2012, http://www.cnet.com/news/verizon-offers-rural-americans-a-pricey-4g-broadband-alternative/.
36. Hussain et al., *The Cost of Connectivity*.
37. Malecki, "Digital Development in Rural Areas, 202.

38. New Deal Network, *TVA, Electricity for All,* Franklin and Eleanor Roosevelt Institute, http://newdeal.feri.org/tva/.
39. National Rural Electric Cooperative Association, "Electric Cooperative Growth 1914–present," interactive visualization, http://www.nreca.coop/wp-content/plugins/nreca-interactive-maps/coop-growth/index.html.
40. Kielbowicz and Lawson, "Protecting the Small-Town Press," 39.
41. National Telecommunications and Information Administration, "DCN's CCI Broadband Project," grant listing, U.S. Department of Commerce, http://www2.ntia.doc.gov/grantee/dakota-carrier-network-llc.
42. Dakota Carrier Network, "DCN Partners with Google, Netflix and YouTube to Advance User Experience," news release, March 12, 2014, http://www.dakotacarrier.com/data/upfiles/press/DakotaCarrierNetworkNewsRelease_031014.pdf.
43. Lisa Gonzalez, "California's Smallest Incorporated City to Extend Fiber to Residents," *Community Broadband Networks,* Institute for Local Self-Reliance, September 7, 2013, http://muninetworks.org/content/californias-smallest-incorporated-city-extend-fiber-residents.
44. Christopher Mitchell, "Publicly Owned Broadband Networks: Averting the Looming Broadband Monopoly," New Rules Project, Institute for Local Self-Reliance, March 23, 2011, http://www.ilsr.org/publicly-owned-broadband-networks-averting-looming-broadband-monopoly/.
45. Edward Wyatt, "Communities Fight State Laws That Can Divide Broadband Access," *New York Times,* November 9, 2014, http://www.nytimes.com/2014/11/10/technology/in-rural-america-challenging-a-roadblock-to-high-speed-internet.html.
46. Mitchell, "Publicly Owned Broadband Networks," 5.
47. Tom Wheeler, "Removing Barriers to Competitive Community Broadband," *Official FCC Blog,* Federal Communications Commission, June 10, 2014, http://www.fcc.gov/blog/removing-barriers-competitive-community-broadband.
48. National Telecommunications and Information Administration, *Exploring the Digital Nation: America's Emerging Online Experience,* U.S. Department of Commerce, June 2013, http://www.ntia.doc.gov/files/ntia/publications/exploring_the_digital_nation_-_americas_emerging_online_experience.pdf.
49. Kathryn Zickuhr and Aaron Smith, "Home Broadband 2013," Pew Internet & American Life Project, Pew Research Center, August 26, 2013, http://www.pewinternet.org/2013/08/26/home-broadband-2013/.
50. Kathryn Zickuhr, *Who's Not Online and Why,* Pew Internet & American Life Project, Pew Research Center, September 25, 2013, http://www.pewinternet.org/2013/09/25/whos-not-online-and-why/.
51. National Telecommunications and Information Administration, *Exploring the Digital Nation,* 26–28.
52. Whitacre, Gallardo, and Strover, *Rural Broadband Availability,* 9.

53. Ibid., 68–69.
54. Edward Wyatt, "F.C.C. Chief Aims to Bolster Internet for Schools," *New York Times*, November 17, 2014, http://www.nytimes.com/2014/11/17/business/fcc-chief-aims-to-bolster-internet-for-schools.html.
55. Federal Communications Commission, "Wireline Competition Bureau Announces Entities Provisionally Accepted for Rural Broadband Experiments; Sets Deadline for Submission of Additional Information," December 5, 2014, http://www.fcc.gov/document/wcb-announces-provisionally-selected-bidders-rural-broadband-exps.
56. Todd R. Weiss, "FCC's Rural Broadband Experimental Efforts Get 181 Applicants," *eWeek*, November 11, 2014, http://www.eweek.com/networking/fccs-rural-broadband-experimental-efforts-get-181-applicants.html.
57. Crawford, *Captive Audience*, 267.
58. Ibid.
59. CSMG Consulting, FTTH [Fiber to the Home] Deployment Assessment, prepared for Corning, October 13, 2009, http://www.neofiber.net/Articles/FTTH_Assessment_of_Costs.pdf.
60. Lori A. Dickes, R. David Lamie, and Brian E. Whitacre, "The Struggle for Broadband in Rural America," *Choices* 25, no. 4 (2010), http://www.choices magazine.org/magazine/article.php?article=156.
61. Kuttner, *Broadband for Rural America*, 9.
62. Jed Kolko with research support from Davin Reed, *Does Broadband Boost Local Economic Development?*, Public Policy Institute of California, January 2010, 24. "Moving from no broadband providers to 1–3 providers (the FCC groups one, two, and three providers together in its reporting) is associated with employment growth that is higher by 6.4 percentage points over the seven-year period from 1999 to 2005" (22), http://www.ppic.org/content/pubs/report/R_110JKR.pdf.
63. Ray Rasker, Patricia H. Gude, Justin A. Gude, and Jeff van den Noort, "The Economic Importance of Air Travel in High-Amenity Rural Areas," *Journal of Rural Studies* 25 (July 2009): 343–53,6, http://www.headwaterseconomics.org/3wests/Rasker_et_al_2009_Three_Wests.pdf.
64. Kolko, *Does Broadband Boost Local Economic Development?*, 27.
65. Don E. Albrecht, *Rethinking Rural: Global Community and Economic Development in the Small Town West* (Pullman: Washington State University Press, 2014), 197.
66. Economic Research Service, "Rural America at a Glance, 2013 Edition," Economic Brief No. 24, U.S. Department of Agriculture, November 2013, 6, http://www.ers.usda.gov/media/1216457/eb-24_single-pages.pdf
67. Accessed from https://www.goodreads.com/author/quotes/591907.Joe_Paterno.
68. Philip Dampler, "Special Report: Big Phone and Cable Companies Are Losing Your Calls to Rural America," *Stop the Cap!*, August 28, 2014, http://stopthe

cap.com/2014/08/28/special-report-big-phone-and-cable-companies-are-losing-your-calls-to-rural-america/.

69. Tom Lyden, "Dropped Calls: FCC Says Problem Hits 'Epic Proportions,'" Fox 9 TV, Minneapolis-St. Paul, March 5, 2014, http://www.myfoxtwincities.com/story/24899066/dropped-calls-fcc-says-problem-hits-epic-proportions.
70. Erik Wasson and Bernie Becker, "Postal Service Losses Reach $3.9B in 2013," *The Hill,* August 9, 2013, http://thehill.com/policy/finance/316381-postal-service-losses-reach-39-billion-in-2013.
71. Kielbowicz and Lawson, "Protecting the Small-Town Press," 27.
72. Jonathan Rodden and Jowei Chen, "Unintentional Gerrymandering: Political Geography and Electoral Bias in Legislatures," *Quarterly Journal of Political Science* 8, no. 3 (2013): 239–69.
73. Gautham Nagesh, "House Republicans Say FCC Net Neutrality Laws Are Unnecessary, Overreach," *Wall Street Journal,* June 20, 2014, http://www.wsj.com/articles/house-republicans-say-fcc-net-neutrality-laws-are-unnecessary-overreach-1403293782.
74. Edward Wyatt, "Communities Fight State Laws That Can Divide Broadband Access," *New York Times,* November 9, 2014, http://www.nytimes.com/2014/11/10/technology/in-rural-america-challenging-a-roadblock-to-high-speed-internet.html.
75. Narayana Kocherlakota, "Speech to the State of the West Symposium, Stanford University," Minneapolis Federal Reserve, November 13, 2014, http://www.minneapolisfed.org/news-andevents/presidents-speeches/state-of-the-west-symposium.
76. Katrina Schwartz, "How Rural Schools Paid for Students' Home Internet to Transform Learning," *MindShift,* KQED News blog, December 2, 2014, http://blogs.kqed.org/mindshift/2014/12/how-rural-schools-paid-for-students-home-internet-to-transform-learning/.
77. Copps, *Bringing Broadband to Rural America,* 3.

COMMUNITY

Many of the problems confronting the rural West are regional or national, but most of them have their primary impact on communities and must be addressed by them. Husbanding scarce resources, choosing economic-development paths, even the challenge of providing basic social services are issues with which local communities struggle. The essays in this section deal specifically with community issues in the rural West.

Judy Muller explores the relationship between the small community of Norwood, Colorado, and its local newspaper by focusing on the reaction to a high-school hazing incident. In Norwood—as in many small towns—there was a reluctance, shared by the local press, to confront the scandal and the culture of bullying that nurtured it. A lack of local leadership—which has implications for a wide range of decision making and problem solving—hampered Norwood's efforts to address the scandal effectively, as it restricts many small communities.

J. Dwight Hines investigates an increasingly common phenomenon in the West—the changing nature of communities and the tensions that result from that change. New residents seeking the experiences and amenities offered by the natural beauty of the West have frequently clashed with farmers and ranchers, who value nature for its productive potential. Hines highlights these conflicts by focusing on controversies over water policy in Montana and the reintroduction of wolves in Wyoming, Montana, and Idaho.

In his essay, Burke Griggs explores the division between surface-water and groundwater irrigators on the western plains of Kansas, Nebraska, and Colorado. Surface-water irrigation, with its emphasis on shared work and water, puts a premium on community cooperation. Groundwater irrigators, who tap the Ogallala Aquifer, are more individualistic. The conflict between the two over scarce water mirrors the enduring struggle in the West between the individual and the community.

As Geoff McGhee pointed out in his essay on broadband Internet, much of the rural West can be defined by what it lacks. Among the absent services with which rural westerners frequently cope is readily available health care. It is not uncommon for rural westerners to be far distant—sometimes a hundred miles or more—from health-care providers and hospitals. And for those who lack insurance or are undocumented aliens, distance is the least of their challenges. Marc Schenker tackles the latter of these problems. He finds that Latino immigrants in rural California suffer disproportionately from such chronic health problems as diabetes and obesity. And their ability to get treatment is hampered by poverty, discrimination, and a shortage of providers. Schenker concludes by exploring treatment options for this underserved population, some of them relatively new and imaginative.

Too Close for Comfort

When Big Stories Hit Small Towns

JUDY MULLER

On February 16, 2012, the high-school wrestling team from the small town of Norwood, Colorado, along with the coach and some parents, traveled by bus to Denver for the state wrestling championships. At one point, the coach took the team inside the Pepsi Center for a weigh-in, leaving four students to wait on the bus. What exactly happened next is known only to those boys, but the allegation is that three of them—two fourteen-year-olds and one fifteen-year-old—ganged up on the youngest, a twelve-year-old. They carried him to the backseat of the bus, duct-taped his ankles and wrists together, taped his sweatshirt hood over his head, then used a pencil to shove quarters into the crack of his buttocks.

This would qualify as a news story, no matter where it happened. Given the recent national attention on hazing (e.g., the death of a member of the Florida A&M marching band) and bullying (e.g., the documentary film *Bully*), not to mention sexual assault (e.g., Penn State), it seems all too timely. Now add some additional twists: the twelve-year-old victim in this case is the son of the high school principal; two of the three boys who ganged up on him are sons of the wrestling coach, who also happened to be the school-board president at that time. What's more, these families have been close friends for years, even taking vacations together. In a small ranching community like Norwood, where the school's typical graduating class is about twelve, residents know everyone involved, including the kids. And they take sides.

Perhaps this story would never have split the community so viciously except that the case played out over many agonizing months in the media. As a journalist who has recently written a book on the subject of small-town newspapers,[1] and as a part-time resident of Norwood, I was curious to see what sort of impact local coverage had on such a sensitive topic. Because editors of rural newspapers live next door to the people they are reporting about, they must often choose between getting along and getting at the truth. Those who choose frankness over friendship, I have discovered, often feel the backlash in a very personal way, ranging from a cold shoulder at the grocery store to bullets fired through a window. Violent reactions are rare, of course, but social ostracism is also a painful experience when one lives in a small community. Throw in the occasional angry merchant who threatens to pull advertising, and you add financial pressure as well.

Norwood is a town of about five hundred people—a thousand if you include all the surrounding ranches and homes—about forty miles from the upscale resort of Telluride. The way that the local newspaper, the *Norwood Post,* chose to cover this particular story illustrates how challenging it can be for a local editor—especially one with little journalism experience—to report on an incident that eventually splintered the community and cast an unflattering spotlight on the town by outside media. It also underscores the growing conflicts in rural communities between the insular "macho" culture of ranching life and the more diverse attitudes of newcomers, a theme that is cropping up in the so-called New West more and more frequently, whether it involves uranium miners versus environmentalists or snowmobilers versus cross-country skiers. Rural journalists are often caught in the middle.

Before getting into the details, I should also point out that I experienced something of a Pirandello effect in writing this article, a play-within-a-play feeling where that too-close-for-comfort quandary affected me in a personal way. I have a home in Norwood, my brother and his wife live there, and I have made a lot of friends in the community. At the invitation of the school superintendent, Dave Crews, I have spoken to students about journalism, and I delivered the commencement address two years ago. So writing a critical piece, even one leavened with concern and compassion, about a town where I may retire was not easy. The fact that I have thirty years of reporting experience as a network correspondent doesn't provide any Teflon when it comes to writing about people in a community I have come to love. Nevertheless, I would like to believe I have not pulled any punches in relating this difficult tale, which is based mainly on interviews that I conducted between May and September of 2012.

The incident took place in February. But *Norwood Post* editor Ellen Metrick first heard about it on March 28, when she received an e-mailed letter to the editor, signed "a concerned citizen of Norwood." That e-mail is reproduced here, complete with spelling errors:

> There is a huge cover-up going on at the Norwood School. A 7th grade boy was raped on a bus at the Wrestling State Meet in Denver on February 16, 2012. Three other students who attend the Norwood School taped this boys hands, feet and hood over his head so he could not fight back and was violated. This was reported to the Head Wrestling Coach, who is also President of the School Board, his two sons were a part of this assault. Bobby Harris [the coach and school-board president] has admitted his sons did this but it just was horse play that went to far, a hazing if you will. The parent of the boy that was raped is the Principal of the Norwood School. The three boys were given one day of in-school suspension. The administration never contacted the police to let them know there was a crime committed. The school board has met in executive sessions and feels the principal needs to be on administrative leave. So lets review, the principal's son is raped and the father of the rape victim is punished. This school board has shown no compassion for the child that was assaulted. This school board should be recalled. This could have been your son? How would you feel if this school board disregarded your son? These people are supposed to be protecting our children. Please stand up for this young man. Attend the next school board meeting and let them know you are outraged. Be heard now![2]

Despite the amount of detail in this anonymous e-mail, Metrick did not act on it. "I tucked it away," she told me. "It was anonymous, seemed like someone trying to stir something up that wasn't there or get back at someone and, of course, I didn't want to believe it. I am not proud of the way I handled it. I should have gotten on it right away and notified Andrew Mirrington [her publisher, who lives in Telluride] right away."[3]

Metrick took the part-time job of *Norwood Post* editor several years ago. A published poet with no journalism training, she approached the job with the goal of uniting the community, primarily focusing on news about school events and achievements. "The school is the hub of this community,"[4] she told me two years ago in what turned out to be an ironic and prescient observation. When she was hired, the *Post* was no longer a fully independent newspaper; the publisher had decided to make the *Norwood Post* a weekly eight-page wraparound of his daily paper, the *Telluride Daily Planet,* and to close the paper's small office on the main street of town.

Even so, Metrick says she took the job with a commitment to fairness and giving the town a sense of identity. As she told me several years ago, "Somehow the paper validates the town and our very existence. It says, 'We are here, in print! Look, we won the game; we have this great art teacher!'"[5] This cheerleader approach to the news is not uncommon at small weeklies, at least until a controversial story erupts in their community, forcing them to make a choice about how deeply to dig, how much to tell, and how much is at stake.

Two weeks after Metrick received, and ignored, that anonymous e-mail, the same message was sent to the editor of the *Telluride Watch,* a weekly paper run by two veteran journalists, Marta Tarbell and her husband, Seth Cagin. Tarbell says she reported on it right away, using the e-mail as a starting point for asking questions to school officials in Norwood and authorities in Denver. "I decided to break it online so as not to sound sensationalistic, and I tried to put the most salacious stuff online, instead of in the paper," she said. "My goal was to foster discussion." That it did, with the *Watch*'s website becoming the must-read update location for anyone interested in the story, which was just about everyone in Norwood.

In those first posts in early April, the *Watch* reported that the Denver district attorney was investigating the matter (since it had happened there) and that Denver police officers had traveled to Norwood to interview the boys involved. Tarbell also quoted Norwood Superintendent Dave Crews, who responded to the *Watch*'s inquiry in an e-mail. He declined to comment on specifics because the story involved personnel and students, but he added, "At this time, we have not had any disciplinary incidents at school pertaining to this case. It is a safe environment."[6]

Crews told me he did not expect to see his e-mail posted as part of the *Watch*'s website story. This struck me as astonishingly naïve since anything he put in writing at that point was bound to be considered an official statement. He said people misinterpreted the line about no disciplinary action; after all, he told me, back in February, he had decided to give the boys involved in the "incident" a one-day, in-school suspension. "But the media got hold of my comment and reported we had done nothing about it," he told me. When I suggested that a one-day, in-school suspension might strike people as being as close to nothing as possible, he responded, "In retrospect, we should have reported it [to the authorities]."

His "in retrospect" regrets may have been caused, in part, by media pressure, especially the intense coverage in the *Telluride Watch*, which pointed out in one of its earliest reports something school officials should have known all along: "The Colorado Child Protection Act of 1987 requires school employees who have reason to believe that a child in their care has been assaulted must report their suspicions, in writing and orally, to county social services and/or law enforcement authorities."[7]

So who did report the incident? Tisha LaFramboise, mother of the alleged victim and wife of the school principal, Tom LaFramboise, told me they were the people who had called the Denver police but only after they felt rebuffed by Norwood school officials. The very night their son had told them about the incident, back at the state wrestling championships in February, she said, "Tom called [Superintendent] Crews and said, 'I am not calling as an administrator, but as a parent, and you need to take action here.' We waited for three weeks, and David Crews did nothing. He gave them [the assailants] a one-day, in-school suspension!"

I asked her if she had written that anonymous e-mail. "No," she responded emphatically. "If I had written it, I would have signed my name, and I would not have used the word 'rape' because that was not accurate." She believed the e-mail might have come from a teacher because the incident was common knowledge inside the school before it became public knowledge, and some of the teachers had called her to say how upset they were about the backlash against the principal.

Once the Denver police and district attorney became involved, it was easier for Ellen Metrick to report on events as they unfolded at official levels. But she still refrained from digging for local details; she didn't call Tom LaFramboise (the principal and father of the victim), Bobby Harris (the wrestling coach/school-board president and father of two of the accused boys), or the mother of the third boy involved in the case. "This story traumatized me," Metrick told me. "It would be a lot easier if I didn't know everyone."

On April 10, she decided to ask her publisher for advice about how to approach the story. "We talked on the phone for about an hour. He said, 'You have to cover this,' and we agreed that the coverage would be delicate and appropriate. Because we are a small paper, we don't want to alienate anybody. We want to keep the doors open and have people communicate with each other," she told me.

In late April and early May, she reported (as did the *Watch*) that the Denver police had arrested the three boys involved in the alleged assault. Her article in the *Post*, headlined "Norwood Students Charged with Assault, Kidnapping," quoted D.A. spokesperson Lynn Kimbrough as saying, "These are very serious charges. This is a very serious case." The *Post* article outlined the charges against the boys, ranging in age from fourteen to sixteen: "They were charged with sexual assault, false imprisonment and second-degree kidnapping of their classmate and could face up to two years in a juvenile detention facility. The charges would be class 2 misdemeanors and class 2 felonies if the boys were charged as adults."[8]

Later in the article, Metrick explained, "Under Colorado statute, juveniles charged with class 1, 2, or 3 felonies lose their right to anonymity, giving the public access to arrest and criminal records information. Yet, because they are juveniles, many news sources, including the *Norwood Post*, have not published their names."[9]

The *Telluride Watch* also chose not to print the names of the boys involved, and both papers found creative, somewhat-contorted ways not to mention that two of the accused were sons of the wrestling coach/board president, even though everyone in town knew it and also was aware that the victim was the son of the principal. Lynn Kimbrough, the spokesperson for the Denver D.A., says she was surprised that news media, including the Denver press, chose not to print the names of the accused since the charges were serious enough "to waive confidentiality of the juvenile process." But Kimbrough also understood the reluctance. "I've lived in a small town," she told me, "and my heart goes out to everyone there."

One television station, KREX-TV in Grand Junction, which is more than a two-hour drive from Norwood, did print the names of the accused boys on its website. KREX also published photos of two of the accused boys with their names underneath, taken from Facebook pages. The comments on the station's website reflected a wide split reacting to this decision. "Please protect the identity of the victim," posted one supportive viewer, "but place all photos of the criminals and their parents on a billboard. Expose these idiots before they strike again and ruin someone's life...." However, another read, "Shame on you for showing their faces and names. They have not been convicted, and they are juveniles! This is hurting everyone in our community, and reports like yours just cause more upset."[10]

Back in Norwood, meanwhile, the reactions of the school board and residents were picking up steam. Both the *Telluride Watch* and the *Norwood Post* reported on various developments during April and May, including the decision of the school-board president, Bobby Harris, to "recuse himself" from his position on the board and his job as wrestling coach (both papers managed to do this without mentioning that Harris was the father of two of the accused boys); an executive session of the school board, when more than forty residents signed up to tell board members their concerns over this incident away from the ears of reporters; and an open session when the board heard mostly plaudits from parents and complaints that this incident had overshadowed all the good work done by the Norwood schools.

A reporter from CBS4-Denver suggested on the air that the meeting had a "pep rally" atmosphere. Superintendent Dave Crews commented in the same report that this support did not drown out claims that soon "bubbled up" regarding "a number of other 'taping incidents' from past years," leading officials to suspect a "possible culture of hazing" in the school.[11]

The *Telluride Watch* editor jumped on Crews's reference to hazing in the television report and called the Denver D.A.'s office for a reaction. In a website update, Tarbell quoted spokeswoman Lynn Kimbrough as saying, "Comments that somehow suggest this was just a hazing are somewhat concerning. It implies that somehow hazing is OK, which is misguided. It also diminishes the serious nature of these allegations, and demonstrates a misguided moral compass." The same *Watch* website article also noted that the allegations "have split members of Norwood's tight-knit longtime ranching community down the middle, and reports from inside the school indicate the students are divided every bit as bitterly as the adults. 'The students are voting on which side's story they believe,' said one parent close to the case, and defenders of the alleged assailants seemed to be winning.'"[12]

If you're wondering how such a thing is possible, you need to know about the background rumors I heard from numerous residents that Principal LaFramboise had ignored complaints in the past about the hazing of students (including boys being stripped and wrapped in duct tape) and that many locals were angry that he was ready to call the police only when his own son was targeted. Neither paper reported on this allegation—even to dispel it—which is a major oversight in explaining the complexities of community reaction.

One television station, KKCO in Grand Junction, did report on this allegation, based on interviews its reporter did with some Norwood parents after one school-board meeting. This summary comes from the station's website: "[This is] something that has some parents and students enraged, saying hazing incidents happen all the time and the principal turns the other cheek, only reacting now because his son was the victim.... So, last night, parents and students on both sides met with the Norwood School Board in small private groups, most of them calling for the principal's firing."[13]

That report elicited a number of angry comments from both sides of the debate and all around the country. But one KKCO online comment came from someone in Norwood, who wrote,

> I don't think anyone thinks it's OK because of past events or OK in any shape or form. However, very similar assaults have happened under the principal's direct supervision and his oldest son has been directly involved many times.... The Principal gives out his standard issue speech that 'boys will be boys' and we are 'taking care of it' and 'don't you worry.' NO EXCUSE for what happened and it's tragic. However the principal has failed his youngest son and many other children the same way.[14]

In the months I spent reporting on this incident, I did not find a single parent who could say—on or off the record—he or she had reported bullying or hazing to *this* principal and was ignored. Perhaps they will yet come forward. But surely Tom LaFramboise deserved to be asked about these allegations, and he was not. What did get reported was an effort by the school board (now with a new president) to encourage LaFramboise to take a buyout and leave his position. This came after the *Watch* headlined a story, "Norwood Principal LaFramboise May Be Out." In the article, the Norwood school attorney said no decision had been reached. But the article clearly implied that the principal's possible ouster might be a backlash against his role in this case: "LaFramboise, who is also the school's football coach, persisted in the face of resistance from the school board and administrators in reporting to police a February 16 incident in Denver that led to the filing of felony sexual assault and kidnapping charges against three Norwood students."[15]

Again, the *Watch* managed to tell this story without saying explicitly that LaFramboise was the father of the victim. The board members later voted to offer the principal only a one-year renewal of his contract and stripped him of his football coaching duties. And the board continued to encourage him to take a buyout for early retirement. Finally, just before the new school year began, he was put on administrative leave.

Ellen Metrick also addressed the "culture of hazing" in an April 18 article in the *Norwood Post*. After leading with the fact that Denver police had come to Norwood School to investigate, she added,

> Rumors and discussions abound in the larger community, though the events may only ever be known to those most intimately involved in the incident. A group of parents or community members—it is unclear from the anonymous e-mails received by local newspapers as to who and how many are involved—said they are concerned for their children's safety and "there is a cover-up going on at Norwood School."

She added, "Some parents in the school community said there is a bullying problem at Norwood School, something that was supported by a middle-school student survey conducted two years ago by Norwood High School students." But she also said that "a quick poll of a dozen parents" revealed that most of them were not worried for their children's safety because of this incident. "One parent said the kids are probably safer than ever."[16]

The fact that residents would not allow their names to be used in this article is not unusual in Norwood; Metrick says it is extremely difficult to get people in a small town to make a controversial statement on the record, or any statement, for that matter. She did interview Superintendent Crews, who said there was no effort by the school board to oust the principal and that plans were under way to tighten policy and disciplinary procedures, "leaving little gray area for discernment in future cases."

Compared to the *Telluride Watch*'s aggressive coverage, the *Norwood Post*'s approach may seem overly cautious to appear "balanced." That disparity could simply represent the distance—cultural and geographic—between Norwood and Telluride, between a fairly conservative ranching community and a liberal resort community. Or it might reflect the fact that Ellen Metrick and her husband *live* in Norwood, where she sometimes works as a substitute teacher and where her daughter attends elementary school.

Despite what some professional journalists might call cautious coverage, a number of people in the community admire the way Metrick handled this story. Art Goodtimes, a San Miguel County commissioner whose hippielike appearance makes him stand out in conservative Norwood, knows something about navigating the tricky line between the old and new regional cultures. "I think Ellen has done an excellent job with this story," he told me, "just sticking with the facts." Superintendent Crews agrees: "Ellen did a good job. She wasn't trying to create something huge." And Metrick told me that after her first article on the case appeared—detailing the arrests and investigation—she was approached at Clark's Market (the only one in town) by the mother of one of the boys charged in the case. "She had tears in her eyes," said Metrick, "and she said, 'Thank you for writing such a fair article.'"

As for the Harrises, they told me that while "it's hard to see all the headlines accusing your kids," they thought the *Norwood Post* took the right approach, reporting only the legal developments in the case. "She tried to be fair," says Molly Harris. They were outraged, on the other hand, by those television stations that printed the names of their sons and aired their Facebook photos. "They were treated as guilty," says Molly. And because the Harrises had been advised not to talk with the media, they just had to ignore it. Eventually, they stopped reading and watching the coverage.

Often the way a local paper covers a sensitive story is nuanced. Certainly Metrick would not have written the sort of line that appeared in one *Watch* article—attributed to reporter Gus Jarvis—describing the split in the Norwood community over this story as "an unseen cultural divide wider than Gurley Gulch, which separates the Hitchin' Post from Two Candles,

Norwood eating and drinking establishments patronized by conservative and liberal members of the community, respectively."[17] A great line, I thought, and fairly accurate, but if you lived in town, would you glibly stereotype the population that way? Probably not.

One person who is not a fan of the *Post*'s coverage is Tisha LaFramboise, who told me, "In the beginning, I know Ellen was trying to not get involved, to downplay the controversy. She has never asked to speak with us. I actually really like Ellen," she added, "but she got some of the facts wrong." In particular, she says that Metrick reported that Tisha's husband made the decision, along with the superintendent, to discipline the three boys with a one-day, in-house suspension. Not true, says LaFramboise. They had been encouraging Crews and the school board to report the incident to authorities. Only when they were stonewalled, she says, did they decide to report the incident themselves.

On the other hand, she has high praise for the *Watch*'s coverage. "We've had calls from Australia and Japan, from people who have seen [Tarbell's] stories online, people offering their sympathy and support." But it's small comfort, she says, when the town "has turned against us. We are basically ostracized. [My son] has never changed a bit of his story, not to this day. It has caused us all real grief. Why would he lie about this? Now he wishes it would just go away. He's gone to town maybe three times since this happened." As someone who was born and raised in Norwood, LaFramboise says she is devastated. "The Harrises were our best friends. We vacationed with them. I think the superintendent just thought this would all go away. Bobby Harris has refused to talk to us. Not one school board member has called to ask about our son. Facebook comments to [her son] have been hateful." The LaFramboises eventually decided to send the boy to live with relatives in another Colorado town, she says, because returning to school in Norwood would have been impossible for reasons that had become painfully obvious.

The Harris boys and the third boy charged in the case, on the other hand, returned to the Norwood school after a summer when they were required to wear court-ordered ankle bracelets and allowed to leave their house for only one hour a day. During those long months, says Bobby Harris, they were told by their lawyer to avoid contact with reporters. Metrick made no attempt to contact them. Tarbell did try, but the Harrises say they didn't trust her enough to go "off the record," as she encouraged them to, so that she could at least hear both sides of the story. "We didn't know her," says Harris, underscoring the advantage local editors have, despite that too-close-for-comfort issue.

The Harrises said they decided to talk with me even though, in the words of Bobby Harris, "we don't know you, either, but we know who you are. And I saw you at commencement." That was enough of a local connection, apparently, to win their trust. But they spoke to me only on the condition that specific details about the incident on the bus would not be on the record. Bobby Harris says the version of events that appeared in the media was "grossly exaggerated. Not even close to what has been said in court under oath. The facts are so different from what's being said on the street."

The facts in this "rural *Rashomon*" are difficult to determine. But according to the version allegedly offered by the three boys who taped the LaFramboise boy, the incident began as four friends kidding and taunting one another. "I truly believe they did not do this maliciously," Bobby Harris says. "They were friends messing around. My kids would never have taped up a kid who wasn't their buddy. But there should be limits to hazing. When somebody's upset, when it's not fun for everyone anymore, you have gone too far. I don't condone it." But, concedes Harris, "it [taping of feet and hands] is like a rite of passage with kids who are in athletics." In fact, say the Harrises, one of their sons was once taped up on a bus going to an athletic event...and they say the perpetrator was the oldest LaFramboise boy.

That incident was handled between the families, who have long been close. But now they have been introduced to the juvenile justice system, which characterizes such attacks as more than a group of friends messing around. Harris says they had to learn to decipher the legal language. "Taping is 'unlawful imprisonment.' Taking him to the back of the bus was 'kidnapping.'" The sexual-contact charge comes from the allegation that the pencil made contact with the boy's buttocks. "But one newspaper," says Harris, "wrote that he was 'penetrated with a foreign object.'" That sort of coverage, he adds, fueled the gossip on the street and traumatized his sons.

But the boys were certainly not without their supporters. In an article in the *Watch* on May 8, Marta Tarbell reported that

> Norwood students sporting "Team TTH" T-shirts were told to remove them at the Norwood schools' annual end-of-the-school-

> year barbecue. 'Team TTH' was an explicit proclamation of support for the three students facing felony charges in a February 16 sexual assault on a fellow student in Denver. The alleged assailants, whose initials appeared on the T-shirt, will not return to classes this year.

The article also mentioned that the shirts had been made "at a Norwood establishment specializing in 'uniforms, custom embroidery…'" and that one student who wore a T-shirt to the barbecue was reportedly the son of a teacher in the Norwood schools.[18]

Because this is such a telling incident, indicating the angry split in the community, it seems undeniably newsworthy, but Metrick did not delve into the T-shirt brouhaha. In fact, she says she did not even know about it until she read the article in *The Watch*. Even after finding out about the incident, however, she did not write a follow-up story.

Meanwhile, anonymous comments posted on May 11 on the *Watch*'s website in response to its coverage were often insightful and provided a forum for people to vent their feelings without fear:

> I cannot believe the behavior of students, parents, teachers, and anyone else who sported the t-shirts, which were printed locally, by an upstanding community member. What are you people saying to the boys who performed the lascivious act? Worse, what are you telling the victim?
>
> Before you speak against your neighbor, know the facts and try to avoid mudslinging. Please confront the person who passes judgment on ANYONE involved, whether it be in line at the grocery store or paying for gas.
>
> I think many of us in this community are heartbroken by this incident, the divisions that have arisen, the things we've been forced to explain to our children and the sense of sadness and uncertainty in our community.[19]

And there was also this comment, indicating that not everyone in Norwood was a fan of Metrick's cautious approach to the story: "I salute Seth, Marta and the *Watch* for having the gonads to report this. The other paper has not stood up to this. In my household we call the other paper cowards of the first sort."[20]

It appears that website comment pages may be replacing the "Letter to the Editor" page in weekly papers, at least at the ones that offer them. And with good reason: e-mail comments do not require names, whereas many papers still insist that printed letters to the editor must be signed and verified. The *Norwood Post* has a website, but it is more archival than active, even though there are occasional comments to weekly articles. On this story, the *Post*—with its part-time staff of one—simply could not compete with the almost-daily updates on the *Watch*'s website and comment page. But Metrick did receive one letter to the editor, signed by a former Norwood teacher who had moved away, which she was happy to print.

> Dear Editor:
> As a retired educator and previous member of the Norwood teaching and administrative staffs, I am deeply saddened by the continuing, tragic revelations of abuse and malfeasance in the district. Naturally, I know only what has been made public but the following issues must be addressed:
>
> - A culture of bullying, harassment and hazing has been the norm in the school for a significant time.
> - Four young lives have been unalterably impacted by the casual, tacit acceptance of a school climate, which accommodates brutalizing some students.
> - Those charged with the safety of all students failed to act to change this culture.
> - Once the most recent incident occurred, the decision was made to ignore Colorado Statutes, requiring an immediate report to law enforcement or Child Protective Services.
> - The climate in the community has been affected, as some parents have allowed their children to openly persecute the victim.
>
> A safe and secure learning environment for all students must be the first and constant goal for all educators. Without this security, learning cannot occur and time and scarce resources will be squandered in an effort to undo harm which should have never occurred. Responsible adults must act with due diligence. Parents, teachers and administrators must assure that the school climate, which gave rise to these acts, is radically altered. Anything less will impart the lesson that school violence is acceptable.
>
> William Nickell[21]

I asked Metrick if she had considered writing an editorial about the incident and the "culture of hazing" that kept coming up in discussions around town. Her publisher, Andrew Mirrington, had told her not to write an editorial, she said, because he didn't want the paper out on "the edge." But she did not disagree with his reticent position and was happy to have this strong letter to the editor make the case for reform. In Norwood, just printing such a letter might be considered a courageous stand, but if ever a story cried out for an editorial voice, it seems to be this one, even if it simply asked readers to withhold judgment until the court determined exactly what had happened on that bus.

Again the *Telluride Watch* filled that void with a lengthy editorial on April 29 entitled, "Do the Right Thing." Publisher Seth Cagin did not mince words, denouncing school administrators who had long tolerated bullying with the attitude of "boys will be boys" and praising the courage of the victim's family in this case to upend the status quo by reporting the assault to the authorities. In his words, "This insistence on justice and the Norwood District's resistance to it has turned the assault into an occasion of reckoning for the entire community. Is the Norwood school system a place where hazing and bullying are condoned?"[22]

One can make the case that the local news media—collectively speaking—did manage to do their job in this case: one weekly took an aggressive approach in both its reporting and editorial position, as well as encouraging a discussion of this incident on its website, while the other weekly was more cautious, waiting until events unfolded before reporting them and shying away from editorial comments. But as good as the *Telluride Watch* coverage was, especially in the early weeks of this story, I think that the local paper should have pursued a deeper investigation into the culture of hazing in Norwood. Some of the residents of Norwood harbor distrust of Telluride, and those are the very people who need to be involved in this discussion because they would most likely trust someone who also lives in town. That too-close-for-comfort problem experienced by local editors can also be beneficial: they know whom to talk to and how to elicit the information required to tell a sensitive story.

And there certainly is a deeper story waiting to be told here. In my own cursory reporting, I found a number of Norwood residents who described horrendous examples of bullying going back decades in the Norwood schools. These people had never told their stories on the record before. John Herndon was one. He comes from a longtime ranching family in the area and—before retiring recently—ran a successful construction business in Norwood. He attended Norwood schools from kindergarten to twelfth grade and said, "Sports dominate the culture. Residents made fun of you if you didn't play football. I was 135 pounds and named a guard. All I wanted to do was play rock-and-roll music, but I was forced to play football. This was 1968," he says,

> and I grudgingly went out for the team. When I suffered an injury in a workout, the town doctor, John Peters, told me, "There's nothing wrong with your ankle, just a sprain, but I could put a cast on it." He knew that would help get me out of playing football my senior year. And so I got that cast put on. Even so, men would come up to me on the street and point their fingers at me and call me a sissy-assed chicken shit because after the cast came off, I didn't go back on the team.

Years later, when it came time for their children to enter school, John and Laurie Herndon enrolled their son and daughter, Anjin and Anneka, in the Norwood system. Laurie was teaching in the school at that time, and a lot of years had passed since John had been pressured to measure up to that macho ideal. But when Anjin was still in elementary school, says Herndon, kids started picking on him because he was small: "He got stuffed in trash cans." While their son tried to laugh it off, "when you're the smallest one, and you're the one getting stuffed, it's not fun after a while."

By the time Anjin was in middle school, says Laurie, he started showing signs of depression. He had a friend named Walker Ferguson, a new kid in town, and both boys were bullied. "One kid grabbed Walker," says John, "got him down, and threatened to pull his earring out. I found myself advising my kid to help Walker and fight these guys. Then I was appalled at myself." The Herndons had already complained to the principal (not LaFramboise, who came later), who told them, "Well, Anjin and Walker play basketball, and they did pretty well, so I guess they're not pansies," which was saying, in effect, that their kids should stand up for themselves.

The Herndons' solution was radical. They started their own school along with other parents whose kids had suffered harassment at the Norwood schools. The group included Art Goodtimes, whose son had also been bullied, and Duncan Ferguson and his wife, Susie Billings, who had moved with their two children to Norwood in 1994. "We were advocates of public schools," they told me,

> so we enrolled Coral [age eight] and Walker [age twelve] in the Norwood school. But he would get thumped on every day—physically hit by other kids. Walker begged us not to report this to the principal and superintendent because he felt it would add to the intimidation, but we did report it. The response we got was that Walker needed to learn how to fight because then he would fit right in.

Apparently their son was singled out for abuse because he looked different from the other kids in this rural area—"he wore shorts, ate bagels, had an earring, wore flip-flops."

But the last straw came when John Herndon confided to the Fergusons, "You need to know something" about the volunteer football coach at Norwood: "This guy is offering kids fifty dollars to beat up Walker to convince him to become a team player and join the football team." That did it. Walker's parents went to school-board member Mark Vandenberg (the local veterinarian) with this information. "Mark got three people fired—the superintendent, the principal and the coach—within the year. We were invited to another school board meeting with new people in charge, saying, 'We need people like you to help turn things around.' But we weren't willing to sacrifice our kids, so we started our own school." The Sage Hill School, as they called it, lasted two years. Then funding and staffing problems prompted them to eventually put their children into the Telluride school system, a trend that has become so common that Telluride has put a limit on the number of students who can enroll from outside the district.

There is no small irony in the fact that both Anjin Herndon and Walker Ferguson turned out to be more macho than their tormentors could have imagined. Anjin was recently a photographer on the *National Geographic* team ascending Everest, requiring expert climbing skills. Walker went on to win several junior world titles in the rigorous sport of cycling.

So how did these two couples react to this latest incident involving Norwood kids? "We were saddened," said Susie Billings. "Fifteen years later, the same things are happening, and the town still hasn't gotten it together. The same shenanigans: whether you use duct tape or rope, it's hazing." Laurie Herndon echoed that sentiment: "Same ol', same ol', only more intense," she said. "Where have we not stepped up to the plate? Ken Watt is stepping up. He's taking a leadership role. And this is a community without leaders."

Ken Watt is head of the Norwood Youth Organization, which provides activities for kids. He also has a son in the high school. Along with a couple of other parents, Watt has tried to spark a reform movement of sorts. "We're just not going to put up with [the bullying culture] anymore," Watt told me. His group paid to bring in a motivational speaker to help the community "heal from a recent rift," as the *Norwood Post* delicately described it, and teamed up with the Telluride Foundation, a charitable group, to fund a visit from two University of Colorado professors who specialize in conflict management and team building.

In a *Norwood Post* article on August 2 headlined "The New Note for the New School Year," Metrick wrote that the school board "vows to be proactive and positive." The board, under new leadership, revised the students', staff's, and coaches' handbooks to reflect tougher standards, she reported. And she quoted Ken Watt, "who pointed out that not only the school is affected by the February wrestling championship incident that made state news. 'The potential economic impact of this is huge: If you don't have a good school, people don't want to come. This is a community project. The school board can't do it alone.'"[23] In perhaps the most significant move of all, the Board of Education hired William Nickell, a former teacher in the Norwood schools and the author of the one outraged letter to the editor of the *Norwood Post*, to return to Norwood to serve as principal for one year.

Meanwhile, the judicial process finally came to an end. The two older boys, then sixteen and seventeen, pled guilty in August 2012 to third-degree misdemeanor assault and were sentenced to two years of probation, fifty hours of community service, and joint payment of restitution. In December, the third boy, then fifteen, avoided trial by pleading guilty to a misdemeanor count of sexual contact/no consent. He was sentenced to ongoing probation, fifty hours of community service, participation in a victim-empathy class and "boundaries" group, and restitution to the victim's family.

The victim's family, in the end, left town. LaFramboise had lost his job as principal, their youngest son had been placed in a school in another town and was living with relatives, and the discomfort of remaining in Norwood was simply too intolerable.

Both local weekly newspapers covered the judicial process, but as far as reporting on the social disruption in the community and the long history of hazing and assault, neither paper seems interested in deeper analysis. The *Telluride Watch* has never really covered ordinary activities in Norwood, anyway, such as sports and community events. The bullying scandal was an exception.

Certainly Metrick is more comfortable reporting the solution than the problem, and now she hopes to become part of it. She accepted a position as a middle-school English teacher in the Norwood schools and passed the editorial reins to Patrick Coleman, a young man who recently moved back to the area from Oregon to help his mother run the family ranch. He had worked as a reporter for a weekly, the *Portland Mercury*. He said he was very excited about running the *Norwood Post*, even though it was a part-time job. As for the messy story he was stepping into, he commented, "I don't want to be quiet; I want to address this first."

In one of his first articles, he wrote about parents joining together to form a PTA for the Norwood schools.

> In a small town, 14 Facebook "likes" can actually make a difference. That's how many people have given the virtual thumbs-up to Norwood's first Parent Teacher Association in at least a decade.
>
> It all began with the well-publicized events surrounding Norwood High School's ill-fated wrestling trip. "Last year, when all that trouble happened, I realized that parents needed to be more involved in school," said [the PTA founder] Mandee Shirley.[24]

Coleman may have had what it takes to bridge cultures in Norwood; with roots in the area, he was considered somewhat of a local, but he had yet to form the sort of friendships that might make him pause with tough reporting decisions. No matter how professional the editor, however, it is in that crucible where one must choose between truth and popularity that real courage is forged at small-town papers, and it can be a lonely place.

When I interviewed Metrick about her reporting on this story, she said that if she had it to do over again, she would have started asking questions immediately, following up on the anonymous e-mail. "Morally," she told me, "I should have gone to [Superintendent] Dave Crews right away. If he knew about it, he should have done something. And if not, why not?

A lot of parents, staff, and teachers who were in Denver—at least fifteen adults—knew about it that night."

The most successful weeklies in small towns establish themselves as the place to go for well-sourced facts, as opposed to rumors; for a community conversation, perhaps carried out on a website where people feel free to comment without being identified; and for an editorial voice to arouse collective conscience and rally a ruptured community. If that voice, that reportage, is not thriving at the local level, others will hijack the story—e.g., a television station in a nearby city that doesn't hesitate to name the juveniles and post their photos, as well as another station that can't get the basic facts right and is willing to report unsubstantiated rumors.

And the story was, indeed, hijacked by outside media—a full year later. On June 20, 2013, a story headlined, "Sodomy Hazing Leaves 13-year-old Victim Outcast in Colorado Town," appeared on Bloomberg.com and was then recirculated by the *Denver Post*, the *Huffington Post*, and the *Daily Mail Online* in the United Kingdom. The story included numerous factual errors, including a statement that the whole town had turned against the victim and his family. Angry hate mail and phone calls poured in from around the country, aimed at local businesses, town officials, and the families of the assailants.

But this time, the editor of the *Norwood Post* did not ignore the problem; Patrick Coleman wrote a strong editorial about the Bloomberg story, which he said "paints an undeniably ugly picture of the assault and its aftermath," adding, "and, in truth, only an ugly picture could be painted of the events." And for the first time since three boys had ganged up on another boy on a school bus two years earlier, repeating a decades-long pattern of abuse, the local newspaper finally made an editorial statement:

> We must agree, as a community, with one loud voice, that physical violence in any context, whether sexual, spousal or as a result of hazing or bullying, is never acceptable.
>
> We must agree that no parent concerned about their child's mental and physical health after an assault should feel it necessary to leave their community due to harassment.[25]

If ever there was a classic example of why "watchdog journalism" makes a difference, this story is it. Once the *Telluride Watch* and other media outlets began covering this case, the school officials in Norwood had to start answering uncomfortable questions. Without the persistent coverage, it's likely that they would have tried to deal with this incident as an in-house disciplinary problem. The media attention—now expanded to a national and international stage—shamed them into action. But even now, after the juvenile court has dealt with the legal issues, and the reconstituted school board is promising to reform the hazing culture, it would be all too easy for the local news media to heave an editorial sigh of relief and concentrate on positive developments to heal the community.

The editorial baton has been passed yet again at the *Norwood Post*; Patrick Coleman and his family have moved out of state. But he and his predecessor, Ellen Metrick, have also passed on a powerful lesson to the new editor—healing doesn't happen when the truth remains hidden, when a long history of macho bullying is allowed to fester and erode the reputation of a school and, by extension, the community. The truth may make us squirm, but—as we saw with the Penn State scandal—looking the other way only makes it worse. Much worse.

Notes

1. Judy Muller, *Emus Loose in Egnar: Big Stories from Small Towns* (Lincoln: University of Nebraska Press, 2011).
2. Anonymous e-mail received by Ellen Metrick, March 28, 2012; copy provided to author.
3. All the interviews for this article were conducted between May and September of 2012.
4. Muller, *Emus Loose in Egnar*, 234.
5. Ibid.
6. "D. A. Reports Investigation, Decision-Making Process Still Ongoing," *Telluride Watch*, April 12, 2012.
7. Ibid.
8. "Norwood Students Charged with Assault, Kidnapping," *Norwood Post*, April 26, 2012.
9. Ibid.
10. KREX-TV, April 27, 2012, http://www.krextv.com.
11. CBS4-Denver, April 17, 2012, http://www.cbs4.com.
12. "Three Norwood Students Charged with Sexual Assault," *Telluride Watch*, May 3, 2012.
13. KKCO-TV, April 27, 2012, http://www.nbc11news.com.
14. Ibid.
15. "Norwood Principal Laframboise May Be Out," *Telluride Watch*, May 4, 2012.
16. *Norwood Post*, April 18, 2012.

17. Gus Jarvis, "CBS4 in Denver Breaks Code of Silence Surrounding Norwood Sex Assault," *Telluride Watch*, May 7, 2012.
18. Maria Tarbell, "Tensions Persist in Norwood in Wake of Sexual Assault Charges," *Telluride Watch*, May 8, 2012.
19. "Comments from Readers," *The Watch*, May 8, 2012, http://www.telluridenews.com/the_watch/.
20. Ibid.
21. Letter to the Editor, *Norwood Post*, May 24, 2012.
22. Seth Cagin, "Do the Right Thing," *Telluride Watch*, April 29, 2012.
23. Ellen Metrick, "The New Note for the New School Year," *Norwood Post*, August 2, 2012.
24. *Norwood Post*, September 13, 2012.
25. Patrick Coleman, "Letter from the Editor," *Norwood Post*, June 26, 2013.

On Water and Wolves

Toward an Integrative Political Ecology of the "New" West

J. DWIGHT HINES

Introduction: Where is the New West?

Within the American West, the contemporary process of rural gentrification is exacerbating preexisting social, geographic, and environmental disparities. The sites of this gentrification are the so-called amenity-rich counties that dot the regional expanse and form an "archipelago," or chain of rapidly changing island communities in the midst of a relatively static agricultural/industrial sea.[1] It is this archipelago that most people are referring to when they use the term *New West*.[2] These communities typically are named for their principal town, although they quite often encompass adjacent areas, and the names form a list of the most iconic sites in the region: Aspen, Vail, Park City, Jackson (Hole), Sun Valley, Taos, Missoula, and Bozeman, among others.

The emergence of the New West represents a major break from the previous era not just because it is the product of locally dramatic in-migration but because the people who are moving in practice life by a different cultural logic than previously predominated in the region. In some small communities, the balance is clearly tipping away from previous ways of thinking and acting toward the imported approach. A transition is occurring from one rational landscape focused on an industrial form of capitalism to another that is emerging in conjunction with an ascending postindustrial regime.

Thus, the current phase of rural restructuring is best described as the transition from the prior dominance of a regime of production and consumption of natural resources and commodities to the increasing emergence of one centered on the production and consumption of what can be called "experiences." Defining this distinction between the so-called Old and New Wests in these terms allows us to focus on gentrification as an expression of the abiding cultural logic of postindustrial society that transcends the rural/urban divide and thereby points to societywide changes.

Gentrification and the New West Archipelago

When coined, the term *gentrification* referred to the mid-twentieth-century displacement of working-class Londoners by a new upper-middle-class, or urban, gentry.[3] In applying the term to the rural American West, I want to emphasize the class character of this contemporary form of counterurbanization: rural gentrification is the colonization and transformation of the primarily (if not exclusively) industrial working- and middle-class social and physical space of the rural United States by members of the ex-urban postindustrial middle class, or PIMC.[4]

The bulk of the newcomers that I have chronicled in my decade-long research come from sub/urban middle-class backgrounds, are college educated, and work in the professional or service industries (e.g., financial, managerial, educational, creative);[5] they are economists, lawyers, contractors, artists, baristas, commercial entrepreneurs, all occupations associated with the postindustrial middle class.[6] It is these people, who are engaged in creating, manipulating, and developing images and symbols, who are especially predisposed to be the primary and most ardent consumers of these products we can call *experiences*.[7] Many newcomers seek and employ them to justify gentrification.

Thus, as the demographic balance tips in many communities toward a preponderance of the PIMC, the land is increasingly valued as a site of the production and consumption of experiences as opposed to the production and consumption of material commodities, e.g., minerals, timber, agricultural products, as was done previously. This shift, which is occurring throughout the archipelago, manifests itself in any number of conflicts related to land and resource use. I have chosen to focus on two elements—water and wolves—that, each in its own way, concentrate our attention on the evolving situation within the American West.

Water: The Georgetown Lake Controversy

Water, because it is the longest-standing and most quintessential resource of conflict in the semiarid American West, is the place to start. I want to reiterate that an important way to make sense of all of the conflicts described in this essay is seeing them as clashes between competing cultural perspectives and their material manifestations. Rural gentrification is inspiring a modification in what people of the West consider to be proper natural-resource use. While this shift has not entirely cast aside preexisting land-use regimes—much less dented them in the still Old West regions—it has, in some places, begun a possible tectonic shift. To demonstrate this movement, I offer a case drawn from southwestern Montana, where a long-standing water-use protocol is being challenged.

Georgetown Lake is a human-made reservoir that straddles the line between Granite and Deer Lodge Counties in southwestern Montana. It is located at more than six thousand feet near the top of the Flint Creek drainage, north and west of Butte. Flint Creek flows north out of the lake for thirty-some miles before it joins the westward course of the Clark Fork River.

The lake was created in 1901 when the Montana Power Company (MPC) dammed Flint Creek to generate electrical power for its mines and smelter in nearby Anaconda. The construction of the dam was a boon for the local economy; not only did it provide cheap energy to process copper ore, but it also benefited local sheep and cattle ranchers, who gained water rights on Flint Creek. The dam meant that the distribution of water, upon which ranchers rely to irrigate their crops, could spread over the summer, instead of being almost entirely dependent upon snow melt, as it is on Rocky Mountain streams without water impoundment.[8]

In 1988, the MPC discontinued producing electricity at the site. In 1997, the Granite County Commission (GCC), the five-member group of elected officials charged with administering the county, acquired the dam with the idea of restoring power generation. In 2000, before the permitting process to reestablish energy production was complete, juggling Georgetown Lake's volume with Flint Creek's in-stream flow resulted in a conflict between local industrial and postindustrial interests in southwestern Montana.

The conflict became public in the summer of 2000 on the heels of four years of drought, when the Granite County commissioners responded to pressure from local homeowners, business people, and recreationalists to reduce the release from Georgetown Lake from its standard midsummer flow of more than fifty cubic feet per second (cfs) to less than thirty cfs. Lowering the outflow was the commissioners' attempt to balance the concerns of the residents and recreationalists of Georgetown Lake with the needs of ranchers who relied upon Flint Creek to water their stock and irrigate their fields. No one on either side was completely happy with the decision.

On one side, local ranchers were frustrated by lowering the in-stream flow from its traditional midsummer volume; they thought the decision was a clear-cut "taking" that threatened their economic survival.[9] The local water commissioner, John Ohrmann, said at the time that the "irrigation situation was really critical...we are fighting for our livelihood."[10]

On the other side, lake residents and recreational business concerns joined to oppose the continued draining of the lake at the previous rate. The members of both groups shared the fear that drawing the lake down too far would threaten the local trout and salmon populations that made the reservoir the most popular sport-fishing site in western Montana. They recognized that if an alpine lake gets too low during the summer and fall, the fish do not have sufficient oxygen and food to survive under the ice when the winter freeze comes; what is more, a lower-level lake at the end of one year takes an abnormally wet winter and spring the following year to regenerate it. Droughts have persisted for up-to a dozen years in some parts of the American West, so wise, long-term management of water resources is constantly at a premium.

A recently chartered homeowners' association on the lake epitomizes the postindustrial emphasis of these new residents; the covenants of the association express its purpose is

> to ensure use of the Property for attractive recreational and residential purposes only; to promote health and happiness; to prevent unnecessary impairment of the environment; to maintain the tone of the Property in its native form and preserve its natural beauty as far as possible; to secure to each Owner the full benefit and enjoyment of their Lot with no greater restriction on free use of the same than as necessary to ensure the same advantage to other Lots.[11]

What is interesting about this document is its adamancy to establish the legitimacy of experiential pursuit as part of the mandate of this rural residential neighborhood. This statement differentiates this site and style of residence from previously predominant residential behavior within a more strictly industrial regime of production and consumption.

Local homeowners, recreationalists, and business people differed slightly in their reasons for maintaining the lake's volume. Both of these reasons revealed a postindustrial regime of production and consumption of experiences. The lake residents and Montana recreationalists principally sought to preserve their experience of trophy fishing, while the business owners primarily wanted to safeguard their economic interest in the people who sought these experiences. Karen Funston, the owner of Georgetown Lake Lodge—a local hotel and restaurant that caters to people from around the state who come to fish—echoed the water commissioners' concern regarding resource use when she said, "There is a lot of people who have a lot to lose…there is a lot at stake."[12]

Another rationale also existed for the agenda of the water-conservation coalition, and it even more clearly exemplifies the postindustrial perspective of Georgetown Lake residents. Rural gentrifiers wanted not only to experience fishing on the lake but also to maintain and maximize its aesthetic beauty in its high-altitude setting. As the summer heated up and there was less inflow to the lake due to the high-mountain snowpack running out, as well as the increased demand for outflow to sate the ranchers' irrigation needs, the lake level annually dropped dramatically. The band of exposed earth around the lake grew. This happened every year, some years more than others. The residents bemoaned the increasing distance between the full shoreline of early spring and the summer one. One lake resident, whose home sits right next to the high-water mark, expressed his dissatisfaction: "No one likes to look out over an empty bathtub; and that is just what it looks like in August: an empty bathtub."

For this subset of the water conservation group, it was not necessarily the health of the fish population as much as the limitation of the alpine aesthetic that inspired them to lobby the GCC. These newcomers were clearly communicating their desire not to see their experience of the rural West compromised by the ranchers' industrial-production interests. By seeking to influence the outflow from the reservoir, they were clearly articulating their desire not to see the industrial production of agricultural commodities (i.e., alfalfa and, ultimately, beef cattle) continue to trump the postindustrial production of aesthetic commodities (i.e., the experience of the lake's alpine beauty).

When the news of this issue hit the statewide press in late 2001, it prompted a vocal response from nearby gentrifying communities. One rancher I asked about the controversy (and specifically about reactions like the bathtub quote), shook his head, muttered a four-letter word, and said, "I am not sure if people like that have the sense gawd gave a goose." He and many other natives considered prioritizing recreation or aesthetics over resources for industrial production to be the acme of illogical behavior.

By contrast, a local newcomer and an ardent fisherman applauded the Georgetown provocateurs for their attempt to challenge the traditional priorities of the Old West. "I think it's about time that we got people out in support of such measures," he told me, "There needs to be more action taken to maintain Montana's natural resources and not see them exploited solely by the ranchers and miners."

Although not completely successful in satisfying all sides of the dispute, the Grant County commissioners' decision to limit the Flint Creek flow put off the conflict for the rest of 2000. Their hope was that with any luck a wet winter would break the drought in Montana, and the benevolence of Mother Nature would alleviate further agitation. They were not so lucky. The winter of 2000–2001 was even drier than the previous half dozen, and water managers throughout Montana were forced once again to make hard decisions.

On October 15, 2001, U.S. District Judge Don Malloy in Missoula issued a temporary restraining order to the GCC that required the commission to reduce Georgetown Lake outflows enough to prevent lowering the level. The order had been prompted by the commission's refusal on October 2 to follow the recommendation of its own advisory group—composed of irrigators, members of the homeowners' association, and state and federal administrative agencies—to reduce immediately the discharge volume at the Flint Creek Dam from thirty cfs to ten cfs. The Butte-based George Grant Chapter of Trout Unlimited (TU) and the Georgetown Lake homeowners (GLH) filed the request for legal action.

It is interesting to note that no business concerns were overtly involved in the 2001 legal petition (unlike the informal request made the previous year). Instead, the petitioners were the recreational advocates of TU and the local experiential residents from the homeowners' association. The composition of these two groups is important because they represent the changing perspective within Montana communities caused by recent rural gentrification. TU is a national organization that has a significant presence (twelve local chapters) in Montana, a state that is widely renowned for the quality of its trout fishing. TU focuses on the creation and maintenance of fishable habitat both through access and riparian restoration. Its priority is establishing access to the experience of recreational and sport fishing; it has no interest in developing or advocating for the production of fish as an aquacultural commodity. Not surprisingly, the majority of its members—which, in general, come from a wide swath of local society—are middle-class newcomers to Montana.

At the same time that they sought the restraining order, these two groups also pursued an injunction in federal district court to make the conditions of the temporary judgment permanent. As a result, Judge Molloy issued a permanent injunction in October 2001. The injunction required that the GCC maintain Georgetown Lake's level at no less than one foot below full pool level at the end of May. This ruling, which to date remains unchallenged by the Granite County commissioners and has become the de-facto administrative protocol for Flint Creek, has some likely profound repercussions for resource management in the Rocky Mountain West. It signals a reversal of the predominant priorities of local society.

Wolves

The controversy over wolf reintroduction to the Greater Yellowstone Ecosystem (GYE) is much less a struggle over wolves and much more a conflict between social groups.[13] In important ways, the continuing debate surrounding the management of wolves within the states surrounding the GYE reflects the ongoing conflict between local natives and newcomers.

Going along with the thesis of this chapter, the rhetorical attention given by rural gentrifiers to support reintroduction and conservation management of wolves indicates that they also subscribe to the post-industrial ideal of the production and consumption of experiences, whereas middle- and working-class natives believe that the production and consumption of saleable commodities (e.g., livestock, timber, minerals) constitutes the best use for the lands of the American West. This conflict is rooted in a class-cultural dynamic that pits classes and class factions against one another in contests (legal, political, and social) to determine who will exert greater control over the ways in which the landscapes of the GYE are managed.

Wolf Reintroduction to Yellowstone National Park

The North American gray wolf (*canis lupus*) is an indigenous species whose range encompassed most of the continent prior to European colonization. Extensive hunting throughout the frontier period both to prevent predation of livestock and express deep-seated cultural biases led to radical reduction of its numbers and range. By the twentieth century, the wolf survived in only a few pockets in the United States, most notably in mountainous regions of the American West. In 1926, the last wolf was trapped in Yellowstone National Park (YNP), although several individuals survived in the park until the mid-1930s.[14]

With the rise of the U.S. environmental movement in the 1960s came the call to reintroduce the wolf to the wildlands of the Rocky Mountains. As early as 1968, the U.S. National Park Service (NPS) expressed its recognition of its role in the production of ecosystems and its desire to deal with their missing components.[15] By the early-1970s, Nathaniel H. Reed, assistant secretary of the interior for national parks and wildlife, was convening meetings in YNP to discuss wolf reintroduction. Despite these nascent rumblings, national and regional sentiment, as well as local political will, was significantly opposed to the idea.

The late 1970s and early 1980s saw gradual development of the idea of wolf reintroduction in addition to a rise in popular support. By 1978, NPS biologist John Weaver had proposed the specific idea to transplant wolves from Canada or Minnesota to restore a viable population of this predator to YNP. In 1980, an initial plan for reintroduction was drafted, and John L. Spinks, deputy regional director of the U.S. Fish and Wildlife Service (FWS), signed a revised version in 1987. On the popular front, sentiment had also shifted by the late 1980s. A survey of YNP visitors indicated overwhelming support for wolf reestablishment.[16] In addition, a study of Wyoming residents showed that almost half favored wolves.[17]

Even after these developments, the first dramatic shift in political will toward reintroduction only came in 1988 when former U.S. Senator James McClure of Idaho endorsed the idea. He noted that there were already breeding pairs of wolves in Glacier National Park (in northern Montana), and he thought it appropriate that they return to YNP.[18] Then Congressman Wayne Owens of Utah introduced a bill that called for relevant agencies to begin the environmental impact statement (EIS) for wolf reintroduction to YNP. From that point, support grew in official circles with significant voices like Wyoming Senator Alan Simpson joining the burgeoning chorus.

In 1990, Congress appropriated $375,000 to support the development of a wolf introduction and management plan for YNP and central Idaho wilderness areas. In 1995 and 1996, the NPS succeeded, in conjunction with the FWS, in introducing 66 individual wolves into the northern reaches of YNP.[19] The numbers of animals and breeding pairs rose so rapidly that by 2000, they had already reached the initial FWS goals of 300 individuals and 30 packs. Since then numbers have continued to rise with the most recent *Rocky Mountain Wolf Recovery 2010 Interagency Annual Report* (RMWRI) indicating that there were at least 1,651 individuals in 244 packs with 111 breeding pairs in Montana, Wyoming, and Idaho.

Interestingly enough, while the overall numbers in the northern Rocky Mountain states have increased, the numbers in YNP have fallen from a high of 94 in 1997 to fewer than 40 in 2010. Biologists hypothesize that this decline ironically is an indication of the wolves' success because they have effectively culled the park's ungulate herds, especially elk. As their sources of easy prey have dwindled, wolves have been forced to move outside their federally protected domain. This point is bolstered by the precipitous drop in the number of elk in YNP, particularly in the so-called northern herd, which saw its population decline significantly since wolf reintroduction. This circumstance—beyond inspiring more wolves to move outside the park—has incurred the ire of local professional outfitters, who rely upon big game to attract out-of-state hunters. However, although the numbers of the northern and southern Yellowstone elk herds have declined since wolf reintroduction, they are still well above the goals set by the FWS.[20]

Ongoing discussion about wolves in Wyoming and Montana some seventeen years after reintroduction is not something people favoring conservation could have anticipated. In many respects, the wolf is now the victim of its own success. As numbers have risen and wolves have expanded their territory beyond YNP, they have left the protection of U.S. Forest Service (USFS) lands and even the GYE, which in turn has thrown them into further conflict with residents—especially ranchers and hunter/outfitters—of the surrounding states. This has shifted the debate from whether or not the wolves should be brought back to how they should be managed.

On the antiwolf side, the expansion of range beyond public lands confirmed the worst-case scenario: wolves were uncontrollable, and they would reoccupy significant swathes of the Rocky Mountain West. Increasingly these people called for delisting the wolf as a federally mandated endangered species and turning management of the animals back to the individual states. In 2009, the FWS agreed to delist the animal and give control back to the states of Idaho and Montana, which had drafted management plans that met the basic guidelines—of 150 wolves and 15 breeding pairs—thought necessary for population maintenance proposed by the RMWRI. However, the FWS balked at giving Wyoming the same permission since that state persisted in its intention to designate the wolves outside the GYE as predators and permit their unregulated killing.

Shortly after the initial delisting, U.S. District Judge Donald Malloy halted it on the grounds that the FWS had failed to follow the legal process for delisting an endangered species. Nevertheless, the U.S. Congress reinstated the delisting through a budgetary rider drafted by Senators Jon Tester (D) of Montana and Mike Simpson (R) of Idaho. Thus, at present, the wolf is managed as a trophy-game animal by Montana and Idaho, which both hold annual hunts to control numbers. In late 2012, the FWS delisted wolves in Wyoming and turned their management over to the state, which created a system of regulation similar to those in Montana and Idaho.[21]

Crying Wolf: The Divergent Perspectives on the Value of Wolves in Yellowstone

Over the last decade of my research in the northern Rocky Mountains, it has become evident that wolf reintroduction and management are two issues that glaringly serve as markers for the emerging cultural conflict between postindustrial middle-class and industrial working- and middle-class Americans within the New West.[22] What makes these debates more challenging is that—as the result of almost two decades of rural gentrification—many of the alternate voices of postindustrial America are not coming from around the United States but from fellow local residents. The fact that many more of these voices emerge from neighbors makes the conflict certainly more complex and in some cases more rancorous.

When addressing the topic shortly after reintroduction, Matthew Wilson identified three principal issues that were driving the debate over wolves in YNP;[23] these were "(1) differential access to social power, (2) conflicting ideas about private property, and (3) divergent beliefs about humankind's proper relationship with the natural environment" between the members of two social movements—the environmentalists and the so-called wise-use adherents—seeking to impose their ideals of proper land use.[24]

I would add a fourth issue, which springs from the emerging difference between the two competing ideals of proper land use, especially for the public domain. This difference stems from the burgeoning value of experiences in an increasingly postindustrial world. While the members of the wise-use movement are largely constituents of the industrial working and middle class,[25] not all members of the latter are part of the former. In a similar vein, neither is the postindustrial middle class simply composed of members of the environmental movement.

As with many such debates, the rhetoric of the two sides is composed of multiple voices and therefore encompasses many slightly divergent arguments. As I have discussed, several types of experiences draw ex-urban, postindustrial middle-class Americans to the rural West.[26] Among them is the natural environment but also included are ideals pertaining to the experiences of rural community and small-town life and the physical and social landscape of the ranching industry, which do not necessarily inspire overt environmental activism.

The rest of this essay sketches the extent of this debate while retaining a sense of its central core. Despite the shift in emphasis from establishing the wolf population (prior to the mid-2000s) to managing it, both the pro-wolf postindustrial perspective and the antiwolf industrial point of view have remained remarkably consistent.

The Industrial Perspective on Wolves

In contrast to the pro-wolf position, those westerners who are against the wolf propose a more-or-less singular argument: reintroducing and maintaining the animal threatens the true purpose—what they describe as the "highest and best use"—of the land, especially the public lands of the American West. This overall worldview fractures into specific opinions according to what industry a given person considers is the correct way to use the land (usually by affiliation). Therefore, industrial Americans say that public lands of the West are best used primarily, if not exclusively, to produce agricultural goods, minerals, timber, and/or big-game wildlife (as saleable commodities).

With the advent of management in Idaho and Montana, local antiwolf activists have become bolder. This has led to local proposals on ways to improve the plans agreed to by state and federal governments. Antiwolf advocacy groups in both states want to permit more and different ways to hunt wolves. These movements have defined the situation as a "taking" issue. By proposing that the loss of livestock and/or wildlife represents taking private property by the federal and/or state governments, wolf opponents seek to tap into the rich vein of libertarian opinion and resentment of federal government influence in the rural American West.

In western Montana, a group of livestock producers are pressuring the Ravalli County Commission to adopt a system to reward people who kill predators in the Bitterroot Valley. The plan proposed by the Livestock Protection Group will fund a hundred-dollar bounty on wolves and mountain lions. It is unlikely that a county law like this would be able to supersede the jurisdiction of Montana Fish, Wildlife & Parks (FWP),[27] but the attempt reveals how bold the antiwolf position has become.

In Missoula County, immediately north, antiwolf advocates have a similar plan. Toby Bridges, the self-professed leader of a group of "sportsmen against wolves," has accused FWP of "working closely with radical environmental groups, the majority of which are extremely anti-hunting."[28] One of these groups, the Yellowstone to Yukon Conservation Initiative, Bridges said, strives to "make it where you can't live on the land" and to "reduce human use of the West."[29]

A similar scenario is playing out in the state senate in Idaho. A Republican lawmaker has introduced a bill to allow ranchers to use live bait to hunt wolves. The bill would also permit anyone whose livestock or family pets have been bothered or killed by wolves to shoot the animals from airplanes using night scopes and luring them with live bait within thirty-six hours.[30] Revealing the animosity between natives and newcomers, antiwolf advocate Jay Pearce proclaims, "We've danced their [pro-wolf] dance. It's now time to dance with our own people."[31]

One seeming exception to the industrial mind-set came in 2011 when Idaho Governor Butch Otter signed a bill declaring an emergency due to the number of wolves in the state. The legislation stated that

> the uncontrolled proliferation of imported wolves on private land has produced a clear and present danger to humans, their pets and livestock, and has altered and hindered historical uses of private and public land, dramatically inhibiting previously safe activities

> such as walking, picnicking, biking, berry picking, hunting and fishing.... it is the intent of the legislature to regulate the presence of Canadian gray wolves in Idaho in order to safeguard the public, wildlife, economy and private property against additional devastation.[32]

It is telling that the governor does not just state the potential of wolves to affect livestock production but includes nonproductive activities such as picnicking and berry picking as being compromised as well. While I do not see this necessarily as evidence that Otter has adopted a postindustrial perspective, this example does reveal that the changing demographics of the New West archipelago can compel politicians to respond to the ideology of their gentrifying constituents.

Hidden behind the rhetoric is the idea—at least from the antiwolf camp—that wolves are a sovereignty issue. But underlying that is a more fundamental difference between the way industrial Rocky Mountain natives and postindustrial newcomers want to use the land and, by extension, its resources.

The Postindustrial Perspective on Wolves

Within the pro-wolf camp, there are at least two distinctive positions: what I am provisionally calling vociferous and latent. The vociferous position is evident in statements by an organization like the Greater Yellowstone Coalition (GYC), which was formed in 1983 as a confederation of sixty-plus independent nonprofit organizations. It is dedicated to keeping the GYE "healthy and wild" by keeping it "whole."[33] The GYC's flagship programs involve predator advocacy; grizzly bears and wolves are the primary species they focus on. A few statements from the GYC should make its ideology clear.

The GYC's stated values regarding wolves are threefold:

1. Wolves are critical to the overall health of the Greater Yellowstone Ecosystem as a keystone species, restoring ecological balance. Most notably wolves improve the health of their prey through selecting weak, old, diseased and injured animals.
2. Wolves also change the habits of prey such as elk by reducing their numbers and changing distribution. These changes have contributed to a rebirth in the growth of cottonwood, willow, aspen and shrubs,

subsequently benefiting grizzly bears, pronghorn, beaver, cutthroat trout, songbirds, scavengers and small mammals.

3. Wolves have proven to be a substantial economic draw for Yellowstone and Grand Teton gateway communities, with an estimated $35.5 million annually attributed directly to visitors coming to the three-state region solely to see wolves. In Yellowstone, 50 percent or more of the more than 3 million annual visitors are specifically interested in the possibility of seeing a wolf. Eco-tourism has developed as a valuable business in communities surrounding Yellowstone. Like grizzly bears, wolves are an irreplaceable symbol of vanishing wildness, and their restoration to Greater Yellowstone in 1995–96 nearly 70 years after they were eliminated is a shining example of a conservation success story.[34]

It is important to note that all three of these values are ultimately predicated on the intangible experience they provide to tourists and people concerned with the United States' status as a conservation leader. The GYC develops the second point in a section on its website entitled "Wolves and Economics":

> Travel and tourism make up a significant portion of Wyoming's economy. More than 7 million overnight visitors traveled to Wyoming in 2008, and visitors to Wyoming spent $2.7 billion, or $7.4 million each day in 2007. Wildlife watching is one of the top reasons people choose to visit Wyoming. In fact, 31 percent of visitors to Wyoming in 2008 participated in wildlife watching.[35]

Subsequently the GYC proposes that "for many visitors to Yellowstone watching wolves is a significant attraction…44 percent of visitors to Yellowstone National Park in 2005 wanted to see wolves.… In winter, when wolves are most visible in the park, 59 percent of visitors came to Yellowstone specifically to see or hear wolves."[36] By establishing that wolf tourism is a significant industry in and around YNP, the GYC is seeking to reframe the wolf argument as a debate between competing capitalist agendas, rather than an expression of rural/urban cultural difference.

The more moderate or latent pro-wolf position is expressed by any number of people living in the New West archipelago. It is characterized by resignation to the fact of the wolves' presence in the northern Rocky

Mountains. This resignation includes the awareness that the future management of the wolves demands a significant compromise from both extremes in the debate.

Acceptance of the situation comes from people on the industrial side of the divide such as Dean B. Peterson, who says, "I do not dislike or hate the animal." Peterson, a fourth-generation rancher in Montana's Big Hole, adds that "...the wolf is here to stay now, and my feeling is that those people who want it here should share the costs."[37]

This is largely happening. Ed Bangs, wolf-recovery specialist for the FWS, notes that as many as 40 percent of Montana's estimated 497 wolves were killed in 2010; the year before, wolves had killed more than 353 head of livestock in the state. The Montana Department of Livestock reimburses owners for each confirmed kill. In 2009, the total paid in compensation was more than $128,000.[38] A similar program in Idaho also reimburses livestock owners for wolf depredations.

A similar view is expressed by Davis Reagan, a New West in-migrant, who states,

> As far as I can tell, I'm right in the middle when it comes to having wolves here in Montana. I support their reintroduction and am glad they are here again. They are beautiful animals and efficient predators with truly impressive intelligence and resilience. But I also believe they should be managed for the benefit of all equally, including ranchers/livestock owners. If they are removed from EPA protection I do not have a moral or other objection to the State having a hunting season with a set number of animals that can be taken.[39]

Conclusion

The often-sharp rhetoric surrounding the theory and practice of wolf management in the GYE is one useful lens onto the burgeoning class and class-faction dynamics of an increasingly postindustrial world. So, too, is the dynamic surrounding other resource-management practices in the American West, such as changing water use at Georgetown Lake. These examples reveal the increasing influence of the postindustrial perspective and the tension this has precipitated with the previously dominant industrial perspective.

These issues, which are really one issue expressed across several domains, are just a few of many more that are playing out along the class-cultural fault lines of the emerging New West. Together they portend potentially radical—if not rapid—-change of the political ecology of the archipelago. Throughout this essay, I have sought to emphasize that the relevant repercussion of ongoing rural gentrification is not that it inspires a transition from production to consumption but that the types of production and consumption that it inspires are changing. Thus, what differentiates many recent newcomers to the New West archipelago from prior inhabitants is the relative emphasis they place on commodities and experiences. This shift constructively refocuses our attention on the distinctive characteristics of an emerging segment of society—the PIMC—and its impact on the American West.

Notes

1. Sonya Salamon, *Newcomers to Old Towns* (Chicago: University of Chicago Press, 2003).
2. The idea of the New versus the Old West is problematic due to the ambiguity of the terms, as I have discussed elsewhere: J. Dwight Hines, "Rural Gentrification as Permanent Tourism: The Creation of the 'New' West Archipelago as Post-Industrial Class-Cultural Space," *Environment and Planning D: Society & Space* 28, no. 3 (2010): 509–25; Hines, "The Post-Industrial Regime of Production/Consumption and the Rural Gentrification of the 'New' West Archipelago," *Antipode* 44, no. 1 (2012): 74–97.
3. Ruth Glass, *London: Aspects of Change* (London: Centre for Urban Studies, 1963).
4. J. Dwight Hines, "In Pursuit of Experience: The Post-Industrial Gentrification of the Rural American West," *Ethnography* 11, no. 2 (June 2010): 285–308.
5. Ibid.; Hines, "Rural Gentrification as Permanent Tourism," 509–25.
6. Hines, "Post-Industrial Regime of Production/Consumption," 74–97; Hines, "The Postindustrialization of the Class-Cultural Space in the 'New' West Archipelago," chap. 7 in *The Politics of Space and Place: Exclusion, Resistance and Alternatives*, ed. Chiara Certomà, Nicola Clewer, and Doug Elsey (Cambridge: Cambridge Scholarly Press, 2012), 172–92.
7. Dean MacCannell, *The Tourist* (Berkeley: University of California Press, 1976); Mike Featherstone, "Towards a Sociology of Postmodern Culture," in *Postmodernism Jameson Critique*, ed. H. Haferkamp (Washington, DC: Maison-neuve, 1989.
8. On watercourses with irrigation systems, ranchers can get additional cuttings of hay per season and thereby reduce the cost of maintaining livestock during the long, cold winters that affect these latitudes and altitudes.
9. Beginning with the frontier era and lasting throughout most of the twentieth

century, the resource extractors and commodity producers held near-exclusive economic sovereignty in Montana. However, from the beginning of the European-American occupation of the Rocky Mountains, residents existed who were not involved with agricultural, mining, or any locally productive economic activity. This set of recreational and/or retired homeowners slowly increased throughout the century but remained a small minority until recently. The first lots on Georgetown Lake were sold to seasonal residents, local second homeowners, and summertime visitors from outside Montana. As the number of houses on and around the lake increased, so did the percentage owned by full-time, year-round residents.

10. Associated Press, "Lake's Water Pits Irrigators against Recreationists," *Missoulian*, June 16, 2000.
11. "Declaration of Covenants and Restrictions for Badger Bay at Georgetown Lake Subdivision," 2005, copy in the author's possession.
12. AP, "Water Pits Irrigators against Recreationists."
13. Matthew A. Wilson, "The Wolf in Yellowstone: Science, Symbol, or Politics? Deconstructing the Conflict between Environmentalism and Wise Use," *Society & Natural Resources* 10, no. 5 (1997): 453–68.
14. John L. Weaver, "The Wolves of Yellowstone," National Resources Report 14, National Park Service (Washington, DC: Government Printing Office, 1978).
15. Glen F. Cole, "Mission-Oriented Research in the Natural Areas of the National Park Service," Research Note 6 (Mammoth, WY: Yellowstone National Park, 1969).
16. D. A. McNaught, "Wolves in Yellowstone Park? Park Visitors Respond," *Wildlife Society Bulletin* 15 (1987): 518–21.
17. A. J. Bath, "Public Attitudes in Wyoming, Montana and Idaho toward Wolf Restoration in Yellowstone National Park," *Transactions of the 56th North American Wildlife and Natural Resources Conference* (Washington, DC: Wildlife Management Institute, 1991), 91–95.
18. M. R. Cutler, "Welcome the Wolf?" *Defenders* 63 (1988): 9.
19. It is important to note—as Rik Scarce does in "What Do Wolves Mean? Conflicting Social Constructions of *Canis Lupus* in 'Bordertown,'" *Human Dimensions of Wildlife: An International Journal* 3, no. 3 (2008), 26–45—that, at the time of reintroduction, wolves in the GYE were given the status of "experimental, nonessential" by the FWS, as opposed to being listed as an endangered species. This decision has had significant repercussions because it gave the agency leeway—up to and including the power to kill "problem" wolves—to manage the population.
20. Wyoming Game and Fish Department, *Annual Report*, 2008, http://wgfd.wyo.gov/web2011/wgfd-1000485.aspx.
21. On September 23, 2014, U.S. District Court Judge Amy Berman Jackson ruled that Wyoming's wolf-management plan was not legally sufficient and returned population administration to the FWS until the state could guarantee its 2012 rule limiting take of gray wolves.
22. Wilson, "Wolf in Yellowstone," 453–68.

23. Wilson's work in general is insightful; however, as Scarce, "What Do Wolves Mean?," 30, notes, Wilson's analysis ultimately reduces all parties' motivation to economics, which is a perspective that neither Scarce's research nor mine supports.
24. Wilson, "Wolf in Yellowstone," 454.
25. The wise-use movement was a "social movement that contested access to rural land and resources in the United States from the late 1980s through the mid-1990s, particularly on federal lands in the American West," according to James McCarthy, "First World Political Ecology: Lessons from the Wise Use Movement," *Environment and Planning A* 34, no. 7 (2002): 1281–82. Furthermore, it "is an umbrella term for a coalition of organizations... [whose] agenda concentrated on efforts by rural commodity producers to maintain their historical, privileged access to and control over the federally owned lands in the region" (1282).
26. Hines, "Pursuit of Experience," 285–308; Hines, "Rural Gentrification as Permanent Tourism," 509–25; Hines, "Post-Industrial Regime of Production/Consumption," 74–97.
27. Perry Backus, "Livestock Producers Group Hopes to Put Bounty on Wolves, Lions," *Ravalli Republic*, February 22, 2012.
28. Rob Chaney, "Activist Wants to Plan to Control County's Wolves," *Missoulian*, February 23, 2012.
29. Ibid.
30. Rocky Barker, "Wolf Bill Could Backfire on Idaho," *Idaho Statesman*, February 25, 2012.
31. Rocky Barker, "How Many Wolves Are Just Right in Idaho?," *Idaho Statesman*, October 5, 2011.
32. "Otter Signs Bill Declaring an Emergency in Idaho Due to Wolves That Pose a 'Clear and Present Danger,'' *Idaho Statesman*, April 19, 2011.
33. Greater Yellowstone Coalition, "Wolves: Still Fighting for their Place in Greater Yellowstone," copy in the author's possession.
34. Ibid.
35. Greater Yellowstone Coalition, "Wolves and Economics," copy in the author's possession.
36. Ibid.
37. Leslie Kaufman, "After Years of Conflict, a New Dynamic in Wolf Country," *New York Times*, November 4, 2011.
38. Eve Byron, "With Wolves Entrenched, Debate Has Shifted," *Independent Record*, February 1, 2010.
39. Statement by Davis Reagan, Defenders of Wildlife website, https://www.defenders.org (no longer available).

Irrigation Communities, Political Cultures, and the Public in the Age of Depletion

BURKE W. GRIGGS

Introduction

All farmers get their water from somewhere. In the East, water just falls from the sky, but across the arid West, farmers must get it elsewhere. For centuries it has come with difficulty from the West's sparse and irregular river systems, which depend upon variable, but annual, melt from mountain snowpack, local precipitation, and reservoirs. Since the 1950s, most irrigation water has come dependably from the ground, from shallow alluvial systems and deeper aquifers, first in deceptively ever-increasing volumes, but now in permanently ever-decreasing ones.

The depletion of the West's groundwater is a national problem of high order. Geologists have sounded alarms, and policy wonks have prescribed legal and technocratic solutions; Washington has sent emissaries and money, and western politicians have promised change. But obscured behind this credentialed and often-posturing expertise is a simple, hard, but useful fact: it matters a great deal where western irrigators get their water.

It matters because the source of that irrigation water largely defines the political culture of the community that depends on it. The relationship between irrigation and political culture is an ancient one.[1] The two most influential exponents of irrigation in the American West—John Wesley Powell and Elwood Mead—stressed that the relationship was as real as western aridity itself and should guide the development of irrigation projects on western river systems.[2] Accordingly, western states and the United States, largely through the Bureau of Reclamation, built surface-water irrigation projects for nearly a century. Across the Great Plains, Reclamation engineered most of its projects during the 1940s and 1950s to realize its original vision of rural society, where citizen irrigators would own modest farms organized around the irrigation project's reservoirs and canals.[3]

Less than twenty years later, however, the groundwater revolution transformed most farmers' relationship with their water supply, and that transformation, depending upon one's view, either promised or threatened to make that original vision obsolete. Regardless, many rural communities now face a future threatened by permanent groundwater depletion. Because the groundwater revolution has produced a groundwater crisis, we must refocus our attention on the relationship between irrigation agriculture and political culture.

This essay is an attempt toward renewing that focus. It surveys the way irrigation agriculture has created two distinct communities and political cultures across the Great Plains: those based on its river systems and those based on groundwater. While scholars and other experts have long studied the political culture of irrigation, they have paid far less attention to this important distinction.[4] Because surface-water irrigation communities and their political culture came first, they established most of western water law, built (or had built for them) most of the West's irrigation infrastructure, and framed the legal and regulatory systems that secure property rights in water.[5]

Since the 1950s, however, groundwater irrigation and its distinctive political culture have assumed a dominant position across the Great Plains, where as much as 90 percent of irrigation water comes from the ground.[6] That dominance has challenged and transformed western water law, threatened western water infrastructure, and frustrated the regulatory systems of most western states, regardless of their distinct water law codes.

As groundwater pumping has caused declines in stream flows, reservoirs, and groundwater levels across the Great Plains, these political cultures have begun to clash. An especially revealing theater of this conflict is the Republican River, which gathers groundwater across the plains of northeastern Colorado, southern Nebraska, and northern Kansas. On the legal level, this conflict has produced a series of "water wars" between Kansas and Nebraska.[7]

Yet water, like war, ignores political and legal boundaries. While the legal dispute pits one state against another, it is rooted in the deeper and more intractable conflict between surface-water and groundwater irrigation communities across the Republican River Basin. The Supreme Court resolves such lawsuits as a matter of course, but this deeper conflict will remain. Indeed, the hydrologic future of this basin, like other western river basins such as the Rio Grande and the Arkansas, may not depend upon *whether* upstream states comply with their legal obligations to downstream states. Rather, that future will depend largely upon *how* they comply—by reducing their groundwater pumping and surface-water diversions, by importing water from somewhere else, or by some combination of all three. These choices matter a great deal; they may even determine the viability of the rivers themselves.

Who will make these choices? Across the rural West, the contrasts and conflicts between surface-water and groundwater irrigation communities raise hard but unavoidable questions about the public and its river basins. What is this public: a regional, basinwide, and therefore interstate public? Is it a statewide public, and therefore determined by political borders that are blind to the course of western drainages? Or is it—at least at its most intensely felt level—a local public, limited to those who hold water rights? For unlike natural resources such as hard-rock minerals or oil and gas, water in the West is typically dedicated to the people as a public resource subject to the private appropriation and beneficial use that create a water right. And unlike other natural-resource use rights, such as timber leases in national forests or grazing rights on federal land, most water rights are state-law property rights, insulated from federal jurisdiction.

Water can thus be the most public but the least publicly protected of all western resources. As these irrigation communities continue their conflicts within their various theaters, and western states make policy choices about how to comply with their interstate water obligations, they will have to choose among these competing and divergent concepts of the public. The concept of the public that prevails will determine those policy choices, and those choices will in turn decide the future of rivers that—for now—still run across the Great Plains.

Surface Water Irrigation Communities and Their Political Culture

Prior Appropriation, from Custom to Constitution

The history of surface-water irrigation communities begins with their claim to water, a claim central to their political culture. That claim and the doctrine that gives it legitimacy—prior appropriation—are rooted in a sensibility about the beginning of the West and so merit discussion. Prior appropriation is the fundamental doctrine of most western water law. It combines two rules: the rule of capture and the rule of priority. Under the rule of capture, a person who diverts and captures unclaimed water from its source and then puts that water to beneficial use obtains a property interest in the use of that water, a water right.[8] Under the rule of priority, first in time is first in right. In dry years, there is no equitable sharing of a water shortage—as there is in the eastern doctrine of riparian rights—because this sharing would make all users so short of water that no one could make beneficial use of his share. Rather, a senior water right receives its full allocation before a junior right receives any. In the West, priority *is* equity.[9]

Prior appropriation became the predominant law of western water because westerners consistently relied upon it, from the California gold rush of 1849 through the end of the nineteenth century. In working water-intensive mining claims in California, beyond the reach of state and federal authorities, miners applied a mining custom to water: the first to divert and use water from a stream had an exclusive right to it.[10] However, this custom ran afoul of California law, which had established English common law riparianism, and so the courts first ruled accordingly.[11]

Yet the claims kept coming, and in the landmark case of *Irwin v. Phillips*, the California Supreme Court held that the right of a prior appropriator to divert water from a stream, convey it to another site, and use it there was a superior claim to that of a rival whose land bordered the stream and who would otherwise have prevailed as a riparian owner under the common law.[12] The court explained its position by stressing "the peculiar condition" of the mining camps and their customs, a condition without precedent in English common law.[13] The doctrine became orthodoxy immediately; just two years later, it had become "too long settled to admit of any doubt or discussion at this time."[14]

The doctrine quickly spread across the rest of the West. In Colorado, it collided with Spanish and Spanish-American water law, which in times of drought allocated supplies according to need, rather than temporal priority.[15] Due to the Mexican War and obvious differences in ethnicity, religion, and language, Anglo-American westerners did not recognize Hispanic water law as legitimate.[16] The other rival law came from the Mormons, whose legal customs held that the right to use water belonged to the group, rather than its individual members.[17] Across the San Luis Valley, fights over water erupted over these competing doctrines.[18] The potential for conflict continued after Colorado Territory was established in 1861, when the territorial legislature enacted water laws that largely accorded with Spanish and Mormon doctrines and made water rights inseparable from land.[19]

At the statewide level, however, prior appropriation demanded recognition; otherwise, the property rights that depended upon it might be called into question, leaving titles to land and water rights uncertain, especially those of powerful irrigation companies. Therefore, Colorado enshrined the doctrine in its constitution.[20] The Colorado Supreme Court, in its landmark prior appropriation case, marginalized rival doctrines with the same logic that its California brethren had employed in 1855: as a custom, prior appropriation was old enough. "We think... [the rule of prior appropriation] has existed from the date of the earliest appropriations of water within the boundaries of this state," declared the court.[21] Influenced by these precedents, Kansas recognized prior appropriation in 1876—the year that Colorado made it a constitutional right.[22] Nebraska followed in 1889 and incorporated the doctrine in its constitution by amendment in 1920.[23] These enactments acknowledged the political and cultural authority of prior appropriation, which promised to secure reliable legal rights to the highly variable flows of western rivers—at least for their most senior appropriators.

Irrigation, Disposition, and Reclamation

For the next half century, surface-water irrigation communities developed across the Great Plains. In Colorado, that development began along the South Platte and the Cache la Poudre Rivers, assisted by favorable conditions and statutes granting irrigation companies valuable legal rights and protections.[24] In 1870, the Union Colony's Greeley Irrigation Company began its community irrigation system, which watered thirty thousand acres along the Cache la Poudre. Similar projects developed along the South Platte and Arkansas Rivers. By 1884, Colorado had developed more than a million acres of irrigated land.[25] In western Kansas, the five main irrigation canals on the Arkansas River had been developed by the 1880s, irrigating around sixty-five thousand acres with whatever water managed to flow out of Colorado. Surface-water irrigation communities also sprang up in the valleys of more remote basins, such as the North Fork Republican River in Colorado, the South Platte in Nebraska, and even the Cimarron River Valley in southwestern Kansas.[26]

These private developments coincided with the federal government's ham-fisted attempts to promote irrigation by granting millions of acres on unrealistic terms. The Desert Land Act (1877) set arbitrary boundaries.[27] It invited fraud by not requiring proof of actual cultivation.[28] And it granted far too much land—640 acres on top of the other claims available to the homesteader.[29] This was far more land than any settler could cultivate, much less irrigate. Speculation soon displaced settlement, and fraud and failure delivered most holdings into the portfolios of corporations. Ninety-five percent of the final proofs of irrigation and settlement under the Desert Land Act were fraudulent.[30]

The Carey Act (1894) sought to reform these flaws.[31] It made between one and three million acres of federal land available to the western states on condition that the receiving state—whether directly or through private companies—would develop irrigation canals and works and then sell off the irrigated land in quarter sections.[32] The act reduced speculation by requiring that water rights be attached to the irrigated land, and it promoted better irrigation projects by requiring the state engineer to supervise their design and construction.

These improvements had limited success in Wyoming, Idaho, and Utah, but most projects failed because the Carey Act's reforming initiatives were too costly.[33] Irrigators faced mortgages that combined land purchase with the high costs of developing the irrigation project, and few could make their payments.[34] By 1900, most of the West's land had been claimed—and thanks to the laws of western water and federal disposition, more than ten times its water supply.[35]

Despite federal support, large-scale irrigation across the Great Plains faced three difficult obstacles. The first concerned the legal structure of ownership: land titles derived from the federal government, but water rights came from the states. The result was a split estate, where one party, often an irrigation company, held the water rights under state law, while another party, usually the homesteader or an assignee, obtained the federal land patent.[36] Powell and Mead stressed that split estates promoted water monopolies and other speculative abuses and that successful irrigation required combining land titles with water rights.[37]

But overcoming this obstacle produced a second one: private irrigation companies usually lacked the financial and engineering resources to build effective irrigation projects, even under the Carey Act.[38] Successful projects needed experts to design and build them on a large and efficient scale, and they required financing that could unite land titles with water rights.[39]

The final obstacle was the doctrine of prior appropriation itself. It had produced vague, mistaken, and grossly excessive claims to water, far more than western streams could provide even in wet years.[40] Because many reservoirs had storage water rights that were junior to most of the irrigation rights on a steam, prior appropriation made it difficult to store water in dry years, when it was most needed and valuable.[41] Lawyers and litigation discredited the doctrine's founding myth—that it was well suited to manage western waters for orderly irrigation.[42] Yet by 1900, the doctrine was deeply anchored in state law, and millions of acres of irrigated land relied upon it. Resolving these obstacles required federal supervision.

Congress responded with the Reclamation Act of 1902.[43] It made the federal government, through the new Bureau of Reclamation, the creditor, designer, and builder of large-scale irrigation projects. Federal financing came from a fund generated by the sale of public lands. The act directed the secretary of the interior to survey, locate, and build irrigation projects and then open these improved public lands to settlement under the homestead laws. Resident farmers would irrigate small tracts whose water supply was ensured by federal projects; they would then repay the government for its investment at heavily subsidized rates. Through this structure (which was also applied to private, already-settled lands), Reclamation's finance and design would resolve the problems of undercapitalized and poorly designed projects. As for the speculative dangers of the split estate and prior appropriation, the act required water rights for Reclamation projects to be fused with land and explicitly devoted to irrigation.[44] Supreme in finance, expertise, and law, Reclamation would establish and protect irrigation communities across the West.[45]

Yet aside from the North Platte Project in Wyoming and Nebraska (1905), Reclamation did not have a substantial presence across the Great Plains for several decades. Indeed, the next thirty years seemed to make irrigation less critical as Great Plains agriculture entered its second manic

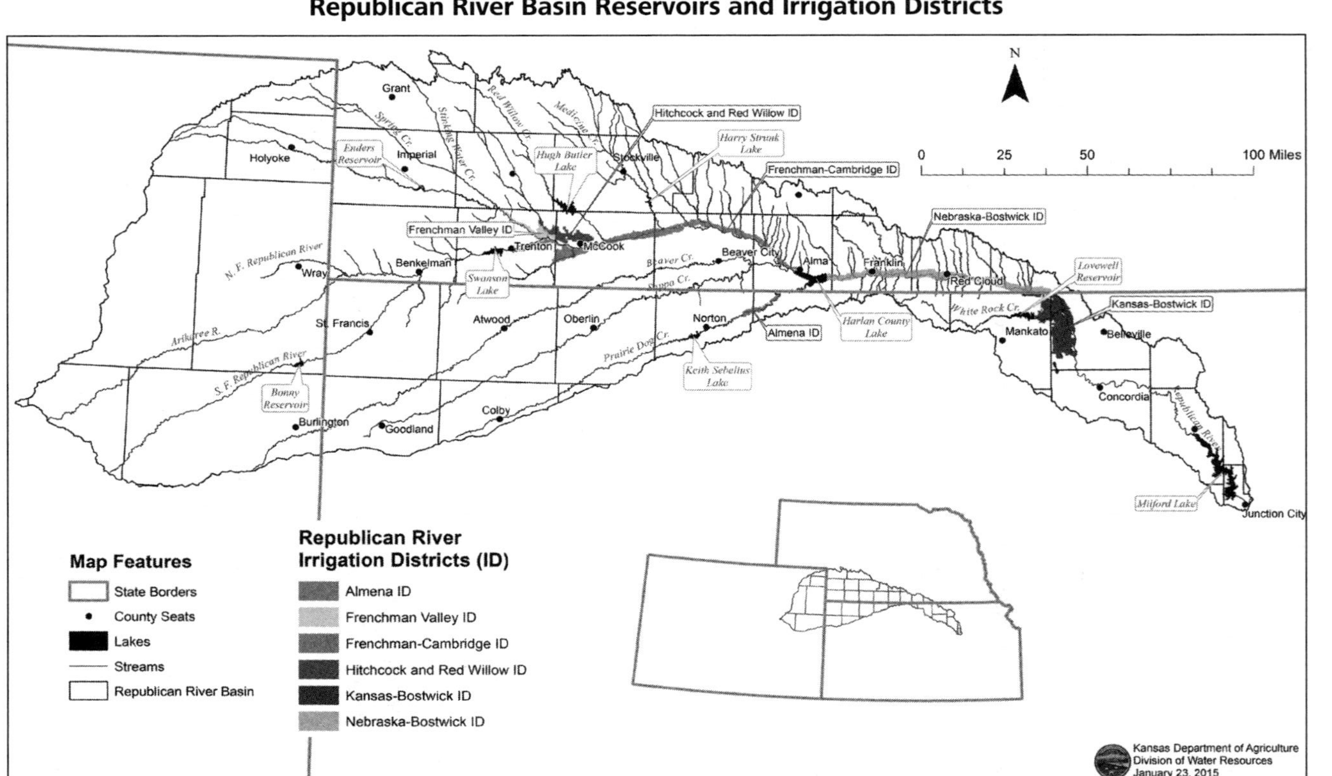

Map depicting the Republican River Basin reservoirs and irrigation districts. Courtesy of the Division of Water Resources, Kansas Department of Agriculture.

phase—the "great plow up." Steam- and gasoline-powered tractors, pulling deep plows and mechanized farm equipment vastly and recklessly expanded cultivated acreage across the region. For a time, farming was both productive and profitable because of an anomalous combination of unusually wet and temperate weather, high wartime wheat prices, and the speculative excesses of the Roaring Twenties.[46]

The Great Depression and the disasters of the "dirty thirties" put an end to that fragile anomaly, destroyed the viability of Great Plains agriculture, and brought the Bureau of Reclamation to the region as a whole. The great plow up had destabilized Great Plains soils, which blew away during the dust bowl era and buried farms during the Republican River flood of 1935.[47] These disasters motivated the states and Reclamation to plan a comprehensive system of multipurpose reservoirs to supply irrigation water and control flooding. Local boosters immediately embraced what Powell, Mead, and the Reclamation Act had recognized a generation earlier: only federal means and power could build such infrastructure. Unlike drainages such as the South Platte and the Rio Grande, where numerous private irrigation ditches predated the Reclamation Act, most of the rivers of the Great Plains were relatively undeveloped. This fact encouraged planners to consider the region's river basins as a whole, unimpeded by the complexities of extensive, preexisting irrigation projects and their water rights. This situation was ideal for Reclamation's focus on river-basin planning and accounting.[48]

The response to these natural and man-made disasters produced a decade of cooperative federalism, with federal water projects and state water planning operating in tandem across the Great Plains. On the federal side, the most important piece of legislation was the 1944 Flood Control Act, which planned the development of the entire Missouri River Basin through a series of irrigation, flood-control, and navigation projects.[49] On the state side, the 1940s produced the Republican River Compact of 1943 and the Arkansas River Compact of 1949. These compacts established federal guarantees that the states' water allocations and Reclamation's irrigation projects would be protected at the same time.[50]

Secured by the Republican River Compact and enabled by the Flood Control Act, private irrigation districts expanded within the basin, and Reclamation built new irrigation districts during the following decades.

These are classic works of civil engineering, built for irrigator-citizens who populate a recognizable community of private farms within a public irrigation project. Within the Republican River Basin alone, federal money and expertise built nine dams and reservoirs and thousands of miles of canals and laterals to subsidize—often at profligate cost—complex irrigation and flood-control projects. In a region that had long been characterized by demographic and natural extremes that militate against an enduring public—the booms of original settlement and the great plow up, followed by the depopulating droughts of the late 1880s and the dust bowl, and then the flood of 1935—Reclamation's projects promised a stability predicated upon this allocated, engineered, and regulated water supply. Here and elsewhere, Reclamation projects also enhanced the water supplies of preexisting irrigation communities. As a result, few surface-water irrigation communities across the Great Plains could claim they were separate or independent from the public beyond their boundaries—the wider public that largely financed them—and the cooperative federalism that had built them in the first place.[51]

The Political Culture of Great Plains Surface-Water Irrigation Communities

Compared to its projects farther west, such as those in the Colorado and Columbia River Basins, and especially in California, Reclamation's projects across the Great Plains have received little attention, probably because they are not stupendous. Sited in wide and shallow valleys, these projects serve comparatively modest irrigation districts. This seems a mundane point, but given the conflicting and sometimes hyperbolic opinions that the Bureau of Reclamation has provoked, some grounding may be justified.[52] Whether heroic or villainous, Reclamation built irrigation communities across the Great Plains that have enjoyed a mostly stable water supply for more than sixty years. For all of the political machinations that went into their construction, these irrigation communities have largely endured at a time when many rural communities are under significant pressure to survive.

This is not a mundane point. Compared to other irrigation communities across the Great Plains, they have existed a fairly long time, and their present state carries the stamp of the social and civil engineering that made them possible. It is important, and fairly easy, not to romanticize these communities. But it is equally important, and less easy, to recognize their distinct political culture, which has five principal characteristics.

First, surface-water irrigation communities such as those across the Republican River Basin are still mostly recognizable, clustered around the projects on a local and visible scale. Reclamation's visionaries wanted to build nucleated communities composed of small holdings, irrigated and intensively farmed. As Mead put it, "Where farmers live in villages, they are able to realize a happy combination of town and country life, and to dwell under conditions which are favorable to a growth of the best forms of civilization."[53] While no one—not even Floyd Dominy, the unrepentant, steamrolling commissioner of Reclamation during its high, imperial phase—could plausibly describe these districts as full of happy villagers, they do remain largely populated by resident farmers.[54] For most of the twentieth century, the Reclamation Act required the owners of irrigated lands to reside on those lands or nearby.[55] They were also subject to the acreage limitations of the homestead laws, which set a floor of 40 and a ceiling of 160 acres.[56]

The residency requirement and the acreage limitation sought to reverse the nineteenth-century trend of social dispersion, where settlers' desire to obtain as much land as possible frustrated the formation of schools, churches, and social life. The United States Supreme Court repeatedly reaffirmed that goal: to ensure that the "enormous expenditure" for Reclamation projects "will not go in disproportionate share to a few individuals with large land holdings. Moreover, it [the Reclamation Act] prevents the use of the federal reclamation service for speculative purposes."[57] These rules lasted for eighty years until the abolition of the residency requirement and significant relaxation of the acreage limitation in 1982.[58] Nonetheless, surface-water irrigation communities across the Great Plains largely remain residential, grouped ones.

The Kansas Bostwick Irrigation District is a representative example. It supplies irrigation water to 244 owners of district lands, who farm nearly 43,000 acres in north-central Kansas—an average farm is 176 acres. The acreage limitations in the district applied until 1982, and Reclamation enforced them, requiring owners to sell their excess land. The residency requirement also applied, as did Kansas laws forbidding the corporate ownership of farmland; as a result, about half of the local residents still farm their own land or district land owned by other local residents, or they are retired from farming and live nearby.[59] These numbers stand modestly in contrast to the gaudy corruption of California, where corporate landownership and Reclamation's neglect of its own laws have combined to distort the social vision of the Reclamation Act beyond recognition.[60]

Second, surface-water irrigation communities are organized along corporate lines, where a corporate entity mediates between the water supply of the district and the individual owners of irrigated land. This corporate structure characterizes both private irrigation companies, such as those on the Arkansas River in Colorado and Kansas, and Reclamation districts, such as the Bostwick Irrigation Districts on the Republican River in Nebraska and Kansas. The ditch or the district, not the individual landowners, typically holds the water right under which lands for the entire district are irrigated.[61] Districts make corporate decisions about system maintenance and the irrigation calendar.

At the operational level, individual landowners make daily calls for water from the reservoir or main canal headgate during the irrigation season, and district managers and ditch riders respond to those calls, route water deliveries, and account for them. The operational realities of surface-water irrigation require a high degree of coordination to ensure that water is delivered efficiently and on a timely basis. This coordination takes palce among individual irrigators within one district and among adjacent districts as well.[62]

Third, surface-water irrigation communities are intended to be permanent. They hold water rights that are real property rights. The high capital costs of building and maintaining surface-water irrigation projects could not be justified if their water supply was not dependable over time. That is especially the case with Reclamation projects, which stress their permanent irrigation and flood-control benefits to justify their substantial subsidies.[63] Alongside that fiscal reality is the requirement that irrigated land be forever tied to its water rights, despite the efforts of speculators to sever them. While this requirement lapsed for private irrigation districts long ago, it remains valid for Reclamation projects.[64]

Fourth, surface-water irrigation communities tend to be legally conservative. They support the fundamental principles of classic western water law, primarily because they hold most of the oldest water rights in their water neighborhoods. Likewise, they tend to oppose legal changes that may undermine their ability to exercise the priorities and other rights they enjoy. The entrance of Reclamation did not substantially alter this conservatism because the Reclamation Act has consistently deferred to state water law. Indeed, Reclamation projects effectively made the federal government a guarantor of the districts' water supply.[65]

Finally, surface-water irrigation communities are under threat across the Great Plains because they have become vulnerable to the hydrologic and political impact of groundwater irrigation. The reservoir inflows upon which they depend have gradually declined over the last several decades due to excessive groundwater pumping, despite the senior priority of their water rights. Moreover, groundwater irrigators have purchased and retired part or all of the water rights of many ditch companies and irrigation districts, while those that remain have been unevenly protected by state engineers.

Groundwater Irrigation Communities and their Political Culture

The Groundwater Revolution

Reclamation applied a progressive social vision to the ancient technology of surface irrigation. By contrast, groundwater irrigation communities owe their existence to modern technology—the high-capacity, centrifugal water pump, propelled by electricity or internal combustion, which can pump thousands of gallons per minute from the vast and previously unexploited aquifers of the West, especially the Ogallala. This technological breakthrough took place at the very time that Reclamation's Great Plains projects were coming on line during the 1950s.

At first, irrigating with groundwater required little more than a decent well and a powerful pump to flood the fields; later, center-pivot systems made irrigation more versatile, precise, and efficient. The impact of the pump and pivot can hardly be overstated. More than the tractors of the great plow up, groundwater irrigation sharply reduced the need for farm labor. Where one industrious farm worker could surface-irrigate little more than 200 acres by opening ditches with a shovel or using siphon tubes and gated pipe, one operating an early center pivot could water a full section—640 acres.[66]

Center pivots also vastly expanded the reach of irrigated agriculture across the Great Plains. Compared to gravity-fed, flood-irrigation systems, center pivots can distribute water more evenly and much more precisely, applying water as well as fertilizer according to the specific needs of the crop and the moisture content of the soil. They are also more efficient, delivering a higher percentage of water to the root zone of the crop: where flood irrigation systems are at best 65 to 70 percent efficient, modern center pivots with drop nozzles and draglines raise that level to 90 percent. Groundwater irrigators have exploited this increase to expand irrigated acreage and intensify crop density, raising yields.

Center pivots also conquer gravity: their motorized wheels can crawl over sloping and uneven uplands, enabling the irrigation of millions of acres of previously unirrigable land. And the finely modulated spray of their nozzles allows effective irrigation of both coarse and sandy soils without washing them away. As a consequence, lands formerly considered unfit for farming, such as those above the southern banks of the Arkansas River in southwestern Kansas, now yield more than three hundred bushels of corn per acre.

For all of these reasons, modern groundwater irrigation has transformed much of the Great Plains from risky dryland farms and spotty shortgrass rangelands into a large portion of the most dependably profitable irrigated land in North America. Only a Luddite would fail to appreciate this transformation. Groundwater irrigators on the Great Plains are among the most technologically adept farmers in the world. One sufficiently capitalized farmer in western Kansas can activate his irrigation system according to data provided by soil-moisture probes and then control his pivots through his smartphone, all from the comfort of his condominium in Denver.[67]

The technology of groundwater irrigation, together with the huge volume of the Ogallala Aquifer, enabled anyone who owned land above it to irrigate. Between the mid-1950s and the mid-1970s, everyone appeared to have enough groundwater, which is protected and in many places immune from annual variations in precipitation. Up to a point, groundwater irrigators could compensate for drought by pumping more. As a result, groundwater irrigation has enabled the overexploitation of water resources in a way that is not possible with surface water.

The Legal Response to the Groundwater Revolution

Because groundwater behaves differently from surface water, the groundwater revolution created fundamental problems for western water codes. Unlike the annual fluctuations of streams and rivers, which vary according to precipitation, aquifers fluctuate far less, and depletions to their water supplies can lag behind pumping for decades. The Ogallala Aquifer, which is mostly unconnected to the streams and rivers of the Great Plains, is only affected by pumping; its waters are thousands of years old and basically unreplenishable. Mostly unaware and relatively unconcerned with these groundwater sources, the architects of western water law did not foresee whether the water could be tapped out. After all, the right to use water assumes that there is water to use.[68]

Across the states of the Republican River Basin, the groundwater revolution and the unique features of the Ogallala Aquifer produced basic changes in western water law and policy. The sheer size and drought-proof dependability of the aquifer encouraged irrigators, regulators, and policy makers to ignore the inevitable reckoning inherent in the prior appropriation doctrine. Starting in the 1950s, state legislatures amended their water codes to encourage the development of groundwater without setting a limit on the depletion of the aquifer. The opportunity to exploit the Ogallala Aquifer was too good to pass up, and the problems of depletion could be put off until later. Some states withdrew Great Plains groundwater sources from the public domain and placed them under local control, creating a new type of water-based public in the process.

These changes raised a fundamental question: was groundwater a public resource? In Colorado, the answer seemed to be yes and to rest on constitutional bedrock. The waters of any "natural stream" and the "waters of the state" were public resources subject to prior appropriation; hence, it seemed reasonable to conclude that groundwater sources were "waters of the state."[69] The groundwater revolution, however, produced legislation that redefined those waters. In 1969, the Colorado Legislature defined the constitutional meaning of waters of the state to include groundwater supplies that were tributary to natural streams but to exclude other types of groundwater.[70] Tributary groundwater would be governed by prior appropriation and receive the same protection as surface-water rights.[71]

The other major type of groundwater was labeled "designated groundwater"—groundwater that did not underlie a flowing stream, such as the aquifers of eastern Colorado, where pumping did not quickly affect surface water and water rights.[72] Because strict application of the prior appropriation doctrine would frustrate the development of these groundwater supplies, Colorado limited the doctrine: senior water rights would be entitled to "reasonable groundwater pumping levels" but not to the "maintenance of historical water levels."[73] Economic development came at the policy price of withdrawing a substantial portion of Great Plains groundwater from the public domain and compromising prior appropriation.[74]

From a different origin, Kansas arrived at a similar decision. Kansas originally followed two legal water doctrines. Eastern Kansas adhered to the riparian doctrine, where the reasonable use of water was an attribute of riparian property, while higher, drier, western Kansas followed the prior appropriation doctrine. These doctrines coexisted with increasing unease until 1944, when the Kansas Supreme Court ruled that—as a whole— Kansas water law did not grant the state the power to regulate groundwater.[75]

This decision prompted a comprehensive review of Kansas water law, one focused largely on whether groundwater was a public resource. Kansas answered that question decisively in 1945 by enacting the Kansas Water Appropriation Act (KWAA).[76] The KWAA dedicated all of the waters of Kansas, including groundwater, to the people of the state, subject to prior appropriation as enforced by the chief engineer.[77] A central tenet of the original KWAA is a basic rule of prior appropriation: if a junior water right impaired a senior right by affecting its access to or use of water, the chief engineer had the statutory duty to administer, or curtail, the use made under the junior right.[78]

The groundwater revolution soon forced this basic and decisive rule to yield to a peculiar compromise. Like their neighbors in Colorado, Kansas policy makers recognized that the widespread pumping of Ogallala Aquifer groundwater would soon impair senior rights by lowering the water table, giving the holders of those rights the power to invoke their priority, requiring the chief engineer to shut off junior rights and prohibit further groundwater development.[79] The economic potential of the Ogallala Aquifer demanded that prior appropriation be compromised, and so the Kansas Legislature redefined impairment accordingly. In 1957, the hydrological definition of impairment gave way to an economic one: junior rights could henceforth reduce groundwater levels as long as the reduction did not go "beyond a reasonable economic limit."[80] Yet in the same session, the legislature also boosted the legal status of a water right, redefining it as a real property right.[81]

These amendments, together with a liberal policy of granting water rights applications, resulted in a massive—but totally legal—overappropriation of Ogallala Aquifer groundwater.[82] People did not seem to mind;

even Kansas chief engineer Guy Gibson believed that "water rights were like belly buttons—everyone ought to have one."[83] Groundwater levels across the Great Plains of Kansas began to decline as a consequence, creating a paradox: groundwater pumpers gained the legal right to permanently diminish the Ogallala Aquifer, even as that property right attained the legal status of permanence.

As for Nebraska, groundwater had never been considered a statewide public resource, so fewer adjustments were necessary to accommodate the groundwater revolution. Although it enshrined prior appropriation in its state constitution, Nebraska never extended that doctrine to groundwater, which it regulated instead by the doctrine of reasonable use.[84] Along with this legal and doctrinal distinction between surface water and groundwater was a jurisdictional one: Nebraska has always maintained that local governments should exclusively regulate groundwater supplies.

The legal and jurisdictional gap between surface water and groundwater in Nebraska is intentional and longstanding. As John Riddell, a Nebraska assistant attorney general, told his Kansas colleagues in 1944, "As to ground water, practically speaking, we do not have any law. There is no question but what in the future something will have to be done about that, probably the sooner the better."[85] Later statutes have clearly stated that groundwater is connected to surface water, but the Nebraska Supreme Court has consistently refused to protect the holders of senior surface water rights from impairment by groundwater pumpers.[86]

Local Publics and the Creed of Local Control

The second change wrought by the groundwater revolution was political. If groundwater was not a statewide public resource, who should exercise jurisdiction over it? State legislatures answered this question largely by delegating jurisdiction to local districts or enhancing the powers of existing ones. In so doing, they created a new type of water-related public, one that placed the local economic benefits of groundwater irrigation above concerns about the sustainability of supplies. Where Reclamation had stressed basinwide planning and federal involvement, local control became the creed of groundwater irrigators across the Great Plains.

Colorado has delegated the control of designated groundwater to local irrigators. While a state agency, the Colorado Ground Water Commission, issues well permits, it is dominated by "resident agriculturists" who live in the designated basins.[87] The power really rests in local groundwater-management districts, which can "exercise all regulatory and administrative authority" over irrigation wells.[88] And in the event that a well owner places a priority call against others in his water-rights neighborhood, neither the commission nor the state engineer can administer those rights; instead, the Colorado Supreme Court has ruled that the local groundwater-management district must do it.[89] The implication of this decision is clear: when direct priority is most an issue—typically the job of the state engineer—local control is exclusive. That is in marked contrast to the long-established system for surface water and tributary groundwater, which makes no local compromises.

Despite its central state control over groundwater, Kansas also created local groundwater districts. After a false start in 1968, Kansas enacted the Groundwater Management District Act in 1972.[90] This legislation sought to establish some local control over regulating and developing groundwater rights by forming local groundwater-management districts, or GMDs. Five GMDs were formed in western Kansas. They can assess taxes on their membership, which is limited to holders of groundwater rights.

Allied with farm and agribusiness interests that support groundwater pumping at its current levels, Kansas GMDs have become a powerful force in state water politics, one that the chief engineer must reckon with on a regular basis.[91] In partnership with the chief engineer, they have established well-spacing rules and closed large areas to new water rights, largely to protect current levels of groundwater pumping under existing water rights. However, the problem of overappropriation remains, while the regional impairment of wells is getting worse.[92]

In response to these concerns, local GMDs led a successful effort to amend the act in 1978 to allow intensive groundwater-use control areas, or IGUCAs. This amendment intended to enable local irrigators to take the lead in reducing groundwater depletion by convincing the chief engineer to reduce pumping to sustainable levels, even if these cutbacks conflicted with prior appropriation by reducing senior as well as junior rights.[93] Unfortunately, the tool has proven too powerful for the GMDs to use: no GMD has sought to establish an IGUCA, nor have any of its members. And while the chief engineer has established eight IGUCAs across western Kansas, none of these overlie the nonrenewable supplies of the Ogallala Aquifer, where the problem of depletion is worst.[94]

The absence of an IGUCA over the Ogallala Aquifer reveals the irony of local control in Kansas. The GMD Act gave local districts substantial power to reduce groundwater depletion, but by choosing not to exercise that power, the GMDs have returned it to the chief engineer, whose power and duties regarding an IGUCA arouse suspicion from local irrigators. If the chief engineer began to establish an IGUCA over the Ogallala Aquifer on his own, the GMDs would almost certainly oppose him.

Because Nebraska has never claimed central authority over regulating groundwater, the state has never needed to delegate that authority; local control of groundwater has always been the law. While the Nebraska Department of Natural Resources (DNR) controls surface water and water rights, groundwater is governed by a different set of laws, which are administered by natural resource districts (NRDs), large, multicounty state subdivisions.[95] As Nebraska law states, "Local entities are the preferred regulators of activities which may contribute to ground water depletion."[96] The growth in groundwater irrigation in Nebraska has brought a commensurate increase in the power of the NRDs. Each NRD has its own taxing authority and grants, administers, and regulates groundwater permits. State involvement in groundwater regulation depends on local NRD approval of state policies through local rules and regulations.[97] As a result, the managers of the local NRDs collectively exert much more power over irrigation than does the DNR.

The Political Culture of Groundwater Irrigation Communities

Groundwater irrigation appeals to farmers because it enables them to access water without expensive dams and canals and without federal intervention and regulation.[98] Across the Great Plains, the groundwater revolution produced irrigation communities that are markedly distinct from their surface-water counterparts. Regardless of the different state water codes under which they operate, these communities have substantial local control over groundwater; indeed, the less renewable their water supplies, the more removed these communities became from the wider public of the state. They have generated a distinct political culture that is inextricable from groundwater itself. That culture has five principal characteristics.

The first and most important characteristic is their economic dominance. For example, since 1970, the amount of surface-water-irrigated acreage in Nebraska has remained relatively constant at roughly 1 million acres;

however, groundwater irrigation in the state expanded from about 500,000 acres in 1950 to 7 million in 1990.[99] Because irrigated agriculture is far more productive than dryland farming, it yields greater secondary economic benefits. The expansion in groundwater-irrigated acreage has generated economic growth in industries that supply irrigators with what they need: capital, insurance, irrigation-related farm machinery, seed, chemicals, and power for the pumps. Most of these suppliers have an economic interest in continuing groundwater irrigation at the maximum level, even if it reduces the long-term water supply beneath the irrigators' land.

Second, groundwater irrigation communities are more dispersed than surface-water ones. Where a surface-water community is necessarily organized around the structures of the irrigation project and its limitations, groundwater communities have no such constraints. There is no common water storage or delivery system, so groundwater irrigation communities lack the corporate structure and operation of their surface-water counterparts. Most farmers in surface-water irrigation communities receive the same allotment of water per acre as their neighbors. By contrast, groundwater supplies on the Great Plains are highly variable. Some irrigators in southwestern Kansas have enough groundwater to enable them to pump eighteen inches of water per acre every year for a hundred years, while others nearby may be struggling to irrigate fully now and may be out of water in ten years.

So groundwater irrigation communities are not as physically recognizable as surface-water ones. They are communities of atomized individual irrigators: while their farms may lack a common physical connection to the water supply, they share an orientation to the regulatory structures that control that supply. Groundwater irrigation communities are thus more abstract than surface-water ones, but they are no less real; indeed, they are ably represented by their groundwater districts.

Third, groundwater irrigation communities are comparatively impermanent and mobile. Surface-water power and irrigation projects are capital intensive and designed to be permanent—to "endure as long as time endures."[100] While the investment required for groundwater irrigation is substantial, it is relatively inexpensive compared to surface-water irrigation, and the equipment is depreciable as a capital expense. If conditions change, the irrigator can move that equipment to another tract or sell it. Major groundwater irrigators such as dairies and feedlots have moved during the last several decades in response to changes in groundwater levels and regulations.[101]

Yet groundwater irrigation communities are also strongly marked by a fourth characteristic—their close connection to their local economies and markets. In Kansas at least, the power of these local economies and markets helps explain their communities' quiescent approach to prior appropriation. Senior water-rights holders can protect themselves by requesting that the chief engineer administer junior water rights, but groundwater irrigation communities in Kansas have not behaved according to the administrative assumptions of prior appropriation. As individuals, farmers with senior groundwater rights have generally refrained from making calls to protect their wells against impairment by nearby junior wells. As communities, they have long pursued a deliberate policy of inaction to avoid the consequences of reducing junior groundwater rights.

This action may seem economically irrational, but there are good reasons for it. It can be much more complicated to identify and assign impairment in a groundwater-dominated system than in a surface-water one.[102] Is the impairment beyond a reasonable economic limit?[103] Answering this question requires time and analysis. Prior appropriation in a surface-water system has immediate and predictable consequences; but in a groundwater system, especially one such as the Ogallala Aquifer, its effects are delayed and uncertain and can be too wide ranging and draconian for many groundwater irrigators to consider. Making a groundwater call can also have greater impact than making a surface-water one: largely because the water-rights neighborhoods across the Ogallala Aquifer are severely overappropriated, protecting a senior groundwater right at its fully authorized quantity may require many nearby junior rights to be shut down for a long time. Groundwater irrigation communities in Kansas are acutely aware of this potential consequence, and so few major irrigators have filed impairment complaints.[104]

This collective inaction is a tribute of sorts to groundwater irrigation communities, but it also reveals the way their individually held water rights relate to their local economic situation. A typical groundwater irrigator in Kansas grows corn, soybeans, and grain sorghum and sells that crop to feedlots and ethanol plants, which usually have substantial water rights of their own. Any administrative or legal action that might recalibrate local groundwater rights according to the actual, declining water supply threatens to upset this economic system, treating its participants disproportionally according to the priority of their water rights.

This inaction reveals the final characteristic of groundwater irrigation communities: their attitude to classic western water law and regulation. Surface-water irrigation communities tend to be legally conservative because their senior water rights enjoy strong property-rights protections under state water law and—where applicable—the Reclamation Act. Groundwater irrigation communities do not generally enjoy this protection. And because administering groundwater rights according to prior appropriation may produce unpredictable results, groundwater irrigation communities usually view water law not as something that protects property rights, but rather as governmental regulation that limits and interferes with their water use. Acting through their groundwater districts, they have significantly curtailed the influence of state engineers and the prior appropriation doctrine.

And where surface-water irrigation communities prize their valuable senior rights during water shortages, groundwater ones typically stress the need to treat all groundwater irrigators equally to reduce water use.[105] Indeed, many groundwater irrigators have argued to abandon prior appropriation altogether by comparing groundwater to any mineral resource that should be mined without regard to sustainability. One hundred fifty years after California blessed the analogy of mining customs to water use, these irrigators have forced that analogy to its logical extreme: no one in his or her right mind keeps gold in the ground.

The Collision of Political Cultures in the Republican River Basin

The overdevelopment of groundwater across the Great Plains began to reduce the region's stream and river flows as early as the 1960s.[106] By the 1980s, interstate conflicts over these declining river systems started to reach the Supreme Court, which decides interstate disputes.[107] Texas sued New Mexico over the Pecos River, and Kansas sued Colorado over the Arkansas.[108] These lawsuits followed the typical pattern of interstate water litigation: the downstream state sues the upstream state (or states), alleging that excessive upstream use, usually caused by underregulated groundwater pumping, is violating its rights by depleting downstream supplies. The fight over the Republican River Basin is no exception.

Interstate lawsuits appear to be simple. The Constitution draws the battle lines clearly as fights between sovereign states, and the eleventh amendment usually requires the states to include all their often-divergent water interests in the suit. In the Republican River Basin, however, these constitutional battle lines are no longer accurate. Behind and underneath them is a deeper, unconventional conflict, where irrigators' allegiances to their parent state are becoming less important than their connection to their water supply. Groundwater irrigation communities in Colorado and Nebraska have taken control of the relevant water law and policy in their portions of the basin to forestall reductions in groundwater pumping. Threatened and vulnerable, surface-water irrigation communities are looking beyond their state governments to find other means to reduce the excessive groundwater pumping that is threatening their irrigation projects.

The Supreme Court will not resolve this deeper conflict. Presented with an interstate case, the court's job is to decide it; it rarely digs further. From the court's distant, elevated perspective, the end of compliance with an interstate compact justifies the means that a state takes to achieve it—as long as those means are legal.[109] As a result, the future of this interstate river basin relies most upon the way the states choose to comply with the compact. Upstream states can balance their compact budgets by reducing usage by both surface-water and groundwater communities, by reducing groundwater pumping significantly, by shutting down surface-water irrigation projects, or by importing water from outside the basin.

To protect its groundwater irrigation communities, Nebraska and Colorado have chosen the last two methods. Kansas sued Nebraska to protect its surface-water irrigation communities along the Republican River. Its success in court has caused Nebraska to comply, using means of compliance that will deliver water to Kansas but which threaten the future of surface-water irrigation in Nebraska. Such nominal compliance, obtained by overpumping groundwater at the expense of the basin's long-term hydrology, may produce a Pyrrhic victory—the end of the Republican as a functioning Great Plains river.

The Conflict on the Surface

The fight over the Republican River began with excessive groundwater development. By the end of the 1970s, Colorado and Kansas had responded to groundwater declines by closing their portions of the basin to new wells,

Irrigated Acreage in the Nebraska Portion of the Republican River Basin and Declines of River Flows into Harlan County Lake, 1948–2012

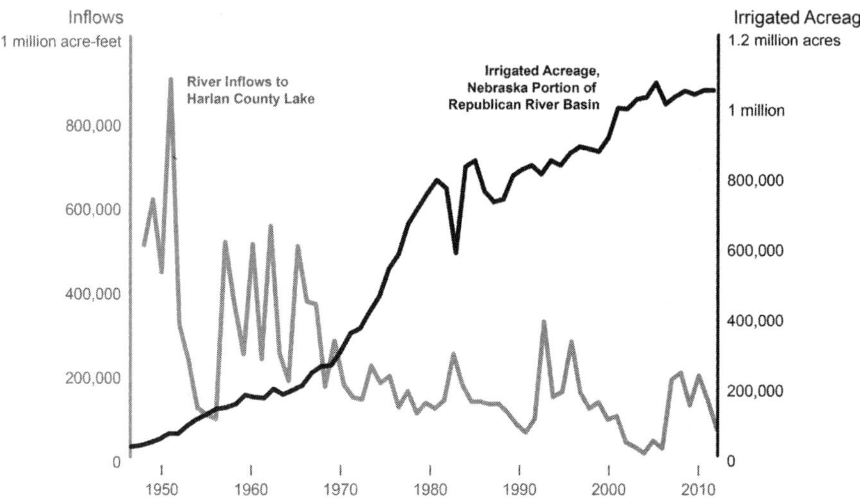

Chart reflecting the irrigated acreage in the Nebraska portion of the Republican River Basin and the declines of river flows into Harlan County Lake over the past sixty-five years. Courtesy of the Nebraska Department of Natural Resources, 2014.

limiting their number to about four thousand in each state. By contrast, Nebraska did not impose restrictions. As a result, the wells in Nebraska increased more than 50 percent, from around twelve thousand to more than eighteen thousand, and irrigated acreage increased even more.[110] This increased pumping intercepted groundwater base flows that would have otherwise supported the surface waters of the basin. Inflows to the tributaries and main stem of the river, as well as lakes and reservoirs, declined accordingly. The graph shows how this increase in irrigated acreage and groundwater pumping caused a drop in the basin's largest reservoir, Harlan County Lake, which supplies water to irrigators in the Nebraska Bostwick and Kansas Bostwick Irrigation Districts.

While inflows can vary according to annual fluctuations in precipitation, the overall trend is undeniable: the increase in groundwater pumping beyond sustainable levels produced a significant decline in both surface flows and groundwater levels in Nebraska. In Perkins, Chase, and Dundy Counties, groundwater levels have fallen more than fifty feet.[111]

These declines reached a critical point during the 1990s. In 1998, Kansas sued, alleging that groundwater pumping in Nebraska had deprived Kansas of the water to which it was entitled under the compact.[112] The compact, however, contained a problem: enacted decades before groundwater pumping became significant, it did not mention groundwater. Was groundwater even included in the compact's allocation of the basin's water supply? Both Nebraska and Colorado presented legal defenses that largely conformed to their state water laws. Nebraska stated that the compact was limited to surface water and excluded all groundwater, while Colorado claimed that the compact at most included only alluvial groundwater; Kansas argued that the compact included all of the groundwater within the basin. The court ruled mostly for Kansas on this issue, deciding that the compact required an accounting of groundwater pumping that caused depletions to the river's flows.[113] Following that threshold decision, the states began to negotiate the remaining issues in the case.

These negotiations produced a comprehensive settlement agreement, the Final Settlement Stipulation of 2002, or FSS. The FSS formally integrated the basin's groundwater supplies within the allocations of the compact. Through the FSS, the states imposed a general moratorium on additional wells within the basin. They established accounting procedures to calculate groundwater consumption according to the states' respective allocations, and they produced a computer groundwater model that estimates the impact of groundwater pumping basinwide. The court trumpeted this settlement as superior to any result that litigation could have produced. Interstate cooperation had apparently produced that rarest of things: interstate comity, the Panglossian goal of every interstate water compact.[114]

Yet despite the lawsuit, the court's decision, and the FSS, Nebraska did not reduce its groundwater pumping. As the graph reveals, Nebraska continued to increase its irrigated acreage even after the FSS was signed in 2002. Dry years returned to the basin, groundwater irrigators compensated for drought by increasing their pumping, and Nebraska again violated the compact. In 2005 and 2006, Nebraska overused its allocations by more than 35,000 acre-feet per year. As a result, the long-term depletions to surface-water supplies caused by groundwater pumping continued to increase in both Nebraska and Kansas.[115]

In 2010, Kansas returned to court to enforce the compact and the FSS. After trial in 2012 and 2013, Special Master Willam J. Kayatta Jr. found that Nebraska had failed to comply with both the compact and the FSS in 2005 and 2006, and he awarded damages to Kansas of $5.5 million—the Kansas Bostwick Irrigation District had suffered most of the loss. More crucial was the way the special master viewed the future: he did not intervene in Nebraska's own water policy. He denied Kansas's request to have the court order Nebraska to reduce groundwater pumping on 302,000 acres, an amount that Kansas experts believed was sufficient to balance the basin's hydrology and ensure compliance with the compact over the long term. Instead, he recommended a strong and novel contract remedy: if Nebraska failed to comply with the compact in the future, it should be forced to give Kansas the profits it had gained through noncompliance.[116]

In 2015, the Supreme Court approved the special master's recommendation. The Supreme Court found that Nebraska had "recklessly gambled with Kansas's rights" and ordered the state to pay accordingly, thereby establishing a landmark precedent in the history of interstate water litigation.[117]

The Deeper Conflict over Compliance

Will Kansas's legal victory be enough to protect its portion of the basin's water supplies? This is the $200 million question. While the Supreme Court ruled for Kansas, it did not overrule Nebraska law and order reductions in the state's groundwater pumping. In all likelihood, the court just postponed the interstate legal fight for another day, allowing Nebraska (and Colorado) to figure out how best to comply with the compact in the meantime.

The fight is by no means over; on the contrary, the decision has highlighted the issue of future compliance. Colorado and Nebraska, where groundwater interests dominate their portions of the basin, have devised plans that protect their current groundwater pumping levels by shifting the burden of compliance to surface-water irrigation projects. In response, surface-water irrigation communities in Nebraska have sued in state court, sought help from Reclamation, and even assisted the state of Kansas to obtain protection from these compliance plans.

The interstate legal fight over the future of the Republican River has thus produced an intrastate conflict between surface-water and groundwater irrigation communities within Nebraska. And due to the dominance of groundwater interests there, the future probably holds a sad and paradoxical end, where legal compliance with the compact comes at the expense of the river itself and the surface-water communities that depend upon it. This is not what the compact's framers intended; they believed emphatically in a perpetual river.

Both Colorado and Nebraska have struggled to comply with the compact because their excessive groundwater pumping has depleted surface flow and groundwater base flows across their portions of the basin. To achieve compliance over the long term, these states have a choice. They can reduce groundwater pumping to correct this hydrologic imbalance, but that option will significantly reduce the amount of acreage irrigated by groundwater. Instead, they have chosen a more complicated option that is engineered to protect groundwater pumping from forced reductions. This option obtains the water necessary for compact compliance from elsewhere: by sacrificing water supplies devoted to surface-water rights and by pumping groundwater from the Ogallala Aquifer directly into the river.

Nebraska's approach to compliance lies in its "integrated management plans," or IMPs.[118] While these plans involve coordinating Nebraska's segregated laws for surface water and groundwater, that coordination remains largely under local control.[119] As a result, the IMPs have not seriously addressed the problem of excessive pumping. While they include provisions that require pumping reductions as a last resort, in practice, they sacrifice surface-water supplies when water runs short. In dry years, when Nebraska needs to reduce water use, the IMPs require that all surface-water rights in the basin be cut off *before* shutting off any groundwater wells.

During the water-short year of 2013–14, that is just what Nebraska did. Rather than reduce groundwater pumping, the Nebraska DNR issued closing notices for all surface-water rights in Nebraska's portion of the basin, including those held by Reclamation projects.[120] These projects went without water for much of 2013 while Nebraska groundwater irrigators did not suffer any pumping reductions. In the name of integrated water management, Nebraska has chosen to sacrifice its most senior water rights in the basin—surface rights.

This choice reveals the stark power divide in Nebraska water law. While the DNR has the legal duty to protect senior surface-water rights according to prior appropriation, neither that duty nor that doctrine extends to groundwater. Because the DNR has no jurisdiction over groundwater pumping, it cannot order the local NRDs to reduce pumping in dry years. As a result, Nebraska's principal response to the cause of its noncompliance with the compact—excessive groundwater pumping—is to shut down the very rights most affected by that pumping—senior surface rights. The architects of the IMPs have decided that cutting off senior water rights during shortages is preferable to curtailing junior groundwater pumpers.

Nebraska has singled out surface-water rights because they fall under the jurisdiction of the state through the DNR. As a result, in dry years, when the legal protections afforded by the compact matter most, the IMPs transform the reservoirs of federal irrigation projects— such as the Frenchman-Cambridge Irrigation District and the Nebraska Bostwick Irrigation District—into little more than large holding ponds to deliver water to Kansas. In late 2013, after holding unused water in basin reservoirs for nearly a year, the DNR ordered Reclamation to flush water out of Harlan County Lake so it would flow down into Kansas to meet Nebraska's compact requirements. The DNR ordered the release even though that water could not be put to beneficial use in Nebraska or Kansas: irrigation season had ended months earlier, and the flush drained water supplies that had been stored for irrigation the following year.[121] Groundwater irrigators, meanwhile, pumped throughout the year at their usual levels. The DNR does not regulate them.

The power of Nebraska's groundwater irrigation interests dwarfs that of its surface-water irrigation projects. Groundwater irrigators have secured local control through the NRDs; the NRDs have gained control over the IMPs; and the IMPs protect groundwater pumping at the expense of surface-water irrigators. Groundwater interests in Nebraska have exploited the legal segregation of surface-water and groundwater to control the state's compliance strategy.

The IMPs clearly reflect the political realities of water in Nebraska. State political leaders—governors, attorneys general, and directors of natural resource agencies—are often tempted to disregard their compact obligations to other states, rather than face the political consequence of making the unpopular decision to reduce groundwater pumping.[122] A state supreme court can also be a formidable obstacle to state regulation of groundwater pumping; indeed, that is what happened in Colorado, despite its more sophisticated approach to groundwater.[123]

Colorado has also subordinated surface-water rights to groundwater interests in its portion of the basin. Groundwater districts have

The results of the draining of Bonny Reservoir in March 2012. The Colorado Division of Wildlife later buried all of the fish. Photo courtesy of the author.

purchased surface water rights that once diverted water from the North Fork and the South Fork of the Republican River and retired them permanently.[124] On the South Fork, Colorado has taken a more dramatic step by draining Bonny Reservoir, a Reclamation project where it holds all the water rights.

These surface-water rights are not connected to an irrigation project; Reclamation conceived of one to operate in tandem with private ditches that predated the reservoir but never built it. Rather, the rights in Bonny are recreational ones, dedicated to fishing, wildlife, and boating. Due to upstream groundwater pumping, stream flow on the South Fork has been declining for decades, reducing the level in the reservoir. By 2000, Colorado faced a choice with Bonny: reduce upstream groundwater pumping to preserve and possibly restore it, or drain it to free up water for groundwater pumping.[125] By choosing the second option, Colorado no longer suffers the evaporative and seepage losses that count against its compact allocations.

Subordinating surface-water supplies to groundwater pumping is the necessary first step in these compact compliance plans, but it is far from sufficient. The second step consists of a series of "augmentation plans," in which both Colorado and Nebraska have invested around $200 million. The augmentation plan originated in Colorado, where it has become a popular water-management tool. It enables junior groundwater pumpers to secure their water rights and keep pumping during shortages as long as they have a legally binding plan to "augment" the water supply—to provide substitute water to senior rights holders that are affected by out-of-priority pumping.[126] By the time the Republican River Compact was litigated in 1998, augmentation plans had spread across Colorado's eastern river basins. At a late point in the settlement negotiations, Colorado introduced the concept of augmentation plans at the interstate level, and the states agreed to allow them.[127]

Envisioned as a limited exception to the states' moratorium on groundwater development, augmentation plans are becoming the dominant tool by which Colorado and Nebraska comply with the compact. These plans pump water from the Ogallala Aquifer, which is mostly unconnected to the alluvial waters of the Republican River Basin and so does not count as water supply under the compact. That water is then shunted into tributaries of the river, where it augments the basin's water supply. These plans compensate for reduced stream flow, caused by groundwater pumping, by pumping even more groundwater (from a different source) to replace the depleted stream flow. Put another way, they legally solve the problem of a diminished river by replumbing it—connecting it to a different source altogether.

To build its augmentation plan, Colorado established the Republican River Water Conservation District (RRWCD), a local political entity that controls Colorado's portion of the basin, includes several groundwater-management districts, and contains nearly half a million irrigated acres.

Colorado then loaned the RRWCD millions of dollars at low interest rates to develop a compliance plan. Using that loan and money raised by its own substantial land taxes, the RRWCD spent around $51 million to purchase and retire surface-water and groundwater rights in the district so that they would not interfere with junior groundwater pumping.

Next, it spent more than $20 million to build the Colorado Compact Compliance Pipeline, or CCP. This project pumps as much as 25,000 acre-feet of Ogallala Aquifer water from a battery of high-capacity wells, pipes it to a point just west of the Nebraska border, and then dumps it into the North Fork Republican River. As that water hits the state line gauge, it compensates for Colorado's groundwater overuse under the compact. The RRWCD has spent nearly $100 million on the project, which should enable Colorado to comply with the compact while allowing most irrigators to maintain their groundwater pumping at current levels.[128]

For the retained believers—the leaders of the RRWCD, their engineers, their lawyers, and their state officials—the CCP is a clinical and perfectly legal solution to an intractable problem: the limitations of the hydrologic cycle. These experts point out the reality of accumulated groundwater depletions: even if Colorado stopped all groundwater pumping in its part of the basin, it could not comply with the compact for decades without the CCP.[129] The CCP may well provide its backers with more than a century of water; time will tell.

From a layman's perspective, Colorado's approach to compliance may seem absurd. It drains a federal reservoir on the South Fork while pumping nonrenewable Colorado groundwater into a pipeline on the North Fork—so that Colorado can pump more groundwater, further dewatering northeastern Colorado under the legal cover of augmentation, and ultimately replacing a real, if struggling, river with a bad replica of one.

Yet the perspective that matters is the local one. Dennis Coryell, the president of the RRWCD, speaks plainly about the interests and assumptions of his groundwater irrigation community. "We were given two tasks. One was to assist the State in reaching compact compliance. The other was to sustain the agricultural-based economy in the Basin," he says. Given those goals, the only option was to drain Bonny and tap the Ogallala Aquifer. "No one wants to pump our precious groundwater and send it down the river, but we have no other choice," he explains.[130] For Coryell and his neighbors, the "agricultural-based economy" is the current situation of groundwater irrigation at its present pumping levels; they acknowledge no other kind. Reduced levels of groundwater irrigation are not politically possible given the amount of irrigation water that corn requires in eastern Colorado. As long as corn is king across the Ogallala Aquifer, neither sustainable irrigation levels nor dryland farming will be an acceptable option.

And so Colorado had no other choice but to drain Bonny Reservoir, and the RRWCD had no other choice but to build the CCP. These are not decisions based on water supply. They are grounded in the economic expectations of irrigated agriculture—rates of return, purchases of agricultural equipment and supplies, and tax revenues, which all support a belief that the present value of money exceeds the future value of water. Keep these expectations in mind, and the CCP makes sense.

Where Colorado has concentrated its augmentation efforts on one large pipeline, Nebraska has built two so far and may build more. The first pumps as much as 15,000 acre-feet of Ogallala Aquifer water into a dry streambed high on Rock Creek, a remote tributary of the Republican River in Dundy County. From there the water seeps and flows into the main channel of the river above Swanson Reservoir; whatever water enters the river from this pumping project counts as a credit to Nebraska under the compact.[131]

A second pipeline, the Nebraska Cooperative Republican-Platte Enhancement Project, or N-CORPE, can pump 65,000 acre-feet of deep groundwater every year from beneath the Platte and Republican River Basins to meet the state's multiple interstate obligations. On the Platte, the groundwater helps ensure compliance with an interstate agreement with Wyoming, Colorado, and the United States, one designed to protect endangered species by setting minimum instream flows.[132] On the Republican, N-CORPE water shores up Nebraska's accounting balance under the compact. The Rock Creek and N-CORPE projects pumped nearly 63,000 acre-feet of water into the Republican River system in 2014.[133]

Because the Nebraska augmentation projects pipe groundwater to streambeds far upstream from Kansas, something has to be done to shepherd that water downstream. To that end, augmentation in Nebraska contains a distinct twist. Even though this water technically qualifies as surface water under Nebraska law, senior surface-water rights holders in Nebraska cannot divert it to satisfy their rights; that is expressly prohibited. Augmentation water thus creates a cruel spectacle for Nebraska surface-water irrigators. After seeing stream flow decline for decades due to groundwater pumping, they can only watch as this augmentation water flows downstream past their headgates, and irrigators who depend on Reclamation reservoirs can only watch that water evaporate until Nebraska sends it downstream to Kansas. From the augmentation wells to the state line, no surface-water irrigators can divert that water in dry years, even if their priorities date to 1890.[134] First in time, last in right.

Caught between the pincers of this two-pronged compliance strategy, surface-water irrigation communities in Nebraska have come to the grudging conclusion that they cannot rely upon their own state to protect their water rights. The DNR has ceded control of the Republican River to the NRDs, whose IPMs subordinate surface water to groundwater. In a state where groundwater irrigates seven times more land than surface water does, the Nebraska Legislature will probably not offer relief. Left unprotected, some of these communities have taken the bold step of supporting Kansas—or at least its efforts to reduce excessive groundwater pumping in the basin.

In the 2012–13 litigation, one of the largest irrigation districts on the Republican River in Nebraska testified in support of Kansas. The Frenchman-Cambridge Irrigation District (FCID) stores about 145,000 acre-feet of water in four reservoirs and routes that water through nearly four hundred miles of canals and laterals to sixty-six thousand acres. It holds forty-one different Nebraska water rights, whose priorities date back to 1890.[135] Over time, depletions due to the overdevelopment of groundwater irrigation have crippled the district's infrastructure and dried up return flows; more recently, the IMPs have made that situation worse by shutting down the district in dry years. At the trial, the FCID also provided testimony showing that groundwater development had substantially reduced the amount of land the district could irrigate and the DNR had also excluded surface-water irrigators from the IMP process.[136] Officials from Reclamation provided similar testimony, arguing that Nebraska's overdevelopment of groundwater, as well as its IMPs, threatened the long-term water supply upon which Reclamation facilities in Nebraska depend.[137]

Nebraska vigorously opposed this testimony, offering a different vision altogether. It argued that the declining hydrological condition of Reclamation projects in Nebraska had little to do with the state's record of compliance or its compliance strategy, because its obligations under the compact and the Reclamation Act were distinct and severable; and the former always trumped the latter. For Kansas and the Bureau of Reclamation, the security of Reclamation's water supplies and Nebraska's ability to comply with the compact were legally, historically, and hydrologically inseparable. Faced with such a choice, the Nebraska surface-water irrigation communities within the FCID assisted Kansas to protect the district's *Nebraska* water rights—ones held by Reclamation.

That alliance reveals the way the conflict between surface-water and groundwater irrigation communities can supplant state-based allegiances with water-based ones. The interstate conflict over the Republican River has generated a proxy war between these communities, and it does not observe political borders.[138] Neither does the river: it responds to the different effects of groundwater and surface-water irrigation across the basin. The discrepancy between political boundaries and hydrological reality has created a parallel discrepancy between the sovereignty of the states and the hydrological integrity of the basin as a whole.

Just how these discrepancies are resolved will probably determine the future of the Republican River. Colorado and Nebraska have made their sovereign decisions to overpump groundwater, dry up the river, and replace its flows with water pumped from the Ogallala Aquifer. Kansas, along with some surface-water irrigation communities in Nebraska, opposes these decisions because they upset the dependability of surface flow upon which its surface-water irrigators depend. Reclamation, for its part, has done almost nothing.[139] The states answer to their respective publics; in the Colorado and Nebraska portions of the basin, groundwater irrigation communities have appropriated theirs. Barring federal intervention, they may well prevail in the long run, regardless of what the Supreme Court says.

Conclusion

The conflict between Great Plains irrigation communities can end three ways. If groundwater irrigation communities prevail, then their surface-water counterparts will no longer be viable as depletion transforms the water rights upon which they depend into legal fiction. If surface-water communities prevail, then groundwater communities may suffer substantial economic losses during the decades of suspended or reduced pumping that will be necessary to restore the hydrologic integrity of Great Plains river systems. The first result would repudiate the states' and Reclamation's commitments to its surface-water irrigation communities, while the latter outcome would suspend the use of billions of dollars' worth of individual groundwater rights and their economic benefits. The first result is entirely possible, if legally dubious; the latter outcome is politically impossible and economically irrational.

There is room for compromise between these extremes. That compromise must protect surface-water irrigation communities from the excessive pumping that threatens them; yet it must do so without imposing severe reductions in the pumping upon which groundwater irrigation communities depend. Colorado and Nebraska have followed the lead of their locally controlled groundwater irrigation communities, but their compliance strategies are producing a Potemkin river, replumbed on the surface by Ogallala Aquifer groundwater but depleted of its own flows.

Downstream and vulnerable, Kansas has sought repeatedly to restore these flows by reducing groundwater pumping upstream. Its compliance path leads to a diminished river but one that is at least intact as a hydrological system. The Supreme Court has now decided the conflict between Kansas and Nebraska for a second time, but it has also decided to avoid, so far, the conflicts between these irrigation communities and their diverging paths of compliance. It will not decide the fate of the river. The river lacks standing.

The problem returns us to the original purpose behind Reclamation—to build enduring irrigation communities across the rural West. For fifty years, the groundwater revolution severely tested that purpose and raised candid questions about whether it was obsolete. Irrigation is above all a business, as the Reclamation Reform Act of 1982 conceded.[140] But the decline of Great Plains aquifers should revive our interest in these communities because this decline is both a public crisis and a crisis of the public. Where pumping threatens to separate groundwater base and alluvial flows from stream flows, the presence or absence of those surface flows indicates whether the river—as a hydrological whole—can sustainably support present levels of pumping. If it cannot, then it cannot endure, and the different irrigation communities that depend on its water supply cannot coexist. Will the Bureau of Reclamation protect the river systems upon which its projects depend? Or will the states and Reclamation, in a most cynical act of cooperative federalism, walk away from the projects and the purposes behind them?

The drought has gone underground, and neither rain nor technology can end it. On the other side of the groundwater revolution, there is no cycle—historical, hydrological, or otherwise—to reverse. If groundwater and surface-water irrigation communities are to survive and coexist across the Great Plains, they will have to accept what Powell and Mead made abundantly clear more than a century ago: aridity requires a public that is committed to its rivers. To sustain this public—one that connects these divergent communities—the arid West requires more modest expectations from both of them and greater cooperation between them. That may be more than they are willing to sacrifice. In that case—if the idea of a durable public across the Great Plains no longer deserves protection—the groundwater crisis will take care of itself.

Notes

1. See, for example, Julian Steward, ed., *Irrigation Civilizations* (Washington, DC: Pan-American Union, 1955), a collection of monographs exploring the relationship between irrigation and society in ancient China and Mesopotamia, and pre-Columbian Peru and Mesoamerica.
2. John Wesley Powell, *Report on the Lands of the Arid Region of the United States: With a More Detailed Account of the Lands of Utah*, rev. ed. (1879; repr., Lincoln: University of Nebraska Press, 2004), 33–36, chap. 2.; Elwood Mead, *Irrigation Institutions: A Discussion of the Economic and Legal Questions Created by the Growth of Irrigated Agriculture in the West* (New York: Macmillan, 1903), chap. 3.
3. Donald Worster, *Under Western Skies: Nature and History in the American West* (New York: Oxford University Press, 1992), 62.
4. For example, see Natural Research Council, *A New Era for Irrigation* (Washington, DC: National Academy Press, 1996).
5. See Donald Pisani, *From the Family Farm to Agribusiness: The Irrigation Crusade in California and the West, 1850–1931* (Berkeley: University of California Press, 1984); Norris Hundley Jr., *The Great Thirst: Californians and Water: A History*, rev. ed. (Berkeley: University of California Press, 2001).
6. This figure is for Kansas. Charles A. Perry, *Effects of Irrigation Practices on Water Use in the Groundwater Management Districts within the Kansas High Plains, 1991–2003* (Washington, DC: U.S. Geological Survey, 2006), 1.
7. The metaphor is overused, but the Supreme Court depends upon it. The court only accepts interstate water lawsuits if the "dispute between States [is] of such seriousness that it would amount to *casus belli* if the States were fully sovereign." Texas v. New Mexico, 462 U.S. 554, 571 n.18 (1983).

8. For an early explanation of the rule of capture applied to water, see Acton v. Blundell, 152 Eng. Rep. 1223 (1843).
9. Frank J. Trelease, "State Water and State Lines: Commerce in Water Resources," *University of Colorado Law Review* 56, no. 3 (1985): 347, 349.
10. Samuel C. Wiel, *Water Rights in the Western States* (San Francisco: Bancroft Whitney Publishing Company, 1905), 2–4; Wells A. Hutchins, *Water Rights Laws in the Nineteen Western States* (Washington, DC: United States Department of Agriculture, 1972–77), 1:164.
11. Eddy v. Simpson, 3 Cal. 249 (1853).
12. 5 Cal. 140, 146 (1855).
13. Hoffman v. Stone, 7 Cal. 46, 48 (1857).
14. Hill v. King, 8 Cal. 336, 338 (1857). The Supreme Court of the United States agreed, blessing the pioneers as "emphatically the law-makers, as respects mining, upon the public lands in this State." Jennison v. Kirk, 98 U.S. 453, 457–58 (1879).
15. Michael C. Meyer, *Water in the Hispanic Southwest: A Social and Legal History, 1550–1850* (Tucson: University of Arizona Press, 1996), 20–23, 147–64; see also John O. Baxter, *Dividing New Mexico's Waters, 1700–1912* (Albuquerque: University of New Mexico Press, 1997).
16. See Malcolm Ebright, *Land Grants & Lawsuits in Northern New Mexico* (Albuquerque: University of New Mexico Press, 1994), chap. 1.
17. Mead, *Irrigation Institutions*, 42–44, 233.
18. Virginia McConnell Simmons, *The San Luis Valley: Land of the Six-Armed Cross*, 2nd ed. (Boulder: University Press of Colorado, 1999), 219–24.
19. See 1861 Colo. Sess. Laws 67, § 1; 1862 Sess. Laws 48, § 13. Mead noted the 1861 laws that required water rights to be permanently fixed to the lands where they were used; similar laws were adopted in Wyoming in 1876. Mead, *Irrigation Institutions*, 83.
20. Colo. Const. art. XVI, §§ 5, 6 (1876).
21. Coffin v. Left Hand Ditch Co, 6 Colo. 443, 1882 WL 231 (1882). For a fuller discussion of this apparent contradiction, see Gregory A. Hicks and Devon G. Pena, "Community Acequias in Colorado's Rio Culebra Watershed: A Customary Commons in the Domain of Prior Appropriation," *University of Colorado Law Review* 74, no. 3 (Spring 2003): 387, 400.
22. Kan. Laws 1876, ch. 58.
23. Neb. Laws 1889, § 1, art. 1 (1889); Neb. Const. art. XV, § 6 (adopted 1920): "The right to divert unappropriated waters of every natural stream for beneficial use shall never be denied except when such denial is demanded by the public interest."
24. Mead stressed that the success of private irrigation projects in Colorado and Utah was largely due to the favorable conditions on the Front Range and the Wasatch Front, which enabled ditch builders to establish small-scale irrigation at low cost. Mead, *Irrigation Institutions*, 63.
25. Ibid., 144.

26. Erasmus Haworth, *Underground Waters of Southwestern Kansas*, Water Supply and Irrigation Papers of the United States Geological Survey No. 6 (Washington, DC: Government Printing Office, 1897), 62–63.
27. Desert Land Act, 19 Stat. 377 (1877), 43 U.S.C. § 321 et seq. (2014). While Colorado fell within the Desert Land Act's scope in 1891, Kansas and Nebraska never did, even though the western regions of these two states have basically the same climate as eastern Colorado. 26 Stat. 1096, 1097 (1891).
28. Desert Land Act, 19 Stat. 377 (1877), 43 U.S.C. § 321 (2014). The act still defines "desert land" as "all lands exclusive of timber lands and mineral lands which will not, without irrigation, produce some agricultural crop," a fact ascertained either by the sworn testimony of two credible witnesses or the secretary of the interior or his designee. Ibid., § 322 (2014). The vague and ambiguous language made fraud inevitable and has been repeatedly ridiculed by all commentators.
29. After 1877, a patentee could use the Preemption, Homestead, Timber Culture, and Desert Land Acts to obtain 1,120 acres—nearly two sections, more than half of that allegedly irrigated. Chastened, Congress restricted the Desert Land Act to 320 acres and repealed the Preemption and Timber Culture Acts. 26 Stat. 1095 (1891).
30. Mead, *Irrigation Institutions*, 17; Marc Reisner, *Cadillac Desert: The American West and Its Disappearing Water*, rev. ed. (New York: Penguin Books, 1993), 44.
31. Carey Act, 28 Stat. 372 (1894), 43 U.S.C. §§ 641–48 (2014).
32. The Carey Act did not improve the arbitrary nature of the Desert Land Act. Following its precursor, it excluded Kansas and Nebraska but included Colorado. 43 U.S.C. § 641 (2014). Colorado was allowed up to two million acres, including the treaty lands formerly held by the Uncompahgre and White River Utes. 37 Stat. 38 (1911), 43 U.S.C. § 645 (2014); 34 Stat. 1056 (1907), 35 Stat. 644 (1909), 43 U.S.C. § 647 (2014). Nevada was allowed two million acres. 36 Stat. 1417 (1911), 43 U.S.C. § 645 (2014). Wyoming was also allowed up to two million acres, 35 Stat. 347 (1908), 43 U.S.C. § 645 (2014). Idaho was allowed up to three million acres. 35 Stat. 577 (1908), 35 Stat. 347 (1908), 43 U.S.C. § 645 (2014). Arizona and New Mexico became eligible for Carey Act grants in 1909. 35 Stat. 638 (1909), 43 U.S.C. § 646 (2014).
33. Mead, *Irrigation Institutions*, 24–27. Mead's optimistic view of Carey Act projects in Wyoming was based on his appreciation for the state's administrative regulations for water in general—regulations he largely authored. Ibid., 247–74; see especially 272.
34. Ibid., 345. Corruption was almost certainly a factor in this distress. See "Remarks of Spencer L. Baird," attorney for the Bureau of Reclamation, at Conference of the Governor's Committee on the Appropriation of Water in Kansas, Topeka, October 16–17, 1944, p. 6 (transcript on file with the author).
35. Mead, *Irrigation Institutions*, 145–59 (regarding Colorado).
36. The potential conflict between federal and state law worried Mead as much as the split estate itself. Ibid., 62.

37. Ibid., 22–23; Powell, *Report on the Lands of the Arid Region*, 53–55.
38. James Earl Sherow, *Watering the Valley: Development along the High Plains Arkansas River, 1870–1950* (Lawrence: University Press of Kansas, 1991), 79–92; Mead, *Irrigation Institutions*, 310 (regarding Idaho).
39. Mead, *Irrigation Institutions*, 19, 27.
40. Ibid., 145–59 (regarding Colorado).
41. Ibid., 169–71.
42. Ibid., 299, 307.
43. Reclamation Act of 1902, 32 Stat. 388 (1902), 43 U.S.C. § 371 et seq. (2014).
44. Ibid., § 8, 43 U.S.C. § 372 (2014).
45. Between politics and the realities of financing reclamation projects, the act has been regularly and significantly amended. The standard legal discussion of the Reclamation Act is Amy K. Kelley and Reed D. Benson, "Federal Reclamation Law," in *Waters and Water Rights*, ed. Robert Beck and Amy K. Kelley (Dayton: LexisNexis, 2012), § 41. See also Joseph Sax, "Selling Reclamation Water Rights: A Case Study in Federal Subsidy Policy," *Michigan Law Review* 64, no. 1 (November 1965): 13; Amy Kelley, "Staging a Comeback—Section 8 of the Reclamation Act," *U.C. Davis Law Review* 18, no. 1 (Fall 1984): 97; Lawrence J. MacDonell, *From Reclamation to Sustainability: Water, Agriculture, and the Environment in the American West* (Boulder: University Press of Colorado, 1999); Reed D. Benson, "New Adventures of the Old Bureau: Modern-Day Reclamation Statutes and Congress's Unfinished Environmental Business," *Harvard Journal on Legislation* 48, no. 1 (Winter 2011): 137–84.
46. See Donald Worster, *Dust Bowl: The Southern Plains in the 1930s* (New York: Oxford University Press, 1979); Timothy Egan, *The Worst Hard Time: The Untold Story of Those Who Survived the Great American Dust Bowl* (New York: Mariner Books, 2006).
47. Worster, *Dust Bowl*, 17.
48. Reisner, *Cadillac Desert*, 134–36. The general lack of large-scale hydropower opportunities in most Great Plains projects distinguishes them from those in the Colorado and Columbia River Basins, where Reclamation could use revenue forecasts from electricity generation to conceal the high costs and comparatively low benefits of the irrigation projects.
49. Flood Control Act, 58 Stat. 887 (1944), 33 U.S.C. §§ 701 et seq. (2014). See Marian E. Ridgeway, *The Missouri Basin's Pick-Sloan Plan: A Case Study in Congressional Policy Determination* (Urbana: University of Illinois Press, 1955); Henry C. Hart, *The Dark Missouri* (Madison: University of Wisconsin Press, 1957); John E. Thorson, *River of Promise, River of Peril: The Politics of Managing the Missouri River* (Lawrence: University Press of Kansas, 1994).
50. President Franklin D. Roosevelt vetoed the 1941 version of the Republican River Compact because it contained language curtailing federal jurisdiction and did not "specifically reserv[e] to the United States all of the rights and responsibilities which it now has in the use and control of the waters of the basin." H.R. Doc. No. 690, 77th Cong., 2nd Sess. (April 2, 1942) (veto

message), at 2. (In this and earlier versions of the compact, the states had sought a declaration that the river was not navigable and thus largely immune from federal jurisdiction.) The states and Congress addressed the president's concerns by adding Articles X and XI to the compact, which contain the specific reservations of federal rights, power, and jurisdiction that he had demanded. Congress passed this version, and the president signed the amended compact into law. 57 Stat. 86 (1943).

51. On the Republican River, the Frenchman Valley and H & R W Irrigation Districts were integrated into the Frenchman-Cambridge Irrigation District, a Reclamation project in Nebraska. Pre-Reclamation irrigation districts within the Arkansas River Basin have also grown to depend upon federal irrigation and flood-control projects. These include the Colorado ditch companies downstream from Trinidad and Pueblo Reservoirs and the Associated Ditches of Garden City, Kansas, which have diverted water from the Arkansas River since the nineteenth century. The Kansas ditches largely depend upon releases from John Martin Reservoir in Colorado—a United States Army Corps of Engineers project operated in conjunction with the administration of the Arkansas River Compact (1949).
52. That literature mostly reflects Reclamation's largest and most ambitious (but sometimes disastrous) projects. The writers include boosters and statist champions: Bureau of Reclamation, U.S. Department of the Interior, *Lake Powell, Jewel of the Colorado* (Washington, DC: Government Printing Office, 1965); Michael Robinson, *Water for the West* (Chicago: Public Works Historical Society, 1979); career apologists: Henry J. Tebow, *My Love Affair with the Bureau of Reclamation* (New York: Carlton Press, 1985); academic critics: Donald Worster, *Rivers of Empire: Water, Aridity, and the Growth of the American West* (New York: Oxford University Press, 1992); MacDonnell, *From Reclamation to Sustainability;* Karl Brooks, *Public Power, Private Dams: The Hells Canyon High Dam Controversy* (Seattle: University of Washington Press, 2009); crusading journalists: Reisner, *Cadillac Desert,* especially 104–19; Blaine Harden, *A River Lost: The Life and Death of the Columbia,* rev. ed (New York: Norton, 2012); and dark, but funny, novelists: Edward Abbey, *The Monkey Wrench Gang* (1975; repr., New York: Harper Perennial, 2006).
53. Mead, *Irrigation Institutions,* 382–83.
54. Dominy was fully aware of the divide between the yeoman-farmer intentions of the Reclamation Act and its subsequent abuses, especially in California. "Congress never faced up to revising the law [the Reclamation Act of 1902 and the Reclamation Reform Act of 1982], so we ended up watering private-land developers instead of subsistence farmers." Tom Wolfe, "Mr. Dominy, Are You a Hero or a Villain?," *High Country News,* October 26, 1998, accessed May 22, 2015, http://www.hcn.org/issues/141/4583.
55. Reclamation Act of 1902, 32 Stat. 388, § 5, 43 U.S.C. § 431 (2014).
56. Ibid., §§ 3, 5. The acreage requirement was later relaxed to allow a married

couple jointly to claim 320 acres. 74 Stat. 732 (1960), 43 U.S.C. § 423h (2014). Kelley and Benson, "Federal Reclamation Law," § 41.03(a), at n.84.

57. Ivanhoe Irrigation Dist. v. McCracken, 357 U.S. 275, 297 (1958).
58. Reclamation Reform Act of 1982, 96 Stat. 1263 (1982), 43 U.S.C. § 390aa et seq., 43 U.S.C. §§ 390bb(9), 390dd(1)–(2), 390kk (2014). See also Kelley and Benson, "Federal Reclamation Law," § 41.03(c).
59. Kenneth Nelson, superintendent of the Kansas Bostwick Irrigation District, Courtland, Kansas, e-mail communication to author, November 26, 2014.
60. For example, the Southern Pacific Railroad controlled more than 100,000 acres of the Westlands Water District in 1979, where less than 3 percent of all farms controlled 31 percent of the land. Kelley and Benson, "Federal Reclamation Law," § 41.03(a), at n.71.
61. For example, the Republican River Compact explicitly recognized the rights of the Pioneer Irrigation Ditch on the North Fork of the Republican River. Republican River Compact, 57 Stat. 86, art. V (1943). Similarly the priority date of the Kansas Bostwick Irrigation District's water right was formally recognized by the compacting states in 2002. Kansas v. Nebraska and Colorado, No. 126 Orig., "Final Settlement Stipulation," December 15, 2002, at § 5.A.1.
62. The Associated Ditches of Kearny and Finney Counties in Kansas, which irrigate from the Arkansas River, provide a good example of coordination among legally distinct, but hydrologically connected, surface-water irrigation companies. For all of their internecine battles, they have operated under a series of consent decrees dating back to the nineteenth century, which include provisions for routing water through each other's ditches. See *Arkansas River Surface Water Distribution Plan*, Kansas Department of Agriculture, accessed October 31, 2013, http://agriculture.ks.gov/divisions-programs/dwr/interstate-rivers-and-compacts/kansas-colorado-arkansas-river-compact.
63. In describing the benefits of its projects, the Bureau of Reclamation usually makes a point that its reservoirs have saved hundreds of millions of dollars in flood damage. As of 1998, for example, Reclamation calculated that the reservoirs in the Bostwick Project had saved $281 million. "Bostwick Division," Bureau of Reclamation, U.S. Dept. of the Interior, April 4, 2013, accessed November 25, 2014, http://www.usbr.gov/projects/Project.jsp?proj_Name=Bostwick+Division.
64. For example, one early Kansas statute held that any water right severed from the land was considered abandoned. Kan. Laws 1870, ch. 79; Mead, *Irrigation Institutions*, 290. The requirement that water rights remain fixed, or appurtenant, to the irrigated lands of Reclamation projects remains valid federal law. 43 U.S.C. § 372 (2014).
65. Many of the legal disputes between landowners in Reclamation projects and the Bureau of Reclamation revolve around who is eligible to receive project water and under what terms. See Kelley and Benson, "Federal Reclamation Law," §§ 41.05, 41.06.

66. William Splinter, "Center Pivot Irrigation," *Scientific American*, June 1976, as summarized in James Aucoin, *Water in Nebraska: Use, Politics, Policies* (Lincoln: University of Nebraska Press, 1984), 39.
67. This does not imply that surface-water irrigation systems remain trapped in the age of tube siphons and gated pipe. Where feasible, most of the farmers using these systems have converted to sprinklers with similar gains in both labor and water efficiency.
68. See Kan. Stat. Ann. § 82a-701(f) (2014).
69. Colo. Const. art. 16, §§ 5, 6 (1876); Adjudication Act of 1879, 1879 Colo. Sess. Laws, 99–105; Safranek v. Limon, 228 P.2d 975, 977 (Colo. 1951).
70. Colo. Rev. Stat. § 37-92-103(13) (2014). This is part of the Water Rights Determination and Administration Act of 1969, Colo. Laws 1969, p. 1200, Colo. Rev. Stat. § 37-92-101 et seq. (2014).
71. 1965 Colorado Ground Water Management Act, Colo. Rev. Stat. § 37-90-137 (2014).
72. Ibid., § 37-90-103(6) (2014).
73. Ibid., § 37-90-102(1) (2014).
74. It should be noted that the alluvial supplies of the South Platte and Arkansas Rivers remained within the "waters of the state." Two other categories of groundwater—nontributary and not nontributary—include the stacked aquifers within the Denver Basin, which supply water to the newer communities along the suburban Front Range. Due to their high economic value as municipal water sources, the Colorado Legislature did not apply the doctrine of prior appropriation to them; ownership of these resources is connected to the overlying land and assumes a hundred-year depletion period. Colo. Rev. Stat. § 37-90-102(2) (2014).
75. State, ex rel. Peterson v. Kansas State Board of Agriculture, 149 P.2d 604 (Kan. 1944).
76. Kansas Water Appropriation Act, Kan. Stat. Ann. § 82a-701 et seq. (2014). For discussions of the act, see John C. Peck, "The Kansas Water Appropriation Act: A Fifty Year Perspective," *Kansas Law Review* 43 (November 1995): 735–56; Burke W. Griggs, "Beyond Drought: Water Rights in the Age of Permanent Depletion," *Kansas Law Review* 62 (June 2014): 1263–1324.
77. Kan. Laws, 1945, ch. 390, § 6, Kan. Stat. Ann. § 82a-706 (2014).
78. Ibid., ch. 390, § 11, Kan. Stat. Ann. § 82a-711 (2014).
79. Kansas Water Resources Board, *Report on the Laws of Kansas Pertaining to the Beneficial Use of Water* (Topeka: State Printing Office, 1956), 91.
80. Kan. Laws, 1957, ch. 549, § 16, Kan. Stat. Ann. § 82a-711 (2014); compare the original Kan. Stat. Ann. § 82a-711, which required the chief engineer to reject a water-rights application if "the water sought to be appropriated would impair vested rights, prior appropriations, or be detrimental to the public interest." Kan. Laws, 1945, ch. 390, § 11.
81. 1957 Kan. Laws, ch. 539, § 1, Kan. Stat. Ann. § 82a-701(g) (2014).

82. Water-rights applications under the original Kansas Water Appropriation Act numbered just 334 between 1945 and 1950. By contrast, the Kansas Division of Water Resources recorded 5,730 applications during the 1950s, 6,433 during the 1960s, and 16,226 in the 1970s, most for irrigation rights from the Ogallala Aquifer in western Kansas. John C. Peck, "Groundwater Management in Kansas: A Brief History and Assessment," *Kansas Journal of Law & Public Policy* 15, no. 3 (Spring 2006): 441, 443.
83. Scott Ross, water commissioner of the Kansas Division of Water Resources, personal communication with the author, August 14, 2012.
84. Osterman v. Central Nebraska Public Power and Irrigation Dist., 268 N.W. 334 (1936); In re: Metropolitan Utility Dist. of Omaha, 140 N.W.2d 626 (1966). For recent misgivings expressed by the Nebraska Supreme Court on this issue, see Spear T Ranch v. Knaub, 691 N.W.2d 116 (2005).
85. "Remarks of John Riddell," Nebraska assistant attorney general, at Conference of the Governor's Committee, 1944, p. 95 (see note 34).
86. Neb. Rev. Stat. § 46-703(1)–(4) (2014); Spear T Ranch v. Knaub, 691 N.W.2d 116 (Neb. 2005); In re: Complaint of Central Nebraska Public Power, 699 N.W.2d 372 (Neb. 2005); Central Nebraska Public Power and Irrigation Dist. v. North Platte Natural Resources Dist., 788 N.W.2d 252 (Neb. 2011).
87. Colo. Rev. Stat. § 37-90-901 et seq. (2014); Ibid., § 37-90-104(3)(b) (2014). The state engineer is the executive director of the commission.
88. Colo. Rev. Stat., § 37-90-111.5 (2014); Ibid., § 37-90-130 (2014).
89. Upper Black Squirrel Creek Ground Water Management Dist. v. Goss, 993 P.2d 1177, 1186 (Colo. 2000).
90. Groundwater Management District Act, 1968 Kan. Laws, ch. 403 (repealed 1972); 1972 Kan. Laws, ch. 386, §§ 1–16, Kan. Stat. Ann. § 82a-1020 et seq. (2014).
91. Kansas is the only state where the Division of Water Resources is under the Department of Agriculture, a situation that compounds the problem. Kan. Stat. Ann. § 74-606b (2014). Some of the most important decisions of the chief engineer, a classified employee under Kansas civil-service laws, are subject to review by the secretary of agriculture, a political appointee. Kan. Stat. Ann. § 82a-1901 (2014).
92. See Michael K. Ramsey, "Kansas Groundwater Management Districts: A Lawyer's Perspective," *Kansas Journal of Law & Public Policy* 15, no. 3 (Spring 2006): 517, 522.
93. Kan. Laws, 1978, ch. 437, §§ 2, 4, Kan. Stat. Ann. §§ 82a-1036, 82a-1038 (2014); Leland E. Rolfe, "Comparing and Contrasting the Roles of the Division of Water Resources and the Groundwater Management Districts in Groundwater Management and Regulation, *Kansas Journal of Law & Public Policy* 15, no. 3 (Spring 2006): 505–9.
94. For a summary of Kansas IGUCAs, see http://agriculture.ks.gov/divisions-programs/dwr/managing-kansas-water-resources/intensive-groundwater-use-control-areas and its links, accessed January 6, 2014.

95. See Neb. Rev. Stat. § 61-206(1) (2009): "The Department of Natural Resources is given jurisdiction over all matters pertaining to water rights for irrigation, power, or other useful purposes except as such jurisdiction is specifically limited by statute." For the NRDs, see Neb. Rev. Stat. § 2-3213(1) (2007).
96. See Neb. Rev. Stat. § 46-702 (2011).
97. See Neb. Rev. Stat. §§ 2-3201 et seq. (2014).
98. Aucoin, *Water in Nebraska*, 36.
99. Vincent H. Dreeszen, "Water Availability and Use," in *Flat Water: A History of Nebraska and Its Water*, ed. Robert D. Kuzelka, Charles Flowerday, Robert Manley, Bradley Rundquist, and Sally Herrin, Resource Report No. 12, Institute of Agriculture and Natural Resources (Lincoln: University of Nebraska Press, 1993), 84.
100. Bureau of Reclamation, *Lake Powell*, 9.
101. Dairies are a good example of the mobility of groundwater irrigators. See "Remarks of Robert Irsik," member of the Kansas Water Authority and a prominent dairyman, at the Governor's Conference on Water and the Future of Kansas, Manhattan, Kansas, October 30, 2012.
102. See Kan. Admin. Regs. 55 55 5-4-1a (2014).
103. See Kan. Stat. Ann. §§ 82a-711, 82a-708b (2014).
104. As yet Kansas has no reported legal case of groundwater impairment, but this may change. A recent Kansas Court of Appeals decision—Garetson Brothers v. American Warrior, Inc., no. 111, 975 (Kan. App., April 3, 2015)—upheld a senior groundwater right holder's injunction against a junior groundwater right.
105. See "Order of Designation Approving the Sheridan 6 Local Enhanced Management Area within Groundwater Management District No. 4," Division of Water Resources, Kansas Department of Agriculture, April 17, 2013, 17–18, accessed May 15, 2015, http://dwr.kda.ks.gov/LEMAs/SD6/LEMA.SD6.OrderOfDesignation.20130417.pdf.
106. By 2009, groundwater pumping had dried up most of the previously perennial streams of Kansas west of the hundredth meridian. Kansas Geological Survey, "Major Perennial Stream Changes from 1961 to 2009," map, accessed May 15, 2015, http://www.kgs.ku.edu/HighPlains/HPA_Atlas/Aquifer%20Basics/Perennial%20Stream%20Changes%201961%20to%202009.jpg.
107. Under the United States Constitution, the Supreme Court has original jurisdiction over cases between two states. U.S. Const., art. III, § 2, cl. 1. Under federal law, the court's jurisdiction over these interstate cases is also exclusive—no other court can decide the case. 28 U.S.C. § 1251(a) (2014).
108. Texas v. New Mexico, No. 65 Orig. (1983–90), contested New Mexico's violations of the Pecos River Compact; Kansas v. Colorado, No. 105 Orig. (1984–2009), contested Colorado's violations of the Arkansas River Compact. For an excellent account of the Pecos River litigation, see G. Emlen Hall, *High and Dry: The Texas-New Mexico Struggle for the Pecos River* (Albuquerque: University of New Mexico Press, 2002).

109. Hinderlider v. La Plata River and Cherry Creek Ditch Co., 304 U.S. 92, 106–8 (1938). In that case, the Supreme Court stressed two related principles: 1) private water rights held under state law are determined by whatever adjustments an interstate compact imposes, even when the water rights predate the compact, and 2) the state can comply with its compact budget by deciding what it deems to be the necessary intrastate reductions in water use. Nonetheless, these decisions must be legal. *Hinderlider* does not give state engineers the discretion to violate federal law. Reclamation Act of 1902, 32 Stat. 390 § 8 (1902), 43 U.S.C. §§ 372, 485h(c) (2014).
110. Kansas v. Nebraska and Colorado, No. 126 Orig., "Final Report of the Special Master with Certificate of Adoption of the Republican River Compact Administration (RRCA) Groundwater Model," September 17, 2003, at 18.
111. See "Groundwater-level Changes in Nebraska—Predevelopment to Spring 2013," map, accessed January 6, 2014, http://snr.unl.edu/data/download/water/GWMapArchives/2013GWMaps/Predevelopment_to_Spr2013.pdf.
112. Kansas v. Nebraska and Colorado, No. 126 Orig. Kansas's lawsuit was directed at Nebraska, but because Colorado is a party to the compact, it was necessary to include Colorado in the case.
113. See Kansas v. Nebraska and Colorado, No. 126 Orig., "First Report of the Special Master" (Subject: Nebraska's Motion to Dismiss); 530 U.S. 1272 (2000).
114. Kansas v. Nebraska and Colorado, "Final Settlement Stipulation," 2002, approved by Decree of May 19, 2003, 538 U.S. 720 (2003).
115. Kansas v. Nebraska and Colorado, No. 126 Orig., "Kansas Brief in Support of Motion for Leave to File Petition" (May 2010), at 10–15. The Nebraska Bostwick Irrigation District shares Harlan County Reservoir with its Kansas counterpart, the Kansas Bostwick Irrigation District.
116. Kansas v. Nebraska and Colorado, No. 126 Orig., "Report of the Special Master" (November 15, 2013), at 103–87. The legal term for this unusual contract remedy is *disgorgement.*
117. Kansas v. Nebraska & Colorado, No. 126 Orig., 547 U.S.__ (slip opinion, February 24, 2015), at 10–17.
118. See *Integrated Management Plan Jointly Developed by the Department of Natural Resources and the Upper Republican Natural Resources District* (effective November 1, 2010), accessed May 15, 2015, http://www.dnr.ne.gov/iwm/integrated-management-plan-jointly-developed-by-the-department-of-natural-resources-and-the-upper-republican-natural-resources-district-effective-november-1-2010.
119. See Neb. Rev. Stat. § 46-719 (2011).
120. Nebraska Department of Natural Resources, "In the Matter of Water Administration of the Republican River Basin: Order [placing] Compact Call Year in Effect," January 1, 2013, 2, accessed May 15, 2015, http://dnr.ne.gov/republican-river-basin-compact-call-year-in-effect-2; ibid., January 2, 2014, 2, accessed May 15, 2015, http://dnr.nebraska.gov/orders-order-for-republican-river-compact-call-year-2.

121. Nebraska Department of Natural Resources, "Nebraska Sends Republican River Water Downstream after Kansas Rejects Deal to Aid Its Water Users," news release, May 3, 2013, accessed May 15, 2015, http://www.dnr.ne.gov/nebraska-sends-republican-river-water-downstream-after-kansas-rejects-deal-to-aid-its-water-users.
122. See, for example, the work of the incomparable Steve Reynolds, New Mexico state engineer. Hall, *High and Dry*, 108–29.
123. Colorado attempted in the 1960s to regulate groundwater pumping on the Arkansas River, and the Colorado Supreme Court overcame and/or reversed these efforts. It took Kansas's lawsuit against Colorado to force the state either to curtail postcompact groundwater development or replace the depletions caused by overpumping. (The fact that the waters of the Arkansas River Basin in Colorado are classified as tributary groundwater and thus within the jurisdiction of the state engineer only emphasizes this point.) Kansas v. Colorado, No. 105 Orig., "First Report of the Special Master" (July 1994), at 118–19.
124. These include rights on the Pioneer Ditch on the North Fork and the Hale and Newton Ditches on the South Fork. The Pioneer Ditch was considered important enough in 1943 to have its water rights included in the compact. Republican River Compact, 57 Stat. 86, art. V. (1943), at 121.
125. According to Mike King, executive director of the Colorado Department of Natural Resources, draining Bonny Reservoir was the hardest choice he ever had to make. Deb Daniel, "Compact Compliance Pipeline Dedicated," *Julesburg Advocate*, September 6, 2012, accessed May 15, 2015, http://www.julesburgadvocate.com/ci_21482136/compact-compliance-pipeline-dedicated.
126. Colo. Rev. Stat. Ann. § 37-92-103(9) (2014). See Cache LaPoudre Water Users Association v. Glacier View Meadows, 550 P.2d 288 (Colo. 1976); Kelly Ranch v. Southeastern Colorado Water Conservancy Dist., 550 P.2d 297 (Colo. 1976).
127. Kansas v. Nebraska and Colorado, "Final Settlement Stipulation," 2002, at § III.B.1.k.
128. Most of the information in these two paragraphs comes from the RRWCD website, accessed September 15, 2014, http://www.republicanriver.com.
129. In re: "Non-Binding Arbitration Pursuant to the Final Settlement Stipulation," Kansas v. Colorado and Nebraska, No. 126 Orig., Colorado Compact Compliance Pipeline Dispute, Arbitrator's Final Decision, October 7, 2010, at 7.
130. Daniel, "Compact Compliance Pipeline Dedicated."
131. "Water Begins Flowing in Rock Creek Augmentation Project," *McCook Gazette*, February 28, 2013, accessed May 15, 2015, http://www.mccookgazette.com/story/1945715.html.
132. See *Platte River Recovery Implementation Program*, accessed November 29, 2014, https://www.platteriverprogram.org.
133. See Russ Pankonin, "Augmentation Pumping from Lincoln County Project Complete," *Imperial Republican*, April 9, 2015, 1, accessed May 15, 2015, http://www.imperialrepublican.com/index.php?option=com_content&view=arti

cle&id=7898%3Aaugmentation-pumping-from-lincoln-county-project-complete&Itemid=63. (More than 20,000 acre-feet were pumped from the Rock Creek project in 2014); Kamie Stephen, "N-CORPE Ceases Republican River Compliance," *North Platte Telegraph*, April 22, 2015, accessed May 15, 2015, http://www.nptelegraph.com/news/local_news/n-corpe-ceases-republican-river-compliance/article_036cd71f-bb18-5c85-883a-f98e3506d3d8.html. (More than 42,000 acre-feet were pumped from the N-CORPE project in 2014).

134. Nebraska Department of Natural Resources, "In the Matter of Water Administration" January 2, 2014, 2.
135. See *Frenchman-Cambridge Division*, Bureau of Reclamation, accessed October 31, 2013, http://www.usbr.gov/projects/Project.jsp?proj_Name=Frenchman-Cambridge%20Division.
136. Kansas v. Nebraska and Colorado, No. 126 Orig., "Prefiled Testimony of Kansas Witness Brad Edgerton," July 26, 2012, at 5–22, on file with the author.
137. Kansas v. Nebraska and Colorado, No. 126 Orig., "Prefiled Testimony of Kansas Witness Marvin Swanda," July 13, 2012, at 12–23; ibid., "Prefiled Testimony of Kansas Witness Aaron Thompson," July 15, 2012, at 16–27, on file with the author.
138. The Frenchman-Cambridge Irrigation District has also sought relief from the Nebraska DNR in court, so far unsuccessfully. See Frenchman Cambridge Irrigation Dist. v. Nebraska Dept. of Natural Resources, 801 N.W.2d 253 (Neb. 2011).
139. Whether Reclamation will protect its projects in the basin remains to be seen, but the Department of the Interior has at least become officially concerned about the legality of Nebraska's approach to compact compliance. Anne J. Castle, assistant secretary for water and science, U.S. Department of the Interior, to Brian P. Dunnigan, director of the Nebraska Department of Natural Resources, September 30, 2014, letter on file with the author.
140. For a discussion of this issue, see Kelley and Benson, "Federal Reclamation Law," § 41.03; and more generally, MacDonnell, *From Reclamation to Sustainability*.

Health Disparities among Latino Immigrants Living in the Rural West

MARC SCHENKER

Introduction

Immigrant Latinos represent a large, growing population in the rural western United States, and they experience numerous health disparities in comparison to urban Latino populations and nonimmigrant groups. These disparities include public-health problems, such as the prevalence of chronic diseases, as well as issues with health-care delivery. Some of the public-health challenges confronting immigrant Latinos result from the intersection of their status as rural residents and also immigrants. Approaches to addressing health disparities among Latinos living in the rural West must recognize their different educational, linguistic, cultural, behavioral, and legal background, as well as respect their medical beliefs.[1]

As immigrants remain in this country, many of the health advantages they experienced in their countries of origin diminish. Among Latinos, this trend has been described as the "Hispanic paradox." Examples include a shorter life expectancy, increased pregnancy problems, and more chronic diseases. Poverty is a major underlying factor contributing to poorer health experienced by rural Latino immigrants, particularly recent ones. An axiom in public health states that "wealth equals health," and this is the case in the United States as well as elsewhere. Other factors contributing to the adverse health of rural immigrant Latinos are the discrimination they suffer, particularly the undocumented, and the inequities in public-health facilities and health care that all rural residents face.[2]

This essay first addresses the demographics and health status of Latinos in the rural West, focusing on factors associated with their health problems. It then describes the constellation of factors that contribute to health disparities among immigrant Latinos, especially the new arrivals. Finally, it details some effective approaches to addressing the health needs of this population. Some of the data for this essay comes from California, the state with the largest immigrant Latino population. The western states or the entire country provide other data sources.

Demographics and Health Status

There are currently more than 50 million Latinos in the United States, representing a 43 percent increase over the past decade. By 2050, the Latino population is projected to be 133 million. More than half the country's population growth in the last decade came from Latinos. The states with the largest Latino populations are in the Southwest, although their numbers are growing in all parts of the country. Four states are more than 25 percent Latino: California, Arizona, New Mexico, and Texas—the states that share a border with Mexico. Other states with significant percentages of Latino residents include Florida, New York, Illinois, Colorado, and Nevada. While the rate of immigrant-Latino population growth has slowed in the United States since the recession of 2008, more than 38 percent of California residents are Latino, which equals more than 14 million people and is overwhelmingly the largest Latino population in the country. Of this total, more than 1 million live in rural areas. The Latino population in nonmetropolitan areas grew at the fastest rate of any racial or ethnic group during the 1990s and after 2000.[3]

Size and growth have varied for different Latino subpopulations, but the largest group of immigrants from Latin America comes from Mexico. California also has the most Latinos from Guatemala and El Salvador. The nine counties with majority Latino populations in California (Imperial, Monterey, San Benito, Fresno, Madera, Merced, Kings, Tulare and Colusa) are characterized by large rural populations, agricultural work, and low economic status.

Throughout the rural West, many small communities are more than 80 percent Latino. These communities are often in unincorporated agricultural areas and are dominated by Latino institutions and commerce. These Latino communities provide labor to regional agriculture and service industries but are often "invisible" to their more demographically mixed neighbors.[4]

Of the more than 50 million Latinos in the United States, an estimated 12 million are undocumented immigrants. Research on their documentation status and health care is difficult because of the obvious legal sensitivity involved. It is possible that rural areas have a greater percentage of undocumented Latinos than urban ones. This conclusion is based on the fact that increasing percentages of recent immigrants from Mexico are undocumented, and agricultural work is often the first occupation for Latino immigrants. Documentation status is associated with several risk factors for poorer health and reduced access to health care. For example, undocumented immigrants are less likely to seek medical care or other social services, which has a direct negative impact on their health.[5]

Undocumented immigrants also tend to concentrate in low-wage jobs that do not provide health care. Almost 60 percent of undocumented Latino immigrants have no health insurance, a rate four times higher than among immigrants with a green card. Thus, poverty and undocumented status combine to reduce preventive and treatment health care among this most vulnerable population. The situation is intensified by the Affordable Care Act, which prohibits undocumented immigrants from purchasing health care in its exchanges. Recent executive action to limit deportations for up to five million undocumented immigrants in the United States does not change the restrictions on health-care access.

The situation is similar for immigrant Latino children. The Deferred Action for Childhood Arrivals (DACA) program of August 2012 provided temporary permission to stay in the United States to those immigrants who were fortunate enough to qualify. However, the Affordable Care Act continues to block these individuals from buying health insurance—even private insurance—in the act's health exchanges.

States have taken different approaches to dealing with the worsening inequalities created by the Affordable Care Act. Twenty-three states have decided not to expand Medicaid under the Affordable Care Act, even though it would cost nothing for the first three years and then never more than 10 percent of the expense. Data from several states reveal that failure to expand Medicaid is associated with increased mortality. It is likely that this lack of Medicaid, and the resulting increase in morbidity and mortality, will disproportionately impact the rural poor, including Hispanic populations.[6]

In contrast, some states have chosen to expand Medicaid as well as their care to the poor and undocumented. Six states provide health insurance to all children regardless of their legal status, and fifteen states offer full prenatal and maternity care. While these extended services will certainly benefit poor, rural Latino families, the effect is limited because it leaves the majority of undocumented immigrants still without access to health care.

Factors Contributing to Health Disparities

The California Health Interview Survey (CHIS) found that 27.7 percent of Latinos in the state consider their health to be fair or poor, as opposed to 11.7 percent of non-Latino whites. This may underestimate the actual difference since the CHIS underrepresents the most transient, migrant population in the state. There was only a small difference in self-reported health between urban and rural Latinos, but substantially more rural (24.8 percent) than urban (20.4 percent) Latinos said they were limited in the kinds of work or other physical activities they could do because of their health. A total of 7.2 percent of rural Latinos reported that they could not work for at least a year due to physical or mental impairment, as opposed to 4.8 percent of urban Latinos. Among rural Latinos, 8 percent reported that they have a health problem that requires special equipment, compared to 5.9 percent of urban Latinos.[7]

One factor disproportionately and adversely affecting the health of rural Latinos is agricultural work. The vast majority of hired agricultural workers in the West are Latino, and they reside in rural areas. In California alone, there are more than 500,000 farmworkers, approximately 90 percent of whom are Latino. Numerous studies have documented the acute and chronic health hazards of agricultural work for this population. For example, the fatality rate for agricultural workers is approximately four times that of all other industries combined.[8]

A profile of the average rural farmworker in California highlights the vulnerability of this population. The most recent National Agricultural

Workers Survey, 2008–12, indicates that the average age of the population is 37.9 years with 91.4 percent born in Mexico. Almost 93 percent speak Spanish as their first language, and median educational attainment is sixth grade. More than one-fifth of this working farmworker population have family incomes below the poverty level, i.e., they are working poor. Approximately one-fourth of farmworkers in California have health insurance, but this number falls dramatically for those hired by labor contractors (under 5 percent) or who are undocumented. In general, undocumented farmworkers have lower incomes than authorized ones along with worse health care and housing.[9]

Environmental conditions may also be worse for rural Latinos and negatively impact their health. While there is no indication of more persons per dwelling among rural than urban Latinos, living conditions for rural immigrant farmworkers include many informal and substandard types of housing. For example, a survey of California farmworkers found that 11 percent resided in informal dwellings, which are defined as residences not recognized by the United States Postal Service or county tax assessors. Some of these are trailers or mobile homes with amenities similar to permanent dwellings, but the category also includes sheds, garages, and abandoned equipment or animal facilities. An additional 2 percent of respondents resided in the autos they drove to and from work.[10]

The Commission on Agricultural Workers (CAW) noted numerous inadequate types of farmworker housing in its 1993 report:

> Whether in labor supply communities or upstream areas, the number of farmworkers in need of housing exceeds the available housing stock. The result is overcrowding, the occupation of substandard units and homelessness.... The vast majority of hired farmworkers are housed in seriously inadequate conditions. Most quarters are overcrowded. Other problems include use of dilapidated structures and of buildings not intended for residential use, such as garages and storage sheds.[11]

A 2008 report by William Kandel from the Economic Research Service of the United States Department of Agriculture updated and confirmed these findings. It noted that noncitizen farmworkers had higher numbers of families per dwelling than did citizens, in addition to higher rates in trailers and other unconventional housing.[12]

A 2009 study by California Rural Legal Assistance underscores the fact that little has changed in farmworker housing since the CAW report. The study's authors address a wide range of harmful health effects and their possible association with housing in rural areas. These health conditions include adverse respiratory symptoms and diseases related to indoor air pollution, excessive heat and cold, injury, and the negative effects of poor drinking water, sanitary facilities, and garbage and waste disposal. A 2012 study describes the conditions that produced California's rural farmworker slums and documents the way inadequate housing has been rooted in the exploitation and disposability of farm labor in California.[13]

A critical issue among rural Latinos, as it is for many rural residents living in isolated or sparsely populated areas, is the absence of a nearby health-care center. CHIS found that 7.1 percent of rural Latinos had traveled to another county for medical or dental care in the past year, a rate higher than the 5 percent of urban residents who had done so. This suggests that rural Latinos have less-accessible health-care options.

The behavior of rural Latino immigrants may also contribute to the health disparity they experience. There is no difference in observed cigarette-smoking rates between rural and urban Latinos in California. However, CHIS found greater rates of binge drinking in the past year among rural (37 percent) versus urban (32.7 percent) Latinos. Higher alcohol intake, particularly binge drinking, may be associated with a variety of acute and chronic diseases as well as traumatic injuries, for example from motor-vehicle accidents.

Obesity and diabetes are an epidemic affecting the entire country, but the problems are more severe among Latinos. CHIS found that 64.1 percent of rural, compared to 58.1 percent of urban, Latinos are overweight. Tragically, greater overweight and obesity rates are associated with heart disease, infection, and ultimately shorter life expectancy. The causes of the obesity epidemic are complex, as are the explanations for the higher rates of obesity and diabetes among Latinos. While examining this phenomenon is beyond the scope of this essay, the epidemic appears to be greatest among rural immigrant Latinos, which is of great concern because of the associated increase in morbidity and mortality.

Many other types of public or preventive health problems are worse among rural Latinos. They fail to receive established preventive care, such as vaccinations, dentistry, and eye refraction. This disparity may stem from poverty, lack of awareness, and/or limited preventive care in rural areas. For example, higher rates of rural (7.6 percent) than urban (3.7 percent) Latinas did not think that human papilloma virus (HPV) caused cervical cancer, which suggests ignorance of basic medical information. Concomitantly, more rural (14.5 percent) than urban (11.5 percent) Latinas have never had a pap smear.

Differences in health and health care are also apparent among rural children and teens and may reflect greater rates of poverty, limited availability of early childhood education programs, and higher numbers of undocumented Latinos in rural areas. Smaller percentages of rural Latino children attend preschool, nursery school, or Head Start than comparable urban Latino ones. A prospective cohort study recently found that children who attend preschool programs achieve higher incomes and education levels and have less substance abuse and criminal activity. The association was strongest for males and children from impoverished families.[14]

Underlying many of these health disparities is poverty among Latino households. The CHIS data document small differences in poverty rates between urban and rural Latinos but dramatic ones between Latino and non-Latino populations. For example, 23.4 percent of rural Latino households reported incomes of fifteen thousand dollars or less, compared to 21.8 percent of urban Latino ones. These statistics are significantly higher than the comparable rates of 9.3 percent and 9.4 percent for urban and rural non-Latinos.[15]

Finding Solutions

How do we begin to reverse the large and growing health disparity between rural Latino immigrants and the rest of the population? The effort needs to begin with a paradigm shift to programs that focus on the health of immigrants. The fundamental reason for such a shift, aside from its obvious social justice, is that health and disease know no boundaries, either human or geographic. The recent global epidemics of H1N1, Ebola, and SARS that have rapidly traversed borders and even continents have graphically made this point. To think that public-health efforts or health care can be selectively provided for only some residents is naïve and dangerous. We need to move from the old idea of protecting the population of the receiving nation from immigrants bringing in diseases to a new multidimensional approach that is inclusive and multinational.

The health of immigrants needs to be monitored, and health systems need to be sensitive to their linguistic, cultural, and economic needs. Many databases do not include information on immigration status and thus do not allow analyses of the unique health needs of this population. We must understand the underlying causes of the health disparities as well as design interventions that are culturally acceptable. Legal frameworks that focus on health need to be developed. For example, immigrant workers are often excluded from receiving worker's compensation for workplace injuries, even when they are entitled to it. This situation may benefit employers economically in the short term but ultimately may result in greater cost to the health system and society.

Creative approaches are possible, such as utilizing the workplace for educational and intervention programs. *Promotoras* or community health workers can be extremely effective in reaching immigrant populations and educating immigrant Latinos in a cost-effective way. Promotora interventions have been used for a wide variety of diseases and even for environmental problems. Binational health-insurance schemes are another way to successfully provide health care for many of the country's immigrant workers. Some agricultural producers in the West have created systems that provide health care to immigrant Latino workers and their families for just a few dollars a week. The growers profit because the health of their workers improves, and the workers benefit because of the obvious advantage of having safe, compassionate, affordable health care.[16]

Another innovation attempted by some growers is a workplace obesity- and diabetes-prevention program. Similar to workplace programs that discourage smoking, this effort can improve both the physical and mental health of the workers as well as benefit employers economically by lowering absenteeism and injury rates and increasing worker productivity. The programs, of course, need to be tailored to the population, i.e., poorly educated, immigrant, and Spanish-speaking workers with specific cultural beliefs. Evaluating these programs is also critical to assess short- and long-term benefits.

A long-term solution to poverty among rural Latinos and an approach to reducing health disparities may result from focusing more resources on early childhood education. As already mentioned, attendance in preschool programs may increase income and improve educational achievement, thus breaking the cycle of poverty related to poorer health.

Targeting outreach to rural immigrant Latino populations is another approach that has been implemented to address their public-health needs. The largest of these programs, Binational Health Week, utilizes more than ten thousand volunteers to reach 500,000 people with health fairs, screenings, and other health services. The popularity of the event attests to the fact that it is filling an unmet need. Ventanillas de Salud is a program that provides health advice and referrals to clients at every Mexican consulate in the United States. A mobile program, Ventanillas Movil, also supplies services to more rural areas from some of the consulates.

Rural immigrant Latinos are a large and important population in the United States, but one whose health is falling victim to the dangers of immigration, poverty, and rural life. It is time to focus on filling the needs of this growing population. Some solutions are being implemented, but more are needed to address the multiple causes of Latino immigrant health disparities.

Notes

1. Louisa Franzini, John C. Ribble, and Arlene M. Keddie, "Understanding the Hispanic Paradox," *Ethnicity & Disease* 11, no. 3 (Autumn 2001): 496–518; Edna A. Viruell-Fuentes, "Beyond Acculturation: Immigration, Discrimination, and Health Research among Mexicans in the United States," *Social Science & Medicine* 65, no. 7 (October 2007): 1524–35.
2. Viruell-Fuentes, "Beyond Acculturation"; Franzini, Ribble, and Keddie, "Understanding the Hispanic Paradox"; John F. Dovidio, Agata Gluszek, Melissa-Sue John, Ruth Ditlmann, and Paul Lagunes, "Understanding Bias toward Latinos: Discrimination, Dimensions of Difference, and Experience of Exclusion," *Journal of Social Issues* 66, no. 1 (March 2010): 59–78; Edna A. Viruell-Fuentes, Patricia Y. Miranda, and Sawsan Abdulrahim, "More Than Culture: Structural Racism, Intersectionality Theory, and Immigrant Health," *Social Science & Medicine* 75, no. 12 (December 2012): 2099–106; and Sharon L. Larson and John A. Fleishman, "Rural-Urban Differences in Usual Source of Care and Ambulatory Service Use: Analyses of National Data Using Urban Influence Codes," *Medical Care* 41, no. 7 suppl. (July 2003): III65–III74.
3. Sharon R. Ennis, Merarys Rios-Vargas, and Nora G. Albert, "The Hispanic Population: 2010," *2010 Census Briefs* (Washington, DC: U.S. Census Bureau, May 2011), 1–16, http://www.census.gov/prod/cen2010/briefs/c2010br-04.pdf; Kenneth Johnson, *Demographic Trends in Rural and Small Town America*, Carsey Institute Reports on Rural America 1, no. 1 (Durham: University of New Hampshire, 2006).

4. David L. Brown and Louis E. Swanson, *Challenges for Rural America in the Twenty-First Century* (University Park: Pennsylvania State University Press, 2003).
5. Leighton Ku and Sheetal Matani, "Left Out: Immigrants' Access to Health Care and Insurance," *Health Affairs* 20, no. 1 (January–February 2001): 247–56, http://www.content.healthaffairs.org/content/20/1/247.full.
6. Benjamin D. Sommers, Sharon K. Long, and Katherine Baicker, "Changes in Mortality after Massachusetts Health Care Reform: A Quasi-Experimental Study," *Annals of Internal Medicine* 160, no. 9 (May 2014): 585–93.
7. Center for Health Policy Research, "California Health Interview Survey" (Los Angeles: Center for Health Policy Research, University of California Los Angeles, 2013), http://www.healthpolicy.ucla.edu/chis/Pages/default.aspx
8. Marc B. Schenker, "Preventive Medicine and Health Promotion Are Overdue in the Agricultural Workplace," *Journal of Public Health Policy* 17, no. 3 (1996): 275–305; Don Villarejo, Stephen A. McCurdy, Bonnie Bade, Steve Samuels, David Lighthall, and Daniel Williams III, "The Health of California's Immigrant Hired Farmworkers," *American Journal of Industrial Medicine* 53, no. 4 (April 2010): 387–97; Bureau of Labor Statistics, *Census of Fatal Occupational Injuries (CFOI)—Current and Revised Data,* (Washington, DC: Bureau of Labor Statistics, U.S. Department of Labor, 2014), http://www.bls.gov/iif/osh cfoi1.htm.
9. U.S. Department of Labor, "National Agricultural Workers Survey: Farm Worker Tables" (Washington, DC: United States Department of Labor, 2010), https://naws.jbsinternational.com.
10. Don Villarejo and Stephen A. McCurdy, "The California Agricultural Workers Health Survey," *Journal of Agricultural Safety and Health* 14, no. 2 (April 2008): 135–46.
11. United States Commission on Agricultural Workers, *Report of the Commission on Agricultural Workers* (Washington, DC: United States Commission on Agricultural Workers, 1993), 105–7.
12. William Kandel, *Profile of Hired Farmworkers, A 2008 Update,* Economic Research Report No. 60, (Washington, DC: Economic Research Service, U.S. Department of Agriculture, 2008), 28–30.
13. Don Villarejo, Marc Schenker, Ann Moss Joyner, and Allan Parnell, *(Un)Safe at Home: The Health Consequences of Sub-Standard Farm Labor Housing* (Oakland: California Rural Legal Assistance, Inc., December 31, 2009), http://www.aginnovations.org/images/uploads/CRLA-UnSafeAtHome052610.pdf; Sarah M. Ramirez and Don Villarejo, "Poverty, Housing, and the Rural Slum: Policies and the Production of Inequities, Past and Present," *American Journal of Public Health* 102, no. 9 (September 2012): 1664–75.
14. Arthur J. Reynolds, Judy A. Temple, Suh-Ruu Ou, Irma A. Arteaga, and Barry A.B. White, "School-Based Early Childhood Education and Age-28 Well-Being: Effects by Timing, Dosage, and Subgroups," *Science* 333, no. 6040

(July 15, 2011): 360–64, http://www.viriya.net/jabref/school-based_early_childhood_education_and_age_28_well-being_-_effects_by_timing_dosage_and_subgroups.pdf.

15. Center for Health Policy Research, "California Health Interview Survey."
16. Thomas A. Arcury, Antonio Marin, Beverly M. Snively, Mercedes Hernández-Pelletier, and Sara A. Quandt, "Reducing Farmworker Residential Pesticide Exposure: Evaluation of a Lay Health Advisor Intervention," *Health Promotion Practice* 10, no. 3 (Jul 2009): 447–55, http://www.ncbi.nlm.nih.gov/pmc/articles/PMC3088730/; "Binational Health Week," Health Initiative of the Americas, School of Public Health, University of California, Berkeley, http://hia.berkeley.edu/index.php?page=binational-health-week.

THE RURAL WESTERN ECONOMY

The economy of the rural West has become increasingly diversified, but it continues to depend largely on natural beauty—to attract tourists and amenity-seeking residents—and natural resources, such as grasslands, mineral and petroleum deposits, and timber. The two essays in this section look at different ways of exploiting natural resources, both of which promise long-term sustainability to rural western communities. They also suggest a central role for government, which has always been a key force in resource development in the West.

Mark and Julia Haggerty explore the increasingly significant energy economy of the rural West with an eye toward assuring that states develop fiscal policies that address immediate impacts on communities and provide for economic health in localities once the energy boom is over. They point out the varying impacts of fossil-fuel and renewable energy development and suggest ways that states and localities can shape their fiscal policies to derive maximum benefit from both.

Focusing on two rural communities in Oregon, Michael Hibbard and Susan Lurie examine the possibilities of the New Natural Resource Economy, which manages the West's natural resources in a more benign and sustainable manner than has happened historically. They argue that communities that apply principles of conservation, diversification, and multifunctionality to their resources can achieve long-term economic and social stability. They also suggest some steps local, state, and federal governments can take to encourage the New Natural Resource Economy.

Energy Development Opportunities and Challenges in the Rural West

MARK N. HAGGERTY AND JULIA H. HAGGERTY

Introduction

As a region, the rural West plays a key role in oil and natural-gas extraction, expanded renewable-energy generation, and energy transportation, including transmission lines, pipelines, and rail. This chapter examines ways that rural western communities can maximize economic opportunities from energy development. The jobs, income, and tax revenue these projects provide can revitalize rural areas with otherwise-limited economic opportunities. But, as an economic-development strategy, energy is not without challenges.

As a general rule, wealth from energy resources has rarely translated into a long-term economic advantage for the rural West. We argue that energy can and ought to generate long-term benefits for communities and that securing them relies on tax policy. Yet energy fiscal policies at the state level are failing in fundamental ways. Communities often do not receive the revenue needed to mitigate the acute impact of energy development in the right amount, time, or location. Revenue is also volatile, responding to changing prices and production levels. States are generally not doing enough to ensure communities have predictable returns over time.

Meaningful reform requires regional solutions. Alignment, rather than competition, among state fiscal policies will improve benefits from energy development across the region. Fiscal-policy goals must specifically address the needs of different localities through direct distribution and long-term savings that help communities. Improved access to information and innovative planning can enhance knowledge about local impact and regional cooperation.

This essay takes a threefold approach. First, we situate the rural West in the region's changing economy and describe the emerging energy landscapes. Second, we discuss the role of state energy fiscal policy and offer case studies of renewable energy infrastructure and unconventional oil extraction that highlight its unevenness and the implications for communities. We conclude by discussing reforms that can help leverage better returns to rural communities from regional energy development.

Part 1: Uneven Economic Growth Is Leaving Parts of the Rural West Behind

The West has been the fastest-growing region in the country during the last four decades, but progress has not been evenly distributed. Particularly in the rural West, distance from markets limits opportunities to participate in the changing U.S. economy. Structural changes in the production economies of timber and agriculture have also created hardships in many rural areas. As a result, many relatively isolated, resource-based communities have experienced a long-term decline in income and wealth and increased poverty.[1]

Energy-development opportunities are dependent on local socioeconomic characteristics. In fast-growing, diversified parts of the West, energy development poses a unique set of challenges related to quality of life, competition with other industries, and uncertain environmental impact. In rural areas with fewer economic options, energy development is more attractive because it makes larger contributions to jobs and income. At the same time, rural communities with limited local government infrastructure risk being overwhelmed by rapid growth and industrial activity. For these reasons, it is in these rural and isolated parts of the rural West that the promise and peril of energy development come into sharpest focus.

Economic Restructuring

What are the main drivers of economic prosperity in the West and the challenges facing rural communities? From 1970 to 2010, service industries created more than two million new jobs or nearly 100 percent of job growth in the nonmetropolitan West. In the last decade, financial services, tech-

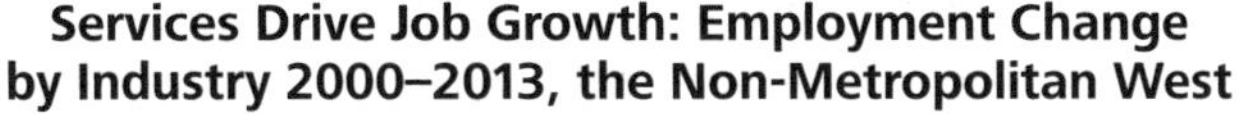

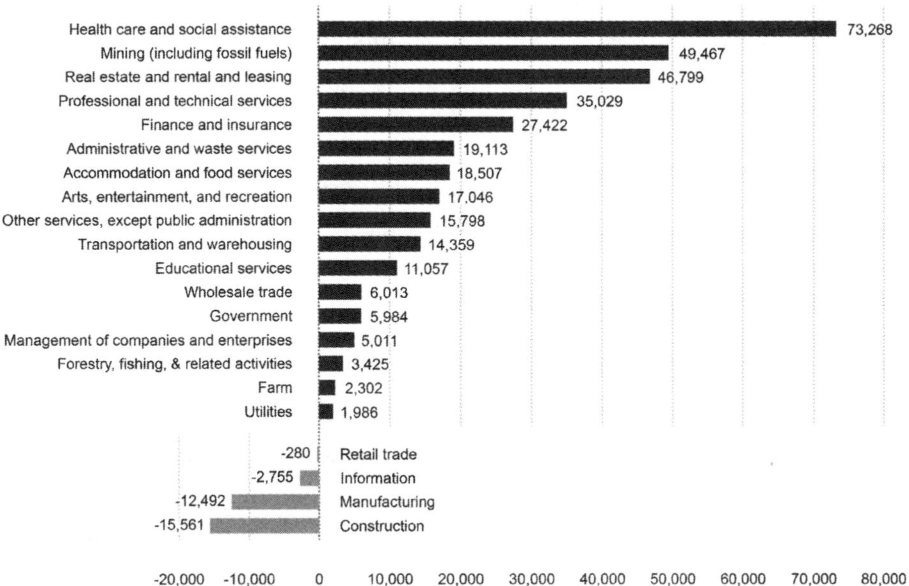

This graph depicts the employment change in various industries in the non-metropolitan West between 2000 and 2013. Service occupations added the most new jobs, with the exception of mining.

nology, health care, education, and accommodations generated the most new jobs according to the following graph.[2]

Restructuring the U.S. economy around services is rewarding communities with highly educated workers and connections to national and global markets. Cities and rural areas connected to markets via airports have experienced the majority of the related growth in high-wage service jobs and nonlabor income.[3] Remote rural communities are at a competitive disadvantage in the new economy of the United States because they are not well connected to markets and typically do not attract the investment and employment associated with either new residents seeking amenities or innovative economies.[4]

Meanwhile nonservice industries, as a whole, continue to shed jobs. In 2010, agriculture and resource extraction, including oil, natural gas, coal, mining, and wood products, accounted for only 7 percent of total employment in the nonmetropolitan West.[5] Rural restructuring, discussed in Michael Hibbard and Susan Lurie's chapter, "The New Natural Resource Economy," is reducing the returns from this work as well, measured in the number of jobs, lower wages earned in natural-resource development, and persistent rural poverty.

Energy in the New Economy

Energy development appears to be bucking the trends of other nonservice industries. Energy industries pay higher-than-average wages, and jobs are expanding across the West. For example, in Sublette County, Wyoming, during the natural-gas boom, energy development accounted for the largest number of jobs and paid the highest wages, about 50 percent more than the county average, as revealed in the following chart.[6] For rural communities losing jobs in other natural-resource areas and unable to compete for high-wage service jobs or attract new residents seeking amenities, energy provides an important option.

But energy development presents challenges for rural communities. Often the size of the labor force and amount of housing and support services demanded by the energy industry far exceed what small rural areas can provide. In-migrants typically take most of the jobs, and wages and wealth leave the area, rather than remaining locally.[7] Some rural communities wary of overbuilding to accommodate population growth during the oil boom have embraced an "offshore" housing model. Out-of-state workers live in temporary "man camps" and commute to the drilling sites each day. Industry and contractors provide basic services and infrastructure that can be removed after the drilling ends and workers return to their homes. The same kinds of temporary arrangements often accompany major energy-generation and transmission projects, where employment is short term and isolated from the local economy.[8]

The situation is different in emerging service centers, such as Williston, North Dakota; Rock Springs, Wyoming; and Grand Junction, Colorado; which fare better at capturing and retaining workers. Many of the long-term and high-wage workers supporting the oil fields, including engineers, contractors, and managers, live in these service centers.

In rural communities less likely to capture and retain energy-related jobs, the largest and most lasting benefit of energy development is financial. Tax revenue and royalties from extraction and large industrial facilities

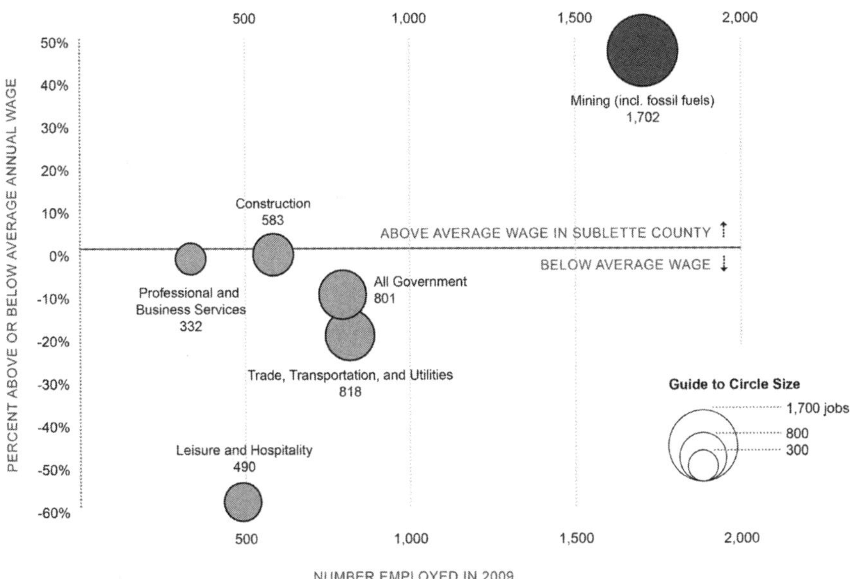

This chart depicts employment and income from various occupations in rural Sublette County, Wyoming, where a natural gas boom dominated during much of the 2000s. It reveals that the high wages and plentiful jobs associated with mining were not duplicated by other industries.

can make a large contribution to state income and can persist long after the boom ends or building a facility is completed. For example, the following chart reveals that in Montana and Wyoming, jobs in oil and gas extraction account for 1.7 and 8.5 percent of total employment respectively but contribute 12 and 37 percent of state and local government tax revenue.[9]

Energy Fiscal Policy and Community Benefits

Energy fiscal policy refers to the way state and local governments tax energy extraction, generation, and transmission and how they spend the proceeds. Energy fiscal policy has a major impact on communities seeking to benefit from energy development for two main reasons. First, communities need resources to manage the acute impact of rapid industrialization and population growth during booms. Second, energy revenue should provide lasting benefits after the boom ends.

Share of Total Employment, Income, Gross Domestic Product, and Tax Revenue Contributed by Oil and Natural Gas Extraction in Montana and Wyoming in 2010

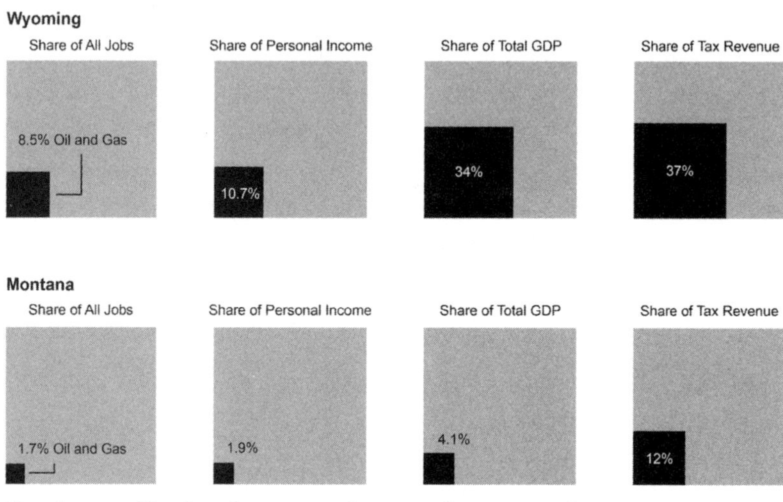

This chart profiles the relative contributions of mining to jobs, income, gross domestic product (GDP), and tax revenue in Montana and Wyoming. It shows that the largest advantage of new resource extraction is fiscal.

Many studies have documented a set of boomtown effects: social disruption;[10] public-safety and infrastructure problems, including negative impact on roads, water systems, and housing;[11] increasing disparity in wealth;[12] public-health risks;[13] and uncertain environmental consequences, including impact on water quality and quantity and wildlife and habitat loss.[14] While large-scale utility projects, like wind farms and transmission lines, disrupt local services less, they often generate community controversy because of their size. A potential increase in property tax revenue is often an influential factor in public discussions about the costs and benefits of new utility projects.[15]

Impact can be more severe in rural areas, where a lack of infrastructure can create higher costs. For example, rural roads are often the first victims in oil and natural-gas booms, and the pace and scale of drilling activity keep applying pressure throughout the entire development period, which may last decades.[16] In North Dakota's oil field, three quarters of the roads the trucks travel are two-lane gravel ones not designed to handle industrial traffic related to drilling, fracking, and hauling away oil. Counties are still struggling to maintain these roads years into the boom. In Texas, even paved roads are experiencing tremendous wear and tear, and local resources are so strapped that the state has recommended allowing them to revert to gravel.[17] These realities point to the need for the state to deliver resources in the time, place, and amount necessary to mitigate the immediate impact of energy development.

Counties experiencing energy development also worry that a bust will follow the boom, posing a new set of challenges associated with long-term volatility.[18] While early studies of mining-dependent areas revealed positive benefits of mining on employment and income, subsequent studies complicated that picture by highlighting differences across time periods, regions, types of mining, and characteristics of the community. This essay cannot undertake an exhaustive discussion of the literature, but the work of William Freudenburg provides a fair conclusion reached by sociological and econometric studies. Writing with his student, Lisa Wilson, in 2002, Freudenburg observed that research does "not support the widespread expectation that mining can be expected to increase the prosperity of isolated rural communities."[19]

This conclusion about long-term effects on rural communities is unchanged by subsequent research. In a recent econometric analysis, we found statistical evidence that participation in the energy boom of the early 1980s, coupled with continued participation in oil and gas extraction, had negative effects on income, educational attainment, and crime rates in counties in the six major energy-producing states of the West.[20]

However, studies have yet to specifically detail the mechanisms that produce poor economic results of energy development. The volatility of commodity prices, the potential for cost-price squeeze, and *flickering*, or periodic operating shutdowns due to prices fluctuating below operational costs, may be factors.[21] More recent research indicates that energy development may be associated with a higher risk of long-term economic disruption, including "crowding out" other industries due to competition for wages, services, and infrastructure; environmental damage that limits long-term growth; and problems associated with social stress.[22]

A more helpful framework is political analysis of the influence of institutions on exacerbating the challenges of what has been called the resource curse. As James Robinson and his colleagues have shown, a predictable model of political behavior involves a focus on exploiting resources for short-term political gain. This is most obvious in resource-dependent countries, where political appropriation of oil revenue contributes to inefficient investment and weak economic performance. The argument is bolstered by the fact that some countries have avoided the resource curse, turning windfall profits into strong economic growth. This result indicates that the most important question may not be the size or duration of resource windfalls but what communities do with the revenue.[23]

Renewable energy facilities have received less attention in scholarly studies, although projections of local economic benefits from permitting processes abound. The first empirical analysis of ex post facto economic benefits of wind farms in the Great Plains states found a small, but significant, income advantage.[24] It would be unwise to extrapolate from this study to the West as a whole, where ownership and royalty opportunities vary considerably according to whether facilities are on public or private land. However, two important and valid conclusions from both impact analyses and published studies are that (1) local employment benefits from renewable energy facilities are marginal, and (2) private and public revenue figures prominently in the anticipated benefits of new electric facilities.

It is understood that a strong connection exists among taxation, local institutions, and overall economic benefits. However, this chapter does not analyze the mechanisms relating fiscal to economic performance. Instead, we provide a grounding in fiscal policy and its implications for revenue amounts and distribution. This initial work is important. New shale natural gas and tight oil resources have a very different production character than conventional oil, exacerbating the negative impact of inefficient fiscal policies developed in the 1980s. Tax policies affecting renewable energy infrastructure in all but one state reflect very little consideration of local issues.[25] Furthermore, imposing state constitutional limits on the ability of local governments to raise revenue and increase budgets may be making it more difficult for communities to benefit from windfall profits by mandating their inefficient use.

The West's Emerging Energy Geography

Before discussing specific fiscal policies and their impact on local government, it's important to describe the emerging energy landscape of the West. The West is endowed with both significant fossil fuel and renewable solar and wind energy. Moving these products to markets largely on the coasts is likely to require large new investments in improving transmission lines, pipelines, and rail connections. Regardless of what direction future energy policy or markets take, the rural West will continue to feature prominently in energy extraction and generation.

Fossil Fuels

The advent of unconventional natural gas and oil has reshaped the extraction landscape. *Unconventional* refers to oil and gas extracted by means other than conventional vertical wells drilled into reservoirs of liquids trapped by geologic features. This chapter defines unconventional oil and gas as trapped in tight shale rocks and extracted using advanced horizontal drilling and hydraulically fracturing or *fracking* the rock, allowing the freed oil to be pumped to the surface. Improvements in these technologies and high prices have reopened production in places with long histories of conventional oil and gas exploration and are pushing into areas with less experience or infrastructure to accommodate the extensive and intensive nature of unconventional drilling. Nearly two-thirds of all rigs active in North America in 2013 are drilling horizontal wells, up from only 8 percent at the start of 2004.[26] In key deposits, like the Eagle Ford in Texas, the effort devoted to horizontal drilling versus vertical wells is even greater.[27]

Renewable Energy Resources

Renewable-energy development opportunities are widely dispersed in many parts of the West. To date, the sweet spots in renewable-energy generation have largely been areas with high-quality resources and access to transmission methods such as the inland Northwest and eastern California; there are additional pockets in other states. However, there are plans for many large-scale developments that will impact rural areas in Wyoming, Montana, Idaho, Colorado, New Mexico, and Arizona, as well as the coastal states. The fruition of those plans relies heavily on unpredictable factors such as public-policy support for renewables and development costs. One factor in the West is the Obama administration's emphasis on identifying appropriate places for renewable-energy development on public lands. While this is a reasonable use of public resources, it does narrow local economic opportunities for private landowners by depriving them of potential lease revenue.

Transmission

The term *pass-through counties* is a good way to describe many rural areas of the West likely to host new and expanded transmission methods, including power lines, pipelines, and rail connections. Transmission projects, like energy generation and drilling, contain potential benefits and a variety of associated risks and inconveniences for pass-through counties. Local impact does not reflect national priorities and values, or entirely local ones, either; instead, it is the result of state and local fiscal policy and varying landowner compensation. While this chapter only partially addresses transmission implications, it is crucial that future conversations and research focus on the fact that any kind of energy buildup has implications for pass-through counties.

Oil and gas development occurs where resources are located, often in areas remote from markets. The oil and gas industry has proven highly adept at finding paths to market. For example, developers were able to initiate new natural-gas pipelines linking gas hubs both east and west of the Rocky Mountains in time to synchronize with emerging market opportunities. More recently, developers in the Bakken oil field have compensated for imported oil shortages by shipping crude oil by railroad.

Renewable-energy generation to date has correlated with the availability of transmission methods to link production with markets. New high-voltage transmission lines have proven far more difficult to develop than oil and gas pipelines or flexible trucks and trains. Still, major new transmission lines have been constructed to enable renewable-energy development in Montana and California. Serious plans are under way for several more, including new projects and upgrades to existing transmission lines. The proposed projects will facilitate renewable-energy development in central New Mexico, southern Arizona, south-central Wyoming, and central Montana.

Looking Forward

Changing technology, prices, and shifting policy debates will shape these emerging energy landscapes. Whatever direction energy policy takes—whether continuing to emphasize unconventional fossil fuels, or adopting a carbon tax that privileges renewable energy—the West will participate in extracting, generating, or transporting energy to markets.

Community leaders in the places where development will occur expect that they will be better off because of energy development. Yet local governments have little or no influence over the kind of development that takes place, where it is located, or when it happens. They can work to understand what is likely to happen, and they can ensure that they and their constituents benefit.

Two case studies of unconventional oil development and renewable-energy generation and transmission across several western states are illuminating.

Case Study: State Taxation of Unconventional Oil

This case study has three important points. First, extracting unconventional oil is dramatically more costly and intensive than conventional oil. The changed nature of development is heightening and extending community impact. Second, most fiscal policies were crafted before the current boom and are useless in providing necessary revenue to manage community challenges. And finally, state policies are dramatically different, which should help them align their goals and approaches to meet community needs.

Unconventional Oil Requires More Wells over Larger Areas Than Conventional Development

Applying unconventional technology to the Bakken formation in Montana and North Dakota, the Eagle Ford in Texas, and other shale deposits has helped reverse declining domestic oil production in aging conventional fields in Alaska, Texas, and California.[28] Unconventional oil does not come easily. Shale deposits are much less accommodating than conventional oil fields, demanding dramatically more wells, drilled at higher cost, to bring the oil to the surface. In *The Oil Drum Blog* on January 1, 2013, Rune Likvern compares the need for constant drilling to maintain production to the Red Queen from *Alice's Adventures in Wonderland,* who told Alice, "It takes all the running you can do to keep in the same place."[29]

Unconventional oil wells are characterized by a steep production curve that features relatively high initial levels that decline quickly.[30] The following graph shows a typical decline curve based on 789 wells completed between June 2000 and November 2012 in Montana's Elm Coulee field, part

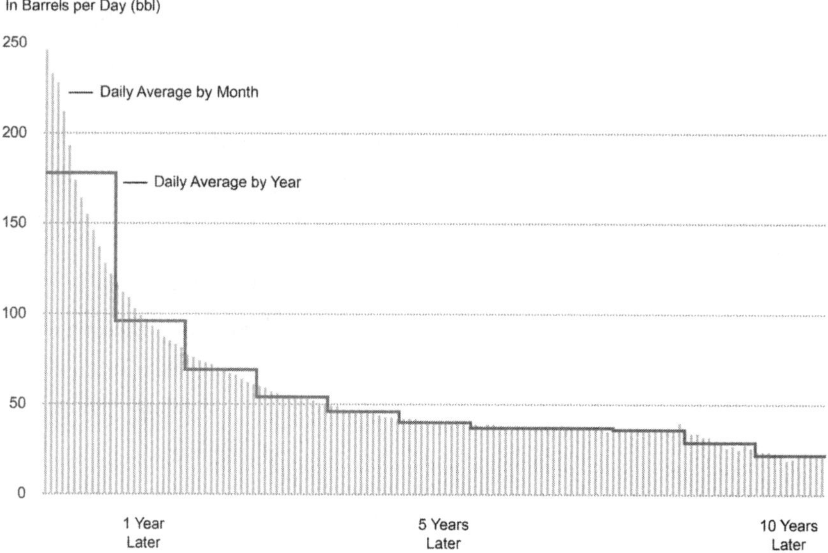

This graph charts the average daily production from a newly completed oil well in Montana's Elm Coulee field over its first ten years. Typical of all horizontally completed and hydraulically fractured shale-oil and natural-gas wells, production declines steeply over the first several years.

of the larger Bakken formation. Production peaked at 246 barrels per day initially, declining to 122 barrels at the end of the first year, 42 barrels after five years, and 24 barrels after ten years.[31]

The second graph illustrates cumulative oil production and the producing well count in Montana's Elm Coulee field from June 2000 to November 2012. Total production flattens and begins to decline in 2006, even as the number of producing wells continues to grow at a rapid rate to compensate for the reduced output from individual wells.[32]

The contrast in productivity between conventional and unconventional wells is demonstrated by comparing figures from Alaska's Prudhoe Bay conventional oil field. Prudhoe Bay had produced nearly 11 billion barrels of oil from just 1,114 wells by 2006—nearly 10 million per well.[33] By comparison, estimates project that tens of thousands of wells—between 33,000 and 48,000—need to be drilled over several decades to extract a similar amount of oil from the Bakken field.[34] The industrialized region in

Cumulative Average Daily Oil Production (bbls/day) from Horizontally Completed Wells and Producing Well Count, Montana Elm Coulee (Bakken Field)

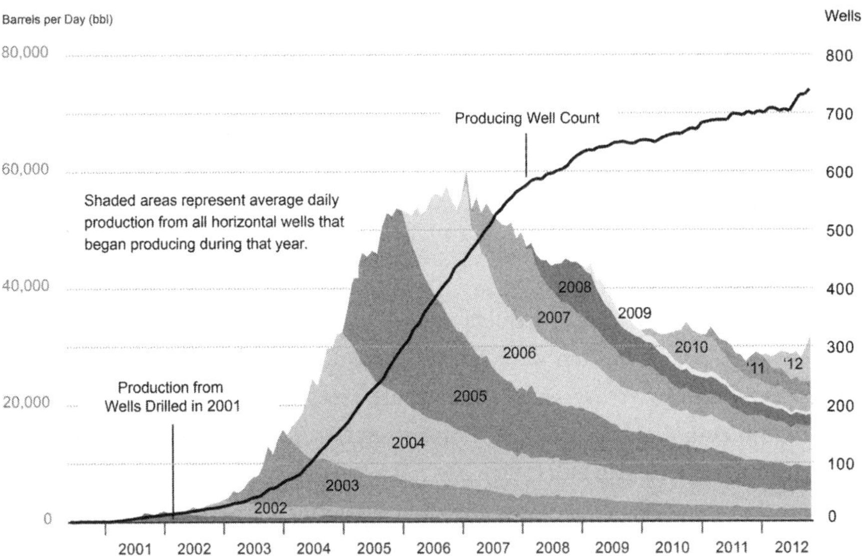

This graph records cumulative production from all wells in the Elm Coulee field on an annual basis. The steep decline associated with individual wells requires continuous drilling of new wells to maintain total production levels.

Alaska covers about 200,000 acres, while the full extent of the Bakken is closer to 128 million acres.

State Fiscal Policies Are Failing in Several Ways

Local governments receive tax revenue from unconventional oil production in several major oil-producing states. State energy fiscal policies can be assessed using four criteria: the amount, time, location, and predictability of revenue distributions to local governments where extraction occurs. The first three criteria—amount, timing, and location—relate directly to a community's efforts to mitigate boomtown impact. Predictability of revenue over time reveals the way states are managing volatility.

Existing taxation and distribution policies are remarkably variable among states, and the differences affect the results for communities. Comparing fiscal policies in Montana and North Dakota illustrates the most important differences among states. This analysis is part of a larger research project comparing state fiscal policies across seven oil-producing states.[35]

The first graph shows how Montana and North Dakota's tax policy would apply to the average unconventional oil well if it were drilled using a constant oil price of eighty-five dollars per barrel. The next chart reveals that the revenue is distributed according to four priorities: the state share, the local government share, permanent investments, and tax expenditures (defined as the value of incentives, deductions, or relief provided in the tax code).

Amount

The graph shows that North Dakota would collect nearly $700,000 more than Montana over ten years from a typical oil well. Tax collection is so different for two reasons: North Dakota's base tax rate is higher—two production taxes combine for a rate of 11.5 percent.[36] Montana collects a single production tax with an average base rate of 10.4 percent.[37]

More significantly, both states offer a drilling incentive that lowers the base tax rate for eighteen months after completion of new horizontal wells, but North Dakota's incentive is tiered to price. Current high prices mean the incentive is not currently available in North Dakota.[38] Montana offers the incentive without condition, so it is always in effect. Drilling incentives were mostly adopted before the current boom and are not responsive to the changing dynamics of unconventional oil or natural gas.[39]

Despite higher collections in North Dakota, the chart reveals that local governments in Montana would actually receive about 50 percent more revenue from a typical well than their counterparts in North Dakota. Montana directs 35 percent of total production tax revenue to local governments, totaling $695,557. Only $451,651, or 21 percent of total production tax revenues, reaches local governments in North Dakota directly.

North Dakota's low direct-distribution threshold has required the governor's office and state legislature to provide significant assistance to localities in each of the last two biennial sessions. In 2012 and 2013, energy-impacted counties received $1.2 billion from the state, about 59 percent of the total projected oil revenue of $2 billion over the same period. Most of this money—$850 million—took the form of one-time transportation, water, and housing grants and tax incentives. While these distributions are significant, biennial appropriations do not give communities the

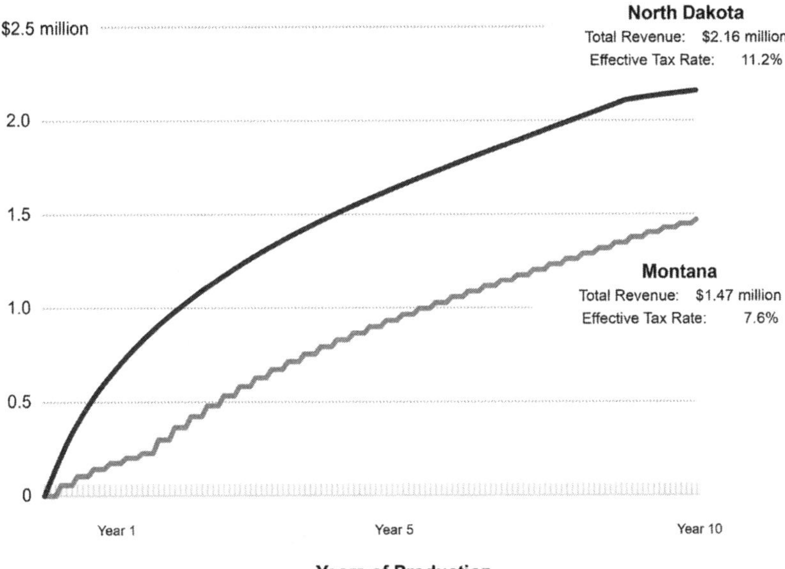

This graph depicts tax revenue derived from a typical oil well according to the current fiscal policies in Montana and North Dakota. Since North Dakota's tax rate is higher, it receives a greater financial benefit.

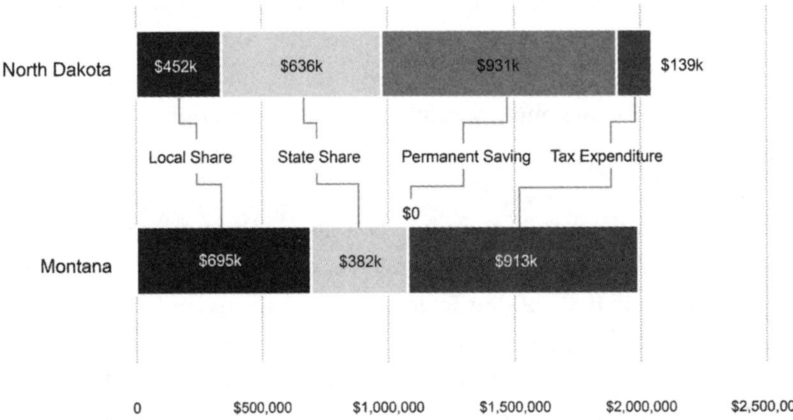

This chart reflects the way tax revenue from oil production is allocated to state and local governments in North Dakota and Montana and compares the value of investments in permanent savings funds to tax expenditures. There are dramatic differences between the two states, partly because Montana has no permanent savings fund.

certainty they would receive from a system of direct distributions based on impact and a tax policy that recognizes the unique needs of oil-impacted communities.

Timing

Drilling impacts roads, water systems, and other infrastructure, but revenue flows only after wells have been completed and begin producing. The time required to plan, design, and construct infrastructure and the uncertainty about future revenue and demand exacerbate this lag,[40] as do tax policies, and communities find themselves always playing catch-up and suffering effects that could otherwise be avoided.

North Dakota collects and distributes production taxes monthly, minimizing the lag to the greatest possible extent. In Montana, it takes nearly two years after a well has been completed before significant revenue reaches communities. Taxes are first fully assessed at the end of the first quarter following the eighteen-month incentive period and are then distributed to counties in the following quarter, or twenty-four months after well completion.

Location

Revenue returns to local governments are complicated by taxes and distribution formulas based on the location of production, not the level or type of impact in industrialized regions. For example, Montana makes direct distributions to county governments and local school districts where production occurs. Cities and adjacent counties that experience population growth and industrial impact typically receive only a small share of energy revenues.

North Dakota's distributions largely followed the same pattern until the 2013 legislative session made significant changes. Reforms increased direct distributions to oil-impacted cities and towns and significantly raised the impact grant fund from $100 to $250 million in the 2013–14 biennium, providing more flexibility to base revenue on needs.[41] Montana's legislature also considered these issues in 2013 but failed to change direct distribution formulas or deliver more money to impacted communities from other sources.

In the Bakken area, the state line dividing Montana and North Dakota—and the oil underlying the two states—presents an additional challenge. Much of the oil—and its production tax revenue—is gathered in North Dakota. Montana's nearby towns are bedroom communities for the oil field; they are feeling impact but not receiving revenue.[42]

Volatility

One of the main goals of energy taxation is to help manage the revenue volatility from oil extraction.[43] If states fail to manage revenue well, they are less likely to be better off in the long term from oil extraction. States can reduce and manage volatility in two ways: avoid incentives and taxes that exacerbate fluctuations in the production value of oil and invest a portion of revenue into a trust fund that provides long-term fiscal stability. Montana does poorly in these areas, while North Dakota excels.

Montana invests no production tax revenue into a trust fund, choosing to spend all of its oil and gas income in the year it comes in. A significant portion of annual revenue (46 percent) is returned to industry and property owners across the state in incentives and tax relief. Property tax relief is guaranteed at a fixed level, even if fluctuating production taxes come in lower than that amount, meaning Montana has essentially swapped a stable revenue source for less dependable production taxes and exposed communities to greater fiscal risk.

North Dakota, by comparison, is investing 43 percent of production tax revenue in the Legacy Fund, a permanent savings trust that will help the state manage volatility and translate one-time oil wealth into lasting fiscal reserves. The following chart shows the savings rate for an equivalent amount of oil produced by a typical well across seven oil-producing states, including Montana and North Dakota.

Policy Lessons

The wide disparity in state approaches to oil fiscal policy results in dramatically different amounts of revenue to local governments at different times, based on varying criteria, and with more or less certainty over time. Montana and North Dakota's fiscal policies are ripe for reform since they were largely drafted before the current boom. For example, Montana's last major overhaul of taxation policy occurred in 1999, and important horizontal-drilling incentives were adopted even earlier in 1993.[44] At the time, oil prices were low, and little new production was anticipated. Montana and North Dakota, as well as other states across the West dependent on oil and

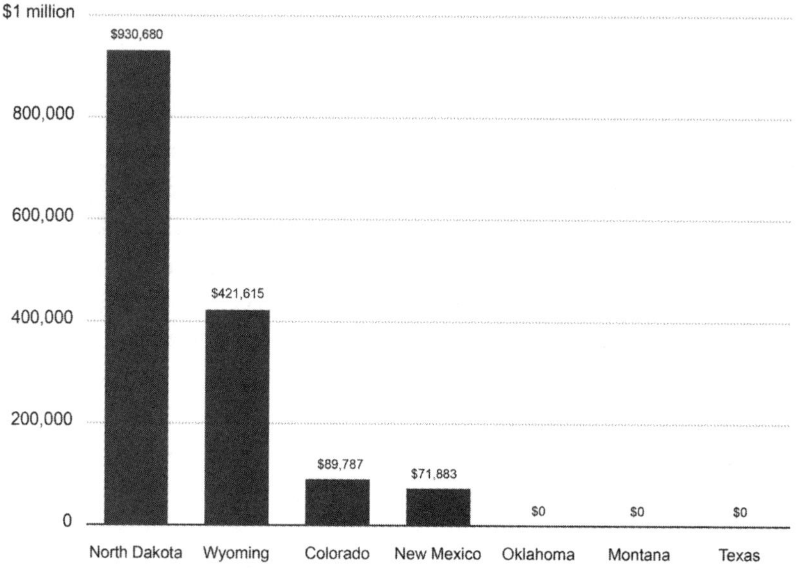

This chart depicts the relative contributions seven states would make to permanent savings funds according to current tax policies if a similar oil well was drilled in each state. Several states—primarily North Dakota and Wyoming—direct a significant portion of revenue to savings while others—Oklahoma, Montana, and Texas—do not.

gas for tax revenue, looked to new drilling techniques to stimulate energy activity.

High prices in the last decade, combined with the advent of horizontal drilling and fracking, led to the current boom in drilling and production. The tax policies written twenty years ago are no longer relevant to the changed production dynamics and increasing community costs associated with unconventional oil.

Placing community needs and long-term goals at the center of fiscal policy formulation triggers two reform agendas: first, a larger share of revenue needs to be directed quickly to communities to mitigate impact and meet their needs. Second, creating stable fiscal institutions to achieve long-term goals requires saving more money in most states and discussing how to best use oil revenues. Communities should expect to receive less mitigation funding over time but obtain a portion of investment income directly to reach economic-development goals.

Case Study: Renewable Energy Facilities and Rural Economic Prospects

The possibility that significant new renewable energy facilities will be constructed in rural parts of the West suggests these projects will be important in economic development. Renewable energy facilities for both power generation and electric transmission present an altogether different scenario for rural areas than fossil-fuel extraction. They are essentially short-lived, major construction projects that do not bring the same employment and income benefits. Construction labor is often highly specialized, and workers move from project to project, limiting the local employment benefits. Because of the short duration and location-specific nature of these projects, they do not have the boomtown impact associated with oil and gas drilling, either.

This does not mean that large electricity facilities are easy to permit and locate—often there are significant local concerns and opposition caused by real or perceived impact to property values, aesthetics, and the environment. However, they are such capital-intensive projects that the potential tax benefits make them appealing to many rural areas. In the case of renewable energy facilities, the largest and most lasting benefit is property-tax revenue to the local government and income to landowners from leases and royalties.

Whether or not the construction of renewable energy facilities will meaningfully contribute to revenue in rural western counties depends on both the existing economy and state laws that dictate how local governments can use utility property taxes. Our research suggests that the actual opportunity varies highly across western states.

This section of the chapter offers an overview of (1) the geographic conjunction of renewable resources, potential pass-through locations, and struggling rural economies, and (2) an estimate of the property tax benefits to these places. A strong rationale exists for a serious regional discussion about a more systematic approach to compensating the places that host the region's clean energy future.

Location of High-Quality Renewable Energy Resources in the West

Rural counties are well represented among the western locations with high-quality renewable energy resources and those potentially affected by new interstate high-voltage transmission lines. The following table assigns an economic-performance score to the twenty counties in the West with

Economic Performance Scores of Counties within the Top Twenty (by Number of Acres) with High-Quality Wind and Solar Resources

	1	2	3	4	5
WIND	Laramie, WY				
WIND	Torrance, NM	Teton, MT			
WIND	Guadalupe, NM	Las Animas, CO		Platte, WY	
WIND	Glacier, MT	Cheyenne, CO	Lincoln, NM	Albany, NY	
WIND	Blaine, MT	Baca, CO	Sedgwick, CO	Eddy, NM	
WIND	Prowers, CO	Kern, CA	Logan, CO	Weld, CO	Converse, WY
	← Low	**ECONOMIC PERFORMANCE AND OPPORTUNITY**			**High →**
	1	**2**	**3**	**4**	**5**
SOLAR	Iron, UT	Beaver, UT	Millard, UT	San Bernardino, CA	Los Angeles, CA
SOLAR	Socorro, NM	Nye, NV	Lincoln, NV	Riverside, CA	
SOLAR	Luna, NM	Esmeralda, NV	Pima, AZ	Dona Ana, NM	
SOLAR	Hidalgo, NM	Mojave, CA	Maricopa, AZ		
SOLAR	Alamosa, CA	Kern, CA			
SOLAR	Imperial, CA				
SOLAR	La Paz, AZ				

Source: WREZ hub wind and solar data, accessed from Phase 1 GIS data portal at http://mercator.nrel.gov/wrez/, November 7, 2012.

the greatest number of acres devoted to high-quality solar and wind energy, according to a plan formulated by the Western Governors' Association.[45] According to this analysis, of the top twenty counties in the number of acres of high-quality wind resources (class 4 and class 5), five are high performing, three are average, twelve are low performing, and seven are among the worst in the West. Among the top twenty counties in the number of acres of high-quality solar resources (greater than 6.5 daily normal insolation values), three are high performing, four are average, thirteen are low performing, and eight rank among the worst in the West.

Proposed transmission lines that link remote renewable energy to grid hubs and load centers necessarily traverse a variety of counties along the way. For example, the proposed TransWest Express, one of the longer lines, crosses more than a dozen counties on its way from central Wyoming through Colorado and Utah to its destination in Clark County, Nevada.

State Tax Policy

Headwaters Economics recently evaluated the relationship between tax policy and potential tax benefits to rural counties hosting renewable en-

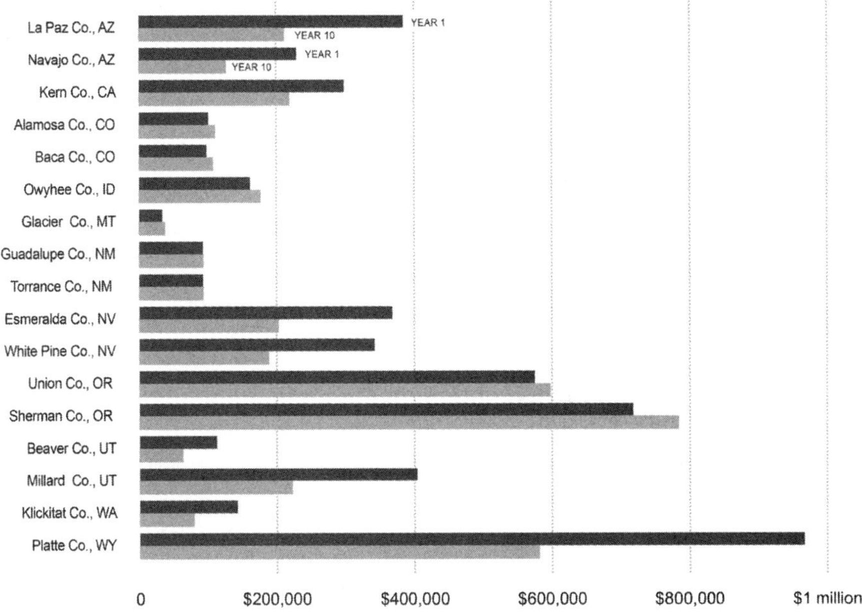

This graph records the potential tax revenue associated with a $100 million investment in renewable-energy-generating facilities in seventeen rural counties across the West. The same level of initial investment generates very different amounts of property-tax revenue.

ergy facilities.[46] The key findings appear on these two graphs that compare estimated property tax revenue and the impact of that revenue on existing collections from the same investment amount in generation facilities in seventeen rural western counties with high renewable energy potential. The estimated revenue varies significantly as does the impact.

This research demonstrates that the same level of initial investment generates very different amounts of property tax revenue in otherwise comparable rural counties. For generation facilities, the revenue ranges from $32,000 to close to $1,000,000 for the hypothetical first year. For transmission investments, amounts range from $112,000 to $871,000.

The implication of varying revenue impact is that the tax advantage is highly uneven and bears little relationship to the economic challenges and opportunities of individual counties. The opportunity from new utility

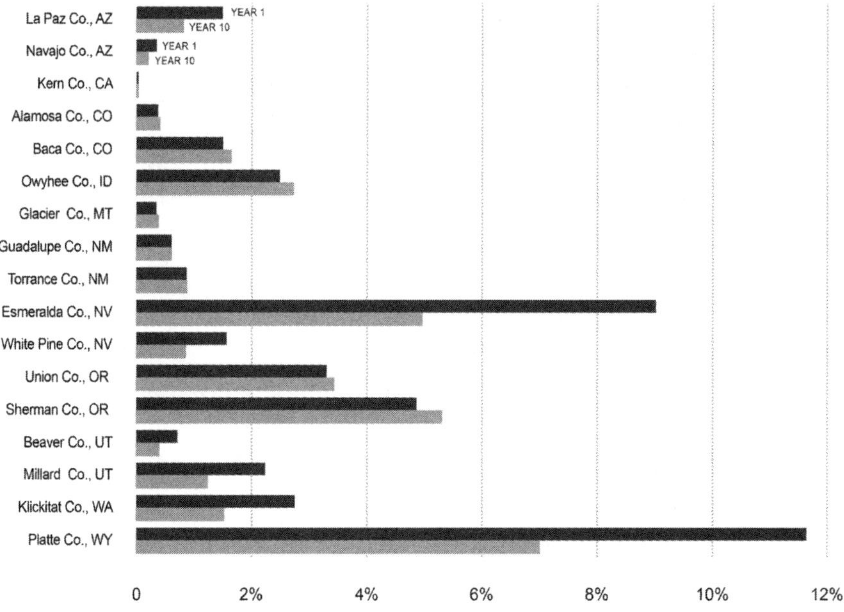

This graph estimates the disparity in the value of tax revenue from renewable-energy-generating facilities as a share of total revenue in the same seventeen counties. The similar $100-million-level of initial investment generates very different contributions to total revenue.

investments is substantial for some rural counties, especially those with small tax bases and high rates. In other rural counties that have a broader tax base and those restricted from capturing new revenue by the state and spending limitations, the opportunity is negligible.

When depreciation enters calculations of taxable value, the drop in revenue can be steep. One-time spikes in valuation can create risk and challenges, especially in places where the new revenue is large in relation to what already exists.

The impact of renewable-energy property-tax incentives varies according to their design. While all but one state program tend to lower potential revenue as compared to income that could be expected from a conventional energy facility, in some cases, they provide benefits by stabilizing revenue over time. As a rule, where states offer tax incentives to lure renewable energy facilities, the return to local areas is significantly lower than in states where these facilities are taxed on a par with conventional ones.

One key exception is Oregon's Strategic Investment Program (SIP). Our chart estimates reflect the success of this program. The SIP works by limiting the property-tax liability of large projects and instead assessing formula-based payments—community service fees—that can be targeted to specific local governments. The SIP approach provides several benefits: first, it stabilizes tax revenue for fifteen years, avoiding the decline typically associated with depreciation. Second, local governments (and even quasi-government organizations like 4-H that are party to the agreement) have more flexibility in using the payments than they would with property taxes. For their part, project developers also benefit through lower tax liability in early years when they are typically paying financing costs and lower expenditures overall on total taxes. The state offers a helpful step-by-step analysis of using the program.[47]

Policy Lessons

Our initial research demonstrates a serious disconnect between the advantages offered to developers and the goals of local communities in many western states. As with fossil-fuel extraction, highly variable returns indicate that states need to consider local economic-development goals when formulating tax policy related to energy generation and transmission facilities.

The regional nature of energy production and consumption also demands a regional approach. The 2009 American Recovery and Reinvestment Act funded a significant new effort to coordinate regional transmission planning that has made enormous progress in integrating data on a regional level and addressing concerns beyond conventional engineering and reliability. But regional planning needs to expand to consider criteria related to local economies.

Discussion and Policy Questions

The West will continue to host various kinds of energy development, regardless of future policy directions or market conditions. Rural areas are endowed with unconventional oil and natural gas and renewable energy resources, and they lie in the current and future path of the pipelines, power lines, and railroads that link these resources to markets.

Turning energy development into long-term economic prosperity is not easy, and local benefits depend on fiscal policies designed at the state level. Fiscal competition and a lack of clear economic-development goals conspire to exacerbate the challenges communities face in managing the effects of development and securing lasting benefits.

In any case, the highly variable tax-revenue potential generates several policy questions.

States Should Coordinate More and End Tax Competition

A dominant force in state fiscal-policy formulation is the assumption that competition largely determines where industries choose to locate activity.[48] Despite the popularity of industry-specific tax incentives in local economic development, studies questioning the effect of these "first-wave strategies" are extensive and long standing.[49] The efficacy of incentives varies significantly depending on the industry and the nature of the incentives.[50]

In the case of oil, particularly, research findings generally agree that production is inelastic with respect to tax incentives for several reasons.[51] Production taxes are downstream ones and have little effect on the upstream investment of capital in exploration and technology that leads to new production. Also state production taxes are deductible from federal income tax, reducing the effectiveness of state incentives.

Anecdotal evidence also suggests that new renewable energy facilities are immune to the charms of tax incentives because they have developed in line with market and grid operation, rather than property-tax abatement opportunities.[52] Consider that Wyoming, with a high property tax and a local production tax on wind energy, has more than 3,100 megawatts (MW) of installed wind power and several thousand more in the works, while Montana—with comparable wind assets and far more generous tax abatement—has 645 MW.[53]

The effects of tax incentives for communities, on the other hand, are large reductions in revenue and delays in the time between project completion and when significant tax revenue accrues to communities. States should coordinate taxation policies. National policy goals, ranging from energy security to reducing carbon emissions, are better addressed with incentives (e.g., the wind-energy tax credit) or disincentives (e.g., a carbon tax) in federal taxes.

Local Economic Development Should Be a Primary Goal of Energy Policy

To date, decision makers have paid too little attention to the impact of state fiscal policies on local governments. For example, a recent energy-development proposal from the Western Governors' Association highlights the importance of energy security and jobs but does not address fiscal challenges and policies with the notable exception of North Dakota, where deficient fiscal policies have caused massive one-time transfers from the state government to affected communities.[54]

Because returns to local governments are not a specific goal of state fiscal policy, communities often do not dependably receive revenue in the correct amount, time, and location to manage development impact or produce lasting benefits. Proper consideration of the impact of local development and long-term goals will produce reforms that address taxation and spending policies.[55]

Fiscal policy could become a central feature of regional planning about energy of all types. For example, Vision West ND, a consortium of local elected officials and professional staff, is developing a regional plan for North Dakota with funding from the U.S. Department of Housing and Urban Development. Regional organizations like the Western Governors' Association that have addressed transmission projects can continue to work toward regional energy planning.

Volatility and the Stability of Fiscal Institutions Should Be Managed

Too much revenue can also present challenges to communities. In the United States, windfall profits from natural resources are often used to maintain lower taxes in the rest of the economy, exposing rural communities to greater risk of price volatility and policy uncertainty.[56] In previous booms, western communities also experienced overborrowing and overbuilding that creates debt and infrastructure costs that cannot be maintained when revenue inevitably declines.[57]

After the funds necessary to meet the acute impact of resource booms are allocated, the maximum amount of remaining revenue should be invested in trust funds to offset fiscal variations inherent to natural resources and provide ongoing benefits from the depletion of nonrenewable resources.[58] The investment income earned from savings can supply stable and lasting resources to achieve multiple goals, including tax relief, investment in education and infrastructure, providing incentives for more energy development, economic development in other areas, and funding for restoration and conservation. Making these reforms a reality will help maximize the coming opportunity from energy development—whatever form it takes—across the diverse western landscape.

Notes

1. W. R. Freudenburg and R. Gramling, "Natural Resources and Rural Poverty: A Closer Look," *Society and Natural Resources* 7 (1994): 5–22.
2. Bureau of Economic Analysis, *Regional Economic Accounts*, table CA25N, U.S. Department of Commerce, 2014, http://www.bea.gov/regional/. See also Enrico Moretti, *The New Geography of Jobs* (Boston: Houghton Mifflin Harcourt, 2012).
3. John Cromartie and Peter Nelson, *Baby Boom Migration and Its Impact on Rural America*, Economic Research Report No. 79 (Washington, DC: Economic Research Service, U.S. Department of Agriculture, August 2009), http://www.ers.usda.gov/media/155249/err79_1_.pdf; Hannah Gosnell and Jesse Abrams, "Amenity Migration: Diverse Conceptualizations of Drivers, Socioeconomic Dimensions, and Emerging Challenges," *GeoJournal* 76, no. 4 (August 2011): 303–22.
4. Rapid growth in rural communities based on the changing economy and the role of market access, education, and amenities is discussed in Ray Rasker, Patricia H. Gude, Justin A. Gude, and Jeff van den Noort, "The Economic Importance of Air Travel in High-Amenity Rural Areas," *Journal of Rural Studies* 25, no. 3 (July 2009): 343–53; David A. McGranahan, Timothy R. Wojan, and Dayton M. Lambert, "The Rural Growth Trifecta: Outdoor Amenities, Creative Class and Entrepreneurial Context," *Journal of Economic Geography* 11, no. 3 (May 2011): 529–57.
5. Bureau of Economic Analysis, *Regional Economic Accounts*, table CA30, U.S. Department of Commerce, 2012, http://www.bea.gov/regional/.
6. Bureau of Labor Statistics, "Employment and Average Annual Wages by Sector in Sublette County, Wyoming, 2009," *Quarterly Census of Employment and Wages*, U.S. Department of Labor, http://www.bls.gov/cew/. See also Headwaters Economics, *Fossil Fuel Extraction and Western Economies* (Bozeman, MT: Headwaters Economics, April 2011), http://headwaterseconomics.org/wphw/wp-content/uploads/Fossilfuel_West_Report.pdf.
7. Jeremy G. Weber, "The Effects of a Natural Gas Boom on Employment and Income in Colorado, Texas, and Wyoming," *Energy Economics* 34, no. 5 (September 2012): 1580–88.
8. William Carrington, "The Alaskan Labor Market during the Pipeline Era," *Journal of Political Economy* 104, no. 1 (February 1996): 186–218.
9. Data sources: for employment, Census Bureau, "Employment in Mining:

Oil and Gas Extraction," *2012 County Business Patterns* (Washington, DC: Census Bureau, U.S. Department of Commerce, 2012); for income, Bureau of Economic Analysis, *Regional Economic Accounts*, 2012, U.S. Department of Commerce, http://www.bea.gov/regional/; for GDP, Bureau of Economic Analysis, *Gross Domestic Product (GDP) by Industry* (Washington, DC: U.S. Department of Commerce, 2012); for tax revenue, Montana Department of Revenue, "Gross Production Tax Collections," *Biennial Report, FY 2013* (Helena: Montana Department of Revenue, 2013), and Office of the State Tax Commissioner, State of North Dakota, *Comparative Statement of Collections, FY 2013 Biennium* (Bismarck: Office of the State Tax Commissioner, 2013).

10. The 1980s energy bust in the West produced an important set of sociological studies documenting boom-and-bust stress in rural communities and opportunities for recovery: Ralph B. Brown, Shawn F. Dorins, and Richard S. Krannich, "The Boom-Bust-Recovery Cycle: Dynamics of Change in Community Satisfaction and Social Integration in Delta, Utah," *Rural Sociology* 70, no. 1 (March 2005): 28–49; Andrew Gulliford, *Boomtown Blues: Colorado Oil Shale*, rev. ed. (Boulder: University of Colorado Press, 2003); Michael D. Smith, Richard S. Krannich, and Lori M. Hunter, "Growth, Decline, Stability, and Disruption: A Longitudinal Analysis of Social Well-Being in Four Western Rural Communities," *Rural Sociology* 66, no. 3 (September 2001): 425–50.
11. A number of white papers produced during the natural gas boom have considered the fiscal situation facing local governments in places such as Colorado and Wyoming. Two relevant studies are BBC Research & Consulting, *Northwest Colorado Socioeconomic Analysis and Forecasts*, Report Prepared for the Associated Governments of Northwest Colorado, April 10, 2008; and Ecosystem Research Group, *Sublette County Socioeconomic Impact Study, Phase II—Final Report*, Report Prepared for Sublette County Commissioners, September 28, 2009.
12. Alex James and David Aadland, "The Curse of Natural Resources: An Empirical Investigation of U.S. Counties," *Resource and Energy Economics* 33, no. 2 (May 2011): 440; Weber, "Effects of a Natural Gas Boom."
13. Charles W. Schmidt, "Blind Rush? Shale Gas Boom Proceeds amid Human Health Questions," *Environmental Health Perspectives* 119, no. 8 (August 2011): a348.
14. Brett L. Walker, David E. Naugle, and Kevin E. Doherty, "Greater Sage-Grouse Population Response to Energy Development and Habitat Loss," *Journal of Wildlife Management* 71, no. 8 (November 2007): 2644–54; Adam Garmezy, "Balancing Hydraulic Fracturing's Environmental and Economic Impacts: The Need for a Comprehensive Federal Baseline and the Provision of Local Rights," *Duke Environmental Law & Policy Forum* 23, no. 2 (Spring 2013): 405–39.
15. Michael C. Slattery, Eric Lantz, and Becky L. Johnson, "State and Local Economic Impacts from Wind Energy Projects: Texas Case Study," *Energy Policy* 39, no. 12 (December 2011): 7930–40.

16. Upper Great Plains Transportation Institute, *An Assessment of County and Local Road Infrastructure Needs in North Dakota*, Report Submitted to the 63rd North Dakota Legislative Assembly, North Dakota State University, September 20, 2012, http://www.visionwestnd.com/documents/StudyonCounty RoadInfrastructure_002.pdf.
17. Aman Batheja, "A New Boom for Oil, but a Bust for Texas' Rural Roads," *New York Times*, September 12, 2013.
18. Ramit Plushnick-Masti and James MacPherson, "Booming Oil Towns Prepare for Inevitable Bust," *Denver Post*, October 15, 2013.
19. William R. Freudenburg and Lisa J. Wilson, "Mining the Data: Analyzing the Economic Implications of Mining for Nonmetropolitan Regions," *Sociological Inquiry* 72, no. 4 (Fall 2002): 549–75, 571.
20. Julia Haggerty, Patricia H. Gude, Mark Delorey, and Ray Rasker, "Long-Term Effects of Income Specialization in Oil and Gas Extraction: The U.S. West, 1980–2011," *Energy Economics* 45 (September 2014): 186–95.
21. Freudenburg and Wilson, "Mining the Data."
22. Don Macke, "Redefining the 'Crowding Out' Effect: Economic Development Capacity and Long-Term Resilience in the Face of an Energy Boom," Center for Rural Entrepreneurship and Rural Policy Research Institute, February 26, 2012, http://www.energizingentrepreneurs.org.
23. James A. Robinson, Ragnar Torvik, and Thierry Verdier, "Political Foundations of the Resource Curse," *Journal of Development Economics* 79, no. 2 (2006), 447–68; Lorenzo Pellegrini and Reyer Gerlagh, "Causes of Corruption: A Survey of Cross-Country Analyses and Extended Results," *Economics of Governance* 9, no. 3 (July 2008): 245–63.
24. Jason P. Brown, John Pender, Ryan Wiser, Eric Lantz, and Ben Hoen, "Ex Post Analysis of Economic Impacts from Wind Power Development in U.S. Counties," *Energy Economics* 34, no. 6 (November 2012): 1743–54.
25. See Julia H. Haggerty, Mark Haggerty, and Ray Rasker, "Uneven Local Benefits of Renewable Energy in the U.S. West: Property Tax Policy Effects," *Western Economic Forum* 13, no. 1 (Spring 2014): 8–22.
26. Baker Hughes, *North America Rotary Rig Count, U.S. Count by Trajectory*, January 9, 2004 to September 13, 2013, dataset, http://phx.corporate-ir.net /phoenix.zhtml?c=79687&p=irol-reportsother.
27. R. W. Gilmer, R. Hernandez, and K. R. Phillips, "Oil Boom in Eagle Ford Shale Brings New Wealth to South Texas," *Natural Gas* 2 (2012): 3–7, http:// www.dallasfed.org/assets/documents/research/swe/2012/swe1202b.pdf.
28. U.S. Energy Information Agency (EIA), "Field Production of Crude Oil (Thousand Barrels) by Area," U.S. Department of Energy, dataset, 2013, http://www.eia.gov/petroleum/.
29. Rune Likvern, "Is Shale Oil Production from Bakken Headed for a Run with 'The Red Queen?'" *The Oil Drum*, September 25, 2012, http://www.theoil drum.com/nodc/9506.

30. Criticism about shale-well decline and the implications for field production is growing. See Likvern, "Is Shale Oil Production Headed for a Run?"; J. D. Hughes, *Drill, Baby, Drill: Can Unconventional Fuels Usher in a New Era of Energy Abundance?* (Santa Rosa: Post Carbon Institute, 2013); Chris Helman, "Why America's Shale Oil Boom Could End Sooner Than You Think," *Forbes*, June 13, 2013.
31. Montana Board of Oil and Gas Conservation, "Production Data for Elm Coulee Horizontally Completed Wells," 2000 to 2012, dataset, Department of Natural Resources and Conservation, analysis by Headwaters Economics.
32. Montana Board of Oil and Gas Conservation, "Elm Coulee," dataset, Department of Natural Resources and Conservation, analysis by Headwaters Economics.
33. British Petroleum, "Prudhoe Bay Fact Sheet," August 2006, http://dec.alaska.gov/spar/perp/response/sum_fy06/060302301/factsheets/060302301_factsheet_PB.pdf.
34. Oil and Gas Division, North Dakota Industrial Commission, Presentation to North Dakota Oil Gas and Coal Producing Counties, October 6, 2011.
35. Headwaters Economics, *How States Return Revenue to Local Governments from Unconventional Oil Extraction*, January 2014, http://headwaterseconomics.org/wphw/wp-content/uploads/state-energy-policies-report.pdf.
36. "What is the current severance tax rate for oil and gas produced in North Dakota?," Oil and Gas Frequently Asked Questions, Office of State Tax Commissioner, State of North Dakota, http://www.nd.gov/tax/misc/faq/oilgas/#Question1.
37. The "working interest" is the share of total production from a well retained by the drilling company while the "nonworking interest" is the share of production retained by the land or mineral right owner. The working interest and nonworking interest shares pay different severance tax rates to the state (9 percent and 14.8 percent respectively). Assuming the nonworking interest owner retains 16.67 percent of the production from a well, the weighted average severance tax rate applied to total well production is 10.4 percent. Montana Legislative Fiscal Division, *Oil and Gas Production Tax, November 2014*. http://leg.mt.gov/content/Publications/fiscal/Oil-Gas/Oil-Gas-Combined.pdf.
38. "Oil Extraction Tax Incentive Becomes Ineffective November 1, 2009," Office of the Tax Commissioner, State of North Dakota, http://www.nd.gov/tax/oilgas/pubs/horizontalnewwellmemo.pdf?20130807121541.
39. Mark J. Kaiser, "Modeling the Horizontal Well Severance Tax Exemption in Louisiana," *Energy* 40, no. 1 (April 2012): 410–27.
40. BBC Research & Consulting, *Northwest Colorado Socioeconomic Analysis*.
41. "2013–15 Oil and Gas Tax Revenue Allocation Flowchart," North Dakota Legislative Council, http://www.legis.nd.gov/files/resource//15.9055.01000.pdf?20150507163728.

42. Jennifer Oldham, "Montana Towns Struggle with Oil Boom Cost as Dollars Flee," *Bloomberg Business Week*, October 9, 2013, http://www.bloomberg.com/news/articles/2013-10-10/montana-towns-struggle-with-oil-boom-cost-as-dollars-flee.html.
43. Ronald A. Wirtz, "Saving for a Rainy, Oil-Free Day," *Fedgazette*, Federal Reserve Bank of Minneapolis, October 13, 2013, 12–15, http://minneapolisfed.org.
44. Montana Petroleum Association, "Issue Brief: Tax Picture for the Oil and Gas Industry in Montana," 2012, http://www.montanapetroleum.org/assets/PDF/articlesReports/MPAIssueBriefs-TaxBackgroundInformation.pdf; Kaiser, "Modeling the Horizontal Well Tax Exemption."
45. This essay does not intend to predict the location of future development. The potential for developing renewable energy resources to support utility projects relates to the quality of the resource, naturally, but many other factors as well, such as transmission access and demand. Still, this case study emphasizes the overlap between struggling remote rural areas in the West and high-quality renewable energy resources.
46. Haggerty, Haggerty, and Rasker, "Uneven Local Benefits of Renewable Energy."
47. See the Strategic Investment Program website at http://www.oregon4biz.com/Oregon-Business/Tax-Incentives/SIP/ and specifically the tax-treatment worksheet: http://www.oregon4biz.com/assets/docs/SIPexample.pdf. Additional information provided by planner Susie Anderson, Gillam County, Oregon, and assessor Ross Turney, Sherman County, Oregon.
48. Bryan Horwath, "Whiting VP: ND Should Cut Oil Tax by Half," *Dickinson Press*, September 26, 2013; Craig Giammona, "Big Oil's Alaska Problem," *Fortune*, July 24, 2013.
49. Zheng Lingwen and Mildred Warner, "Business Incentive Use among U.S. Local Governments: A Story of Accountability and Policy Learning," *Economic Development Quarterly* 24, no. 4 (November 2010): 325–36.
50. Timothy J. Bartik, "Solving the Problems of Economic Development Incentives," *Growth and Change* 36, no. 2 (Spring 2005): 139–66.
51. Ujjayant Chakravorty, Shelby Gerking, and Andrew Leach, "State Tax Policy and Oil Production," in *U.S. Energy Tax Policy*, ed. Gilbert E. Metcalf (Cambridge: Cambridge University Press, 2011), 305–37; Shelby Gerking, William Morgan, Mitch Kunce, and Joe Kerkvliet, *Mineral Tax Incentives, Mineral Production and the Wyoming Economy*, Report to the Mineral Tax Incentives Subcommittee, Wyoming State Legislature, December 2000, http://www.eadiv.state.wy.us/mtim/StateReport.pdf.
52. Federal tax policies, including investment and production tax credits, clearly drive renewable-energy development; however, these policies affect federal income-tax liability and reduce, at meaningful scales, the cost of renewable-energy electricity contracts. Metcalf, *U.S. Energy Tax Policy*.
53. American Wind Energy Association, personal communication with the author, February 2013.

54. Western Governors' Association, *10-Year Energy Vision: Goals & Objectives*, Denver, June 2013, http://westgov.org/reports/309-energy.
55. Headwaters Economics, *Fossil Fuel Extraction;* Michael O'Hare and Debra R. Sanderson, "Fair Compensation and the Boomtown Problem," *Urban Law Annual; Journal of Urban and Contemporary Law* 14 (January 1977): 101–33.
56. Kevin Hackworth, "Importance of Timber-Related Revenues to Local Governments in Oregon and the Effects of Forests in Oregon on Property Tax Rates" (PhD diss., Oregon State University, 1989).
57. Chip Brown, "North Dakota Went Boom," *New York Times Magazine*, February 3, 2013.
58. Robin Boadway, and Michael Keen, "Theoretical Perspectives on Resource Tax Design," in *The Taxation of Petroleum and Minerals: Principles, Problems and Practice*, ed. Philip Daniel, Michael Keen, and Charles McPherson (New York: Routledge, 2010), 13.

The New Natural Resource Economy

A Framework for Rural Community Resilience

MICHAEL HIBBARD AND SUSAN LURIE

Introduction

One of the greatest challenges facing rural communities in the early twenty-first century is their declining socioeconomic condition. It is a concern across the developed world. According to the United Nations, the population of the world's more developed countries was about evenly divided between urban and rural residents in 1950; it is less than 25 percent rural today and is projected to drop to under 15 percent by 2050.

Paralleling the global trend, the rural population of the United States has declined from a little more than one third of the total in 1950 to about 15 percent in 2012.[1] The decline in the rural population has been accompanied by socioeconomic decline. For example, a study of 176 Australian regions between 1976 and 1991 found substantial differences in income and wealth across the rural/urban divide, and a comparative study of the United States and Japan found that in both countries, poverty has become the norm in communities where the economic base relies on *primary production*, which is defined as extracting or harvesting products from the earth. In the United States specifically, the gap in earnings per job between metropolitan and nonmetropolitan workers was 26.3 percent in 1969; by 2008, it had increased to 32.9 percent. Moreover, the median household income in rural U.S. counties is less than two-thirds that of urban households, and the median value of a rural home is less than half that of an urban one.[2]

Not all rural communities are in decline, of course. Those located in amenity-rich areas have become centers for tourism, recreation, retirement, and long-distance commuting and are experiencing unprecedented growth in population and wealth. But the economy of most rural areas centers on primary production, the generation of raw material and basic foods. The associated activities include agriculture (both subsistence and commercial), mineral extraction, forestry, fishing, and quarrying. Packaging and processing the raw materials or foodstuffs are also considered part of primary production.[3] With the exception of a few places experiencing oil and gas booms, rural areas dependent on primary production are struggling.

Historically rural communities were tied economically to primary activities. However, since World War II, the increasing dominance of commodity production—the industrialized approach to agriculture and natural resource management, including specialization, standardization, and consolidation to heighten efficiency—has transformed the rural economy by disconnecting primary producers from rural communities: commodity production encourages direct links between producers and urban centers, bypassing the rural communities that were once essential as transportation, processing, and supply hubs. Thus, many rural communities have been severed from the larger economy and made economically redundant. They are searching for new economic activities to fill the gap left by this transformation in primary production.

Recent developments in environmental planning and resource management are creating an important opportunity. A range of innovative ideas have emerged during the last twenty years—watershed restoration, community forestry, sustainable and unique agriculture, natural resource–based products, and payments for ecosystem services, to mention several examples—focused on producing environmentally sustainable agriculture and managing natural resources. They have important socioeconomic implications for the rural communities where these activities are carried out. They may constitute the beginnings of one element of a new rural economic base, a *new natural resource economy* (NNRE) that can help diversify the economies of rural communities while also protecting and enhancing their environmental, social, and cultural assets.

Although many of the constituent components of the NNRE have received a good deal of attention, there has been no overarching analysis, no attempt to map the whole territory. The activities and businesses that comprise the NNRE may not be new; what *is* new is considering them collectively as an emerging economic sector, one that can help diversify rural economies and increase local resilience as a complement to the traditional natural resource economy. This essay discusses the NNRE as a discrete economic sector and identifies barriers to its development, based on a scoping survey conducted in Oregon in early 2011 along with case studies of two rural communities.

The Rural Dilemma

As a starting point, it is useful to describe what it means to be rural. The myriad definitions advanced by economists, historians, and other observers boil down to two components. The first is physical. It includes settlement patterns (low population density, small size, closeness to nature) and economic base (primary production). The second element of being rural is sociocultural, demonstrating particular values and kinds of social relationships such as neighborliness and self-sufficiency. The shifting rural economy threatens both of these essential elements of rural communities.

The economic history of rural communities in industrialized nations broadly parallels that of cities. The industrial revolution shaped agriculture and natural resource extraction in much the same way it shaped manufacturing. Prior to industrialization, both urban and rural areas were characterized by small, individually owned operations—craft-based workshops for urban manufacturing, and small farms, timber lots, and fishing boats in the rural economy. The technological advances of industrialization brought specialization, vertical integration, scientific management, and mass production to agriculture and resource extraction as well as to manufacturing.

Initially small towns and rural communities served the needs of primary producers. However, as modern commodity production intensified, the substitution of capital for labor, product specialization, larger operations, and consolidated ownership vastly increased output at the expense of labor. Essentially contemporary commodity production takes fewer farmers, loggers, miners, and ranchers to process more wheat, timber, minerals, and beef. Along with improvements in transportation and communication, modern commodity production has disconnected primary producers from the local communities with which they once had a mutually dependent and beneficial relationship.

Since the rise of modern commodity production, poverty rates have consistently become higher in rural than in urban areas, primarily because of the new economic characteristics, especially labor conditions such as seasonality and piece-rate pay. Rural residents accept the reduced standard of living associated with commodity production because they value both the physical and sociocultural qualities of rural life—low population density, primary production, and closeness to nature, as well as other rural influences on their lives. Thus, many rural communities are seeking ways to rebuild their economic base around agriculture and natural resources. They are searching for new ways of thinking about and using natural resources: a new natural resource economy.

Multifunctional Landscapes and Community Resilience

There has been an important convergence recently between scholars, policy makers, and practitioners in community development on the one hand, and those involved with environmental planning and natural resource management on the other. It began with the observation that the way rural landscapes are used has shifted. Nature is the key asset of most rural communities—timber, water, soil, and minerals but also wildlife habitat and recreational opportunities. Commodity production manages nature with a principal—some would say exclusive—emphasis on the production of food, fiber, lumber, and other products. The decline of commodity production as the economic base for rural communities is fostering new thinking about the human uses of rural space. The dominant use of rural landscapes for production has moved toward a more complex and often overlapping mix of uses—production, consumption, and protection—that has been called *multifunctionality*.[4]

Multifunctionality has important implications for rural communities. Using the resource base for more than commodity production enables rural economies to become more diverse. It also enables uses that support the environmental as well as the economic health of the local community. For example, evidence is growing of the local socioeconomic benefits of ecosystem restoration. We found that every dollar in administrative support that local watershed councils received from the Oregon Watershed Enhancement Board brought an additional $5.09 to the local economy. A fuels reduction program in five southwestern national forests generated 500 jobs in 2005. More generally, each $1 million invested in forest or watershed restoration generates between 15.7 and 23.8 jobs and $2.1 and $2.4 million dollars for the local economy. All portions of the local economy benefit as investment dollars circulate: multipliers have been calculated from 1.4 to 2.4, depending on the exact nature of the restoration project.[5]

Payment for ecosystem services is also growing in importance. For instance, using natural hydrological processes such as water filtration and purification, flow regulation, erosion and sediment control, and habitat provision has been shown to reduce capital, operation, and maintenance costs for water utilities and their customers.

The consolidation and vertical integration that characterize commodity production in agriculture have also stimulated new ways of using resources. In the well-known case of meat production, four packers (Tyson, ConAgra, Cargill, and Farmland) control more than 80 percent of the North American beef market. Many producers of grass-fed beef have emerged in response, from the family-owned, but gigantic, 150,000-acre Hearst Ranch on the central California coast, to marketing co-ops such as Country Natural Beef and Tallgrass Beef Company, to individual ranches around the country. In managing their "working landscapes" to meet the U.S. Department of Agriculture (USDA) certification requirement that grass-fed cattle receive only grass and forage, these operators must also address such issues as soil and water conservation and protection of wildlife habitat.

This is an example of the "agriculture of the middle," in contrast to either commodity production or very small-scale operations such as community-sponsored agriculture farms (CSAs) and roadside stands. Industrial-scale commodity production largely bypasses local and regional economics, importing from urban suppliers and exporting to global markets. Very small producers—even considered in together—do not make a significant contribution to the local or regional economic base. The agriculture of the middle generally targets regional markets; does business with local and regional suppliers, processors, and wholesalers; and is large enough to impact the regional economy.[6]

Consistent with multifunctionality, environmental restoration, ecosystem services, and the agriculture of the middle are efforts to build on an expanded concept of the potential of rural landscapes and their resources to support communities, opening the door for the NNRE. The NNRE views rural regions and their resources as long-term assets rather than raw material for production. It draws on them for production, consumption, and protection that utilize natural resources in ways that sustain them economically and socially while restoring and safeguarding the ecosystems that are the foundations of the goods and services provided by the local economy. Its practical purpose is to build a more diverse local economy and thus a more resilient community.

Until quite recently, a healthy natural resource–based community was thought to be stable. The typical example is the forest community, where the local mill is supplied with timber managed for even flow and sustained yield. But the experience of the last quarter century shows commodity production is *un*stable, destabilizing the economies of communities tied to it. Thus, as thinking about resource management has moved away from commodity production, ideas about the stability of community socioeconomic health have altered.

Scholars and practitioners have recognized that change is ever present and long-term stability is unattainable—for communities as well as industries. Rather than stability, they seek to promote community resilience, the ability to absorb change in ways that preserve or enhance essential functions, structure, and identity. A resilient community is active in developing and using the necessary resources to advance its well-being. A resilient community exhibits a well-developed and well-balanced mix of economic, social, and environmental capital and a diverse local economy that continuously generates new sources of income and jobs to replace those being lost.

Resilience in a local rural economy is characterized by three qualities:

1. The local economy thrives on trade. It exports goods and/or services out of the local area that return revenue for reinvestment. Commodity production sells goods outside the area, but the proceeds do not flow back; rather, they go to outside suppliers, processors, and distributors. The agriculture of the middle also produces goods to trade, but the revenue from exports flows back to local firms.

2. The local economy engages in import replacement. Some of the revenue generated by exports is invested to produce goods and services locally, replacing those that were formerly imported. If the new products are sufficiently successful, they can also find markets outside the local area, becoming part of trade and generating additional revenue.
3. The local economy plugs the leaks—makes sure that needed goods and services are locally available through a combination of retail and subsistence production by people for their own use. This process minimizes outflow of capital to purchase consumer goods and services.

Working together, multifunctionality and economic resilience reveal that the NNRE may be a way for rural communities that have lost their economic base in natural resources and/or agriculture to move forward. To understand economic innovation and community change, we need to examine why new firms emerge, why existing firms develop new products and adopt new technology, and what policies can spur them to do more. Empirical research is needed to understand NNRE fully—what it is and what hinders its development. As a start, we conducted a web-based scoping survey across rural Oregon, supplemented by case studies in two rural communities.

Methods

We invited rural community leaders across Oregon to respond electronically to a set of open-ended questions about several aspects of their local economy. We specifically asked them about new ways people in their community have found to generate income from local natural resources and to identify barriers to local businesses starting and expanding. We field-tested the questions with people involved in economic development in three different rural settings. Our sample consisted of 340 community leaders participating in the ongoing statewide rural development program of an Oregon nonprofit organization. We posted the questionnaire on Google Survey and contacted participants by e-mail, inviting them to go to the site and complete it. After one week, we sent a reminder. We received fifty-nine responses, including at least one from every county in Oregon.

The survey gives a clear sense of the scope of NNRE activities in rural Oregon communities. However, to understand the multifunctional nature of the NNRE, it is helpful to examine the processes in practice. We therefore conducted case studies in two rural Oregon communities. In each place, we held semistructured interviews lasting from one to one and a half hours. Prior to the interviews, we provided a summary of the survey results. We asked participants to comment on the results in relation to their communities and add any information they perceived as important.

We specifically asked them to react to the NNRE categories on the survey, identifying the ones that existed locally and those that did not, including whether there might be an opportunity to develop them. We also asked them to name activities unique to their local area that did not appear in the survey.

Results: NNRE in Practice

The results are presented in three parts: an inventory of the types of currently operating NNRE enterprises, case studies, and policy/program considerations.

Inventory

Forty-seven of the fifty-nine respondents (80 percent) said they knew NNRE businesses in their communities. They reported an extensive range of activities. We have organized the types of currently operating enterprises into the three multifunctional categories of production, consumption, and preservation/protection.

The following table summarizes the NNRE activities in rural Oregon communities. As we have already noted, not all of these business types are new; however, many are. What is new is thinking strategically about the NNRE as an emerging economic alternative. The NNRE offers significant possibilities to diversify rural economies and increase local resilience.

Case Studies

To help rural communities make the most of the NNRE's potential, it is important to understand the range of businesses it comprises and their multifunctional nature, as well as policy and program needs. We examined NNRE in specific landscapes by conducting case studies in contrasting contexts in two rural Oregon communities.

Grant County is an isolated area in eastern Oregon. It is about ninety miles from the nearest interstate onramp and has no bus, rail, or commercial air service. It encompasses an area of about 4,500 square miles, and the

Types of Currently Operating NNRE Enterprises in Oregon

Production (a mix of traditional and newer forms of agricultural and forest output)	Farming/ranching • Native plant nurseries, raising plants for habitat restoration • Sustainably produced food products—including meat, milk, cheese, eggs, fruits and vegetables—sold locally and in metropolitan areas for household, restaurant, and institutional (schools, hospitals, etc.) use • Wine grapes and wine production • Herbs and seeds sold by catalog and online • Suppliers to producers of emerging products (e.g., grape growers and wineries) Forest products • Community-owned multiple-use forest • Post and pole manufacturers utilizing "waste" from thinning and wildfire mitigation activities (e.g., small-diameter logs and species such as western juniper, which have invaded historic rangeland habitats) • Utilizers of slash—biomass—both as hog fuel and by processing it into pellet fuel to generate heat and electricity for schools, hospitals, and homes Alternative energy • Utilization of plantation-grown hybrid poplar trees for electricity generation • Generation of geothermal heat—for state prisons, hospitals, and schools, as well as industrial, business, and residential users • Numerous biomass plants under construction • Numerous wind farms
Consumption (amenity-based landscape uses)	Ecotourism • River/paddle trails, including maps, haul-outs • Kayak companies • Mountain bike guides, hunting guides, fishing guides, hiking guides, birding guides, and horseback guides Harvesting firewood, mushrooms, berries, and other plant life from the forest for personal use (subsistence) Agritourism—farm and ranch stays
Restoration/ Protection (activities that reflect societal goals concerned with sustainability)	Watershed restoration Wildlife habitat protection and restoration Forest restoration Environmental education

population in 2010 was 7,445, down from a peak of about 8,200 thirty years earlier. Public lands, including portions of four national forests, account for more than 60 percent of the county's area. Population density is about 1.6 people per square mile, compared to about 39 people per square mile for Oregon as a whole.

Euro-American settlement of the area began with gold mining in the 1860s. Sheep ranching was prominent in the late nineteenth and early twentieth centuries. By the 1920s and 1930s, cattle ranching and timber harvesting and processing became the dominant economic activities. Commodity production in cattle and timber remain important.

However, production and profitability from both those industries have been in long-term decline since the 1980s. In 1970, earned income constituted three-quarters of total personal income in Grant County, and transfer payments were about 10 percent of the total. Currently, earned income is less than half of total personal income, and transfer payments are nearly 30 percent. Paralleling the shift in income source, per-capita income in Grant County in 1970 was about 90 percent of the U.S. average; today it is only about 75 percent.

Because Grant County is struggling to maintain an economic base, there is wide interest in development. The county employs an economic-development coordinator and has an active chamber of commerce and a grassroots organization, the Grant County Resource Enhancement Action Team (GREAT). As in most communities that have historically relied on natural resources, a segment of Grant County citizens feels strongly that the only hope for the local economy is revitalizing commodity production. However, another group argues that even if commodity production returned to historic high levels, changing markets and technology would block a return to high employment or income. They also contend that returning to commodity production is not politically feasible because of changing societal views of resource management, especially on the public lands that dominate Grant County. They promote new ways to think about and utilize natural assets—for the NNRE, though they do not call it that.

Three initiatives reflect this new way of thinking. The first is the effort to restore watersheds and forests. There has been substantial investment across the Pacific Northwest in recent years to recover salmon and steelhead populations. Stream restoration has been and will continue to be a major part of that effort.

Restoration projects aim to improve salmon and steelhead habitats and increase water quality and quantity, but they have important socioeconomic effects as well. One of the most active restoration locations is the upper Middle Fork John Day River, which bisects Grant County. Between 2007 and 2011, fifteen restoration projects were planned for the main channel of the upper Middle Fork, and twenty-two were scheduled for the tributaries, with a large number of additional projects of varying size to be implemented over the following ten years. It is estimated that twenty contracting firms were involved with these projects and brought $1,251,839 to Grant County in 2007 and $924,719 in 2008; in addition, more than sixty government, tribal, and nonprofit staff members are employed in restoration-related professional positions in Grant County.[7]

Forest restoration is less well developed in Grant County, but its potential is recognized. Blue Mountains Forest Partners (BMFP) was formed in 2006 with help from Sustainable Northwest, a statewide "eco-eco" (ecology-economy) group. It has included Grant County elected officials, conservation organizations, local forest producers and contractors, community residents and landowners, and representatives from tribal and federal land management agencies. The dual mission of BMFP is to enhance forest ecosystem health while creating jobs in and around the Malheur National Forest. One promising approach is wildfire mitigation.

Fuel loading in western forests, including the Malheur, has increased significantly with a consequent need for thinning to remove hazardous biomass and enhance forest ecosystem health. BMFP and others are highly interested in finding markets for the material removed from the forest. While BMFP cannot claim direct credit, an important example of what the organization has in mind is emerging in Grant County. This is the second initiative that embodies the NNRE approach.

The Malheur Lumber Company is the last operating mill in Grant County. In 2009, there were concerns that it, too, would close. In that year, the Oregon Business Development Department awarded the company a five-million-dollar grant for a facility to produce pellets and briquettes. In addition to preserving seventy-five existing jobs, it was projected that the facility would add between thirty and forty new jobs to the local economy. Supply will come from forest fuels. There is currently an oversupply of pellets nationally, so one concern is that the plant may struggle unless the market expands. In response, the local hospital and airport have retrofitted their heating systems to utilize Malheur Lumber's pellets. Local schools may also decide to buy pellets from the plant.

In a telling development, Malheur Lumber announced in August 2012 that it was mothballing the main sawmill—though the pellet mill would continue to operate—because of the lagging log supply from local public forests. A number of private landowners almost immediately offered to provide additional timber because of their concern that they would have no place to sell their wood if the mill closed. This is only a temporary solution, however. To sustain the sawmill and its seventy-five jobs, local residents must find a way to provide logs as well as biomass from public forests.

These 165 jobs—60 restoration, 75 saved mill ones, and 30 created—may not seem significant. However, as a proportion of the local labor force, it equals adding 22,000 jobs to the economy of the Portland metropolitan area. The implication is that the Grant County economy would likely have difficulty staffing a firm considered small in an urban area such as Portland—possibly only a hundred workers. What the community needs is a range of microbusinesses.

The third Grant County initiative that embodies the NNRE approach is beef cattle. Consolidation in the beef industry has left commodity producers in difficult economic straits. Some ranchers—in Grant County and elsewhere—have turned to producing more expensive grass-fed cattle. At least one is a member of the Country Natural Beef marketing cooperative. Other natural beef producers in the area include Strawberry Mountain Natural Beef and Field's Grassfed Beef. They have discovered that consumers willing to pay more for their beef also expect producers to pay attention to other resource management issues such as open-land grazing and watershed maintenance. The upshot is a multifunctional approach that promotes managing their ranches for production, consumption, and protection.

Confederated Tribes of the Umatilla Indian Reservation (CTUIR) is located in northeastern Oregon, adjacent to the town of Pendleton. Historically the Confederated Tribes—the Cayuse, Walla Walla, and Umatilla—occupied separate territories in the Columbia/Snake River Basin and the Blue Mountains. The reservation was established by treaty in 1855.

The tribes ceded 6.4 million acres of land in exchange for an agreement to live together in a permanent homeland. They retained hunting, fishing, gathering, grazing, and other traditional rights on the ceded lands.

Today the reservation encompasses about 270 square miles, and the CTUIR has 2,787 enrolled members, with about 1,500 living on or near the reservation. To put that in perspective, the population of Pendleton is 16,480 and that of surrounding Umatilla County is 75,889.

Like most Indian communities, CTUIR experienced a long period of deep impoverishment following confinement on the reservation. That began to change during the 1970s. Passage of the Indian Self-Determination Act of 1974 gave the tribes control of their planning and programs for the first time. The first CTUIR Overall Economic Development Plan (OEDP) was created in that year, and the first comprehensive plan was drawn up in 1979. Since then, CTUIR has built a viable tribal economy virtually from scratch.

Initially CTUIR invested in agriculture and related industries. However, as its 2009 OEDP comments, those "industries have not proven to be a sound economic base in recent years. When natural resources are commodities traded on the global market the pressures for mechanization are immense—profit margins are slim, and job creation is minimal."[8] Over the last twenty years, CTUIR's economic base has moved largely toward gaming/tourism and, to a lesser extent, other tribal enterprises such as retail and land development. CTUIR now provides more than 1,300 jobs, and the unemployment rate among tribal members living on or near the reservation has gone from an estimated 60 percent in the early 1970s to about 12 percent today, which is comparable to the rate of Umatilla County as a whole. Umatilla County's per-capita income is 83.4 percent of Oregon's, while CTUIR's is 57 percent of the state's average; the lower income is mitigated somewhat by the important role of subsistence activities (hunting, fishing, and foraging for berries, camas roots, and mushrooms) in the tribes' culture.

Its success with what can be described as conventional economic development has given the CTUIR room to ask in the 2009 OEDP, "How do we meet our economic needs while protecting our values?" The tribes' answer is *economic sovereignty*, which is defined as "expanding the Tribes' economic choices in a resource-constrained environment."[9]

The overall CTUIR notion of economic sovereignty is based on trying to gain more control over the reservation economy—by diversifying beyond depending on gaming/tourism, for example, or better understanding and capitalizing on competitive advantages. Some ideas are fairly predictable, such as supporting small business start-ups and expansions and developing a workforce.

However, other components seem directly to embody CTUIR values of responsibility and stewardship. Some examples are

1. to increase the number of acres of the Tribal Farm Enterprise that are farmed using no-till practices;
2. to expand and strengthen the business practices of the Tribal Native Plant Nursery that was created by the CTUIR Wildlife Program to capitalize on opportunities for native-plant restoration by federal and state agencies; and
3. to expand CTUIR involvement in generating renewable energy within the homeland (reservation and ceded lands).

As well as embodying CTUIR cultural, social, and environmental values, these projects also exemplify the NNRE by reflecting a multifunctional view of landscapes. However, the most interesting multifunctional activity engaged in by the CTUIR is restoring First Foods. In CTUIR creation belief, the creator asked the foods, "Who will take care of the People?" Salmon was the first to promise; then other fish lined up behind salmon. Next came deer, camas, and huckleberries. Each First Food represents groupings of ecologically related ones. The traditional First Food serving ritual is based on this order and is meant to remind people of the promise the foods made and the people's reciprocal responsibility to use and take care of the foods respectfully.

The longevity of these foods and serving rituals across many generations indicates their cultural and nutritional value to the CTUIR community. First Foods provide an organizing principle for resource management: the CTUIR Department of Natural Resources has designed policies, population- and habitat-management goals, and actions around restoring and protecting First Foods by maintaining water quality and quantity, riparian habitat for fish, and upland environment for deer, camas, and huckleberries. Through this approach, the Department of Natural Resources confirms the

Types of NNRE Enterprises in Case-Study Communities

Production	Pellet mill (Grant County)
	Grass-fed beef (Grant County)
	No-till farming (CTUIR)
	Native plant nursery (CTUIR)
	Alternative energy (CTUIR)
Consumption	First Foods (CTUIR)
Restoration/Protection	Watershed and forest restoration (Grant County)

simultaneous economic (subsistence), ecological, and social importance of these resources to the tribes.

What we see, then, is that the CTUIR engages in active resource planning and management, including aspects of the NNRE, on the reservation and its ceded lands. It does so not because of economic pressures, which it has largely dealt with over the last twenty years, but for cultural reasons.

The case study findings are summarized in the table above. As with the inventory, the case studies show a wide range of activities, and most are in sustainable forms of production. Together, they also indicate a potential for rural communities to add to their local range of enterprises by using the NNRE as an economic-development strategy.

Policy/Program Considerations

The NNRE is not an alternative to the traditional natural resource approach; rather, it is a complement. However, it is a critical complement because it bolsters rural economies in culturally and environmentally healthy ways. To thrive, the NNRE needs appropriate policy support. As one of our interviewees put it, "Economic development on the frontier is very different than in more populated areas in terms of inventory and use"—that is, the assets that are available and the ways they can be used. Rural communities rely heavily on natural capital, in contrast to urban settings, which depend significantly on intellectual and financial capital for business development. Additionally rural businesses are generally very small—sole proprietorships are typical; half-a-dozen employees verge on medium sized.

Given those realities, we asked survey respondents and case-study interviewees about policy/program issues that require attention to promote the NNRE. They said the most important are these:

1. Prevailing definitions of small business—less than 100 or less than 500 workers, depending on the agency—that shape access to capital through federal and state agencies are not appropriate for rural communities. Different lending criteria and loan amounts and terms that respond to the circumstances of very small businesses are needed.
2. Oregon's rural zoning regulations generally assume large-scale commodity production—high-volume, low-value production on large tracts of land. Minimum lot size is 80 acres for farmland and 160 acres for rangeland. This zoning is not designed to accommodate small-lot, high-value production—for example, specialty crops such as nursery plants, berries, and Christmas trees. As a result, when commodity production becomes less viable for financial and/or environmental reasons, the land is converted to hobby ranches, private hunting preserves, and high-end resorts, rather than for multifunctional use that will increase the health of the local community.
3. Similar regulatory barriers to small-scale production exist. Often licensing fees are prohibitive. Also health and safety regulations are designed for very-high-volume mass production and do not make sense for small businesses and/or specialty production.
4. A major barrier to start-ups, especially those with new products, is the lack of markets. Governments can assist in increasing demand for NNRE products. For example, federal and state governments can require building projects that receive public funds or that they regulate to consider biomass as a heat source.
5. Rather than searching outside the U.S. for green industry, state governments can help rural communities by supporting existing and potential NNRE activities.

Conclusion

This chapter has tried to describe the NNRE as an economic alternative and identify the barriers to its development. Current thinking about rural development encourages communities to move away from using natural resources and to recruit new businesses like light manufacturing and call centers and new populations such as retirees. Our research indicates that

NNRE Contributions to Local Rural Economies

Multifunctional Activity	Export	Import Replacement	Plugging Leaks
Production			
Scoping Survey Results			
• Farming/ranching	•	•	•
• Forest products	•	•	•
• Alternative energy	•	•	
Case study results			
• Pellet mill (Grant County)	•	•	
• Grass-fed beef (Grant County)	•		
• No-till farming (CTUIR)	•		
• Native plant nursery (CTUIR)	•		
• Alternative energy (CTUIR)	•		
Consumption			
Scoping Survey Results			
• Ecotourism	•		
• Forest harvesting for personal use		•	•
• Agritourism	•		
Case Study Results			
• First Foods (CTUIR)		•	•
Restoration and Protection			
Scoping Survey Results			
• Watershed restoration	•		
• Wildlife habitat protection/restoration	•		•
• Forest restoration	•		•
• Environmental education	•		•
Case Study Results			
• Watershed and forest restoration (Grant County)	•		•

rather than moving away from using natural resources, rural communities are finding new ways to develop them. We identified a broad range of activities that suggest the NNRE is an emerging economic alternative that can help diversify rural economies by producing new goods and services to export as well as increasing local resilience by generating new income and jobs and strengthening self-sufficiency.

The table above summarizes the ways that NNRE activities identified in the survey and case studies contribute to the three broad requirements of every healthy local rural economy: producing goods and services that are exported out of the local region and generate revenue; producing goods and services locally that were formerly imported into the local region; and plugging economic leaks through retail and subsistence.

The times seem ripe for the NNRE. Rural communities searching for pragmatic approaches to reinvigorating local economies are finding rural entrepreneurs who have identified opportunities to utilize resources in new ways that preserve locally important natural and cultural assets. However, the barriers to develop NNRE enterprises further need more exploration. In general—as our respondents and interviewees pointed out—state policies and programs need to acknowledge the special needs of rural communities and the unique circumstances facing rural entrepreneurs. They encounter different problems than their urban counterparts in accessing capital and markets, finding appropriate sites for their operations, and negotiating regulations.

This study only opens the subject. All of these issues need in-depth investigation to generate the understanding necessary to design effective state policies and programs to support the NNRE. Perhaps most in need of better understanding is the key asset that underpins NNRE: nature or natural capital—water, soil, timber, minerals, and wildlife. Managing natural capital so that it can be used without being used up—providing jobs and wealth today and into the indefinite future—is the promise of the NNRE. The challenge is finding ways to achieve it.

Notes

Research for this chapter was supported by a grant from the Ford Family Foundation, Roseburg, Oregon.

1. There are a variety of "official" U.S. definitions of *rural,* including those of the Census Bureau, the Office of Management and Budget, and the Department of Agriculture (USDA). All three produce somewhat different estimates of the rural population. We have used the USDA's Economic Research Service definition and population estimates.
2. D. J. Walmsley and H. C. Weinand, "Is Australia Becoming More Unequal?" *Australian Geographer* 28, no. 1 (1997): 69–88; Dana R. Fisher, "Resource Dependency and Rural Poverty: Rural Areas in the United States and Japan," *Rural Sociology* 66, no. 2 (June 2001): 181–202; Emery N. Castle, JunJie Wu, and Bruce A. Weber, "Place Orientation and Rural-Urban Interdependence," *Applied Economic Perspectives and Policy* 33, no. 2 (Summer 2011): 179–204; Maureen Kilkenny, "Urban/Regional Economics and Rural Development," *Journal of Regional Science* 50, no. 1 (February 2010): 449–70.

3. Economists contrast primary production with secondary production, which manufactures goods, and tertiary production, which creates services.
4. For more on multifunctionality, see John Holmes, "Impulses toward a Multifunctional Transition in Rural Australia," *Journal of Rural Studies* 22, no. 2 (April 2006): 142–60; and Geoff Wilson, "Multifunctional 'Quality' and Rural Community Resilience," *Transactions of the Institute of British Geographers* 35, no. 3 (July 2010): 364–81.
5. Michael Hibbard and Susan Lurie, "Some Community Socioeconomic Benefits of Watershed Councils: A Case Study from Oregon," *Journal of Environmental Planning and Management*, 49, no. 6 (November 2006): 891–908; Evan E. Hjerpe and Yeon-Su Kim, "Economic Impacts of Southwestern National Forest Fuels Reductions," *Journal of Forestry* 106, no. 6 (August 2008): 311–16; Max Nielsen-Pincus and Cassandra Moseley, "The Economic Impacts of a Sustained Program of Forest and Watershed Restoration," *Restoration Ecology* 21, no. 2 (March 2013): 207–14.
6. For more information on agriculture of the middle, see Agriculture of the Middle, http://www.agofthemiddle.org/; and Center for Integrated Agricultural Systems, University of Wisconsin-Madison, http://www.cias.wisc.edu/category/ag-middle/.
7. Michael Hibbard and Susan Lurie, *Socioeconomic Measures for Intensively Monitored Watersheds: The Middle Fork John Day Effectiveness Monitoring Project*, Report for the Oregon Watershed Enhancement Board (Eugene: University of Oregon Institute for Policy Research and Innovation, October 29, 2010), http://www.ir.library.oregonstate.edu/xmlui/bitstream/handle/1957/29051/IPRI%20IMW%20Final%20Report%202010.pdf?sequence1.
8. CTUIR, *Economic Sovereignty: Confederated Tribes of the Umatilla Indian Reservation Overall Economic Development Plan 2010–2015* (Pendleton, OR: Confederated Tribes of the Umatilla Indian Reservation, 2009), 3.
9. Ibid., 2.

LAND USE IN THE RURAL WEST

The struggle over the way federal lands should be used, and who should make those decisions, stretches back to territorial days in much of the rural West. It flared during the Sagebrush Rebellion of the 1970s, when ranchers, miners, loggers, and other natural-resource users pressed their states to take over federal lands, especially in the Great Basin. The Sagebrush Rebellion faded away, but questions about controlling and using federal lands have, if anything, become more complex with the rise of environmentalism and recreational tourism.

Leisl Carr Childers personalizes these conflicts in her study of the Fallinis, a Nevada ranching family. The Fallinis graze their cattle on the public domain. During and after World War II, their livelihood was threatened when the government turned part of the area into a bombing range and later tested atomic weapons nearby. Now they are challenged by the Bureau of Land Management's commitment to multiple use of the land, which would open it to recreational users and protect the wild horses that compete with the Fallinis' cattle for precious water and grass. Whether multiple use can actually serve everyone's needs remains an open question.

The Goshute Indians of Skull Valley, Utah, are the subject of David Rich Lewis's essay. Challenged by depopulation and shrinking economic opportunities, the leaders of the Skull Valley band wanted to allow storage of nuclear waste on the reservation. They were opposed by some members of the tribe, who saw the proposal as a threat to Goshute culture, and stymied by the state of Utah, which hypocritically and paternalistically undermined their plan. In the case of the Goshutes, it became clear that even those who own the land cannot really control it.

The Angry West

Understanding the Sagebrush Rebellion in Rural Nevada

LEISL CARR CHILDERS

The Sagebrush Rebellion crashed onto the national stage in the fall of 1979 with radical claims about individual rights and the callousness of federal land management. Rumblings of rebellion had bubbled beneath the American West's political surface since 1976 and the passage of the Federal Land Policy and Management Act (FLPMA), but it was not until September 1979 that it hit the national press in full color. Scooping their rival weekly periodical *Time*, *Newsweek* devoted its September 17 cover and lead article to the "angry West."

The image by photographer Ed Gallucci that graced the front of the issue featured a glaring, denim-jacketed cowboy in a felt western hat, creased the way cattle tycoons wore them. Armed with a rifle slung over his saddle and mounted on a sorrel horse with a tidy star and stripe down its face, the cowboy personified the issue's subtitle: "Get off Our Backs, Uncle Sam." In the background, a skyscraper's glossy windows reflected the vivid blue glow of the late afternoon sky as if the cowboy were on the open range.[1]

The cover story, entitled "The Angry West vs. the Rest," began with an illustration by artist Roy Doty, captioned "The alienated frontier." It featured a map of the region with stylized industries and activities on public lands, such as power plants, oil drilling, mining, farming, recreation, and ranching. In the Pacific Northwest, green pine forests dominated the landscape; in the Southwest, migrant laborers tended irrigated fields, and suburban grids created a checkerboard of development. Cattle ranches dominated the Nevada, Idaho, Texas, and Nebraska landscape, and energy facilities marked by towering smokestacks belching white puffy columns dotted Utah, California, and northern Nevada, where Doty emblazoned the words "shale oil" on the side of a power plant. From Oklahoma to the Dakotas, Washington to California, and everywhere in between, signs read, "Keep Out—Federal Land." Cowboys, farmers, migrant workers, miners, and energy producers all stared at the signs obstructing their paths.[2]

Newsweek editor Tom Mathews began the piece:

> From remote ranches high up in the Rockies to corporate watering holes in the valleys down below to the long coast of the Pacific, a rebellion is brewing. Suddenly, the Old West has become the Angry West, a region racked by an increasingly bitter sense of isolation and political alienation. More and more, Westerners complain that a powerful absentee landlord, the Federal government, is regulating them to death; that a Congress dominated by Eastern interests is riding roughshod over their views on land and water; and that Jimmy Carter's new energy policies threaten to replay the rape of the old frontier. And with tempers ragged all around, the West is spoiling to fight back.

Mathews quoted Governors Richard D. Lamm of Colorado, Scott M. Matheson of Utah, Thomas L. Judge of Montana, Bruce E. Babbitt of Arizona, Robert List of Nevada, and a panorama of senators, representatives, mayors, lawyers, journalists, and educators, who all said the same thing: individual states could manage public lands better.[3]

The *Newsweek* issue captured some of the seething dissatisfaction many westerners felt about the changing political landscape of public lands management. The image on the cover was a last-minute invention based on an abrupt change in the issue's focus. Originally entitled "The New West," the issue's cover image, as conceived by the photographer, had the same cowboy—played by character actor William Wohrman—on a rearing horse in front of a city skyline. At the end of the photo shoot, Gallucci received word that the issue's title had changed. With very little information about the content of the lead article, he brought back the horse, found a rifle, and worked with Wohrman to portray an angry westerner. With a similar look to Robert Redford, Wohrman wore a glare that had a firm, but undeniable, "that's far enough, mister" element that stopped readers in their tracks. Gallucci's impression of the angry West, represented by a glaring cowboy with a rifle, certainly captured the spirit of the article.[4]

Unlike the photographer, Doty based his illustration on what he read in the accompanying article. Although he had never spent much time in the American West, he had a sense of the region through his experience on a New Mexico guest ranch close to the Mexican border. His portrayal of westerners engaged in a variety of economic enterprises that were located on and utilized the region's public lands and their befuddlement and disappointment when they encountered signs that prohibited their activities was cartoonish because of his style, but accurate.[5]

From their perspective on the eastern seaboard, Gallucci and Doty visually captured the essence of the debate. Westerners were mad because the economic activities they had normally engaged in on the region's public lands were being curtailed. Mathews's article told readers why—too much regulation—and explained what westerners wanted to do about it—turn management of public lands over to the states.

Yet if anyone from *Newsweek* had asked someone besides a western governor or other state official, the story might have read differently and the images might have looked even angrier. The politicians in Mathews's article embroidered generalizations and sound bites out of the actual circumstances many families, especially ranchers, faced in the 1970s American West. Westerners, particularly those from states such as Nevada that contained a large percentage of public lands, were indeed struggling to adapt to the new reality created by FLPMA. Crafted out of a decade's worth of reports and congressional hearings, FLPMA mandated the management of public lands according to multiple use, a policy that permitted a tangled web of different and often conflicting land uses, and declared that the federal government, via the Bureau of Land Management (BLM), would retain and administer the remaining public domain.

But since 1934 and the passage of the Taylor Grazing Act, the federal government by default had been doing exactly that anyway. So why did westerners feel angry about a situation that already existed, and did they really believe that states could manage public lands any better?

Fighting Words

In 1987, Helen L. Fallini, the matriarch of a prominent ranching family in Nye County, Nevada, sat down with oral historian Robert D. McCracken and discussed, among other things, the aftermath of the Sagebrush Rebellion. She encapsulated the ongoing difficulties she felt her family faced in ranching and grazing cattle on public lands in central Nevada by stating, "The thing I see about the whole thing is that if they would leave us alone, go ahead like they are now and let us run our own business, it would be fine. The BLM stepped in, and they have made it so damn miserable for a person to try to run stock of any kind, or do anything anymore.... The BLM has been nothing but a pain in the butt. No matter what you do, it's wrong to them."[6]

The Fallini family was fairly typical of western families—who relied upon access to public lands for their livelihood—in their frustration with the federal government. But they and a handful of other ranchers were unusual because they have been highly vocal in their opposition to federal land-use decisions they disagree with and have actively litigated against these decisions. More than most, the Fallinis' story has appeared in the public record.

The BLM bore the brunt of Helen Fallini's anger because the family's ranching operations required year-round access to public lands, and the BLM has historically administered the vast majority of that land in Nevada. Helen's son, Joe Fallini, has been known to keep a fire extinguisher in his office labeled "BLM Repellent" because, as reporter Keith Rogers put it, "It's symbolic of the Fallinis' decades of wrangling" with the agency.[7]

Helen Fallini's rhetoric about the government interfering in her family's ranch operations was typical of statements by many people in Nevada and other rural areas throughout the American West during the Sagebrush Rebellion. To them, the federal government, and the BLM specifically, had become barriers to their individual success. According to R. McGreggor Cawley, the Sagebrush Rebellion was a grassroots political response that was generated in 1979 to oppose the changing definition of conservation and the growing influence of environmental concerns in federal land-use decision making. The movement largely originated in Nevada but spread throughout the American West. James R. Skillen has defined the Sagebrush Rebellion as "a movement among western states to claim ownership of public lands, and more broadly, to challenge the federal government's growing regulatory role in public lands management." He indicated that there were actually several of these protests throughout the twentieth century after the passage of FLPMA.[8]

Yet Helen Fallini was only partially reacting to changing public lands policy and the increased environmental regulations on grazing enacted by the BLM. Her statement was far more complex than simply placing the responsibility for her ranch's success or failure at the feet of the federal government. She was articulating the frustration and confusion many rural residents felt in the second half of the twentieth century toward federal public lands policy. Embedded in her statement is a cultural reaction to the changing role of public lands in American society. Underneath Cawley and Skillen's statements about the changing political landscape of conservation, the growth of environmentalism, and the desire of western states to control more of the land within their boundaries were shifting ideas about the role of public lands within the nation's political and social economy. Helen Fallini felt these changes very poignantly because public lands and their management are the mechanisms that subject individual rural residents of the American West to national pressures and interests.

Ranchers comprised only a handful of the multiple users of public lands in the American West but represented the oldest group and the only one wholly dependent upon those lands for their livelihood. In central Nevada, where once Helen's family had grazed cattle on the public domain without governmental direction, nuclear testing, wild horse herds, recreational programs, and increasing environmental regulations now crowded public lands use. Where once the Fallinis and other ranchers had made the only consistent economic use of public lands in Nevada—an area generally described and derided as a useless wasteland—environmentalists, urban residents, and politicians had started to vilify them as poachers of public resources. The Fallinis had to compete with other individuals, groups, and government agencies for access to the rangeland their grandfather had used and almost exclusively controlled at the end of the nineteenth century.

Life at Twin Springs Ranch

The Fallini family's story provides an intimate look at these larger cultural and intellectual shifts because what happened to public lands in the American West directly and negatively affected their ranching operations. Their story begins in the late nineteenth century with the Italian immigrant

Giovanni Fallini in front of his home at Eden Creek, Nevada, about 1932. Photo courtesy of Helen Fallini, Nye County Town History Project, and Nye County History online.

Giovanni Batista Fallini. The young Giovanni arrived in Nevada in the 1870s from the alpine region of Europe disputed by Italy and Switzerland. He worked hauling freight for the charcoal kilns around the mining towns of Eureka and Tybo. By 1900, he had moved south to the Reveille mining district—a once-profitable gold and silver region established in 1866 that was experiencing a second boom—had a productive mill, and ran a small grocery store. He homesteaded 160 acres at Eden Creek and enlisted the help of fellow Italian immigrant and neighbor Abramo Arigoni from nearby Ox Spring to build a small stone house. Giovanni mined what he could and did any extra work he could get to earn money to buy cattle, building his herd one animal at a time.[9]

By the early 1930s, Giovanni's sons—William, Raymond, and Joseph (Helen's husband)—had helped their father amass a herd large enough to require full-time attention. The brothers moved the family's base of operations from Eden Creek a short distance north to Twin Springs. This became the center of the Fallinis' livestock range, from which they controlled their herds in the Kawich, Reveille, and Hot Creek Valleys. Most ranchers ran their livestock loosely over the then-unorganized rangeland; placing their headquarters well within the area where their cattle grazed allowed the Fallinis to protect range resources and maintain water supplies. Adding to their property, the family purchased Herman Reischke's land near Warm

Helen and Joe Fallini in Tonopah, Nevada, about 1935. Photo courtesy of Helen Fallini, Nye County Town History Project, and Nye County History online.

Springs and most of the defunct United Cattle and Packing Company's spread in the southern portion of Railroad Valley.

As one of the larger ranching operations in the area, the Fallinis owned multiple water rights, including major springs in the Kawich Range at Crystal Springs, around the Gila and Bellehelen Mines; at Bellehelen, Eden, and Little Meadows Creeks; and at the southern end of Railroad Valley, including Pyramid, Summer, Cedar, Warm and Twin Springs, and Hot and Warm Springs Creek. They also received numerous underground water rights that allowed them to develop a variety of wells for their livestock. These water rights allowed the Fallinis to control the neighboring public rangeland by precluding further homesteading and livestock grazing in the area.[10]

The Fallinis typically ran several thousand head of cattle each year, driving them to the shipping facilities in Tonopah until the advent of truck hauling in the late 1930s. Roundups were done on horseback, and branding, castrating, and other veterinary practices required several sets of hands and much manual labor to treat one calf at a time.

The ranch operated on a seasonal schedule, with calving beginning in late winter and early spring. The Fallinis conducted roundups in July to separate animals selected for sale and shipping from those the family kept until the following year. The remaining herds spent the rest of the summer

The Fallinis' Twin Springs ranch in the 1950s. Photo courtesy of Helen Fallini, Nye County Town History Project, and Nye County History online.

grazing on grassy ranges at cooler, higher elevations. Before the cold set in, the Fallinis gathered their cattle once more to wean the calves and move the herds onto winter range until calving began again the following year.

Winters proved tough if the weather was particularly cold and low temperatures lasted. The Fallinis had to keep the troughs and pipes they had constructed clear of ice to make sure the cattle had access to enough to drink. When feed ran short on the winter range, the family had to purchase hay to supplement the animals' food, an added expense each year they hoped to avoid.[11]

The Fallinis established Twin Springs and built their ranch at a time when the federal government was unsure what to do with the remaining unallocated and unreserved public lands. Between 1879 and 1933, three federal land commissions attempted to grapple with the status of this leftover land. Members of these commissions shared the expectation that the land had to be put to some kind of economic use. Land economist Richard T. Ely argued at the time, "Idle land is never neutral; it always places a burden on private or public owners." The unallocated and unreserved public domain was a source of dissatisfaction—even anxiety—for the federal

The Fallinis rounded up their cattle and drove them to Tonopah, where they were shipped on the Tonopah and Goldfield Railroad. Here cattle await shipping about 1939. Photo courtesy of Helen Fallini, Nye County Town History Project, and Nye County History online.

government and the nation as a whole, especially during the Progressive Era, when underutilization wasted resources as badly as overutilization. Ely's colleague, Benjamin H. Hibbard, criticized the federal government's short-term public lands planning and argued for a stable, comprehensive policy that regulated grazing and mineral development, the only consistent uses of the leftover public domain that he could envision. The recommendations of these land commissions conformed to the visions of both Ely and Hibbard.[12]

All three of the land commissions recognized the importance of using public lands for grazing. The 1934 Taylor Grazing Act codified this priority by making ranching a nationally acceptable use of public lands in lieu of privatization. Between 1935 and 1936, existing ranching operations helped organize the majority of the unallocated and unreserved public land into grazing districts. But the Fallini family and its neighbors in Nye County, Nevada, refused to organize officially under the grazing act. In 1936, the Fallinis, along with several neighboring ranchers, signed a petition requesting their ranches be excluded from organizing any grazing districts.[13]

In 1942, the Fallinis testified before Nevada Senator Pat McCarran's Committee on Public Lands, suggesting that they and their neighbors were suffering increasing hardship at the hands of the federal government and were better off governing the grazing range themselves. They argued that even the newly established Grazing Service had categorized their area as wasteland and maintained it was not worth the cost of administration. This group of ranchers formed the Central Nevada Livestock Association and worked diligently to avoid any federal oversight and additional costs. Many of them were fundamentally concerned that the act's litmus test that determined their range access would not recognize the open grazing system they had come to rely upon. In addition, the overhead cost of most ranchers in the area was so low and the profit margin so tight that even the smallest use fee would be problematic.[14]

The Changing Public Range

The 1940s marked a major change in the Fallinis' ranching operations. Nevada Senators Key Pittman and Pat McCarran and Representative James Scrugham had vigorously lobbied President Franklin Roosevelt to persuade the United States Army to establish a training base in the state. The creation of the Tonopah Bombing Range in 1940 was an important economic asset for Nevada, but it required certain cattle ranchers to give up access to some of the public grazing range they normally utilized. Nevada's congressional delegation sent notice to ranchers that they would have to make "satisfactory adjustments" to their grazing ranges. McCarran wanted to use the state's wealth of public lands to facilitate private development with federal dollars, and the rapidly expanding defense industry provided ample opportunity. Besides securing development of the Tonopah Bombing Range and the related growth of that community, the senator also paved the way for constructing the nation's largest magnesium plant just east of Las Vegas.[15]

The creation of this militarized space affected the Fallinis since their cattle grazed just on the other side of the bombing range's northern boundary, which ran along the Kawich Mountains. The Fallini brothers testified at the hearings on the impact of the range that although the family owned no patented land inside the area designated for the military, their major winter grazing area was inside its boundaries as were some structures, including water tanks, pipes, and some small buildings. The northern boundary of the bombing range also ran right through Cedar Pipeline at the south end of the Reveille Valley, where the Fallinis owned critical water rights. Several thousand of their cattle typically roamed what was to become the northern stretch of the Tonopah Bombing Range. The army considered the Fallinis' access to their winter grazing range unimportant in light of the national crisis produced by the United States' entry into World War II, but the family certainly did not agree. They felt that access to a crucial asset was about to be terminated.[16]

The Fallinis hoped that the army would let them continue their livestock operations on public lands and merely reduce their access to the herds to several times a year. But the army was disinclined to accommodate the ranchers because their safety and that of their cattle could not be assured. The Fallinis expressed willingness to continue running their cattle on the north end of the bombing range at their own risk because it would take an enormous effort to keep their livestock from drifting onto the restricted area. This situation was terribly impractical for both the Fallinis and the military; without miles of fencing and a dramatic increase in costly manpower, the family's cattle simply would continue to forage in the same area they always had until they met a natural barrier such as Pahute Mesa. The Fallini brothers and their neighbor, Jim Butler, complained to McCarran that the army was appropriating their land the same way they had stolen it from the Western Shoshones. William Fallini quipped that the Indians had starved and dryly stated, "I guess we will, too." Nevertheless, the military activated the Tonopah Bombing Range, and operations were in full swing by 1943.[17]

Frustrated, the Fallinis lost the southern part of their grazing range and struggled to keep their cattle off the bombing area. They also lost access to critical water at Cedar Pipeline. To compound matters, the newly created BLM and its director, Fred Johnson, the former commissioner of the now-defunct General Land Office, made it clear in 1946 that federal oversight was no longer optional on public rangeland. Newly appointed Secretary of the Interior Julius A. Krug supported this position and issued an ultimatum to the Fallinis and other ranchers in unorganized parts of Nye County to either organize in a grazing district or face higher fees under Section 15 of the act. The ranchers countered there was "no reason in the world why the government should force the stockmen using this twelve million acres of desert land to accept federal regulation." In their mind, there was "no doubt" they were making the "best possible use" of the land under the current arrangement. Ranchers suggested the land was worthless—"practically desert"—and most believed that once the federal government charged them for using "these desert acres," they would be forced out of business. They countered that the government was "receiving more in the form of income taxes; the state and the counties involved are receiving greater revenue, and more badly needed beef is being raised, than could possibly accrue to these varied interests under any form of control the government could devise."[18]

The Fallinis and other ranchers in central Nevada succeeded in delaying organization for several more years. However, other forces were pressuring the BLM to administer the unorganized rangeland directly. Motivation behind the push to create the last grazing district in Nevada also came from the Atomic Energy Commission (AEC), which needed to protect its newly established atomic testing program and ranchers in the area from the danger it potentially posed. In 1950, the AEC announced its intention to establish a permanent presence in central Nevada at Frenchman Flat in Nye County, considered by the government, atomic scientists, and the military to be the most isolated and favorable place for a continental nuclear test site. The new Nevada Proving Ground was enclosed within the Las Vegas Bombing and Gunnery Range to the south and the Tonopah Bombing and Gunnery Range to the north. Between the two ranges, the area spanning Tickaboo, Kawich, and Emigrant Valleys; Yucca, Frenchman, and Cactus Flats; Pahute Mesa; and as far north as Ralston, Big Smokey, Monitor, Stone Cabin, and Little Fish Lake Valleys was considered too dangerous for any civilians to occupy, especially during active testing.[19]

Operating predominantly in Frenchmen Flat—but posing potential hazard to ranchers in adjacent valleys, including Hot Creek, Railroad, Coal, Garden, White River, and Pahranagat—the AEC published notices warning of highly dangerous activities. Both the U.S. Air Force and the AEC were concerned about trespassers and announced publically that their safety could not be guaranteed. "Every possible effort," the AEC declared, "is being made to clear all persons and all livestock from the area." Establishing one last grazing district, which would abut—but not legally overlap—the military area was the surest way for the two agencies to remove trespassers, particularly ranchers, from the testing range. By the end of May 1951, Secretary of the Interior Oscar Chapman declared that "all factors were considered" but the "orderly and systematic use of the range" was more important and beneficial than allowing ranchers to administer the rangeland. Despite continued protest by the Fallinis and other ranchers in Nye County, the BLM approved organization of the last grazing district.[20]

The nation's continental nuclear testing program severely affected the Fallini family and other ranchers near the test site. They suffered the effects of radioactive fallout during the height of atmospheric testing during the 1950s. At Twin Springs, Helen Fallini was only thirty-five miles north of the test site and said the monitors sent by the AEC to measure radiation levels outside the testing area told her that radioactive fallout "wasn't supposed to hurt us in any way, shape or form."

But the AEC had not considered the outdoor conditions under which ranching routinely occurred. Helen said, "We got that fallout so heavily that it was unbelievable." She suffered from eye trouble she attributed to radiation and wondered, "Why is fallout harmful if it goes over Las Vegas and not harmful if it comes over here?" Her father-in-law, Giovanni, remarked that "if fallout isn't harmful... let it go wherever it wants to go." The Fallinis regularly witnessed fallout clouds from Frenchman and Yucca Flats rising above the mountains to the south. She watched her neighbors, Minnie Sharp and Madison Locke, lose their hair and suffer significant radiation burns. Joseph Fallini said the fallout cloud often completely engulfed everything, burning people and animals and killing birds. His account of radiation exposure ended up in the June 10, 1957, issue of *Life* magazine, along with images he took of his experiences. Joseph may have been the only civilian ever to capture an oncoming fallout cloud on camera.[21]

Restrictions imposed by military training, nuclear testing, and federal grazing oversight were not the last public lands issues facing the Fallini family. By the mid-1960s, the BLM had fully embraced multiple use as a land management tool meant specifically to include recreation in addition to wildlife and grazing management. Unlike his predecessors, Secretary of the Interior Stewart L. Udall defined multiple use as the proper development and use of public lands resources and not necessarily the "combination of uses that will give the greatest dollar return or the greatest unit output."[22]

The Fallinis and other ranching families were not opposed to multiple use provided it remained consistent with the "customary" use of public lands in which they believed ranching had provided the best and highest use. But the 1964 Classification and Multiple Use Act, a measure designed to further organize and streamline administration of the nation's public lands, made wildlife management and outdoor recreation equivalent to—if not greater than—livestock grazing. According to the Department of the Interior, there was no requirement that all uses of public lands be "universally intermingled in common," which meant that in some areas, less-desirable activities could be prohibited. To oversee implementing multiple use, the Udall administration reorganized the traditional grazing-advisory boards, which had assisted the Grazing Service in overseeing the original grazing districts, into multiple-use boards, a step that broadened their membership to include timber, recreation, wilderness, and "other nonlivestock groups." This change severely decreased the influence that ranchers—and the livestock industry—had on managing public lands.[23]

Then in 1971, the Wild Free-Roaming Horses and Burros Act added wild horse herds to the panorama of public lands management. Joseph Fallini Jr., Joseph and Helen's son, had had a rough time grappling with wild horses throughout the 1960s when he took over management of the family's ranch. The Fallini family had always run horses on the range with their cattle, a common practice among the ranches in the region, especially in drier areas such as the Kawich and Reveille Valleys. Some of these animals drifted onto the bombing range to the south during the 1940s, but the Fallinis periodically rounded them up when the military allowed it. Beginning in 1951, the BLM required the family to limit its livestock—both cattle and horses—to the permitted number, but wild horse herds, descendants of horses the Fallinis and other ranchers had released onto the open range, continued to roam the same areas. Each season the Fallinis transferred their cattle and horses from summer to winter ranges and shut off wells to save water and discourage use in the area. Wild horses migrated with the Fallini animals, following water and forage.

To make matters worse, unmanaged herds from the National Wild Horse Refuge (now the Nevada Wild Horse Range), created in 1963 at the north end of the bombing range, drifted onto the Fallinis' adjacent grazing district, the Reveille allotment. These animals used forage and water at the family's expense, competing with the cattle. To ameliorate the impact on their rangeland, the Fallinis customarily rounded up wild horses whenever they strayed out of the refuge and sold them to slaughterhouses.[24]

This is exactly what the 1971 law prevented. Between passage of the Wild Horses and Burros Act and its enforcement in 1974, the BLM required ranchers to remove any privately owned animals to sort out which horses qualified for federal protection. However, this did nothing to reduce the size of the herds near Twin Springs. In the spring of 1976, BLM officials in the Battle Mountain district and the Fallini family met to discuss a possible solution to the emerging wild horse problem in the area. The agency and the Fallinis discussed developing a new recreation area and expanding the existing wild horse refuge to accommodate the growing herds.

But when the BLM rolled out a map of the recreation area's boundaries, it included the Fallinis' Eden Creek property. The Fallinis had not maintained their wells or structures on the boundary of the bombing range for several years because so little water had been available, giving the impression that it was unused. Nevertheless, they still held valid water rights, land, and grazing permits there. Helen Fallini said, "We jumped up and told them like hell." Under no circumstances would the Fallinis allow the BLM to take the Eden ranch for a new recreation area and expanded wild horse range.

The agency advised the Fallinis that it would give them other land in exchange. "We had quite a battle over that that night," said Helen Fallini, "and they were telling all the other people around who were sitting in there how they were going to take it over, and it was going to be a historical site and all that." The Fallinis were deeply offended at the agency's lack of consideration for the family's history and resisted the BLM's efforts to create a public playground that would have swallowed the remaining portion of their homestead in a one-million-acre wild horse refuge and recreation area.[25]

To make matters worse, the Fallinis and other ranchers who relied on grazing resources on public lands were losing the battle over ever-increasing fees. The new federal fee structure developed in the late 1960s was a closer reflection of the market value of grazing resources; it embodied the equity between the different land uses and the desire of the Department of the Interior to manage all public lands closely. But Nevada ranchers in general felt that their ability to earn a living by running livestock on public rangeland was becoming increasingly difficult because of these fees. They argued that making a living in the livestock industry was becoming more and more tenuous because of "increasing competition for the use of the land, as a result of population growth and industrial demands, and frequent withdrawal of large tracts with public use," along with "cancelled or restricted grazing" and larger fees.[26]

In light of the long list of grievances the Fallinis had with the federal government—forced grazing-district organization, loss of range to national defense, exposure to radioactive fallout, damage from growing wild horse herds, potential removal of property to construct a recreation area, and fee increases—it is not difficult to understand how their frustration built over time. Considering how much had changed with public lands management, it is incredible that the Fallinis could still operate their ranch somewhat successfully. In the two generations from the Fallini brothers to Joseph Jr., shifting national interests and demands had transformed public lands in central Nevada from wasteland to grazing range, bombing range, nuclear test site, wild horse refuge, and recreation area.

The Fallinis believed they had a right to continue grazing cattle on the public domain as they had always done since Giovanni Fallini had homesteaded Eden Creek. But when other, equally legitimate, uses of public lands were codified into law, their right to graze cattle conflicted with the rights of other public lands users. The Fallinis felt that the evolution of multiple use from a concept that allowed ranchers to utilize resources on public lands at minimal (or no) cost to a policy that required continual adjustment to accommodate an increasing number of other public land users had shoved ranchers to the bottom of the user hierarchy.

The Smaller Sagebrush Rebellion

In the spring of 1979, Nevada's Select Committee on Public Lands convened hearings to discuss a proposal requiring the federal government to transfer administration of the public domain to the state. The committee heard Nevada residents testify regarding what they thought should be done to improve public lands management. Joseph Fallini Jr., speaking for his ill father, explained that from 1946, when the BLM was formed, to its Organic Act of 1976, "the BLM has acquired one-third of the land mass of Europe, yet that agency was formed for the purpose of being a disposal agency."[27] He believed that in lieu of outright disposal, the private use of the Reveille grazing allotment fulfilled that mission. The protest expressed in these hearings, in the Nevada Legislature's passage of the first Sagebrush Rebellion bill, and the subsequent bills and lawsuits filed against the federal government by other western states, expressed the frustration of ranchers such as the Fallinis.

But the Sagebrush Rebellion in Nevada also became a larger movement throughout the American West that protested something beyond what most ranchers in the state desired. Where the larger political movement advocated that individual states "reclaim their land," the more localized version promoted the status quo created by the Taylor Grazing Act, a greater respect for traditional users and a shared responsibility for the financial burden of public lands.[28]

Seen from the perspective of the Fallini family and other ranchers in Nevada, increasing grazing fees and added layers of multiple use, especially provision for wild horses, unnecessarily threatened their livestock operations. While all of these activities seemed appropriate to serve national interests and environmentally orient public lands management, only public lands ranchers footed the bill directly. Most Nevada ranchers—and especially those in the central part of the state—lived on the very margins of ranching and could not survive without cheap forage. The rising costs of other resources such as fuel, electricity, and food only intensified their dilemma. Why should they pay when the military, outdoor recreationists, and wild horse advocates did not? This situation was not directly reflected in the larger Sagebrush Rebellion, but the region's ranchers constantly struggled with it.[29]

The statement Joseph Fallini Jr. made at the hearings is revealing. The Fallinis and other ranchers in the area believed that utilizing their grazing allotments, although owned by the BLM and the federal government, predated all other uses and groups. Their range had been unallocated and unreserved public land owned by no one but available to people who were able and willing to stake a claim. When Robert McCracken interviewed Helen Fallini in 1987, she suggested that ranching would have been easier if land management could have stayed the way it was prior to the Taylor Grazing Act or at least remained consistent after that time. Maintaining that status quo was best achieved in the Fallini family's mind by locally controlling the rangeland and keeping the cost low.[30]

Confirming her view, Edgar I. Rowland, the Nevada BLM director, who witnessed the heated debates over control of public lands, argued the national Sagebrush Rebellion "wasn't rancher instigated." He said, "Most of the ranchers would prefer at least at the time not to own the land" because they got "a better deal from [the] BLM." Rowland believed the movement to gain control over public lands "was instigated by some people that just wanted to get rid of all federal control in Nevada." "Really," he argued "the ranchers, level-headed ranchers [at least], didn't want this kind of thing." The BLM's discussion paper on the Nevada bill echoed his thoughts; the agency proposed, "Rural members of the [Nevada] legislature regard BLM's attempts to manage natural resources as efforts to alter the status quo."[31]

Measured against the Fallinis' experience, Rowland's interpretation was correct. The Fallinis did not necessarily support state control over public lands in Nevada. What they wanted was to maintain the same cattle operation they had originally established in the early twentieth century. They wanted to work within a land management system that did not demand they constantly change their practices or cede territory to other land users.

In contrast to the Fallinis, Wayne Hage, a participant in the larger Sagebrush Rebellion, came to ranching later in life. Hage was the son of a miner, who had migrated to Nevada from Minnesota in the early 1900s, and a schoolteacher, whose parents had settled in Elko as it struggled to recover from a collapsed mining economy about the time Wyoming ranching baron John Sparks arrived and launched the region's cattle boom. Hage grew up in Elko, a community immersed in the bygone glory days of its mining and ranching past. The young Hage pursued a degree in animal husbandry and worked on a ranch.

After their marriage in 1963, Hage and his wife, Jean, worked on her parents' ranch in Sierra Valley, fifty miles northeast of Reno. In 1978, they were able to purchase the Pine Creek Ranch in Monitor Valley for about two million dollars, along with a number of water rights and grazing allotments managed by the BLM and Forest Service, and launch their own ranching operation, but, according to Hage, "It was one thing after the other, after the other, after the other" from the moment he took possession of the ranch.[32]

The trouble began in 1979 when the Forest Service allowed the state wildlife department to release nonnative elk into the Monitor Range where Hage's grazing allotments were located. The elk competed with the cattle for water and forage. For the next decade, the Forest Service increased its management of the allotments and asked Hage to move cattle out of overgrazed areas. In addition, the U.S. Department of Defense's MX missile project threatened to bisect allotments and tap valuable water sources throughout the central part of the state.

Hage responded by penning *Storm over Rangelands: Private Rights in Federal Lands*, published by the Free Enterprise Press, the publishing division of the Center for the Defense of Free Enterprise and one of the organizations that wanted to roll back environmental regulation on public lands. Hage felt it was "clear that the federal government wanted this ranch and that they were willing to do anything to drive me out." By 1991, the Forest Service had moved to impound Hage's cattle trespassing on the Meadow Canyon and Table Mountain allotments in the Toquima and Monitor Mountains on either side of the ranch. Hage filed suit against the agency because he believed "it is a grazing allotment. A grazing allotment is personal, private property. That's all that needs to be said."[33]

Although Hage's complaints sounded similar to the Fallinis', their positions were in fact very different. Hage and his family argued with federal land-management agencies about ownership of and right to use public lands. In addition to the 7,000 acres he owned and the water rights attached to the property, he also claimed the 750,000 acres that comprised the grazing allotments overseen by the BLM and Forest Service. The new reality created by FLPMA in 1976—presaged by the Forest Service's 1960 Multiple-Use Sustained-Yield Act and confirmed in the subsequent Public Rangelands Improvement Act in 1978, which led to more intensive rangeland management—meant that the Hages could not own the allotments. These laws ensured the federal government would manage public lands in perpetuity. This seemed to be the most difficult aspect of the shift in public lands management: whereas ranchers and miners had once had priority use of public lands, they now shared them with a number of others who had equal rights according to multiple use.

Yet these laws merely codified what had already been happening since 1934 when the Taylor Grazing Act was passed. More to the point, the legal structure that governed public lands ensured that ranchers dependent upon them had to adjust their operations as the political, cultural, and economic climate shifted nationally, creating a highly volatile situation. But this, too, had already been happening. Beginning with range restrictions during World War II and the establishment of the Tonopah Bombing Range through nuclear testing and the expansion of multiple use, which required wildlife, recreation, wilderness, and wild horse management, ranchers had consistently lost out to the needs and interests of the nation. Their dependence on public lands placed them at the mercy of the American public, symbolized by the federal government and the BLM and put them at risk when public lands shifted from unallocated, unreserved, and unwanted territory to the treasured landscape of the nation. From their perspective, they continually gave ground to accommodate an increasing number of people interested in using public lands.

In contrast to the Hage family, the Fallinis did not claim their 663,000-acre grazing allotment in addition to the 2,300 private acres and multiple water rights they owned; they only asked the ability to manage their herds with minimal impact from other public lands uses. This is the reason why they described their difficulties in terms of the increasing complications they faced conducting normal operations, rather than ownership.

Both the Hages and the Fallinis litigated against federal land-management agencies in lawsuits based on their water rights—not their ownership of the water, but their right to use it. Some of these rights predated the establishment of water law in Nevada and therefore were vested. The Fallinis also wanted to ensure the BLM constrained the wild horse population to around 150 head to protect grazing and water and make certain that livestock—bovine and equine—had equal standing. The Hage family's cases predominantly rested on the issue of whether their vested water rights guaranteed them grazing rights that gave them absolute priority. They based their cases on the supposition that grazing at the Pine Creek Ranch had occurred prior to the 1848 Treaty of Guadalupe Hidalgo and that they held land patents from the Mexican government according to the 1863 Treaty of Ruby Valley and the 1887 General Allotment Act. They questioned whether the federal government had any jurisdiction over this land at all.[34]

Where the Fallinis chose to work within the jurisdictional framework of public lands management and influence it as much as they could, the Hages denied that federal land-management agencies had the right to regulate public lands and wanted to extend their ownership to the areas their cattle grazed. The Hage family's approach represents the larger Sagebrush Rebellion, a 1980s ideological movement that promoted removing the federal government from public lands management and eliminating environmental regulations. However, although the national Sagebrush Rebellion seemed to rest on a reasonable intellectual framework constructed from western individualism and property rights, it actually undermined the very definition of public lands and became a political land grab by pro-growth politicians and corporations seeking greater access to natural resources.[35]

The Fallini family did not really want to remove the federal government from public lands management; they just wanted to clarify their position within the multiple-use framework created by FLPMA. They understood and depended upon the relationship between their actual property—their ranch and water rights—and their grazing range, the Reveille allotment. They understood that federal permitting only granted them a prerogative to utilize the grazing range. Their anger and frustration resulted from the increasing distance between the way they had once ranched cattle and the constantly changing priorities of federal land-management agencies, particularly the BLM. On the surface, it seemed as if the environmental movement and increasing government regulation were to blame. However, a more accurate description is that by 1976, those who depended upon public lands for their livelihood, especially ranchers—as well as those who managed them—faced a complicated landscape of intersecting uses, shaped by national interests and multiple pressure groups, that required constant communication, cooperation, and adjustment.

The real source of trouble in the "angry West" was that multiple use had created a continually changing landscape. The BLM's Organic Act defined multiple use as "the management of public lands and their various resource values so that they are utilized in the combination that will best meet the present and future needs of the American people... without permanent impairment of the productivity of the land and the quality of the environment with consideration being given to the relative values of the resources."[36] In this way, the Sagebrush Rebellion was—and still is— a reflection of the growing distance between those, like the Fallinis, who rely upon public lands to make a living and the American public, represented by agencies charged with ensuring those same lands serve the best interests of the nation.

Notes

1. See the cover of *Newsweek*, September 17, 1979; image licensed by PARS International Corp.
2. Roy Doty, "The Alienated Frontier: An Absentee Landlord, Mushrooming Growth and a Desperate Scramble after Land, Water and Energy," *Newsweek*, September 17, 1979, 31.
3. Tom Mathews, "The Angry West vs. the Rest," *Newsweek*, September 17, 1979, 31–34, 37–40.
4. Ed Gallucci, interview with the author, September 27, 2013.
5. Roy Doty, interview with the author, September 3, 2013.
6. Robert D. McCracken, *An Interview with Helen L. Fallini: An Oral History*

(Tonopah, NV: Nye County Town History Project, 1987), 30, 42, https://nyecountyhistory.com/fallini/fallini.pdf.

7. Besides the Fallini family, Ben Colvin and Wayne Hage have been very vocal about their difficulties with public lands policy and the federal government. See Jon Christensen, "Showdown on the Nevada Range," *High Country News*, August 27, 2001; and Sandra Chereb, "Wayne Hage, Nevada Rancher and Sagebrush Rebel, Dies," *Las Vegas Sun*, June 6, 2006. Some of the Fallinis' federal court cases include Fallini v. Hodel, 783 F.2d 1343 (9th Cir. 1986); Fallini v. Hodel, 963 F.2d 275 (9th Cir. 1992); and Fallini v. United States, 56 F.3d 1378 (Fed. Cir. 1995); they predominantly focus on aspects of public lands use that interferes with their ranching operations. Keith Rogers, "Yucca Mountain Rail Line," *Las Vegas Review-Journal*, April 25, 2004.
8. R. McGreggor Cawley, *Federal Land, Western Anger: The Sagebrush Rebellion and Environmental Politics* (Lawrence: University Press of Kansas, 1993), 1–14; James R. Skillen, *The Nation's Largest Landlord: The Bureau of Land Management in the American West* (Lawrence: University Press of Kansas, 2008), 120–23, 120.
9. Giovanni Fallini patented his homestead in 1923; see General Land Office patent 915720, August 8, 1923, http://www.glorecords.blm.gov. His son, Joseph, expanded the family's property by 80 acres with a Desert Land Act acquisition patented in 1964 (see General Land Office patent 27-64-0115) and again in the 1980s with public-lands purchases totaling 750 acres. With the addition of private-land purchases and the nearby grazing range, the Fallinis' property totaled 66,300 acres by the end of the twentieth century. Myron Angel, *History of Nevada with Illustrations and Biographical Sketches of Its Prominent Men and Pioneers* (Oakland, CA: Thompson & West, 1881), 526; McCracken, *Interview with Helen L. Fallini*, 11–13, 16, 18–20, 26, 39; Rogers, "Yucca Mountain Rail Line."
10. The Fallinis acquired many of their water rights from the United Cattle and Packing Company and relatives such as Gustaf Peterson, who had homesteaded 320 acres near the Bellehelen Mine and whose wife, Minnie, was an aunt to the Fallinis. The Fallinis secured their water rights, most of which were underground sources, between 1916 and 1969 and hold Nevada water certificates 318, 388, 521, 665–66, 949, 1077–79, 1110, 1235, 1393, 1937, 2155, 2533, 2892, 2909–2912, 3103–6, 3123, 3253, 3297, 3325, 3383–86, 3430, 3512, 3515, 3521–22, 3536, 3571–73, 3615, 3618–21, 3659–60, 3696, 3797, 3844, 3932, 4213, 4624, 5048, 5209, 5615–16, 5739, 5763, 6872–73, and 6979. McCracken, *Interview with Helen L. Fallini*, 14–15.
11. Ibid., 21, 31–34, 43–44.
12. Richard T. Ely, Ralph H. Hess, Charles L. Keith, and Thomas Nixon Carver, *The Foundations of National Prosperity: Studies in the Conservation of Permanent National Resources* (New York: Macmillan, 1918), 3–10, 27–46; Benjamin Horace Hibbard, *A History of the Public Land Policies* (1924; repr., Madison: University of Wisconsin Press, 1965), 562–70; Richard T. Ely, *Land Economics*

(New York: Macmillan, 1940), 48–73, 222–70; Benjamin G. Rader, *The Academic Mind and Reform* (Lexington: University of Kentucky Press, 1966), 29–53; Richard T. Ely, *Ground under Our Feet* (New York: Arno Press, 1977), 234–41, 279–82; quotation from Ely, *Land Economics*, 72.

13. Thomas Donaldson, "The Public Lands of the United States," *North American Review* 133 (August 1881): 208–10; "Roosevelt Declares Himself on the Public Land Question," *Ogden Standard Examiner*, February 13, 1907; "Stockmen Are Not Unanimous," *Salt Lake Herald*, February 14, 1907; Milton A. Pearl, "Public Land Commissions," *Our Public Lands* 17, no. 2 (Summer 1967): 16–17; Hibbard, *History of the Public Land Policies*, 479–83; "Land Problem Compromised," *Los Angeles Times*, November 28, 1930; "Public Lands Row Flares," *Los Angeles Times*, January 13, 1931; "Land Report Given Hoover," *Los Angeles Times*, February 15, 1931; "Public Lands Change Urged," *Los Angeles Times*, March 9, 1931; White Pine County Farm Bureau to Senator Key Pittman, March 3, 1936, box 92, folder 4, Richard Kirman Papers, Nevada State Archives, Carson City, Nevada; Senate Committee on Interior and Insular Affairs, Administration and Use of Public Lands: Hearings on S. 241, 77th Cong., 1st Sess., June 24–25, 27–28, 1941, 55–56.

14. Hearings on S. 241, 77th Cong., 2nd Sess., October 28, November 19–20, 1942, 1828–34; "Stockmen Oppose Federal Control," *Reno Evening Gazette*, September 16, 1947; "60 Ranchers Attend Meet," *Nevada State Journal*, March 5, 1948; "Central Nevada Stockmen Elect," *Nevada State Journal*, January 17, 1950; Philip O. Foss, *Politics and Grass: The Administration of Grazing on the Public Domain* (Seattle: University of Washington Press, 1960), 175; Marion Clawson, *The Western Range Livestock Industry* (New York: McGraw-Hill, 1950), 121, 378–82.

15. "Interior Depart. Holding Up Bomb Range Work," *Tonopah Daily Times and Bonanza*, July 24, 1940; "Pittman to Seek Roosevelt's Aid in Bombing Action," *Tonopah Daily Times and Bonanza*, July 25, 1940; "McCarran Sees Early Action by Air Corps on Local Range," *Tonopah Daily Times and Bonanza*, July 26, 1940; "$185,000 Airport Project Slated for Tonopah," *Tonopah Daily Times and Bonanza*, August 21, 1940; "Withdrawal of Bombing Site from Public Domain, Nearing," *Tonopah Daily Times and Bonanza*, August 26, 1940; "Bombing Range Land Withdrawal Approved," *Tonopah Daily Times and Bonanza*, October 12, 1940; "Tonopah Seen as Becoming Major Defense Sector," *Tonopah Daily Times and Bonanza*, October 15, 1940; "Roosevelt Signs Bombing Range Order," *Tonopah Daily Times and Bonanza*, October 31, 1940; "Tonopah Airport Project Is Given Approval by FDR," *Tonopah Daily Times and Bonanza*, November 30, 1940; "Details of New Airport Project Here Described," *Tonopah Daily Times and Bonanza*, December 4, 1940; "Tonopah Airport Work Will Start on Monday, Revealed," *Tonopah Daily Times and Bonanza*, December 7 1940; "McCarran Seeks Early Activity on Bombing Range," *Tonopah Daily Times and Bonanza*, February 6, 1941; "Bombing Range Given Support," *Nevada State Journal*, February 22, 1941; "Scrugham Sees

Early Start on Tonopah Project," *Tonopah Daily Times and Bonanza,* March 1, 1941; "Bombing Range Is Given Title," *Reno Evening Gazette,* July 22, 1941; "Nevada's Participation in National Crisis Listed by Bunker," *Nevada State Journal,* August 22, 1941; Gerald D. Nash, *The American West Transformed: The Impact of the Second World War* (Lincoln: University of Nebraska Press, 1985), 7, 22–23.

16. "Crews Survey Bombing Range," *Nevada State Journal,* September 26, 1941; Hearings on S. 241, 77th Cong., 2nd Sess., October 28, November 19–20, 1942, 1826–35.
17. "Army Prepared Bombing Site for Early Use," *Nevada State Journal,* December 22, 1941; "Huge Acreage in Nevada Now Held by Government," *Nevada State Journal,* June 4, 1942; Hearings on S. 241, 1826–35; Robert V. Nickel, "Dollars, Defense, and the Desert: Southern Nevada's Military Economy and World War II," *Nevada Historical Society Quarterly* 47, no. 4 (Winter 2004): 306–7.
18. Oscar L. Chapman, "Public Notice, May 18, 1943," folder 468, Public Lands Foundation Archives, Bureau of Land Management, Phoenix, Arizona; "Stockmen Oppose Federal Control," *Reno Evening Gazette;* "Cattlemen Take New Steps toward Staving Off Federal Control," *Tonopah Times-Bonanza,* November 21, 1947; "Hearing Attended by Army Officials," *Nevada State Journal,* February 12, 1948; "Formation Taylor District at Tonopah Meeting Ends in Postponement," *Tonopah Times-Bonanza,* March 3, 1950; "United Stockmen Select Officers," *Reno Evening Gazette,* March 17, 1950; Foss, *Politics and Grass,* 180–81; Skillen, *The Nation's Largest Landlord,* 15–17.
19. "Warns of Danger in Using All Roads on Big Bombing Range," *Tonopah Times-Bonanza,* December 15, 1950; "Tonopah Base Still on Unactive List," *Tonopah Times-Bonanza,* January 15, 1951; "AEC Will Improve Atomic Test Grounds," *Tonopah Times-Bonanza,* February 23, 1951; "Nye Land Owners Urged to File Claims," *Tonopah Times-Bonanza,* April 27, 1951; Terrence R. Fehner and F. G. Gosling, *Origins of the Nevada Test Site* (Washington, DC: Department of Energy, 2000), 20–21, 44–48.
20. "Warns of Danger," *Tonopah Times-Bonanza;* C. P. Trussell, "Atom Bomb Testing Ground Will Be Created in Nevada," *New York Times,* January 12, 1951; "Nevada's Bomb Range," *New York Times,* January 14, 1951; "Good Deal of Secrecy Surrounds AEC Nye Development," *Tonopah Times-Bonanza,* January 19, 1951; "No Public Announcement Planned of Atom Blasts at Vegas Range," *Reno Evening Gazette,* January 25, 1951; "AEC Will Control All Air Flights over Bombing Range," *Tonopah Times-Bonanza,* January 26, 1951; "Atomic Energy Commission Warns of Trespassing on Bombing Range," *Tonopah Times-Bonanza,* January 26, 1951; "Chapman Turns Down Plea to Delay Grazing District," *Reno Evening Gazette,* March 16, 1951; "Postponing Taylor Grazing Act Turned Down by Chapman," *Tonopah Times-Bonanza,* March 23, 1951; "Taylor Grazing Meeting Set for Tonopah Next Thursday," *Tonopah Times-Bonanza,* May 4, 1951; "New Graze District Organized," *Tonopah Times-Bonanza,* May 18, 1951; Fehner and Gosling, *Origins of the Nevada Test Site,* 46.

21. "A Searching Inquiry into Nuclear Perils," *Life*, June 10, 1957, 4–29; "Nevadans Charge Fallout Danger," *Los Angeles Times*, June 27, 1957; "Radiation Burns Mark Horses," *Los Angeles Times*, June 27, 1957; Richard L. Miller, *Under the Cloud: The Decades of Nuclear Testing* (New York: Free Press, 1986), 247–48, 299–300; McCracken, *Interview with Helen L. Fallini*, 22–23; Philip Fradkin, *Fallout: An American Nuclear Tragedy* (1989, repr., Tucson: University of Arizona Press, 2004), 136; Robert McCracken and Jeanne Sharp Howerton, *A History of Railroad Valley, Nevada* (Tonopah: Central Nevada Historical Society, 1996), 283–86.
22. Stewart L. Udall, "Nevada's Future and Uncle Sam," *Reno Evening Gazette*, February 1, 1964; John A. Carver to Howard W. Cannon, 88th Cong., May 14, 1963, box 18, folder 207, Howard Cannon Papers, Special Collections, University of Nevada, Las Vegas.
23. Charles H. Stoddard, "What the New Legislation Means to You," *Our Public Lands* 14, no. 2 (Fall 1964): 4–6; "Public Land Responsibility Defined," *Reno Evening Gazette*, November 21, 1964; Robert H. Woody, "BLM Effect Tantalizing to Land Board Chief," *Salt Lake Tribune*, December 15, 1964; Skillen, *The Nation's Largest Landlord*, 39–47.
24. McCracken, *Interview with Helen L. Fallini*, 23–25, 31, 33, 42.
25. Gene Nodine to Edgar I. Rowland, memorandum, May 19, 1976, box 709, folder 8, Donal "Mike" O'Callaghan Papers, Nevada State Archives, Carson City; Edgar I. Rowland to Curt Berkland, memorandum, May 26, 1976, box 709, folder 8, O'Callaghan Papers; Bureau of Land Management, news release, July 2, 1976, 90-34, box 1, folder 3, Tina Nappe Papers, Special Collections, University of Nevada, Reno; John Meder to Norman Hall, memorandum, August 13, 1976, box 709, folder 8, O'Callaghan Papers; McCracken, *Interview with Helen L. Fallini*, 30.
26. "Study Group Opposes Fee Boost," *Nevada State Journal*, April 24, 1962; "Protection of Rights Sought by Ranchers," *Reno Evening Gazette*, March 14, 1963; "Grazing Cost Increase Delay Asked by Baring," *Reno Evening Gazette*, December 3, 1965; "Grazing Fees in Western States to Go Up Three Cents," *Reno Evening Gazette*, February 21, 1966; "Bible Lauds Delay in Grazing Fee Increase," *Reno Evening Gazette*, December 18, 1966; "Baring Protests against Change in Grazing Fees," *Nevada State Journal*, November 23, 1968; "Hickel to Delay Grazing Fee Hike," *Nevada State Journal*, November 26, 1969; "Officials Agree Not to Increase Grazing Fees," *Nevada State Journal*, January 29, 1970; "Public Land Laws Outmoded, Review Commission Reports," *Nevada State Journal*, June 24, 1970.
27. Joseph Fallini Sr. died of cancer the same year as the hearings, a condition possibly related to his exposure to radioactive fallout during the 1950s nuclear testing.
28. For more information on the national political movement called the Sagebrush Rebellion, see Cawley, *Federal Land, Western Anger*; Joint Hearing Senate Committee on Natural Resources and Assembly Committee on

Environment and Public Resources, April 4, 1979, 85-04, folder 7, box 1, Sagebrush Rebellion Papers, Special Collections, University of Nevada, Reno; "Sagebrush Revolt," *Newsweek*, September 17, 1979, 38–39; Joseph Ross, "FLPMA Turns 30," *Society for Range Management* 28, no. 5 (October 2006): 16–23; Skillen, *The Nation's Largest Landlord*, 102–32.

29. William Voigt Jr., *Public Grazing Lands* (New Brunswick, NJ: Rutgers University Press, 1976); Michael Frome, "Fight for Natural Beauty Access," *Los Angeles Times*, September 2, 1979; Cawley, *Federal Land, Western Anger*, 71–76.
30. Tina Nappe and Rose Strickland, "Grazing Fee Hearing," January 11, 1978, 90-34, box 2, folder 45, Tina Nappe Papers; McCracken, *Interview with Helen L. Fallini*, 30, 42.
31. Edgar I. Rowland, Interview with the Public Lands Foundation, October 10, 1987, Public Lands Foundation Archives, Bureau of Land Management, Phoenix, Arizona; Office of the Secretary of the Interior to Richard H. Bryan, letter with attachment, July 17, 1979, box 6, file 11, Department of Conservation and Natural Resources, Nevada State Archives, Carson City.
32. "Final Rites for Elko Pioneer," *Nevada State Journal*, December 11, 1930; "Jean Nichols Becomes Bride of Elwood Wayne Hage," *Reno Evening Gazette*, March 27, 1963; "Deaths," *Nevada State Journal*, July 9, 1965; Susan Imswiler, E. Wayne Hage, interview by Susan Imswiler, April 1, 1999, University of Nevada Oral History Program, Reno; James A. Young and B. Abbott Sparks, *Cattle in the Cold Desert* (Reno: University of Nevada Press, 2002), 101–11; Eugene M. Moehring, *Urbanism and Empire in the Far West, 1840–1890* (Reno: University of Nevada Press, 2004), 151–54.
33. E. Wayne Hage, *Storm over Rangelands: Private Rights in Federal Lands* (Bellevue: Free Enterprise Press, 1989); Jon Christensen, "High Noon in Nevada," *High Country News*, September 9, 1991; Hage interview by Imswiler; Jodi Peterson, "One Sagebrush Rebellion Flickers Out—Or Does It?," *High Country News*, September 21, 2012; Matt Rasmussen, "'Rebel' Cowboys Say We Have No Right to Kick Their Cattle off Our Public Lands," *Grist*, September 9, 2014.
34. Fallini v. Hodel, 783 F.2d 1343; Fallini v. Hodel, 963 F.2d 275; Fallini v. Bureau of Land Management, IBLA 96–463 (Interior Board of Land Appeals, 2004); Hage v. U.S., 687 F.3d 1281 (Fed. Cir. 2012), cert. denied, 133 S. Ct. 2484 (2013); U.S v. Hage, No. 2:07-cv-01154-RCJ-VCF (D. Nev. 2013); Tim Findley, "The Horses of Joe Fallini's Dreams," *Range Magazine* (Fall 2010), 36–39, http://www.rangemagazine.com/features/fall-10/fa10-range-horses.pdf.
35. "Rising Voice of the West," *Newsweek*, September 17, 1979, 37; Brian Allen Drake, *Loving Nature, Fearing the State: Environmentalism and Antigovernment Politics before Reagan* (Seattle: University of Washington Press, 2013), 103–7.
36. For a larger examination of the history of multiple use, see Leisl Carr Childers, *The Size of the Risk: Histories of Multiple Use in the Great Basin* (Norman: University of Oklahoma Press, 2015. *Federal Land Policy Management Act of 1976*, Pub. L. No. 579, 94th Cong., 2nd Sess. (October 21, 1976).

Skull Valley Goshutes and the Politics of Place, Identity, and Sovereignty in Rural Utah

DAVID RICH LEWIS

"How do you think this country was built?" Leon Bear, tribal chairman of the Skull Valley Band of Goshute Indians, shot back at documentary filmmaker and reporter Ken Verdoia. Verdoia had just voiced the common public concern that Goshutes were not sophisticated enough to handle the decision to allow high-level nuclear waste on their reservation in rural western Utah. "Not because of stupidity, same with the reservations," Bear continued. "How do you think we survive? Not because of stupidity, so to answer that question...The Goshute people are here and we're going to be here and we're not going anywhere. No matter how stupid people think we are, we're still here."[1]

With those three final words, Bear summed up all Goshute history and his people's experiences with Euro-American colonizers who thought them incapable at best, inconsequential at worst. With those three words, Bear signaled his intent to secure his people's future.

This chapter explores parts of an ongoing debate over storing nuclear and hazardous waste on public and private lands in rural Utah. In particular, it focuses on the Skull Valley Band of Goshute Indians' 1997 agreement to store 40,000 metric tons of high-level radioactive waste on a concrete pad forty-five miles southwest of Salt Lake City. Surrounded by military bombing ranges, nerve-agent storage facilities, and private hazardous-waste sites, the 18,000-acre Skull Valley Goshute Reservation offered little to sustain the band's approximately 125 members. Until the respective parties walked away from this agreement in December 2012, the project promised needed jobs and economic development in rural Skull Valley and surrounding Tooele County and would have added millions of dollars to the band's coffers.

However, the project was more than controversial from the start, pitting Goshutes against Goshutes, urban against rural residents, power consumers against producers, environmentalists against Indians, and Indians against non-Indians. It placed the limited sovereignty of Indian tribes against an increasingly assertive states' rights movement, against federal regulatory and trust mandates, against the interests of the nuclear-power industry. Like all stories humans tell, it seemed simple and straightforward on the surface: who in their right minds would want to store nuclear waste on their land? But peel away the layers, and you arrive at a larger and more complicated story—an Indian story and a tale of the modern rural West—both of which illustrate the contingent and decidedly frustrating choices humans face as they negotiate their lives in the rural landscape.[2]

Rural Native People and Lands

Indians are the original rural Americans, and rural still defines their places and identities. Prior to Euro-American contact, the vast majority lived in dispersed bands and extended affinal groups, moving and staying as their resources and imaginations dictated. Even those living in settled villages (with a few notable exceptions) maintained population densities within the modern definitions of rural. They lived with immediacy in their ecosystems: farming, foraging, hunting, trading, and actively shaping the world around them to sustain life. They identified themselves and others through their understanding of place and the cosmological meanings they gave to landscapes and resources.[3]

Given the agrarian approach of United States American Indian policy, it is not surprising that Indians remained rural decades after the majority of U.S. citizens had moved to the city. Federal policies such as removal, reservation, and allotment emphasized agrarianism, intensifying Indian rural isolation and economic marginality in an increasingly industrial nineteenth-century world. In 1930, only 10 percent of Indians lived in cities—a decade after the country as a whole had turned urban. A decade of depression halved that urban number as Indians returned to find shelter and New Deal jobs on their reservations. World War II industrial jobs and government-relocation programs in the 1950s drew Indians back to the cities, but 70 percent remained in rural communities in 1960. As late as 1980, 51 percent of American Indians still lived outside standard metropolitan areas, far exceeding whites (26.7 percent), African Americans (19.9 percent), Hispanics (12.4 percent), and the national average (25.2 percent), making them the most rural of all major American ethnic groups. Not until 1990, seventy years after the rest of the nation had accepted urban life, did a majority (51 percent) of the 1,959,234 American Indians and Alaskan Natives finally become urban residents. Today roughly 60 percent of American Indians and Alaskan Natives live in metropolitan areas, still the lowest percentage of any ethnic group.[4]

Reflecting the same policies, American Indians have been overwhelmingly western since the mid-nineteenth century. In 1910, 95 percent of the 291,014 Indians and Alaskan Natives lived west of the Mississippi River, 55 percent of them in the western census region. In 1950, 57 percent of the 377,273 Natives lived in the West. By 2010, 41 percent of the 5.2 million people self-identifying as American Indian or Alaskan Native by ancestry (whole or part) resided in the West, and 65 percent lived west of the Mississippi.[5]

Just as many westerners think of themselves as rural (despite the overwhelmingly urban nature of western settlement and the West today), so, too, do Native Americans. Today only 22 percent of Indians and Alaskan Natives reside on reservation trust lands, and as many live in nearby border towns. Few practice extensive farming, livestock raising, or other agricultural occupations, yet most maintain Native identity and share challenges experienced by other rural Americans: geographic isolation; seasonal wages and labor associated with land, animals, or natural resources; limited access to consumer goods or local health services; strong ties to family, community, and land; relative invisibility in the urban-dominant political realm; and a certain stoic acknowledgment of economic and environmental forces they cannot control. Too often all that separates Indians from the larger rural American community is racial, voiced through denunciations of the limited sovereignty that protects Indians on tribal land from the authority of state and local governments.[6]

While American Indians have taken great strides to mitigate the damage done by twentieth-century federal Indian policies, and while tribes have asserted their limited sovereignty and rights to self-determination subject to federal trust responsibilities since 1975, they have struggled to generate meaningful economic development on rural reservations and trust lands and in Native villages. Agricultural participation and production have fallen on reservations where aridity and competition for water, climate extremes, overgrazing, and isolation from commercial markets and credit complicate the legal legacies of federal Indian policies—small allotted field sizes, checkerboard non-Indian inholdings, and complicated leases and heirship cases. Where 50 percent of Indians maintained full-time agricultural operations in 1940, only 10 percent did by 1960. In 2007, only 1.4 percent of Indians (77,437) operated farms or ranches, averaging 946 acres and $51,501 in products sold. Nearly a third of those operators had sales of less than $1,000, and only 4.8 percent made sales of more than $100,000.[7]

In place of agriculture, tribes have established reservation-based industrial and manufacturing enterprises with varying degrees of success, and individual members participate broadly in regional job markets, often moving between reservation and city and back again at different points in their lives. Tribes have taken advantage of reservation oil, gas, water, timber, coal and mineral resources; fish and wildlife; and recreation and tourism. Since the 1980s, casino gaming has become the "white buffalo" for reservation economies, generating millions of dollars, creating thousands of jobs, and bringing vast improvements to housing, schools, and infrastructure. But that economic bonanza has been unevenly distributed geographically and politically, with isolated rural reservations not faring as well as those closer to large metropolitan populations. Some argue—because the 1988 Indian Gaming Regulatory Act requires that tribes negotiate gaming compacts with states—that tribes have had to surrender some of their tribal sovereignty and cultural identity.[8]

The impact of gaming has been tremendous, but it has not magically resolved the underdevelopment and poverty that mark rural reservation communities. Nationwide reservation unemployment averages have hovered between 30 and 50 percent since the 1940s. In 1970, the median income for rural reservation Indians was about $4,500, 62 percent of what urban Indians earned and less than 41 percent of non-Indian income. Reservation unemployment was eight times the national average. By 1990, 31 percent of rural Indians lived in poverty compared to 16 percent of all rural residents and 13 percent of all Americans. Reservation unemployment averaged 38 percent, yet another 46.3 percent of rural Indians were underemployed, and 26.2 percent with full-time jobs were living near the poverty line. As of 2010, 28.4 percent of American Indians and Alaska Natives were living in poverty compared to the national rate of 15.3 percent. They also experienced the attendant problems of higher-than-average health and nutrition problems, criminal and accidental death rates, and lower life expectancy and educational attainment.[9]

What worries some observers is that tribes without abundant natural resources or access to other forms of meaningful development have chosen—or some say have been exploited by economic or environmental racism—to explore less-desirable types of economic development such as housing toxic wastes.[10] And here begins the story that leads from nuclear fission to rural America to Skull Valley, Utah.

A Place for Radioactive Waste

In 1954—at the height of the Cold War—Congress passed the Atomic Energy Act to encourage development of nuclear power, promising to dispose of radioactive wastes and protect the fledgling industry by limiting its liability in the event of an accident. In the 1960s and 1970s, nuclear power plants popped up across the East and Midwest, with a handful in Texas, Arizona, California, and Washington. Spent fuel rods also began to pile up, but governmental disposal plans lagged.

In 1982, Congress enacted the Nuclear Waste Policy Act, directing the Department of Energy (DOE) to establish a national nuclear-waste repository. The act also set up a Nuclear Waste Fund, financed by consumers through a one-tenth-of-a-cent tax per kilowatt-hour of energy on nuclear utility bills. Congress amended the act in 1987 to designate Yucca Mountain, Nevada, as the DOE's primary repository study site. Locals called it the Screw Nevada Bill.[11] Yucca Mountain—land claimed by the Western Shoshones under the 1863 Treaty of Ruby Valley and appropriated by the government without Shoshone consent—was riddled with political, geological, and construction problems from the beginning. Running out of on-site space and certain that a permanent storage facility was still years away, nuclear utilities pushed DOE for a short-term fix. Consequently DOE sent its nuclear-waste negotiator shopping for a temporary monitored retrievable storage (MRS) site to store reactor waste.[12]

By April 1992, eighteen local governmental organizations, representing underdeveloped rural communities across the country, had applied for the DOE's first round of $100,000 MRS study grants. Among the applicants were the commissioners of San Juan County in southeastern Utah. Rural and sparsely populated (two persons per square mile); dominated by federal parks, monuments, and forests as well as the northern portion of the Navajo Nation; and once the site of extensive uranium mining and milling during the height of the Cold War nuclear boom; San Juan County had fallen on hard times. With a quarter of its families living in poverty, San Juan County Commission Chair Ty Lewis saw waste storage as a viable development strategy. The commissioners used the first study grant to consider "every aspect of the monitored retrievable storage facility, including health safety and siting questions." "We haven't made any conclusions," Lewis told the press. "We're open-minded about the whole thing."

Sensing they were squarely in the crosshairs of this situation, Utah officials mobilized against the study grants. Governor Norman Bangerter (R), his successor Michael Leavitt (R), and Utah House of Representatives Speaker Craig Moody (R) all made it clear that bringing high-level radioactive waste to Utah was unacceptable. Moody railed that even the suggestion of studying the possibility was "outrageous" and that the Utah National Guard should be mobilized to block any imports. "We're not interested in any of this very deadly material, not temporarily, not permanently," he said.

Commissioner Lewis pointed out that "the state of Utah has a little responsibility there. I don't know how many tons and tons of yellowcake, etc., left the state,"—referring to the uranium-bearing ore mined and processed in southeastern Utah in the 1950s and 1960s. Lewis argued that its return in the form of spent fuel rods would reignite the local economy in an underdeveloped corner of rural Utah—500 construction jobs, 250 to 300 permanent jobs, annual payrolls of $12 to $15 million, and perhaps $75 to $85 million flowing into the economy over the project's sixteen-year life. "If you want economic development," he said, "this is the best thing that's ever come along." Expressing deep-seated frustration with distant urban legislators ignoring the needs of his county, Lewis shot back, "Everybody wants to help rural Utah economically, but nobody wants to do anything." In 1993, Governor Leavitt formally slammed the door on San Juan

County's application to pursue a second round of study grants, stating that it was "not in the best interest of the state or San Juan County." But for Leavitt, the larger MRS battle was just beginning.[13]

From the start, the DOE's nuclear-waste negotiator recognized this preemptive power of state governments over counties or corporations and so increasingly tailored his MRS pitch to American Indians. Ultimately more than twenty tribes responded, including the Skull Valley Goshutes, Mescalero Apaches, Yakimas, and several Alaskan Native communities.[14] But those applications also raised environmental-justice issues and elicited objections from tribal leaders. "It's genocide aimed at Indian people who will suffer the consequences of poisoning our rivers and our land with nuclear waste," warned Klickitat Chief Johnny Jackson of the Confederated Yakima Nation. "Even if tribes say they just want to study it, the government intends to hook tribal governments with the money. I know from experience that the government never gives you money for nothing." Anishinaabe activist Winona LaDuke spoke out against DOE's targeting of poor rural communities and the federal government's conflict of interest as both project promotor and Indian trustee. Some tribes considered and backed out; a handful used the grants to explore international nuclear operations. Both the Mescalero Apaches and Skull Valley Goshutes were eligible for a final-stage $2.8 million study grant when Congress killed funding in 1994. At that point, nuclear-power utilities took matters into their own hands.[15]

The utilities had more than 32,000 tons of high-level radioactive waste with a half-life of ten thousand years, produced by the industry's 105 active and 12 decommissioned commercial nuclear reactors and stored on-site at sixty-eight facilities in thirty-one states. They also had the federally mandated $3.8 billion nuclear-waste fund but no assurance the government would complete a permanent repository before power plants exceeded their on-site storage capacity. And their proposal to transport waste to a temporary MRS at the Nevada nuclear test site near Yucca Mountain (a bill dubbed "Mobile Chernobyl") was stalled in Congress.[16]

But the nuclear-power industry had its own money and an audience already identified and prepped by the DOE study grants. In 1994, Mescalero Apache Tribal Chair Wendall Chino and his council negotiated a deal with Northern States Power of Minnesota and a consortium of thirty nuclear utilities to construct a private MRS on Mescalero land. Two years later, the agreement fell apart, the victim of threats by New Mexico state officials and intratribal factionalism over "Chernobyl Chino's" leadership.[17]

But at the same moment, DOE Nuclear Waste Negotiator Richard Stallings announced that the Skull Valley Goshutes had agreed to streamline talks on a temporary waste repository. Stallings hailed the Goshute decision, telling the press, "I appreciate the fact the tribe is looking for economic development. Their land has little economic potential." A stunned Governor Michael Leavitt lashed out that "to make an agreement without contacting the state is somewhere between impolite and arrogant," and he promised to object "actively and strenuously." Goshute tribal attorney Danny Quintana pointedly reminded Utahns about tribal sovereign rights and that "the issues of nuclear energy and nuclear power are environmental problems which involve all of us.... This requires decisions made on the basis of fact, not hysteria."[18]

Despite state protests, Skull Valley leaders entered negotiations with Private Fuel Storage LLC (PFS), a Delaware-based limited-liability corporation made up of eight of the largest public utilities operating nineteen nuclear power plants in Minnesota, Wisconsin, Illinois, Ohio, New York, New Jersey, California, and Alabama. By the end of 1996, the Skull Valley band had reached an agreement to lease 820 acres of reservation land for up to forty years to PFS to construct a privately owned and operated independent spent-fuel-storage installation (ISFSI) for consortium members. The parties sealed the deal in May and June of 1997, submitting lease requests to the Bureau of Indian Affairs (BIA) and their application and draft environmental-impact statement to the Nuclear Regulatory Commission (NRC). Both agencies subsequently approved those applications, and the NRC review got under way. The difference in the results between the Mescalero and Goshute cases was that the Mescalero Apaches had a relatively large reservation population and plenty of other resources and development options—a successful casino and ski resort, tourism, hunting, cattle, timber, and natural gas—whereas the Skull Valley Goshutes did not.[19] And that, in part, is the story of Goshute contact history.

Kusiutta

For hundreds of years before white intrusion into the Great Basin, Numic-speaking peoples who called themselves Kusiutta ("people of the dry earth") inhabited the harsh arid region south and west of the Great Salt Lake. Despite derogatory comments by early Euro-American observers,

Goshutes were superbly adapted hunter-foragers with a cultural complex built on generations of accumulated experience with basin ecosystems. They were culturally flexible in organization and outlook by necessity because of the dispersion and variability of subsistence resources across microclimates, seasons, and years. Scarcity and mobility marked their social, political, and material culture. They moved in small affinal groups between water sources, accumulated little, and creatively used their resources.

But that simple material world rested on an elaborate metaphysical one. Their stories connected them to myth-time animal figures who created the world, distributed resources, instructed humans in proper behavior, and gave Goshutes their identity.[20] Their arid environment insulated Goshutes from their neighbors: Utes, who traded, married, and raided them; Spanish slavers who ventured north after Franciscan explorers Dominguez and Escalante; fur trappers looking for streams with beaver; and American overlanders who hurried west across the Great Salt Lake desert without looking back.[21]

Beginning in 1847, Mormon settlers—members of the Church of Jesus Christ of Latter-day Saints—fleeing the pluralism of American society overran the few fertile valleys of Utah. They systematically displaced Utes, Shoshones, Paiutes, and Goshutes from their resources and accustomed lifestyles, initiating a cycle of Indian starvation, raiding, and military reprisal. Mormons drove Goshutes into the desert hills of western Utah and appropriated or poisoned their waterholes, all in the name of protecting white settlers, livestock, and the overland trail. While Mormons, on one level, had a unique theological understanding of and connection to Indians through the Book of Mormon, on another, they responded to Indians—their land use, the hostility generated by resource competition, and their resistance to assimilation—in the same racial ways other Americans did. They shared Mark Twain's characterization of Goshutes as the

> wretchedest type of mankind I have ever seen, ... a silent, sneaking, treacherous-looking race, ... indolent, ... prideless beggars, ... always hungry, and yet never refusing anything that a hog would eat, though often eating what a hog would decline; hunters, but having no higher ambition than to kill and eat jackass rabbits, crickets, and grasshoppers, and embezzle carrion from the buzzards and coyotes; ... a thin, scattering race of almost naked black children ... who produce nothing at all, and have no villages, ... whose only shelter is

> a rag cast on a bush to keep off a portion of the snow, and yet who inhabit one of the most rocky, wintery, repulsive wastes that our country or any other can exhibit.

Twain concluded, "They deserve pity, poor creatures; and they can have mine—at this distance. Nearer by, they never get anybody's."[22]

Failing to exterminate or remove scattered Goshute bands to distant reservations, Mormons allowed federal officials to sign a treaty with the Indians in 1863, permitting this "disappearing remnant" to remain in their desert valleys. After that, with few exceptions, Goshutes were largely ignored, and their population dwindled to as few as 200 individuals in two bands, but they didn't disappear. And even though Goshutes didn't receive formal reservations until the 1910s, the Treaty of 1863 confirmed their legal identity, their territory, and their inherent sovereignty as a recognized tribe within the framework of federal Indian relations.[23]

No one paid much attention to the smaller of the two Goshute bands living on 18,000 acres in Skull Valley until World War II, when the isolation of Utah's West Desert made it perfect for the military. Air crews training at Wendover and Hill Air Force Bases bombed the West Desert. The army opened Dugway Proving Ground, Tooele Army Depot, and later Deseret Chemical Depot to develop, test, and store the nation's chemical and biological weapons. Between 1951 and 1969, there were 1,635 open-air tests involving more than fifty-five thousand chemical rockets, artillery shells, bombs, and land mines, as well as low- and high-altitude aerial-spraying tests. Weapons scientists released half a million pounds of nerve agent (3.5 trillion lethal doses) and scattered weapons over fourteen hundred square miles of public land adjacent to Skull Valley. Accidents were not uncommon. Nerve agents were released at altitude and dispersed widely with target hits of 10 to 30 percent common. In 1968, a Phantom jet leaked twenty pounds of VX nerve agent that drifted into Skull Valley, sickening ranchers and killing wildlife and sixty-four hundred grazing sheep. The government denied responsibility but took the sheep for testing and then buried them back on the reservation without tribal knowledge.[24]

In recent years, the government began consolidating and incinerating its aging biological weapons at the Deseret and Tooele chemical depots. Tooele County officials cashed in on their surroundings and created the hundred-square-mile West Desert Hazardous Industry Area, upwind from

Grantsville and Tooele. Tenants included Aptus Incinerator and Grassy Mountain Hazardous Waste Storage (now combined in Clean Harbors) and Envirocare (now EnergySolutions), which runs a landfill for low-level radioactive waste. And on the southwest side of the Great Salt Lake sits Magnesium Corporation of America, the worst air polluter in the country in the late 1990s, spewing sixty million pounds of chlorine gas and six million pounds of hydrochloric acid into the air annually. Tooele County and the state reaped the economic benefits of these facilities in jobs, taxes, and "mitigation fees."[25]

But the Skull Valley Reservation was also surrounded. "And we were never consulted on those issues whether we liked it or not," said Skull Valley Tribal Chair Leon Bear. "They didn't tell us that these things were dangerous. They didn't come out and tell the Goshute band or the Council, 'How would you guys like to have a hazardous and toxic waste dump by you? Or how would you like to have a low-level radioactive dump by you? Or how would you like to have the biological labs by you? Or the storage of nerve agents by you?'"[26] But that part of the story was about to change.

Skull Valley, PFS, and Radioactive Waste in Rural Utah

Danny Quintana, former attorney for the Skull Valley Band, remembered seeing the DOE's initial proposal for locating MRS sites. "I suggested... that we get the proposal because my intent was to gather the data and put together a report and kill the proposal." Like others, he assumed the DOE intended to dump the nation's nuclear waste on rural counties like San Juan or Indian reservations and then walk away. Longtime Tribal Chair Richard Bear (Leon's father) agreed and decided to pursue the proposal for the grant money alone. But after using $300,000 in grants to investigate the technological issues and long-term impact on their territory and health, Quintana noted that "it became crystal clear that this could be done safely." A MRS built to the world-class standards of facilities in Japan, France, and Sweden would protect and reward them handsomely.[27]

When Congress cancelled the program in 1994, the Skull Valley Goshutes continued educating themselves, touring national and international facilities. "We also went to... Governor Leavitt, and we had told him that this was our plan," said Leon Bear, who was tribal secretary at the time, "and asked him if the state of Utah wanted to be involved we

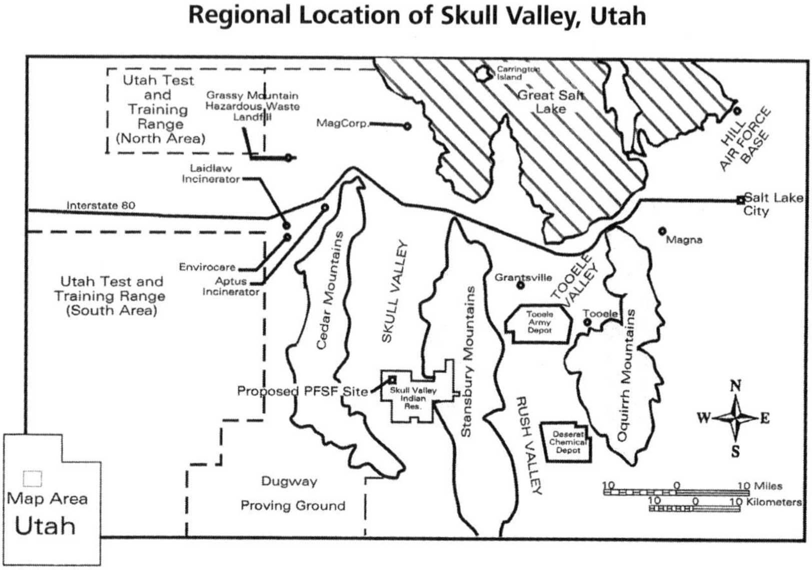

Regional Location of Skull Valley, Utah

Location of Skull Valley, Utah. Reprinted from U.S. Nuclear Regulatory Commission, *Final Environmental Impact Statement for the Construction and Operation of an Independent Spent Fuel Storage Installation on the Reservation of the Skull Valley Band of Goshute Indians and the Related Transportation Facility in Tooele County, Utah*, 2001.

would appreciate it." Leavitt had already squashed San Juan County's ability to pursue the project, and had recently "scolded" Tooele County commissioners for soliciting more hazardous out-of-state waste for disposal at Tooele Army Depot and their West Desert Hazardous Industry Area. But the Skull Valley proposal sent the governor into apoplexy, and he delivered an "over my dead body" ultimatum to the Goshutes that ended all conversation.[28]

On May 20, 1997, then-Tribal Chair Leon Bear and the Skull Valley Goshutes signed a private-sector lease with PFS to accept up to 40,000 metric tons of high-level radioactive waste and store it above ground in an ISFSI for twenty years, renewable to forty.

Ten million spent nuclear-fuel rods—3.5- to 4.5-meter-long zirconium alloy tubes packed with thousands of pencil-eraser-sized uranium pellets and bundled into groups of two hundred—would be removed from their water-cooling tanks and dry-packed into four-inch-thick steel casks, encased in two feet of concrete. Packaged casks from PFS-member utilities would be shipped by rail to the 820-acre Skull Valley ISFSI and placed inside upright stainless-steel cylinders capable of holding 10 tons of waste. Some four thousand cylinders—each eighteen feet tall—would sit spaced for cooling on a 100-acre pad of reinforced concrete, three feet thick and surrounded by a low wall. Two courses of eight-foot-high chain-link fencing would surround the perimeter.

At the time, construction costs were estimated at $500 million, creating four hundred temporary and forty to sixty permanent jobs. Contract payments to the Skull Valley band were confidential, but rumors put the figure between $48 and $240 million, plus preferential hiring for band members. PFS project manager Scott Northand estimated total operating costs at $3.1 billion over the forty-year life of the project.[29]

The Skull Valley decision to host an ISFSI was enormously complicated and deeply contested, even within the tribe. But the basic decision was driven by the same factors that made other rural populations (like San Juan County) explore the DOE proposal: the lack of economic alternatives (in rural Utah and the West in general); the promise of a "clean" industry providing jobs; and the mitigation fees to build infrastructure. Skull Valley Goshutes voted two to one to support the project as a means of revitalizing the band, whose resident population had dropped as low as 15 adult members in the 1960s. "People just gave up," recalled Leon Bear. "They just got up and left. June grass moved in, houses fell apart. Skull Valley pretty much died off at that point." Bear said a few older people like his mother tried to maintain seasonal subsistence traditions of gathering pine nuts and chokecherries, while his father served as tribal chair and worked at Deseret Chemical Depot. "So we did most of our gathering at Safeway," he joked.[30]

When the tribe voted to pursue the project with PFS, only 25 to 30 of 125 Skull Valley band members were living on the reservation; the rest resided in nearby Tooele County towns or along the urban corridor of Utah's Wasatch Front. Goshute unemployment and poverty rates were three times the national average. Thirty percent cuts to federal Indian programs in the mid-1990s and the loss of defense-industry jobs in Tooele County as the Cold War collapsed into America's "peace dividend" hurt the band.

Isolated and surrounded by toxic neighbors, the Goshutes found development opportunities scarce. The band operated a convenience store ironically named the Pony Express Station; they leased land to area ranchers as well as to Hercules Inc. and Alliant Techsystems for test-firing rocket boosters (the Tekoi Test Range); they sold dumpsters to private industries and government agencies; and they ran a solid-waste landfill for urban clients. Corporations approached them about storing mining byproducts or operating hazardous-waste incinerators, and PepsiCo and a local water company both explored building bottling plants in Skull Valley until they heard about nearby Dugway Proving Ground. There was talk of installing an elaborate irrigation system to grow hothouse tomatoes, but it proved too costly, and, as Leon Bear asked journalist Kevin Fedarko, "Would you buy a tomato from us if you knew what's out here? Of course not. In order to attract any kind of development, we have to be consistent with what surrounds us."[31]

At the same time, avenues of economic development open to other rural tribes remained closed to Utah Indians. Since the state of Utah has no legalized gaming or lotteries, tribes cannot establish casinos, bingo parlors, or even racetracks with pari-mutuel betting. Leon Bear called gaming "an equitable possibility" and alternative to nuclear-waste storage, but the state refused to discuss gaming compacts and made little effort to see if any development options might alter the band's decision. Nuclear waste was hot, but gaming was politically hotter in conservative Utah.[32]

With few economic choices and hopelessness, alcohol, migration, and language loss threatening their existence, Skull Valley leaders accepted the ISFSI as a bottom-line tool for cultural survival—to stop a rural tribal community from disappearing. "There is nothing on this land," Bear told a Brigham Young University reporter.

> I believe the benefits from this thing could be awesome, and I want to build up the reservation to the point where everything that we have doesn't have to be substandard anymore.... Tribal members are already expressing that they would come back if there were jobs on the reservation. If more of our people come back to Skull Valley, then things will improve here because they will bring back different ideas and visions that will help guide our future.[33]

"There's a fine line between tradition and economic development," he told *Deseret News* reporters. "Without tradition, there is no past, and without economic development, there is no future."[34] Ultimately, Bear said, "It's up to the people themselves to determine how much culture or traditions they want to maintain."[35]

Goshutes like Bear recognized the potential dangers of an ISFSI despite all the scientific reassurance but weighed that against the benefits of a revitalized tribal community. As Bear explained to reporter David Kestenbaum,

> The initial reaction was, 'Well, why do you want to do that? Isn't it dangerous?' And I said, 'Yes,...but it's just like the coming of the white man, that was dangerous too.' Storage is going to...have to be had in the United States, and it might as well be us. We're gonna get paid to store spent fuel. Yes, a long time ago, we were stewards of the land. Now the stewards are you guys, and I don't think you guys are doing a very good job, to tell the truth.[36]

Frustrated by critics who castigated Goshutes for not acting like "traditional ecological Indians," Bear lashed out: "They want to keep us the way they think of us: living in tepees and riding horses. That's not real. You can't feed your family on a stereotype."[37] "My ancestors ate grasshoppers," said Bear. "I don't want to live like that."[38] Bear insisted that they were acting as environmental stewards for the nation and that "the executive committee would never compromise itself to harm any of our children, the tribe, the land or the territory around it."[39] "We'll always be part of this land. We're not going anywhere. We're survivors."[40] Attorney Danny Quintana agreed, "They're very, very protective of their territory and they know exactly who they are and exactly what they're doing."[41]

Tooele County officials saw these events in a similar light. While statistically part of the Salt Lake City metropolitan area, the character of Tooele County is decidedly rural. In 2000, the 40,735 residents (5.6 per square mile) clustered in the towns of Tooele and Grantsville. Jobs in the county revolved around the federal Tooele, Deseret, and Dugway facilities as well as the private waste-disposal corporations that utilized Tooele's West Desert Hazardous Industry Area. Having lived with and built their county economy around safely handling the nation's most dangerous chemical and biological weapons, Tooele County commissioners chose to partner with Skull Valley and PFS. They saw site construction and operation jobs for their residents, fabricating the huge stainless-steel cylinders to hold the shipping casks on-site, but they also recognized that reservation development would spill over and place huge demands on existing county infrastructure and services.[42]

In May 2000, Tooele County commissioners signed an agreement with PFS that would net the county between $90 and $250 million over the forty-year life of the project. Recognizing that stopping such a facility on sovereign tribal land was beyond the power of the county or state, County Commissioner Gary Griffith recalled, "Our interest was to make sure again that if something was going to happen that we had no control over, we protected our citizens to the best of our ability." He shrugged off Governor Leavitt's disapproval as uninformed and uncaring about the economic interests of rural Utah counties. In the context of things that had been placed in his county without his choice (including toxic tailings from Salt Lake City's Vitro uranium mill that legislators had dumped on Tooele in the 1980s), and the materials his citizens worked with every day, Griffith found the proposed ISFSI innocuous and "purely a business decision." "I would submit to you that it probably would be the safest, cleanest business that we could bring into this county. Because, think about it, it produces not one thing that goes into the atmosphere, into the ground, into the water."[43]

Others, like Tooele County Commissioner Teryl Hunsaker, agreed, adding that they were also serving the state and nation: "We've done more then [*sic*] our share in fighting the wars, and now we're doing more then [*sic*] our share in cleaning up our environment, and when we get through... we will have a better world and we'll have a cleaner Mother Earth."[44]

But opposition to the Skull Valley/PFS project was strong, uniting political parties and diverse advocacy groups along Utah's Wasatch Front. As Attorney Danny Quintana pointed out, "This project is a no-brainer for a politician. It involves high-level radioactive waste. It involves a Native American community and it involves an opportunity to appear green even if they're not. So for a politician to oppose this is a slam dunk."[45]

Governor Michael Leavitt, the Utah Legislature, and Utah's congressional delegation teamed up with environmental organizations like the Southern Utah Wilderness Alliance as well as groups like HEAL Utah, Utah downwinders, and the Green Party to fight the Skull Valley deal. Together they argued that the environmental-impact assessments were flawed; that the region was seismically active; that transporting nuclear waste on state roads was dangerous; that accidents were inevitable and liability unclear; that terrorist attacks or errant military jet crashes could release radiation; and that the Skull Valley site would become, by default, a permanent nuclear-waste dump. All were legitimate concerns, especially in a state that remembered when the federal government had used rural Utahns as Cold War guinea pigs for radioactive fallout from the Nevada Test Site.[46]

But just beneath the surface of these arguments lay the state's financial self-interest and pure politics. Leavitt made that clear: "We don't produce it. We don't benefit from it, and we don't want to store it for those who do." In addition to the fact that U.S. citizens collectively bear the cost of radioactive waste (from locally generated medical and industrial waste to the national power grid, where nuclear fuels generate 20 percent of electricity), Utah had been a welcoming home to hazardous-waste companies that occupied cheap land in rural Utah, paid fees and taxes to the state and nonunion wages to employees, and made handsome campaign contributions to lawmakers to limit state oversight. One of those, Envirocare, was even then being reviewed by state regulators to store hotter Class B and C radioactive waste in its 640-acre Tooele County landfill. The state actively pursued federal appropriations to keep Dugway, Tooele, and Deseret operating, a trio of facilities capable of accidentally unleashing mass destruction against the entire Wasatch Front. Leavitt even named these as an "important economic asset to the state" that would be threatened by the Skull Valley ISFSI. Utah already had a vested interest in storing waste. As historian D. Michael Quinn observed, "When it suited the white majority of Utah to invite hazardous waste in, they did so...now they want to deny both the benefits and the risks to the Goshutes."[47]

Quinn's assessment hinted at an even deeper layer to the state's opposition—a cultural paternalism and racial thread that connected past and present white- and Mormon-Indian relations in Utah.[48] Opponents of the Skull Valley ISFSI claimed that PFS had enticed the Goshutes with money and information they couldn't handle. "I guess our concerns [sic] is, and I don't mean to be unkind to anybody," said Representative James V. Hansen (R) of Utah's first congressional district, "but they [PFS] put an awful lot of money on some of our Indian friends out there...the financial reward was maybe overwhelming to some folks who probably haven't seen much money in their lifetime, and we didn't think that was a proper thing to do."[49]

Other state officials adopted the language of environmental-justice advocates, arguing that the agreement was another example of corporations targeting Indians with the worst byproducts of industrialization. Such arguments fed into paternalistic social and religious beliefs that Indians were incapable victims, children, or dupes—stereotypes that historically had undercut Indian modernity and sovereignty.[50]

Skull Valley leaders responded that "charges of 'environmental racism' and the need to 'protect' and 'save' us smack of patronism [*sic*]. This attitude implies that we are not intelligent enough to make our own business and environmental decisions."[51] Online reader comments to newspaper stories about the Goshute case made it clear that these paternalistic racial attitudes were shared widely enough to be voiced openly.

The state's wholesale assault on the Skull Valley/PFS agreement played out very publicly and personally. Beginning in 1997, Governor Leavitt formed the Office of High Level Waste Storage within the state's Department of Environmental Quality to coordinate opposition to the project. He had the state annex county roads leading to Skull Valley to stop shipments of radioactive waste—creating a metaphorical "land moat" around the reservation. Utah officials petitioned intervention by every involved federal agency and filed a continuous stream of motions and lawsuits to derail the NRC licensing process.[52] In 2001, following NRC approval of the draft environmental-impact statement, the Utah Legislature passed bills to levy steep taxes and security bonds on PFS, to appropriate $1.1 million for outside legal help, and to offer the Goshutes $2 million for rural economic development if they would walk away from the project. However, that last bill contained no fiscal appropriation, frustrating Indian leaders across the state as well as the *Salt Lake Tribune*'s editor, who believed such a good-faith offer to work with the band might change things.[53]

In 2002, Utah voters put a Radioactive Waste Restrictions Act initiative on the November ballot to limit all waste dumping in Utah. State lawmakers (influenced by industry lobbyists who spent millions) ensured the initiative's defeat, arguing that it would hurt existing corporations like Envirocare (that pumped $5 million annually into the Tooele County economy) and keep others from locating in Utah.[54]

At the same time, some of those same lawmakers floated an end run called Plan B. Led by Utah Republican Party Chair Joe Cannon, the group proposed siting an MSR on state school-trust lands in rural Utah, tapping into the Nuclear Waste Fund (estimated at $11 billion), establishing state oversight, then outbidding the Goshutes to circumvent their deal with PFS entirely. "It would be a great shame for Utah to be stuck with this [nuclear waste] and not get a benefit," Cannon told reporter Dan Harrie. Even rural San Juan County jumped back on the bandwagon to be that lucrative Plan B site.[55]

Given the state's stance on the Skull Valley/PFS project, the hypocrisy of Plan B was obvious. Utah Director of Indian Affairs Forrest Cuch stormed, "It is appalling to me and smacks of racism at its highest...an outrage and selfishness and an abuse of power." PFS spokesperson Sue Martin said, "If that's the intent, to rob the Skull Valley Band of economic development they have been working on for 13 years, then that is just shameful." But Plan B discussions continued in private.[56]

By 2003, the state had spent $3.8 million trying (unsuccessfully) to defeat the Skull Valley project in the courts without ever engaging the band in serious negotiations the way they had white corporations looking for tax breaks or ways around environmental-waste regulations.[57] In Washington, DC, the Utah congressional delegation threw Nevada (and the Western Shoshones) under the political bus, voting for a Yucca Mountain national waste repository in return for a pledge (later broken) from Energy Secretary Spencer Abraham to block funds for the Skull Valley ISFSI. The delegation also cynically moved to designate a small wilderness area on federal land adjacent to Skull Valley (after opposing any and all wilderness designations in Utah for decades), thereby blocking a potential rail corridor and completing the state's land moat.[58]

But no one seriously talked to the Goshutes about viable alternatives. While Utah politicians assailed tribal sovereignty, they also claimed the state couldn't help Goshutes with economic development because of that sovereignty. Things might have gone differently, Leon Bear told reporter Kevin Fedarko, "if the people of Utah hadn't spent the better part of the past 170 years treating the Goshutes like pariahs."[59]

As part of its try-everything strategy, the state of Utah also hypocritically supported sincere and legitimate opposition to nuclear waste growing within the Skull Valley Band itself. Early in the process, reservation residents Margene Bullcreek and Sammy Blackbear had challenged the council's decision, charging their leaders had been bribed and misled, that they had failed to disclose terms of the PFS lease, and that young non-reservation Goshute urbanites who had lost their cultural connections to place had foisted the plan on them.[60] In 1997, Bullcreek organized Ohngo Gaudadeh Devia (OGD, meaning "mountain or ridge-top timber," or "timber-setting community"), a grassroots coalition of 21 tribal members and their environmental supporters to counter the 70 band members who supported the project. The state of Utah covered more than $500,000 in legal bills for OGD to challenge the BIA lease approval and file an environmental-justice challenge with the NRC against PFS, all unsuccessfully.[61] Bullcreek and Blackbear waged a very public and acrimonious debate in the press and courts, as well as through several closely contested band elections and resulting investigations into charges of embezzlement and tax evasion, but—through slim majorities and parliamentary maneuverings—the pro-PFS faction retained political control.[62]

Bullcreek and Blackbear framed their most potent arguments in cultural terms as reservation-dwelling "traditionalists," people for whom "seventh-generation" decision making and environmental standards defined Indian identity. "The real issue is not the money," Bullcreek told Kevin Kamps. "The real issue is who we are as Native Americans and what we believe in. If we accept these wastes, we're going to lose our tradition." Bullcreek feared the ISFSI would drive Goshutes away from the rural valley, away from the graves of ancestors that anchored them culturally, and toward an urban melting pot where Indianness would dissolve. "There is peace out here," said Bullcreek of her rural valley. "I felt I had to be outspoken or lose everything that has been passed down from generations. The stories that tell why we became the people we are and how we should consider our animal life, our air, things that are sacred to us. Leon Bear is trying to convince himself that what he is doing is right, but this waste will destroy who we are."[63]

Others picked up that argument, branding Goshute supporters of the ISFSI as urban people who were more like modern whites than "traditional tribal members" with their "inextricable spiritual attachment to the land." The resulting identity war that raged within the tribe over who was "traditional" and who was not invited outsiders to apply ecological Indian stereotypes and deny certain Goshutes their identity; they even questioned the Indianness (and therefore the sovereign authority) of the entire Skull Valley Band.[64]

The most disturbing and insightful political claim Bullcreek and Blackbear made was that PFS had used the band's sovereignty against itself, preventing the state or federal government from protecting Goshutes from the consequences of their own poor judgment. Blackbear went so far as to argue that Goshute "tribal sovereignty has been waived," a statement that fueled a general verbal assault on tribal sovereignty and Indian identity in Utah.[65]

Such arguments over the legal tradition of tribal sovereignty versus the preemptive power of states have become ubiquitous nationally, especially in the current states' rights Sagebrush Rebellion frenzy sweeping the West.[66] Those who directly assail the legal realities of limited sovereignty are easily overcome. More insidious are those who twist the essential meaning of tribal sovereignty from a legal status into a mere formality capable of being ignored when convenient for the "public good." This was Utah's tactic. "Something is dead wrong when a small group of people can ignore the will of 90 percent of our state," complained Utah congressman Merrill Cook (R). Governor Leavitt, who got a crash course in sovereignty from the losing end of every state lawsuit and procedural challenge, continued to insist that "I recognize the sovereignty of this group but let's put it in perspective. This is thirty or forty people who actually live there. We're talking about that by comparison to the public safety of two million people." Attorney Connie Nakahara, who directed the state's legal opposition to the Skull Valley project, put it bluntly: "I guess it's a little bit troubling that they have so much control over what happens to the state." The reverse irony of that statement—the impact of 150 years of state and federal control over the land and people of Skull Valley—went unnoticed.[67]

Epilogue

The furor over the Skull Valley/PFS agreement cooled during the late 2000s. In 2006, under political pressure from Utah's congressional delegation, the U.S. Department of the Interior revoked approval for a rail transfer station on federal land, blocking a key element in the Skull Valley/PFS plan. Interior also expressed lack of confidence that the facility would be temporary in the light of growing doubts about Yucca Mountain. Utah's delegation—led by Senator Orrin Hatch (R), who never met with the Goshutes—coldly gloated that the state had "put a stake right through the heart of this project," that it was "stone cold dead," and that "it couldn't happen to nicer people."[68]

Goshute opponents like Margene Bullcreek expressed relief that nuclear waste wouldn't destroy the tranquility of her valley and looked forward to a "healing process from all the hurt and separation it has caused our relatives." Goshute proponents like Leon Bear were philosophical: "I was told a long time ago by my elders," said Bear, "...if it comes, it comes, and if it doesn't, it doesn't. What does the band have to begin with anyway? We had nothing, we still have nothing." If this deal was over, Bear said, there would be others.[69] Bear and his council were replaced by other Goshutes, who quietly continued to pursue project approval.

In 2010, much to Hatch's dismay, a federal district judge ruled in favor of Goshute/PFS claims that the Department of the Interior's 2006 lease denial had been politically motivated and must be reconsidered. Life flowed back into the project again, especially after President Barack Obama's administration shuttered Yucca Mountain as a national waste repository. But in December 2012, PFS asked the Nuclear Regulatory Commission to terminate its license, ending the possibility of an ISFSI in Skull Valley. Given the political roadblocks thrown in its path, ongoing costs, the defection of a number of member utilities, and the uncertain commitment of a new group of tribal leaders, PFS called it quits.[70]

Today Skull Valley is again as quiet as its name implies. The nation's nuclear utilities now have an estimated 75,000 metric tons of spent nuclear fuel awaiting disposal in a national repository that is even further away from opening. While they now legally store some waste on-site in the dry casks that would have graced Skull Valley, their space has limits, and eventually they'll look to rural America again. Utah's San Juan County remains rural, poor, ignored, underdeveloped, and increasingly dependent on—yet resentful and suspicious of—red-rock tourism, which has tradeoffs for rural communities—what Hal Rothman called a "devil's bargain." So San Juan residents remain interested in other economic-development options, even radioactive ones.[71]

Tooele County's budget has collapsed with the loss of jobs, taxes, and mitigation fees ($5.7 million between 2007 and 2011) since Deseret Chemical Depot incinerated its last weapon in January 2012. EnergySolutions is also paying Tooele fewer fees as federally funded radioactive waste-disposal projects dry up. Utah lawmakers, pleased with defeating the Skull Valley/PFS project—but concerned by the decline of these hazardous-waste facilities—continued to negotiate with EnergySolutions over importing, blending, and storing hotter Class B and C waste. Many also openly supported plans to construct a private nuclear power plant near Green River, Utah. And Plan B (an ISFSI on state school-trust lands) is almost certainly still circulating under the radar in rural Utah, waiting for the right moment to reappear. All of this dissention with Leavitt's simple "over my dead body" message—especially in the wake of the March 2011 Fukushima Daiichi nuclear disaster in Japan—clarifies that the Skull Valley/PFS debate in Utah has always concerned more than just radioactive waste.[72]

The Skull Valley Band of Goshute Indians remains battered and bitterly divided, if less public in their disagreements. Even fewer inhabit the reservation full time, and it is unclear how many of the roughly 100 tribal members and their elected representatives still supported the project when PFS terminated its NRC license. Lori Bear, chair of the Skull Valley Band, expressed her disappointment but recognized that the project had always been a long shot and the council's job remained the same: "to bring jobs and revenue to the Goshute Reservation so our people can be self-sufficient."[73] In the end, Margene Bullcreek, Leon Bear, and the rest of the Skull Valley band wanted the same thing—to create some kind of meaningful economic development to help preserve the Goshutes' physical space, their society and cultural identity, and their sovereign tribal rights.[74]

Change *sovereignty* to *local control,* and you describe most rural communities in this nation today, making difficult choices about their present and future: how best to stabilize population and address physical isolation in an age of mobility and information technology; how to maintain homes and families, schools and community institutions; how to renew basic infrastructure and recapture local businesses and financial institutions; how to create jobs and control natural-resource use that also protects rural health and the environment; how to deal with short-term corporate interests and the regulatory responsibilities of public-lands managers; and how to rekindle the intangible spark that is the social life of a place, that is community itself.

Despite these concerns and experiences shared with other rural Americans, Indians are set apart by the fraught concepts of identity and sovereignty. These are mirrored in the differences between Bullcreek and Bear, echoed in the identity wars that occurred within the Skull Valley Band, and reinforced by the assault from outsiders, who stereotyped Goshutes to assail their capability, modernity, identity, and sovereignty. They reverberate across Indian Country in debates over what it means to be Indian, what difficult choices it takes to maintain cultural identity and sovereignty on top of everything else, and what others have always been willing to do to limit or abrogate that sovereignty. We see it in both historic and ongoing disputes over hunting and fishing rights, tribal resource use and management, casino gaming, religious freedom, and creative property rights. In that way, the experiences of rural reservation residents—and Skull Valley Goshutes—remain separate, unique. The stakes for Goshutes are much higher, given their uncomfortable history of Indian/white relations, the aggressive reassertion of states' rights over federal and tribal authority, the persistent racism that complicates all those interactions, and the mobility that removes people from their rural homes—a movement some Indians fear will become cultural and then biological, a second "disappearing" of Native America.[75]

The reality is that nobody really wanted a high-level radioactive waste dump in Skull Valley, Utah, or, for that matter, anywhere in rural America. What Goshutes wanted—and still need—is the economic promise to help create the physical and cultural community they imagine. Margene Bullcreek and storage opponents firmly believed the waste would poison the reservation and destroy them culturally. "Being traditional is part of what we are as Native Americans, and this is something that has been passed down through the generations," said Bullcreek. "We could have become part of the melting pot a long time ago if the government would have had its way, but throughout the years we have managed to hold onto our identity. And in our identity we respect our land, our air and our animals because they are sacred to us."[76]

On the other hand, Leon Bear and storage proponents saw this compromise as the best way to preserve Goshute identity and sovereignty, to recreate the reservation community Bullcreek wants. "Look, I'm not here to lay down and die like the buffalo," Bear told Kevin Fedarko. "...This is a survival issue for us. But in order to bring my people back to the reservation, we're going to have to provide them with a livelihood. That means real jobs, real houses. As far as being traditional and protecting Mother Earth, I don't understand how we can do that.... There's no way we can go back to living off the land. Not with what they've done to it."[77] "I consider myself to be a traditionalist, too.... I have reverence for the animals, plant life and the Earth. But I also have reverence for the people."[78] "I don't know about seven generations," Bear said. "Without us, there won't be a seventh generation and that's what this is all about."[79]

Bullcreek and Bear are both right. They imagine two ways of being Indian, two strategies for sovereignty, two ways of holding onto place, two paths to the meaning of "we're still here." And that's still only two of the many different ways Indian peoples (and by extension, other rural Americans) imagine their presents and futures. While the Skull Valley story is local and perhaps exceptional in its nuclear consequences and Indianness (including sovereignty), and while it can be told from any number of viewpoints and in any number of ways, it parallels the stories other rural tribes and peoples tell about the very real challenges and very human choices they face. At the heart of each story is a place, a landscape, a sacred geography, an attachment, a way of being and becoming, a meaning, an identity. "The truth about stories is that that's all we are," Native novelist Tom King reminds us.[80] Our stories bind us together—as urban and rural westerners, native and nonnative—even as they divide us on land that was the Native West long before it was the rural West.

Notes

1. Leon Bear, interview by Ken Verdoia, *Skull Valley: Radioactive Waste and the American West*, produced by Ken Verdoia (Salt Lake City: KUED-TV, 2001), interview transcripts, p. 8 (hereafter Leon Bear interview), accessed May 17, 2015, http://www.kued.org/sites/default/files/skull_valley_interviews.pdf.
2. Some portions of this essay first appeared as David Rich Lewis, "Skull Valley Goshutes and the Politics of Nuclear Waste: Environment, Economic Development, and Tribal Sovereignty," in *Native Americans and the Environment: Perspectives on the Ecological Indian*, ed. Michael E. Harkin and David Rich Lewis (Lincoln: University of Nebraska Press, 2007), 304–42. See also the narration of the documentary film *Skull Valley: Radioactive Waste and the American West*, produced by Ken Verdoia, accessed May 17, 2015, http://www.kued.org/whatson/kued-local-productions/skull_valley, script in the author's possession (hereafter Verdoia, *Skull Valley*).
3. David Rich Lewis, "Native Americans: The Original Westerners," in *The Rural West Since World War II*, ed. R. Douglas Hurt (Lawrence: University Press of Kansas, 1998), 12–37; R. Douglas Hurt, *Indian Agriculture in America: Prehistory to the Present* (Lawrence: University Press of Kansas, 1987). For a recent working definition of *rural*, see Rebecca LaGrandeur and Michael De Alessi, "What Is Rural?," Rural West Initiative, Bill Lane Center for the American West, Stanford University, April 2010, accessed September 1, 2012, http://www.stanford.edu/group/ruralwest/cgi-bin/drupal/content/what-rural.
4. Arlene Hirschfelder and Martha Kreipe de Montaño, *The Native American Almanac: A Portrait of Native America Today* (New York: Prentice Hall, 1993),

28; C. Matthew Snipp, *American Indians: The First of This Land* (New York: Russell Sage Foundation, 1989), 83; C. Matthew Snipp and Gary D. Sandefur, "Small Gains for Rural Indians Who Move to Cities," *Rural Development Perspectives* 5, no. 1 (October 1988): 22; Joane Nagel, Carol Ward, and Timothy Knapp, "The Politics of American Indian Economic Development: The Reservation/Urban Nexus," in *Public Policy Impacts on American Indian Economic Development*, ed. C. Matthew Snipp (Albuquerque: Institute for Native American Development, University of New Mexico, 1988), 61; Office of Minority Health, "American Indian/Alaska Native Profile," U.S. Department of Health and Human Services, accessed November 30, 2014, http://minorityhealth.hhs.gov/omh/browse.aspx?lvl=3&lvlid=62. For a more complicated story of the way Native peoples lived in, negotiated, and shaped the growth of a particular urban center through the nineteenth and twentieth centuries, see Coll Thrush, *Native Seattle: Histories from the Crossing-Over Place* (Seattle: University of Washington Press, 2008).

5. Paul Stuart, *Nations within a Nation: Historical Statistics of American Indians* (New York: Greenwood Press, 1987), 57; Tina Norris, Paula L. Vines, and Elizabeth F. Hoeffel, "The American Indian and Alaska Native Populations," *2010 Census Briefs* (Washington, DC: Economic and Statistics Administration, U.S. Census Bureau, U.S. Department of Commerce, January 2012), 5–8.
6. Norris, Vines, and Hoeffel, "American Indian and Alaska Native Populations," 12–13; C. Matthew Snipp and Gene F. Summers, "American Indians and Economic Poverty," in *Rural Poverty in America*, ed. Cynthia M. Duncan (New York: Auburn House, 1992), 155–56; Peter Iverson, *When Indians Became Cowboys: Native Peoples and Cattle Ranching in the American West* (Norman: University of Oklahoma Press, 1994), 182–224; Michael P. Nofz, "Rural Community Development: The Case of Indian Reservations," *Rural Sociologist* 6, no. 2 (March 1986): 69; Robert P. Swierenga, "Theoretical Perspectives on the New Rural History: From Environmentalism to Modernization," *Agricultural History* 56, no. 3 (July 1982): 495–96.
7. C. Matthew Snipp, "Public Policy Impacts and American Indian Economic Development," in *Public Policy Impacts on American Indian Economic Development*, ed. C. Matthew Snipp (Albuquerque: Institute for Native American Development, University of New Mexico, 1988), 5; Nagel, Ward, and Knapp, "Politics of American Indian Economic Development," 42–44; Hurt, *Indian Agriculture in America*, 195–208; Alan L. Sorkin, *American Indians and Federal Aid* (Washington, DC: Brookings Institute, 1971), 18, 66–78; William A. Brophy and Sophie D. Aberle, comps., *The Indian, America's Unfinished Business* (Norman: University of Oklahoma Press, 1966), 63, 80–81; William P. Kuvlesky, Clark S. Knowlton, Thomas J. Durant Jr., and William C. Payne Jr., "Minorities," in *Rural Society in the U.S.: Issues for the 1980s*, ed. Don A. Dillman and Daryl J. Hobbs (Boulder: Westview Press, 1982), 105–6; National Agricultural Statistics Service, "Farms with American Indians or Alaskan Na-

tive Operators Compared with All Farms," *2007 Census of Agriculture* (Washington, DC: U.S. Department of Agriculture, 2007), 5–6.

8. Lewis, "Native Americans," 20–26; Snipp and Summers, "American Indians and Economic Poverty," 165–74; Sorkin, *American Indians and Federal Aid*, 80–96; Brophy and Aberle, *The Indian*, 96–102; Larry Burt, "Western Tribes and Balance Sheets: Business Development Programs in the 1960s and 1970s," *Western Historical Quarterly* 23, no. 4 (November 1992): 475–95; David Rich Lewis, "Still Native: The Significance of Native Americans in the History of the Twentieth-Century American West," *Western Historical Quarterly* 24, no. 2 (May 1993): 211–17; Stephen Cornell and Joseph P. Kalt, eds., *What Can Tribes Do? Strategies and Institutions in American Indian Economic Development* (Los Angeles: American Indian Studies Center, 1992); Charles Wilkinson, *Blood Struggle: The Rise of Modern Indian Nations* (New York: W. W. Norton, 2005); Stephen Cornell, Joseph Kalt, Matthew Kreps, and Jonathan Taylor, *American Indian Gaming Policy and Its Socioeconomic Effects: A Report to the National Gambling Impact Study Commission* (Cambridge, MA: Economics Resource Group, 1998); Steven Andrew Light and Kathryn R. L. Rand, *Indian Gaming and Tribal Sovereignty: The Casino Compromise* (Lawrence: University Press of Kansas, 2005).
9. Harvard Project on American Indian Economic Development, *The State of the Native Nations: Conditions under U.S. Policies of Self-Determination* (New York: Oxford University Press, 2008); Bonnie Jean Adams, "American Indians in Rural America—Conditions and Concerns," in *The Hidden America: Social Problems in Rural America for the Twenty-First Century*, ed. Robert M. Moore III (Cranbury, NJ: Associated University Presses, 2001), 276–93; Brophy and Aberle, *The Indian*, 68, 141, 160–70; Helen W. Johnson, "Rural Indian Americans in Poverty," in *Native Americans Today: Sociological Perspectives*, ed. Howard M. Bahr, Bruce A. Chadwick, and Robert C. Day (New York: Harper and Row, 1972), 25–27; Howard M. Bahr, Bruce A. Chadwick, and Joseph H. Stauss, *American Ethnicity* (Lexington, MA.: D. C. Heath, 1979), 151, 156, 159–60, 165, 170–71, 198–204, 362; Stuart, *Nations within a Nation*, 95–120, 145–202; Snipp, *American Indians*, 206–65; Snipp and Summers, "American Indians and Economic Poverty," 155, 169–71, 174; Marlita A. Reddy, ed., *Statistical Record of Native North Americans* (Detroit: Gale Research, 1993), 485, 663, 685–91, 723, 771, 812–15; Rural Sociological Society Task Force on Persistent Rural Poverty, *Persistent Poverty in Rural America* (Boulder: Westview Press, 1993), 175–78; Jonathan B. Taylor and Joseph P. Kalt, *American Indians on Reservations: A Databook of Socioeconomic Change between the 1990 and 2000 Censuses* (Cambridge, MA: Harvard Project on American Indian Economic Development, 2005); U.S. Census Bureau, "Newsroom: Profile America, Facts for Features: American Indian and Alaska Native Heritage Month, November 2011," U.S. Department of Commerce, accessed November 30, 2014, http://www.census.gov/newsroom/releases/archives/facts_for_features_special_editions/cb11-ff22.html.

10. Donald A. Grinde and Bruce E. Johansen, *Ecocide of Native America: Environmental Destruction of Indian Lands and Peoples* (Santa Fe: Clear Light Publishers, 1995); David Rich Lewis, "Native Americans and the Environment: A Survey of Twentieth-Century Issues," *American Indian Quarterly* 19, no. 3 (Summer 1995): 423–50; Dan McGovern, *The Campo Landfill War: The Fight for Gold in California's Garbage* (Norman: University of Oklahoma Press, 1995); Jace Weaver, ed., *Defending Mother Earth: Native American Perspectives on Environmental Justice* (Maryknoll, NY: Orbis Books, 1996).
11. Randel D. Hanson, "Half Lives of Reagan's Indian Policy: Marketing Nuclear Waste to American Indians," *American Indian Culture and Research Journal* 25, no. 1 (2001): 21–44; John Karl Gross, "Note: Nuclear Native America: Nuclear Waste and Liability on the Skull Valley Goshute Reservation," *Boston University Journal of Science and Technology Law* 7, no. 1 (Winter 2001): 140–67; Ronald Eagleye Johnny, "Showing Respect for Tribal Law: Siting a Nuclear Waste MRS Facility," *Akwe:kon Journal* 11 (Spring 1994): 16–27; Luther J. Carter, *Nuclear Imperative and Public Trust: Dealing with Radioactive Waste* (Washington, DC: Resources for the Future, 1987).
12. Charles J. Kappler, *Indian Affairs: Laws and Treaties,* (Washington, DC: Government Printing Office, 1904), 2: 851–53; Steven J. Crum, *The Road on Which We Came, Po'I Pentun Tammen Kimmappeh: A History of the Western Shoshone* (Salt Lake City: University of Utah Press, 1994); Valerie L. Kuletz, *The Tainted Desert: Environmental and Social Ruin in the American West* (New York: Routledge, 1998); N. S. Nokkentved, "Geological Controversy Haunts Nevada Waste Site," *High Country News,* March 25, 1991, 13; Jon Christensen, "Can Nevada Bury Yucca Mountain?" *High Country News,* July 2, 2001, 1, 8–10; Gerald Jacob, *Site Unseen: The Politics of Siting a Nuclear Waste Repository* (Pittsburgh: University of Pittsburgh Press, 1990); Robert Vandenbosch and Susanne E. Vandenbosch, *Nuclear Waste Stalemate: Political and Scientific Controversies* (Salt Lake City: University of Utah Press, 2007); Allison M. Macfarlane and Rodney C. Ewing, eds., *Uncertainty Underground: Yucca Mountain and the Nation's High-Level Nuclear Waste* (Cambridge, MA: MIT Press, 2006); J. Samuel Walker, *The Road to Yucca Mountain: The Development of Radioactive Waste Policy in the United States* (Berkeley: University of California Press, 2009).
13. "San Juan County, Utah," *Wikipedia,* accessed November 30, 2014, http://en.wikipedia.org/wiki/San_Juan_County,_Utah; Ty Lewis and Craig Moody, quoted in Joseph Bauman, "San Juan County, Goshutes Bristle at Moody's N-Blockade Proposal," *Deseret News,* April 21, 1992, B1; Jim Woolf, "San Juan, Goshutes Consider Building Giant Radioactive-Waste Complex," *Salt Lake Tribune,* July 13, 1992, B1; Woolf, "Leavitt Says San Juan Out as Nuclear Waste Repository," *Salt Lake Tribune,* January 14, 1993, A1. See also Lisa Bourke, "Economic Attitudes and Responses to Siting Hazardous Waste Facilities in Rural Utah," *Rural Sociology* 59, no. 3 (Fall 1994): 485–96.
14. Bunty Anquoe, "New Nuclear Waste Official Pledges Negotiations for Tribes," *Indian Country Today,* December 15, 1993, A3; Hanson, "Half Lives of Reagan's

Policy," 42–43; M. V. Rajeev Gowda and Doug Easterling, "Nuclear Waste and Native America: The MRS Siting Exercise," *Risk: Health, Safety & Environment* 9, no. 3 (Summer 1998): 229–58; Jon D. Erickson, Duane Chapman, and Ronald E. Johnny, "Monitored Retrievable Storage of Spent Nuclear Fuel in Indian Country: Liability, Sovereignty, and Socioeconomics," *American Indian Law Review* 19, no. 1 (1994): 73–103.

15. Johnny Jackson, quoted in Valerie Taliman, "Tribes Denounce Interest in Nuclear Wastes," *Lakota Times*, April 22, 1992, A6; Kevin Kamps, "Environmental Racism, Tribal Sovereignty and Nuclear Waste: High-Level Atomic Waste Dump Targeted at Skull Valley Goshute Indian Reservation in Utah," Nuclear Information and Resource Service, factsheet, last modified February 15, 2001, accessed November 30, 2014, http://www.nirs.org/factsheets/pfsejfactsheet.htm; Ward Churchill and Winona LaDuke, "Native North America: The Political Economy of Radioactive Colonialism," in *The State of Native America: Genocide, Colonization, and Resistance*, ed. M. Annette Jaimes (Boston: South End Press, 1992), 241–66; Lewis, "Native Americans and the Environment," 435–36; Steven M. Hoffman, "Negotiating Eternity: Energy Policy, Environmental Justice, and the Politics of Nuclear Waste," *Bulletin of Science, Technology and Society* 21, no. 6 (December 2001): 456–72.
16. Alex Tallchief Skibine, "High Level Nuclear Waste on Indian Reservations: Pushing the Tribal Sovereignty Envelope to the Edge?" *Journal of Land, Resources, & Environmental Law* 21 (2001): 287–316; Kevin Fedarko, "In the Valley of the Shadow," *Outside*, May 2000, 2, http://www.outsideonline.com/outdoor-adventure/politics/In-the-Valley-of-the-Shadow-9.html; C. Michael Rasmussen, "Note: Gaining Access to Billions of Dollars and Having a Nuclear Waste Backyard," *Journal of Land, Resources, & Environmental Law* 18 (1998): 335–67; Kamps, "Environmental Racism," 2–3.
17. Louis G. Leonard III, "Sovereignty, Self-Determination, and Environmental Justice in the Mescalero Apache's Decision to Store Nuclear Waste," *Boston College Environmental Affairs Law Review* 24, no. 3 (Spring 1997): 651–93; Noah Sachs, "The Mescalero Apache Indians and Monitored Retrievable Storage of Spent Nuclear Fuel: A Study in Environmental Ethics," *Natural Resources Journal* 36, no. 4 (Fall 1996): 881–912.
18. Associated Press, "Goshutes Sign Agreement to Streamline Nuke Talks," *Logan (UT) Herald Journal*, November 13, 1994, 4; Mike Gorrell, "Leavitt to Tribe: Don't Waste Utah," *Salt Lake Tribune*, November 12, 1994, A1; Steve Fidel, "Leavitt Blasts Plan to Store N-Rods in Utah," *Deseret News*, November 12, 1994, B1.
19. Jim Woolf, "Utah's Not Aglow over Goshute Deal to Store N-Waste," *Salt Lake Tribune*, December 25, 1996, A1; K. Marie Porterfield, "Goshute Activists Fight Nuclear Waste Dump," *Indian Country Today*, September 8–15, 1997, A1; Rasmussen, "Gaining Access to Billions of Dollars," 343–45; Verdoia, *Skull Valley;* Michael Satchell, "Dances with Nuclear Waste," *U.S. News and World Report* 120, no. 1 (January 8, 1996): 29–30.

20. Lewis, "Skull Valley Goshutes," 309–17; Dennis R. Defa, "The Goshute Indians of Utah," in *A History of Utah's American Indians,* ed. Forrest S. Cuch (Salt Lake City: Utah State Division of Indian Affairs and the Utah State Division of History, 2000), 73–122; David Hurst Thomas, Lorann S.A. Pendleton, and Stephen C. Cappanari, "Western Shoshone," in *Handbook of North American Indians,* ed. Warren L. D'Azevedo, vol. 11, *Great Basin* (Washington, DC: Smithsonian Institution, 1986), 262–83; Julian H. Steward, *Basin-Plateau Aboriginal Sociopolitical Groups,* Bureau of American Ethnology Bulletin 120, Smithsonian Institution (1938; repr., Salt Lake City: University of Utah Press, 1970), 48–49, 132–41; Carling Malouf, "The Goshute Indians," in *Shoshone Indians,* American Indian Ethnohistory: California and Basin-Plateau Indians, comp. and ed. David Agee Horr (New York: Garland Publishing, 1974), 25–172; Anne M. Smith, ed., *Shoshone Tales* (Salt Lake City: University of Utah Press, 1993), xxv–xxxi, 3–46.
21. Malouf, "The Goshute Indians," 73–79; Defa, "Goshute Indians of Utah," 83–92; Steward, *Basin-Plateau Aboriginal Groups,* 134–35.
22. David L. Bigler, *Forgotten Kingdom: The Mormon Theocracy in the American West, 1847–1896* (Logan: Utah State University Press, 1998); Sondra Jones, "Saints or Sinners?: The Evolving Perceptions of Mormon-Indian Relations in Utah Historiography," *Utah Historical Quarterly* 72, no. 1 (Winter 2004): 19–46; Dan Vogel, *Indian Origins and the* Book of Mormon (Salt Lake City: Signature Books, 1986); Forrest S. Cuch, ed., *A History of Utah's American Indians;* Defa, "Goshute Indians of Utah," 92–100; James B. Allen and Ted J. Warner, "The Gosiute Indians in Pioneer Utah," *Utah Historical Quarterly* 39, no. 2 (Spring 1971): 162–77; Howard A. Christy, "Open Hand and Mailed Fist: Mormon-Indian Relations in Utah, 1847–52," *Utah Historical Quarterly* 46, no. 3 (Summer 1978): 216–35; Christy, "'What Virtue There Is in Stone' and Other Pungent Talk on the Early Utah Frontier," *Utah Historical Quarterly* 59, no. 3 (Summer 1991): 301–6; Mark Twain, *Roughing It* (1872; repr., New York: New American Library, 1962), 118, 120.
23. Malouf, "The Goshute Indians," 108–35; Skull Valley Band of Goshute Indians, "Sovereignty," accessed February 20, 2004, http://www.skullvalleygoshutes.org (site discontinued); Steven J. Crum, "The Skull Valley Band of the Goshute Tribe—Deeply Attached to Their Native Homeland," *Utah Historical Quarterly* 55, no. 3 (Summer 1987): 250–67; Kappler, *Indian Affairs,* 2: 859–60. Goshutes received the 34,000-acre Deep Creek Reservation by executive order in 1914, and the 18,000-acre Skull Valley Reservation in 1917 and 1918.
24. Chip Ward, *Canaries on the Rim: Living Downwind in the West* (New York: Verso, 1999), 98–110; Roy Reed, "Army Admits Its Nerve Gas Killed 6,000 Sheep," *New York Times,* May 22, 1968, 14; Jim Woolf, "Tribe Digs into Mystery of Sheep That Died Near Dugway in 1968," *Salt Lake Tribune,* December 14, 1997, A1.
25. Ward, *Canaries on the Rim,* 62–90, 149–214; Mike Davis, "Utah's Toxic Heaven," *Capitalism, Nature, Socialism: A Journal of Socialist Ecology* 9, no. 2 (June 1998): 35–39; Noriko Ishiyama, "Environmental Justice and American-

Indian Sovereignty: Political, Economic, and Ethnic Struggles Regarding the Storage of Radioactive Waste," (PhD diss., Rutgers University, 2002); Ishiyama, "Environmental Justice and American Indian Tribal Sovereignty: Case Study of a Land-Use Conflict in Skull Valley, Utah," *Antipode* 35, no. 1 (January 2003): 127–28; Bruce Selcraig, "The Filthy West: Toxics Pour into Our Air, Water, Land," *High Country News*, September 16, 1996, 1, 6–10; Jerry D. Spangler and Donna Kemp Spangler, "Toxic Utah," *Deseret News*, eight-part series, February 11–18, 2001.

26. Leon Bear interview, p. 9.
27. Danny Quintana, interview by Ken Verdoia, *Skull Valley*, interview transcripts, p. 84 (hereafter Danny Quintana interview).
28. Leon Bear interview, p. 5; Editorial, "Governor Reiterates 'Don't Waste Utah,'" *Salt Lake Tribune*, August 16, 1993, A6; Associated Press, "Amendment May Doom Goshute Plans for Proposed Nuclear Waste Dump," *Indian Country Today*, October 6, 1993, A6; Gorrell, "Leavitt to Tribe: Don't Waste Utah," A1.
29. Rasmussen, "Gaining Access to Billions of Dollars," 344–46; Verdoia, *Skull Valley*; Fedarko, "In the Valley of the Shadow," 4, 7; Kamps, "Environmental Racism," 3; Skull Valley Goshute Tribe Executive Office, "Native Americans Have the Right to Make Their Own Land-Use Decisions," in *Environmental Justice*, ed. Jonathan S. Petrikin (San Diego: Greenhaven Press, 1995), 65.
30. Leon Bear, quoted in Fedarko, "In the Valley of the Shadow," 6.
31. Defa, "Goshute Indians of Utah," 118–22; Ward, *Canaries on the Rim*, 216–17; Maureen Zent, "Last Stand in Skull Valley," *Edging West*, no. 12 (Summer 1997): 28–29; Skull Valley Goshute Tribe Executive Office, "Native Americans Have the Right," 66–67; Fedarko, "In the Valley of the Shadow," 1, 3, 6.
32. Tony Semerad, "Utah Tribes Want Piece of Gaming Business: Goshutes Study Parimutual Track; Utes Set Sights on E. Utah Casino," *Salt Lake Tribune*, June 30, 1992, B1; Phil Miller, "Tribe to Try Its Hand at Gambling? Seeking a Revenue Source, Utah Goshutes say 'Bingo!'" *Salt Lake Tribune*, October 11, 1997, A1; Leon Bear interview, p. 11.
33. Leon Bear, quoted in Miki Meek, "Goshute Divided on Nuclear Waste Storage," *BYU NewsNet*, September 17, 2000, accessed February 18, 2008, http://byumedia.com/print/story.cfm/11073 (site discontinued).
34. Leon Bear, quoted in Dennis Romboy and Lucinda Dillon Kinkead, "A Time of Change—Industry Plans Cause Discord in, out of Tribes," *Deseret News*, September 26, 2006.
35. Jim Woolf, "Utah Tribe Won't Dump Plan for Its N-Facility: Goshutes Press Ahead with N-Plans," *Salt Lake Tribune*, April 16, 1997, A1. See also Leon Bear interview, p. 8.
36. Leon Bear, quoted in David Kestenbaum, "A Tribe Split by Nuclear Waste," *Morning Edition*, National Public Radio, October 21, 2005, http://www.npr.org/templates/story/story.php?storyId=4967885.
37. Leon Bear, quoted in Tom Knudson, "Environment, Inc.: Drilling Debate Jolts Old Image of Indians," *Sacramento Bee*, December 9, 2001.

38. Leon Bear, quoted in John L. Fialka, "Goshute Indians' Plan to Store Nuclear Waste for Eight Utilities Is Opposed by Utah Governor," *Wall Street Journal*, August 26, 1998, 1.
39. Leon Bear, quoted in Christopher Smith, "Tribes Still Considering Storing Radioactive Fuel," *Salt Lake Tribune*, December 28, 1993, D3.
40. Leon Bear, quoted in Jon Christensen, "Surprises of Sovereignty," *High Country News*, April 3, 1995, 26.
41. Danny Quintana interview, p. 86.
42. "Tooele County, Utah," *Wikipedia*, accessed November 30, 2014, http://en.wikipedia.org/wiki/Tooele_County,_Utah; Ward, *Canaries on the Rim*, 34–50; Smith, "Tribes Still Considering Storing Radioactive Fuel," D3; Gary Griffith, interview by Ken Verdoia, *Skull Valley*, interview transcripts, pp. 26–31 (hereafter Gary Griffith interview).
43. Verdoia, *Skull Valley*; Judy Fahys, "Tooele Signs Deal for N-Waste," *Salt Lake Tribune*, May 25, 2000, B1; Michael Janofsky, "Utah County's Toxic Tradition Is under Threat," *New York Times*, October 20, 2002; Gary Griffith interview, pp. 29, 23.
44. Teryl Hunsaker, interview by Ken Verdoia, *Skull Valley*, interview transcripts, p. 46.
45. Danny Quintana interview, p. 46.
46. Robert Gehrke, "Bishop Engages New Strategy in Attempt to Derail N-Waste Storage," *Salt Lake Tribune*, October 18, 2004, B1; Utah Department of Environmental Quality, "Opposition to High-Level Nuclear Waste," accessed May 12, 2015, http://www.deq.utah.gov/Pollutants/H/highlevelnw/opposition/concerns/deisconcerns.htm; HEAL Utah (Healthy Environment Alliance of Utah), accessed November 30, 2014, http://www.healutah.org; NO! The Coalition Opposed to High-Level Nuclear Waste, *White Paper Regarding Opposition to the High-Level Nuclear Waste Storage Facility Proposed by Private Fuel Storage on the Skull Valley Band of Goshute Indian Reservation, Skull Valley Utah*, November 28, 2000, accessed November 30, 2014, http://www.deq.utah.gov/Pollutants/H/highlevelnw/opposition/docs/2005/09Sep/HLW112800.pdf; Jerry Spangler, "Series to Explore Fight over N-Waste Storage," *Deseret News*, six-part series, January 24–29, 1998, A1; Brent Israelsen, "Leavitt Leads Angry Opposition to N-Waste on Goshute Reservation," *Salt Lake Tribune*, July 28, 2000, A1; Michael Leavitt, interview by Ken Verdoia, *Skull Valley*, interview transcripts, pp. 48–52 (hereafter Michael Leavitt interview); James Hansen, interview by Ken Verdoia, *Skull Valley*, interview transcripts, p. 31–40 (hereafter James Hansen interview); Connie Nakahara, interview by Ken Verdoia, *Skull Valley*, interview transcripts, pp. 63–67 (hereafter Connie Nakahara interview); James McConkie, interview by Ken Verdoia, *Skull Valley*, interview transcripts, pp. 58–62; Joe Bauman, "Nuclear Storage Battle Fires Up," *Deseret News*, March 18, 2005. On Utah's downwind history, see Howard Ball, *Justice Downwind: America's Atomic Testing Program in the 1950s* (New York: Oxford University Press, 1986); Sarah Alisabeth Fox,

Downwind: A People's History of the Nuclear West (Lincoln: University of Nebraska Press, 2014).

47. Michael Leavitt interview, p. 49; Judy Fahys, "Defections Hit Group Opposing N-Waste," *Salt Lake Tribune*, February 9, 2001, C2; Fahys, "N-Waste: How Hot Is Too Hot?" *Salt Lake Tribune*, March 18, 2001, A1; D. Michael Quinn, quoted in Bob Mims, "Different Views: For the Goshutes, a Test of Tradition," *Salt Lake Tribune*, July 17, 2000, D1. See also Spangler and Spangler, "Toxic Utah." Representative James Hansen named these facilities as important Utah assets, and Senator Robert Bennett acknowledged the problems with the project were political, not scientific. See James V. Hansen, "Hansen's Last Stand: Wilderness, Not Waste, for Skull Valley," *Salt Lake Tribune*, May 26, 2002, AA5; Judy Fahys, "Senator Cites N-Dump Politics," *Salt Lake Tribune*, April 27, 2002, as cited in Kenneth A. Rogers and Marvin G. Kingsley, "The Politics of Interim Radioactive Waste Storage: The United States," *Environmental Politics* 13, no. 3 (2004): 600. See also Bourke, "Economic Attitudes and Responses," 485–96.
48. For discussions of this paternalistic relationship in Utah, see Ronald L. Holt, *Beneath These Red Cliffs: An Ethnohistory of the Utah Paiutes* (Albuquerque: University of New Mexico Press, 1992); R. Warren Metcalf, *Termination's Legacy: The Discarded Indians of Utah* (Lincoln: University of Nebraska Press, 2002); Brian Q. Cannon, "Utah's Denial of the Vote to Reservation Indians, 1956–57," in *Utah in the Twentieth Century*, ed. Brian Q. Cannon and Jessie L. Embry (Logan: Utah State University Press, 2009), 245–62; Ishiyama, "Environmental Justice: Case Study," 124–25. For paternalism toward "rich" Indians over time, see Alexandra Harmon, *Rich Indians: Native People and the Problem of Wealth in American History* (Chapel Hill: University of North Carolina Press, 2010).
49. James Hansen interview, p. 37.
50. Ishiyama, "Environmental Justice: Case Study," 130–34; Rufina Marie Laws, interview by Ken Verdoia, *Skull Valley*, interview transcripts, p. 46–48.
51. Skull Valley Goshute Tribe Executive Office, "Native Americans Have the Right," 67.
52. Tracylee Clarke, "An Ideographic Analysis of Native American Sovereignty in the State of Utah: Enabling Denotative Dissonance and Constructing Irreconcilable Conflict," *Wicazo Sa Review* 17, no. 2 (Fall 2002): 52–55; Michael F. Thomson, "Highlight: Placement of High Level Nuclear Waste," *Utah Law Review*, no. 3 (1998): 729–36; Jim Woolf, "Utah Tribe Won't Dump Plan for Its N-Facility: Goshutes Press Ahead with N-Plans," *Salt Lake Tribune*, April 16, 1997, A1; Laurie Sullivan Maddox, "Leavitt, Cook Battle Goshute Waste Storage," *Salt Lake Tribune*, June 27, 1997, A10; Hilary Groutage, "Sign of the Times: No N-Waste Here," *Salt Lake Tribune*, March 22, 1998, C1; Brent Israelsen, "Utah Sues Feds for Data on Goshute N-Plan," *Salt Lake Tribune*, May 28, 1998, A1; Israelsen, "Pols Target N-Waste at Skull Valley," *Salt Lake Tribune*, September 5, 2000, A1.

53. Verdoia, *Skull Valley;* Judy Fahys, "N-Waste Battle Heats Up," *Salt Lake Tribune,* February 26, 2001, A1; Leon Bear interview, p. 7; Danny Quintana interview, pp. 89–91; Forrest Cuch, interview by Ken Verdoia, *Skull Valley,* interview transcripts, pp. 21–22 (hereafter Forrest Cuch interview); "Editorial, Make Goshutes an Offer," *Salt Lake Tribune,* August 7, 2002, AA2.
54. Judy Fahys, "Nuclear Waste Measure Ordered onto Utah Ballot," *Salt Lake Tribune,* August 27, 2002, A1; Fahys and Linda Fatin, "N-Waste Initiative Critics Deny Bias: Envirocare Contributions Make Backers Suspicious," *Salt Lake Tribune,* November 2, 2001, A1; Paul Rolly, "Leaders of Waste-Tax Initiative Have Interesting Histories," *Salt Lake Tribune,* May 26, 2002, AA3; Judy Fahys, "New Approach Planned on N-Waste," *Salt Lake Tribune,* April 13, 2004, B1.
55. Joe Cannon, quoted in Dan Harrie, "Officials Covet N-Waste Profits: If Goshutes Win Approval, Some Quietly Propose 'Plan B' so Utah Reaps Windfall," *Salt Lake Tribune,* September 22, 2002, A1; Judy Fahys, "Plan to Use Trust Lands for N-Waste Reappears," *Salt Lake Tribune,* May 7, 2004, B8; Lisa Church, "San Juan County Commission Revives Plan for Nuclear Waste Site," *Salt Lake Tribune,* April 7, 2005, B1.
56. Forrest Cuch, quoted in Dan Harrie and Judy Fahys, "State Leaders Assail 'Plan B' for Nuclear Waste Storage," *Salt Lake Tribune,* September 25, 2002, A1; Sue Martin, quoted in Judy Fahys and Dan Harrie, "'Plan B' Aims to Outbid Goshutes' N-Waste Site," *Salt Lake Tribune,* February 6, 2003, A1.
57. Judy Fahys, "Walker Takes Reins of Fight against Nuclear Waste Site," *Salt Lake Tribune,* December 1, 2003, A1; Leon Bear interview, pp. 7–8; Danny Quintana interview, pp. 89–91; Forrest Cuch interview, pp. 21–22; Ward, *Canaries on the Rim,* 226–28; Rebecca Walsh and Judy Fahys, "Waste Issue: Disconnect Stokes Debates," *Salt Lake Tribune,* November 23, 2003, A1.
58. Christensen, "Can Nevada Bury Yucca Mountain?," 1, 8–11; Richard W. Stoffle and Michael J. Evans, "American Indians and Nuclear Waste Storage: The Debate at Yucca Mountain, Nevada," in *Native Americans and Public Policy,* ed. Fremont J. Lyden and Lyman H. Legters (Pittsburgh: University of Pittsburgh Press, 1992), 243–62; Valerie Taliman, "Tribes, States Will Fight Nuke Waste Dump," *Indian Country Today,* March 6, 2002, A1; Jerry Spangler, "In Harm's Way: Is Yucca Mountain a Utah Fight?," *Deseret News,* April 28, 2002, A1; Judy Fahys, "Yucca Vote Unlikely to Deter Skull Valley Dump," *Salt Lake Tribune,* July 15, 2002, A1; Fahys, "Yucca Slips, Skull Valley Stock Rises," *Salt Lake Tribune,* August 16, 2004, B1; Robert Gehrke, "Bishop Engages New Strategy in Attempt to Derail N-Waste Storage," *Salt Lake Tribune,* October 18, 2004, B1; Gehrke, "Hatch: Don't Move N-Waste," *Salt Lake Tribune,* April 5, 2005, B1; Bill Schneider, "Right Wilderness, Wrong Reason, Questionable Tactic," *New-West,* February 2, 2006, accessed November 30, 2014, http://www.newwest.net/main/article/right_wilderness_wrong_reasn_questionable_tactic/.
59. Leon Bear, quoted in Fedarko, "In the Valley of the Shadow," 5. For a summary of Utah's tactics, see Rogers and Kingsley, "The Politics of Interim Radioactive Waste Storage," 600–603.

60. Rick Egan, "Goshutes Protest Tribe's Nuclear-Waste Proposal," *Salt Lake Tribune,* May 1, 1997, B1; Jim Woolf, "More Than Half of Goshutes Sue Tribe over Waste Plan," *Salt Lake Tribune,* March 13, 1999, D4; Spangler and Spangler, "Toxic Utah: Goshutes Divided over N-Storage," *Deseret News,* part 4 of a series, February 14, 2001, A1; Judy Fahys, "Family Feud: Skull Valley Goshutes Fight an Internal Battle over the Lucrative Nuclear Waste Storage Proposal," *Salt Lake Tribune,* August 18, 2002, A1, A13–14. See also Lewis, "Skull Valley Goshutes," 326–29.
61. Meek, "Goshute Divided on Nuclear Waste Storage."; Leon Bear interview, pp. 8–9; U.S. Nuclear Regulatory Commission, "Memorandum and Order," Docket No. 72-22-ISFSI, CLI-02-20, October 1, 2002, http://pbadupws.nrc.gov/docs/ML0227/ML022740427.pdf; Kirk Johnson, "A Tribe, Nimble and Determined, Moves Ahead with Nuclear Storage Plan," *New York Times,* February 28, 2005, http://nytimes.com/2005/02/28/national/28tribe.html; Clarke, "Ideographic Analysis of Native American Sovereignty," 57.
62. Brent Israelsen, "Scuffle Threatens to Push Goshutes Deeper into Divisive Power Struggle," *Salt Lake Tribune,* September 1, 2001, A1; Judy Fahys, "Feds Demand Goshutes Open Financial Books on N-Waste Deal," *Salt Lake Tribune,* March 14, 2002, A1; Fahys, "Feds Recognize Bear as Goshute Leader," *Salt Lake Tribune,* April 2, 2002, A1; Fahys, "Family Feud: Skull Valley Goshutes Fight," A1; Donna Kemp Spangler, "A Tribe Divided: Goshutes Fight over N-Waste and Feel Abandoned by State," *Deseret News,* October 6, 2002, A1; Judy Fahys, "More Trouble Ahead for Goshutes," *Salt Lake Tribune,* January 8, 2004, A1; Patty Henetz, "Bear Maintains Grip on Power," *Salt Lake Tribune,* December 6, 2004, B1.
63. Margene Bullcreek, quoted in Kamps, "Environmental Racism," 4; Sammy Blackbear, interview by Ken Verdoia, *Skull Valley,* interview transcripts, pp. 15–17; Fedarko, "In the Valley of the Shadow," 7; Bob Mims, "For Goshutes, the Issue Has Always Been Simple: Survival," *Salt Lake Tribune,* September 1, 2002, A1.
64. John J. Fialka, "Goshute Indians' Plan to Store Nuclear Waste for Eight Utilities Is Opposed by Utah Governor," *Wall Street Journal,* August 26, 1998, 1; Valerie Taliman, "Opponents Call Nuke Deal Environmental Racism," *Indian Country Today,* April 10, 2002, A2; Kamps, "Environmental Racism," 4; Timothy Egan, "New Prosperity Brings New Conflict to Indian Country," *New York Times,* March 8, 1998, 1, 22; Ishiyama, "Environmental Justice: Case Study," 130–32; Noriko Ishiyama and Kimberly Tallbear, "Changing Notions of Environmental Justice in the Decision to Host a Nuclear Fuel Storage Facility on Skull Valley Goshute Reservation," Proceedings of the 9th International High-Level Radioactive Waste Management Conference (2001), http://www.iiirm.org/publications/Articles%20Reports%20Papers/Environmental%20Justice/ChangingNot.pdf; Lewis, "Native Americans and the Environment," 438–40; Shepard Krech III, *The Ecological Indian: Myth and History* (New York: W. W. Norton, 1999), 211–29. For ways that traditionalism gets used for

ideological purposes, see David Rich Lewis, "Reservation Leadership and the Progressive-Traditional Dichotomy: William Wash and the Northern Utes, 1865–1928," *Ethnohistory* 38, no. 2 (Spring 1991): 124–48. For insightful analysis of Indian-environmentalist disagreements, see David Waller, "Friendly Fire: When Environmentalists Dehumanize American Indians," *American Indian Culture and Research Journal* 20, no. 2 (1996): 107–26. On the rhetoric used by both sides in this debate, see Jesse Timothy Weiss, "The Skull Valley Goshute and Nuclear Waste: Rhetorical Analysis of Claims-Making of Opponents and Proponents," (PhD diss., Utah State University, 2004).

65. David Melmer, "Leon Bear Re-elected Goshute Chairman," *Indian Country Today*, December 6, 2000, D2; James May, "Skull Valley Goshutes Sue State of Utah," *Indian Country Today*, May 2, 2001, A1; Clarke, "Ideographic Analysis of Native American Sovereignty," 57.
66. Ishiyama, "Environmental Justice: Case Study," 119–39. On the Sagebrush Rebellion, see R. McGreggor Cawley, *Federal Land, Western Anger: The Sagebrush Rebellion and Environmental Politics* (Lawrence: University Press of Kansas, 1993); Jedediah Rogers, "The Volatile Sagebrush Rebellion," in *Utah in the Twentieth Century*, ed. Brian Q. Cannon and Jessie L. Embry (Logan: Utah State University Press, 2009), 367–84.
67. Merrill Cook, quoted in Timothy Egan, "New Prosperity Brings New Conflict to Indian Country," *New York Times*, March 8, 1998, 22; Michael Leavitt interview, p. 50; Connie Nakahara interview, p. 66; See also Judy Fahys, "Utah Fears Waste Plan Is Shoo-In," *Salt Lake Tribune*, April 22, 2002, A1; Fahys, "Judge Rebuffs State on N-Waste," *Salt Lake Tribune*, July 31, 2002, A1.
68. Orrin Hatch, quoted in Robert Gehrke and Judy Fahys, "Interior Dumps N-Waste Plan," *Salt Lake Tribune*, September 8, 2006; Fahys, "Goshute Says Feds, State Let Them Down," *Salt Lake Tribune*, September 14, 2006, A1; Deborah Bulkeley, "Goshute Leader Calls N-Waste Rulings 'Thin,'" *Deseret News*, September 14, 2006, B1.
69. Margene Bullcreek, quoted in Suzanne Struglinski, "Nuclear Waste Site Looks Doomed," *Deseret News*, September 8, 2006; Leon Bear, quoted in Deborah Bulkeley and Suzanne Struglinski, "Decision to Deny PFS Lease Shocks 2," *Deseret News*, September 9, 2006.
70. Judy Fahys, "Goshute Nuclear Storage Allies Sue Interior Department," *Salt Lake Tribune*, July 18, 2007, A1; Fahys, "Judge's Ruling May Boost Nuke Storage in Utah," *Salt Lake Tribune*, July 27, 2010, A1; Fahys, "Utah Leaders Protest Pro-Nuke Waste Ruling," *Salt Lake Tribune*, July 28, 2010, A1; Fahys, "Interior Won't Fight Ruling on Nuclear Site," *Salt Lake Tribune*, September 28, 2010, A1; Fahys, "Goshutes Elect New Leaders," *Salt Lake Tribune*, February 22, 2011; Fahys, "Utah N-Waste Site Backers Call It Quits," *Salt Lake Tribune*, December 21, 2012, A1; Fahys, "Money, Politics Bury Plans for Utah Fuel-Rod Cemetery," *Salt Lake Tribune*, January 7, 2013. On Yucca Mountain's closure, see Joel Achenbach and Brian Vastag, "Yucca Mountain: A Waste of a Nu-

clear Dump," *Washington Post,* June 14, 2011; Dave Gram, "Nuclear Waste Site Hunt Could Point to a National Repository in Granite," *Salt Lake Tribune,* December 18, 2011; Todd Garvey, *Closing Yucca Mountain: Litigation Associated with Attempts to Abandon the Planned Nuclear Waste Repository,* Congressional Research Service Report for Congress R41675, June 4, 2012, http://www.fas.org/sgp/crs/misc/R41675.pdf.

71. Matthew L. Wald, "Nuclear Waste Is Allowed above Ground Indefinitely," *New York Times,* August 20, 2014, A13; Matthew L. Wald, "Calls to Use Yucca Mountain as a Nuclear Waste Site, Now Deemed Safe," *New York Times,* October 17, 2014, A20. On tourism as a "devil's bargain"—pitting local cultures and needed economic development against the intrusion of outsiders and the loss of local control—see Hal Rothman, *Devil's Bargains: Tourism in the Twentieth-Century American West* (Lawrence: University Press of Kansas, 1998).
72. On Tooele County's problems, see Pat Reavy and Amy Joi O'Donoghue, "Empty Beds, Declining Hazardous Waste Fees Lead to Tooele Layoffs," *Deseret News,* August 30, 2012; Cathy McKitrick and Pamela Manson, "How Tooele County's Boom Economy Went Bust," *Salt Lake Tribune,* July 1, 2013. On EnergySolutions, see Thomas Burr, "Matheson Says 'No' to Nuclear Waste, but Hatch, Bennett, Bishop and Cannon Hedge on Issue," *Salt Lake Tribune,* May 26, 2008, A1; Judy Fahys, "EnergySolutions: Foreign Nuke Waste Already Finds Its Way to Utah," *Salt Lake Tribune,* October 18, 2008; Brock Verakis, "Give Me Your Toxic...Utah Takes N-Waste from States with Their Own Dumps," *Salt Lake Tribune,* May 5, 2009; Judy Fahys, "Green Groups: State to OK Blended Nuke Waste," *Salt Lake Tribune,* August 2, 2011; Editorial, "Who's in Charge? Regulators, Waste Firm too Friendly," *Salt Lake Tribune,* September 13, 2012. On Utah nuclear power-plant proposals, see Judy Fahys, "Green River 'Preferred' Nuke Plant Site: Three Other Utah Locales Also Candidates," *Salt Lake Tribune,* July 23, 2008; Fahys, "Utah Refuses to Block Plans for Nuke Plant Near Green River," *Salt Lake Tribune,* February 29, 2012. On the impact of Fukushima on U.S. debates over nuclear power, see Matthew L. Wald, "Japan Nuclear Crisis Revives Long U.S. Fight on Spent Fuel," *New York Times,* March 24, 2011, A1. On attitudes affecting decision making in Utah on waste sites, see Bourke, "Economic Attitudes and Responses," 485–96.
73. On divisions among the Goshutes, see H. Josef Hebert, "N-Waste Bitterly Divides Utah Tribe," *Deseret News,* June 25, 2006, A1; Fahys, "Goshutes Elect New Leaders"; and Lori Bear, quoted in Fahys, "Money, Politics Bury Plans."
74. See Lincoln L. Davies, "Skull Valley Crossroads: Reconciling Native Sovereignty and the Federal Trust," *Maryland Law Review* 68, no. 2 (2009): 290–376.
75. David E. Wilkins and K. Tsianina Lomawaima, *Uneven Ground: American Indian Sovereignty and Federal Law* (Norman: University of Oklahoma Press, 2001); Richard A. Grounds, George E. Tinker, and David E. Wilkins, eds., *Native Voices: American Indian Identity and Resistance* (Lawrence: University Press of Kansas, 2003); Joane Nagel, *American Indian Ethnic Renewal: Red*

Power and the Resurgence of Identity and Culture (New York: Oxford University Press, 1996); Harmon, *Rich Indians*; Lewis, "Native Americans and the Environment," 423–50.

76. Margene Bullcreek, quoted in Meek, "Goshute Divided on Nuclear Waste Storage."
77. Leon Bear, quoted in Fedarko, "In the Valley of the Shadow," 8.
78. Leon Bear, quoted in Mims, "Different Views: For the Goshutes," D1.
79. Leon Bear interview, p. 11.
80. Thomas King, *The Truth about Stories: A Native Narrative*, CBC Massey Lecture Series (Toronto: House of Anansi Press, 2003), 2.

Contributors

LEISL CARR CHILDERS is assistant professor of history at the University of Northern Iowa, where she coordinates the public history program and teaches about the American West. Her work as the assistant director of the Nevada Test Site Oral History Project and at the Autry National Center in Los Angeles has combined her research in regional and environmental history with her interests in and experiences with ranch life and outdoor recreation.

DAVID B. DANBOM is a historian specializing in American agricultural and rural history. His latest book is *Sod Busting: How Families Made Farms on the 19th-Century Plains* (Baltimore: Johns Hopkins University Press, 2014).

BURKE W. GRIGGS is a water lawyer who represents Kansas in federal and interstate water matters, including Supreme Court litigation, and advises the state on water policy and legislation. In 2013–14, he served as a consulting professor at the Bill Lane Center for the American West at Stanford University. He currently serves as an affiliated scholar at the Bill Lane Center and a nonresident fellow at the Stanford Woods Institute for the Environment, contributing to their joint Water in the West program.

JULIA H. HAGGERTY is an assistant professor of geography at Montana State University. Her research focuses on resource development, governance, and community resilience in the American West.

MARK N. HAGGERTY is a policy analyst at Headwaters Economics, where he explores the economic and fiscal outcomes of natural-resource conservation and development across the West. He holds a BA in economics and an MA in geography from the University of Colorado.

MICHAEL HIBBARD is professor emeritus in the Department of Planning, Public Policy and Management at the University of Oregon.

J. DWIGHT HINES was raised on the wind-swept high plains of the Thunder Basin, the son, grandson, and great-grandson of Wyoming sheep ranchers. He is an associate professor in the Department of Humanities and Human Sciences at Point Park

University in Pittsburgh; his research focuses on the shifting political ecology of the Greater Yellowstone Ecosystem.

DAVID M. KENNEDY is the Donald J. McLachlan Professor of History Emeritus and the founding faculty director of the Bill Lane Center for the American West at Stanford University, where he has taught for more than four decades.

JON K. LAUCK received his PhD in history from the University of Iowa and his JD from the University of Minnesota and is the author or editor of six books, including *The Lost Region: Toward a Revival of Midwestern History* (University of Iowa Press, 2013). Lauck currently serves as an adjunct professor of history at the University of South Dakota, associate and book review editor of *Middle West Review*, and president of the Midwestern History Association.

DAVID RICH LEWIS is a professor of history at Utah State University and editor of the *Western Historical Quarterly*.

SUSAN LURIE is an adjunct research associate in the Community Service Center at the University of Oregon.

GEOFF MCGHEE is the creative director of media and communications at the Bill Lane Center for the American West at Stanford University, where he creates interactive multimedia and web publications on western issues. He formerly worked as a journalist at the *New York Times*, *Le Monde*, and ABC News and was a 2010 John S. Knight Journalism Fellow at Stanford University.

JUDY MULLER is a professor of journalism at USC's Annenberg School. Previously she worked as a network news correspondent for ABC News and CBS News and a commentator for NPR. She is the author of *Emus Loose in Egnar: Big Stories from Small Towns* (Lincoln: University of Nebraska Press, 2011).

MARC SCHENKER is a distinguished professor of public health sciences and medicine at the University of California, Davis. His work largely focuses on health disparities, including hazards (injuries and illnesses) to farmworkers and their families and more broadly to immigrants and temporary workers in various industries.

Selected Bibliography

Our authors consider the works in this bibliography to be essential contributors to their work. Those seeking more extensive references are invited to consult the notes following the individual essays.

Albrecht, Don E. *Rethinking Rural: Global Community and Economic Development in the Small Town West*. Pullman: Washington State University Press, 2014.

Bailey, Liberty Hyde. *Report of the Country Life Commission*. Washington, DC: Government Printing Office, 1909.

Brown, David L., and Louis E. Swanson. *Challenges for Rural America in the Twenty-First Century*. University Park: Pennsylvania State University Press, 2003.

Castle, Emery N., JunJie Wu, and Bruce A. Weber. "Place Orientation and Rural-Urban Interdependence." *Applied Economic Perspectives and Policy* 33, no. 2 (Summer 2011): 179–204.

Cawley, R. McGreggor. *Federal Land, Western Anger: The Sagebrush Rebellion and Environmental Politics*. Lawrence: University Press of Kansas, 1993.

Crawford, Susan P. *Captive Audience: The Telecom Industry and Monopoly Power in the New Gilded Age*. New Haven, CT: Yale University Press, 2013.

Davies, Lincoln L. "Skull Valley Crossroads: Reconciling Native Sovereignty and the Federal Trust." *Maryland Law Review* 68, no. 2 (2009): 290–376.

Defa, Dennis R. "The Goshute Indians of Utah." In *A History of Utah's American Indians*, edited by Forrest S. Cuch, 73–122. Salt Lake City: Utah State Division of Indian Affairs and the Utah State Division of History, 2000.

Dorman, Robert L. *Hell of a Vision: Regionalism and the Modern American West*. Tucson: University of Arizona Press, 2012.

———. *Revolt of the Provinces: The Regionalist Movement in America, 1920–1945*. Chapel Hill: University of North Carolina Press, 1993.

Drake, Brian Allen. *Loving Nature, Fearing the State: Environmentalism and Antigovernment Politics before Reagan*. Seattle: University of Washington Press, 2013.

Ennis, Sharon R., Merarys Rios-Vargas, and Nora G. Albert. "The Hispanic Population: 2010." In *2010 Census Briefs*, 1–16. Washington, DC: U.S. Census Bureau, May 2011. Accessed May 10, 2015, http://www.census.gov/prod/cen2010/briefs/c2010br-04.pdf.

Fisher, Dana R. "Resource Dependency and Rural Poverty: Rural Areas in the United States and Japan." *Rural Sociology* 66, no. 2 (June 2001): 181–202.

Freudenburg, William R., and Lisa J. Wilson. "Mining the Data: Analyzing the Economic Implications of Mining for Nonmetropolitan Regions." *Sociological Inquiry* 72, no. 4 (Fall 2002): 549–75.

Harvard Project on American Indian Economic Development. *The State of the Native Nations: Conditions under U.S. Policies of Self-Determination*. New York: Oxford University Press, 2008.

Hibbard, Michael and Susan Lurie. *Socioeconomic Measures for Intensively Monitored Watersheds: The Middle Fork John Day Effectiveness Monitoring Project*. Report for the Oregon Watershed Enhancement Board. Eugene: University of Oregon Institute for Policy Research and Innovation, October 29, 2010. Accessed May 10, 2015, http://www.ir.library.oregonstate.edu/xmlui/bitstream/handle/1957/29051/IPRI%20IMW%20Final%20Report%202010.pdf?sequence1.

———. "Some Community Socioeconomic Benefits of Watershed Councils: A Case Study from Oregon." *Journal of Environmental Planning and Management*, 49, no. 6 (November 2006): 891–908.

Hines, J. Dwight. "In Pursuit of Experience: The Post-Industrial Gentrification of the Rural American West." *Ethnography* 11, no. 2 (June 2010): 285–308.

———. "The Post-Industrial Regime of Production/Consumption and the Rural Gentrification of the 'New' West Archipelago." *Antipode* 44, no. 1 (2012): 74–97.

———. "Rural Gentrification as Permanent Tourism: The Creation of the 'New' West Archipelago as Post-Industrial Class-Cultural Space." *Environment and Planning D: Society & Space* 28, no. 3 (2010): 509–25.

Hjerpe, Evan E., and Yeon-Su Kim. "Economic Impacts of Southwestern National Forest Fuels Reductions." *Journal of Forestry* 106, no. 6 (August 2008): 311–16.

Holmes, John. "Impulses toward a Multifunctional Transition in Rural Australia." *Journal of Rural Studies* 22, no. 2 (April 2006): 142–60.

Holtgrieve, Donald G. "Frederick Jackson Turner as a Regionalist." *Professional Geographer* 17 (May 1974): 159–65.

Hutchins, Wells A. *Water Rights Laws in the Nineteen Western States*. 2 vols. Washington, DC: U.S. Department of Agriculture, 1972–77.

Ishiyama, Noriko. "Environmental Justice and American Indian Tribal Sovereignty: Case Study of a Land-Use Conflict in Skull Valley, Utah." *Antipode* 35, no. 1 (January 2003): 119–39.

Johnson, Kenneth. *Demographic Trends in Rural and Small Town America*. Carsey Institute Reports on Rural America. Durham: University of New Hampshire, 2006.

Katz, Wendy J., and Timothy R. Mahoney, eds. *Regionalism and the Humanities*. Lincoln: University of Nebraska Press, 2008.

Kilkenny, Maureen. "Urban/Regional Economics and Rural Development." *Journal of Regional Science* 50, no. 1 (February 2010): 449–70.

Krech, Shepard, III. *The Ecological Indian: Myth and History*. New York: W. W. Norton, 1999.

Larson, Sharon L., and John A. Fleishman, "Rural-Urban Differences in Usual Source of Care and Ambulatory Service Use: Analyses of National Data Using Urban Influence Codes." *Medical Care* 41, no. 7 suppl. (July 2003): III65–III74.

Lauck, Jon K. *The Lost Region: Toward a Revival of Midwestern History*. Iowa City: University of Iowa Press, 2013.

———. *Prairie Republic: The Political Culture of Dakota Territory, 1879–1889*. Norman: University of Oklahoma Press, 2010.

Lauck, Jon K., John E. Miller, and Don Simmons, eds. *The Plains Political Tradition: Essays on South Dakota Political Culture*. 2 vols. Pierre: South Dakota State Historical Society Press, 2011–14.

Lewis, David Rich. "Native Americans: The Original Westerners." In *The Rural West Since World War II*, edited by R. Douglas Hurt, 12–37. Lawrence: University Press of Kansas, 1998.

———. "Skull Valley Goshutes and the Politics of Nuclear Waste: Environment, Economic Development, and Tribal Sovereignty." In *Native Americans and the Environment: Perspectives on the Ecological Indian*, edited by Michael E. Harkin and David Rich Lewis, 304–42. Lincoln: University of Nebraska Press, 2007.

McCarthy, James. "First World Political Ecology: Lessons from the Wise Use Movement." *Environment and Planning A* 34, no. 7 (2002): 1281–82.

McCracken, Robert, and Jeanne Sharp Howerton. *A History of Railroad Valley, Nevada*. Tonopah: Central Nevada Historical Society, 1996.

Moretti, Enrico. *The New Geography of Jobs*. Boston: Houghton Mifflin Harcourt, 2012.

Muller, Judy. *Emus Loose in Egnar: Big Stories from Small Towns*. Lincoln: University of Nebraska Press, 2011.

Nielsen-Pincus, Max, and Cassandra Moseley. "The Economic Impacts of a Sustained Program of Forest and Watershed Restoration." *Restoration Ecology* 21, no. 2 (March 2013): 207–14.

Opie, John. *Ogallala: Water for a Dry Land*. 2d ed. Lincoln: University of Nebraska Press, 2000.

Pisani, Donald J. *Water and American Government: The Reclamation Bureau, National Water Policy, and the West, 1902–1935*. Berkeley: University of California Press, 2002.

Ramirez, Sarah M., and Don Villarejo. "Poverty, Housing, and the Rural Slum: Policies and the Production of Inequities, Past and Present." *American Journal of Public Health* 102, no. 9 (September 2012): 1664–75.

Reisner, Marc. *Cadillac Desert: The American West and its Disappearing Water*. Rev. ed. New York: Penguin, 1993.

Scarce, Rik. "What Do Wolves Mean? Conflicting Social Constructions of *Canis Lupus* in 'Bordertown.'" *Human Dimensions of Wildlife: An International Journal* 3, no. 3 (2008): 26–45.

Skillen, James R. *The Nation's Largest Landlord: The Bureau of Land Management in the American West.* Lawrence: University Press of Kansas, 2008.

Skull Valley: Radioactive Waste and the American West. Produced by Ken Verdoia. Salt Lake City: KUED-TV, 2001. Accessed May 17, 2015, http://www.kued.org/whatson/kued-local-productions/skull_valley.

Slattery, Michael C., Eric Lantz, and Becky L. Johnson. "State and Local Economic Impacts from Wind Energy Projects: Texas Case Study." *Energy Policy* 39, no. 12 (December 2011): 7930–7940.

Stegner, Wallace. *Beyond the Hundredth Meridian: John Wesley Powell and the Second Opening of the West.* Boston: Houghton Mifflin, 1954. Reprint, New York: Penguin, 1992.

Steiner, Michael C., and David M. Wrobel, eds. *Many Wests: Place, Culture, and Identity.* Lawrence: University Press of Kansas, 1997.

Walker, J. Samuel. *The Road to Yucca Mountain: The Development of Radioactive Waste Policy in the United States.* Berkeley: University of California Press, 2009.

Walmsley, D. J., and H. C. Weinand. "Is Australia Becoming More Unequal?" *Australian Geographer* 28, no. 1 (1997): 69–88.

Ward, Chip. *Canaries on the Rim: Living Downwind in the West.* New York: Verso, 1999.

Weber, Jeremy G. "The Effects of a Natural Gas Boom on Employment and Income in Colorado, Texas, and Wyoming." *Energy Economics* 34, no. 5 (September 2012): 1580–88.

Whitacre, Brian, Roberto Gallardo, and Sharon Strover. *Rural Broadband Availability and Adoption: Evidence, Policy Challenges, and Options.* National Agricultural & Rural Development Policy Center, U.S. Department of Agriculture, March 18, 2013. Accessed May 10, 2015, http://www.nardep.info/uploads/BroadbandWhitePaper.pdf.

Wilson, Geoff. "Multifunctional 'Quality' and Rural Community Resilience." *Transactions of the Institute of British Geographers* 35, no. 3 (July 2010): 364–81.

Wilson, Matthew A. "The Wolf in Yellowstone: Science, Symbol, or Politics? Deconstructing the Conflict between Environmentalism and Wise Use." *Society & Natural Resources* 10, no. 5 (1997): 453–68.

Worster, Donald. *Dust Bowl: The Southern Plains in the 1930s.* New York: Oxford University Press, 1979.

Young, James A., and B. Abbott Sparks. *Cattle in the Cold Desert.* Reno: University of Nevada Press, 2002.

Index

Numbers in *italics* refer to charts and tables.